Here Lies Jim Crow

CIVIL RIGHTS IN MARYLAND

C. FRASER SMITH

THE JOHNS HOPKINS UNIVERSITY PRESS

BALTIMORE

The Johns Hopkins University Press
2715 North Charles Street
Baltimore, Maryland 21218-4363
www.press.jhu.edu

Library of Congress Cataloging-in-Publication Data

Smith, C. Fraser, 1938–
Here lies Jim Crow : civil rights in Maryland / C. Fraser Smith.
    p. cm.
Includes bibliographical references and index.
ISBN-13: 978-0-8018-8807-6 (hardcover : alk. paper)
ISBN-10: 0-8018-8807-7 (hardcover : alk. paper)
    1. African Americans—Civil rights—Maryland—History.   2. Maryland—Race
relations—History.   3. Civil rights movements—Maryland—History.   I. Title.
    E185.93.M2S65 2008
    323.1196'0730752—dc22   2007040062

A catalog record for this book is available from the British Library.

*Special discounts are available for bulk purchases of this book. For more information,
please contact Special Sales at 410-516-6936 or specialsales@press.jhu.edu.*

The Johns Hopkins University Press uses environmentally friendly book materials,
including recycled text paper that is composed of at least 30 percent post-consumer
waste, whenever possible. All of our book papers are acid-free, and our jackets and
covers are printed on paper with recycled content.

To the memory of Howard Peters Rawlings

Contents

Preface

This book was inspired by a prediction and by an institution's foresight. The prediction came from Albert Murray, the jazz critic and writer, who was my teacher while we were both in the U.S. Air Force in the 1960s. The foresight came from the Maryland Historical Society in the form of its Theodore R. McKeldin—Lillie May Jackson Civil Rights Era Oral History Project.

I learned of the oral histories while working on a book about William Donald Schaefer, mayor of Baltimore as well as governor and later comptroller of Maryland. The interviews are wonderfully expansive observations of the civil rights struggle by some of its most important characters. Insights in these discussions go far beyond the recollections they marshal. Some of the subjects spoke as if they were simply amazed to be asked for their recollections—as if they had never seen themselves or been seen as part of their state's history, a history as closed to them as the Jim Crow—era tea rooms of local department stores. Many were black and, it seemed to me, unaccustomed to having anyone care what they thought. The history project itself turned out to be part of the history and part of the subterranean means of progress toward equality. Here was hard evidence that change was working its way through society—from individuals, to the law, to the customs and thinking and institutional barriers that marked our personal and community consciousness.

For me, there was a further shock of recognition: the realization that Maryland had a lamentably unheralded and unique place in the nation's civil rights history. This started coming into focus as I read the thoughts of William L. "Little Willie" Adams, who is seen from outside the black community as an infamous numbers man. Within the community, Adams holds a far different, even exalted, place. He was a banker to those for whom banking was a foreign idea.

Adams talked about how he and Joe Louis integrated Baltimore golf courses. At the time, I didn't know that Louis was a talented golfer. I didn't know that Willie Adams played golf. I didn't know that Adams and Louis were friends, or that their friendship had helped break the color line in Baltimore and around the nation.

But of course Joe Louis is only one of the famous Americans who worked to defeat Jim Crow—and many of the best known of these leaders were Marylanders. So, this book grows from the historical society's decision to chronicle an important passage in the life of Maryland and the nation. The oral histories have been an indispensable resource.

But there was another, longer-standing, personal motivation: my friendship with Albert Murray, the pre-eminent jazz historian, friend of the writer Ralph Ellison, of the artist Romare Bearden (who made drawings for the *Afro-American* newspaper), and of many others in the world of music and literature. I met Murray in the air force in 1962. I had just graduated from the University of North Carolina. He was nearing the end of his military career, which had begun while he was teaching at Tuskegee Institute in Alabama. Having been integrated by then, the air force was a place where a black intellectual could sustain himself and his family while writing and waiting for retirement. After I met him, he completed more than a dozen well-regarded books of criticism and fiction.

At Laurence G. Hanscom Field, a base outside Boston, I became his student in a class of one. It was an ad hoc, unofficial graduate seminar. We were in Base Supply, bemused by the Strangelovian characters we worked for but not bored. Across a gray steel desk, Murray lectured on William Faulkner, Thomas Mann, André Malraux, Ernest Hemingway, and Ralph Ellison. He talked about Mann and *The Magic Mountain, Joseph and His Brothers, Tonio Kroger, Death in Venice,* and the Faulkner universe. He told me of his friendship with Ellison. We talked somewhat less about politics and civil rights, but he instructed me in the art of gerrymandering, knowledge he picked up during the prosecution of *Gomillion v. Lightfoot,* a redistricting case designed to disenfranchise black voters in the community of Tuskegee, where he had been a student as well as a teacher. We talked about the mind of the South, and not so much about jazz, though it is the area in which his writing after the air force may have its most lasting impact.

After the air force, we fell out of touch for a number of reasons. His life was New York and men of letters and music. Mine was journalism. We lived in different cities. But as the years passed, with their constant issues of race, I periodically wondered about something he had said to me amid the supply manuals, just before the nation would be fully immersed in sit-ins and marches and protests. He had made a prediction. Change would come to the South when one or several young and anonymous white men or women, pebbles in the mighty river of life, would look up at some unpredictable moment and say, "This is not right." The zealously enforced regimen of discrimination would begin to fall.

When I saw him just after the 2004 Republican Convention in New York, I asked if he thought he had been right. Of course I was right, he said. Oh, how right. He didn't suggest that an attack of conscience had swept across the South, and he didn't suggest that pressure exerted by black leaders had not been the main force. But the formal civil rights movement was not the only movement, nor did it have a monochromatic chemistry.

The southern boy he imagined turned out to have power that made his prediction vastly more likely and significant. He told me he had predicted that it would be President Lyndon B. Johnson, too. Would I hand him his copy of *South to a Very Old Place*? He had written the book to expand on an *Atlantic Monthly* article commissioned by editor Willie Morris. The revelation comes in the book during a discussion by "old heads" gathered on a back porch in Mobile, Alabama, in "chinaberry blue Maytime." "Lyndon Johnson, Lyndon Johnson, Ooooold Lyndon Johnson," one of them says.

> They can call him everything but a child of God as long as you please and I still say old Lyndon Johnson, faults and all. They talking about what they talking about and I'm talking about what I'm talking about. I'm talking about the same thing I always been talking about. I'm talking about us, and I say old Lyndon Johnson is the one that brought more government benefits to help us out than all the rest of them up there put together all the way back through old Abe Lincoln . . .

You can say what you want to and I might not be here to see it, but it's going to take one of these old Confederate bushwackers from somewhere right down through in here to go up against these old Southern white folks when they get mad. My Daddy used to say it over and over again. So when old Lyndon Johnson come along and got in there on a humble (had to humble himself to the Kennedys just to get second banana)—and boy that's the onliest way he ever coulda' made it into there, because they were the very first ones to realize that old Lyndon Johnson meant business when he said the time is here to do something. And didn't nobody have to tell them what that meant because they already knew he was one of them and if they made him mad he subject to do some of that old rowdy cracker cussing right back at them.[1]

The record, Murray said, speaks for itself. Johnson's War on Poverty, Johnson's Voting Rights and Open Accommodations Acts, all proved his point. And in case I really wondered if it was true that some southern boy had decided it was time to do something, Murray showed me a letter he got from Jack Valenti, the Lyndon Johnson intimate and movie picture lobbyist in Washington. Valenti's letter says that Johnson pulled him into his study one night at the White House to show him the "Lyndon Johnson, Lyndon Johnson, Old Lyndon Johnson passage" in Murray's book. "We've gotta do something," Johnson said, according to Valenti.

Albert Murray was 88 when he offered me this proof of his foresight. He had thought a moment of enlightenment might come in a less official guise. His confidence seemed characteristic of black faith from the beginning of the struggle, wherever that beginning might be marked in time. A point was reached in U.S. history, in the universal psyche of this nation, where a Lyndon Johnson was inevitable. That was Murray's hopeful point, I think. He chose to see Johnson's policies as the inevitable outcome in a nation where people would eventually see the difference between the founding ideals and practice. This book is a narrative of that evolution in one state blessed with courageous men and women, black and white, who believed as Albert Murray believed.

Here Lies Jim Crow

Laboring Sons:
Jim Crow on a Bulldozer

Not content merely to torment the living, the agents of Jim Crow in Maryland occasionally pecked at the dead. In May 1949 Frederick city officials sent bulldozers rumbling into a cemetery at Fifth Street and Chapel Alley to make way for a playground. Aging members of the Laboring Sons burial society, an African American organization, had asked the City to help them maintain the small cemetery. Instead, what amounted to an officially licensed desecration began. Tombstones fell; bones were unearthed and then covered over. A listing of the names of the deceased began, but the record keeping continued only until, it seemed, workers tired of the task. The names of 161 of the estimated 1,500 souls were recorded. The rest of the gravestones were plowed under as if the other 1,339 deceased black sons and daughters of Frederick were of no consequence. After the markers were buried and the surface smoothed, swing sets and a basketball court were installed. The new playground would be for whites only.

The Beneficial Society of the Laboring Sons of Frederick City incorporated in 1837, named trustees, and bought land for twenty-six dollars. Its members were blacksmiths, barbers, tanners, carters, brick makers, rope makers, shoemakers, gardeners, and waiters. They represented the city's 790 free black people, about 16 percent of the city's population, which stood at about 5,000. When it asked the City for help with the cemetery, the Laboring Sons' leadership must have known it was taking a chance. Respect for the sanctity of the grave did not always extend to black people in Frederick. City fathers had already moved the black cemetery at least one other time, but the Laboring Sons still felt city hall was their best hope.

The careless obliteration of these resting places was particularly grievous because the burial ground was a cherished preserve, as slavery scholar Ira Berlin describes: "Because white Northerners excluded black corpses from their burial grounds, the graveyard became the first truly African-American institution in the northern colonies and perhaps in mainland North America."[1]

Clearly, the nation had not emerged from the shadows of discrimination. Regard for the rights of all was not a part of American attitudes, despite lofty claims to the contrary. But there were straws in the wind. A little-noticed executive order issued by President Franklin D. Roosevelt illustrated what efforts would be needed to bring about change. It required government agencies to abide by fair employment practices—not to discriminate in hiring. Denton Watson argues in his biography of the Baltimore-born civil rights leader Clarence M. Mitchell Jr. that Roosevelt's 1941 order marked the start of the modern civil rights movement.[2]

And in 1948, President Harry S Truman attempted to end segregation in the armed forces—under a threat from the civil rights leader A. Philip Randolph, who told the president his organization would lead young black men in refusing to serve. Even with presidential leadership, several years would pass before military heads agreed to change their policies, one of which limited black enlistments to 10 percent. The wider importance of these presidential orders was their implicit protection for such organizations as the Laboring Sons. The orders were important, pragmatic steps toward what would eventually be called "institutional change." Attitudinal change would come much later.

Public officials in Frederick were not living in a world where anyone thought black people were entitled to the kind of consideration that whites had automatically in similar circumstances. There was no political imperative, nothing like the sensitivity that would grow over the next forty years. Obtaining that sort of consideration was a subtle but fundamental objective of the civil rights movement. It would require the implantation of a missing instinct, a missing assumption that black people were citizens whose rights had to be observed no less carefully than those of any other American. The absence of that assumption was the very reason a dramatic mass movement was necessary. In the coming years, every corner of society, every institution in the nation, would be petitioned—forcefully in many cases—to change.

Americans would never mistake Frederick, Maryland, for the Deep South, but the practices of Jim Crow were no respecters of state boundaries. Living in a border state, Marylanders liked to think of themselves as enlightened, kinder practitioners of slavery. Defenders of racial separation were not in short supply, but Maryland had many citizens who wanted a fairer, more decent society in which laws applied equally to black and white. This segment of anti–Jim Crow sentiment made Maryland closer to the ideal of a free state than the southern states were. Racial antagonism—fear and misunderstanding—was destructive and dispiriting, but there were moderating forces rarely felt in the Deep South. Still, black Marylanders could be forgiven for thinking of their state as Up South. It had many of the same ingrained prejudices and practices, enforced with the same determination, as its sister states in the South.

Fifty years later, the city's principal newspaper, the *Frederick News-Post,* offered its somewhat understated verdict on the cemetery issue: "This doesn't sound like the most respectful and careful treatment of that cemetery . . . something that probably would not have happened in any other area of town or if it was a white cemetery."[3] After the cemetery removal was discovered, there was some indirect criticism of black citizens for not complaining—as if, somehow, that exonerated the offenders. Frederick alderman William O. Lee Jr. says no one—white or black—complained much about Jim Crow when he was growing up. "What could you do? That's the way it was."[4] It's a statement heard down through the years.

"The illusion of [Jim Crow's] permanency was encouraged by the complacency of a long-critical North, the propaganda of reconciliation, and the resigned compliance of the Negro," wrote C. Vann Woodward in *The Strange Career of Jim Crow,* a classic text on what Woodward called "racial ostracism." The system was so deeply embedded in daily life that Jim Crow Bibles were made available in courtrooms to protect whites from physical contact with a holy book held by black hands. Racial discrimination was more religiously and universally enforced than any set of laws could have been.[5] One of the strangest things about Jim Crow's career, Woodward observes, "was that the system was born in the North and reached an advanced age before moving south in force."

The origins of the Jim Crow system have been widely misperceived, the South having been elevated in public perception, by the Civil War and tobacco, to the status of nonpareil discriminator. As Woodward explains: "the Northern Negro was made painfully and constantly aware that he lived in a society dedicated to the doctrine of white supremacy and Negro inferiority. The major political parties, whatever their position on slavery, vied with each other in their devotion to this doctrine and extremely few politicians of importance dared question them. Their constituencies firmly believed that the Negroes were incapable of being assimilated politically, socially, or physically into white society."[6] That assimilation was effectively blocked by the insidious daily proscriptions of Jim Crow. The struggle of black Marylanders to take responsibility for their lives and their communities, as the Laboring Sons had done, was made increasingly difficult. The door to freedom was open, but safe passage was still denied.

CHAPTER 1

Taney and Douglass

O ne of the most important figures in the opposition to full citizenship for black Americans built a flourishing law practice in the relatively northern city of Frederick. Roger Brooke Taney, a native of Calvert County, moved to Frederick in 1802. He became a pillar of the state bar, of the federal government, and of the federal judiciary, serving as chief justice of the U.S. Supreme Court from 1836 to 1864.

As chief justice, he wrote the infamous *Dred Scott* decision of 1857, declaring that—under the U.S. Constitution—black Americans were not citizens of the United States. The framers, he wrote, acted upon the Constitution-era conviction that blacks "had no rights a white person was bound to respect."[1] Taney thought his ruling would carry great significance, calming North-South friction. Catastrophic disruption would be averted. Instead, war came.

Long after the peace, Taney's words echoed through the decades. Various constitutional amendments drained them of their strictly legal significance, but the sentiment—that black people "had no rights a white person was bound to respect"—were embedded in a social and political ethic that allowed public officials, such as those of Frederick, to bulldoze the rights of black citizens.

Taney remains a figure of renown in his adopted city. His house has been preserved, complete with backyard slave quarters, on Bentz Street, located in what has become a black neighborhood. He's buried in one of the town's exclusive cemeteries. Bill Lee grew up just a few doors east and north of the old Taney manse. As a young boy, he had no knowledge of the man's significance for his life and the nation. People were too busy coping with the rigors of their segregated lives to dwell on a long-departed townsman who had been pleased to accept a definition of them as noncitizens and worthy only of deportation to some other country.

Not to notice discrimination was a form of defiance. The black community attempted to establish its own institutions. Lee's grandfather and some of his grandfather's friends opened their own small library in 1916, calling it The Young Colored Men's Reading Club. "They were striving to be educated, to know what was going on. They would assign themselves a book to read, and then they'd read in each other's home and make a report, like a book report. From that grew the Colored Men's Free Library. It was in the home of one of the members on Ice Street. In the first room you walked into, bookshelves were around the wall," Lee says. "Rev. Ignatius Snowden was the librarian, and later his mother took over. They lived in the rest of the house, but the first room, the one a visitor entered first, was the library. No women were allowed except in the summer time when the librarian from the black school would check out books for the summer."[2] A fund-raiser was held one year, and Lee's grandfather wrote a song to assist in directing attention to the effort. He called it the "Free Campaign Song," and it was to be sung to the tune of the "Battle Hymn of the Republic."

We have here in our town, a Colored Library
Run by those who wish to learn you what is best to read
Books of all description you will find upon the shelves
of the Free Colored Library.
[Chorus]

We are working for one hundred dollars strong.
Who will be the first to help the cause along?
Everyone can do their bit so please don't be alarmed.
For the free colored library.

On nineteen hundred and sixteen at one one three Ice Street
A few did pledge themselves on a certain night to meet.
And success has followed as you can see
Of the free colored library.
[Repeat chorus]

Books by men like Washington, Du Bois and Dunbar,
Kelly, Miller, Joseph, Gordon, Bryant
And other writers too you're sure to find
At the free colored library.
[Repeat chorus]

You will also find on file Colored papers too
Such as *Afro-American, Bee,* and *Colored Man,*
Eagle and Defender. Now all of this is true
At the free colored library.[3]

Frederick had no public library for whites or blacks then. But even if
one had existed, blacks would have been excluded. "In my time, I
couldn't go. Blacks were not allowed in the library until the 1950s. I graduated from high school in 1945. That was just the way it was," Lee says.
"Even though his house was in our neighborhood when he wrote that
decision . . . I was almost out of high school before I realized who Roger
Brooke Taney was . . . My feeling was, how can you treat people like
that? How can you think people are the same as cattle, somebody's property? We're human beings."[4]

Lee says he grew up happy, happy with his friends white and black,
untroubled largely by segregation. He was raised by his grandmother,
Bertha, and his grandfather, Clifford Holland, who had a grocery store
on West All Saints Street. "My grandfather never said to me, 'Now remember, you can't go into that restaurant. You won't get served.' Or,
'you can't go in Baker Park.' It was just something you knew." You knew
in part because there was a policeman on the premises to keep you out of
the lovely park with a creek running down the center. Lee and his
friends, some of them white, would play in the streets, roller skating and
making scooters with skate wheels.

Bill Lee and his friends knew the ways of the segregated world—and
spent some time mocking it. Two of Lee's brothers were so light skinned
they could "pass" and often did, to the delight of their friends and kin.
"In my family, on my father's side, we were dark, but on my mother's
side, people were very fair. Of the four children, two were like me and
two were very fair. One of my brothers and another boy in the community who was also fair, they went to the Tivoli anytime they wanted to.
They blended in with the white kids. We joked about it all the time. My

brother's hair was kinky, so he put a cap on. Then he was home free."
Eventually, the Tivoli's owner gave the theater to the city and welcomed
the whole community. "Sometimes we'd get tired of that and someone
would say, 'Let's go up to Baker Park.' What that meant [was that] half
of us would be on the creek side and the other half would be by the armory. Keep in mind there was the cop there to keep us out. Those on the
creek side would be running in the park. The policeman would be so
confused. He'd go after them, and then the other side would go into the
park. He never did catch any of us. That was fun. We knew we were doing
something that was against the law, not permitted at that time."[5]

Like Bill Lee, former U.S. senator Charles McC. "Mac" Mathias grew
up near Baker Park in Frederick, not far from Roger Taney's old home-
stead on Bentz Street. As a boy, Mathias knew nothing of *Dred Scott,* but
he knew Roger Taney was an important man because the City was installing a marble bust of him on the courthouse grounds. Mathias used
to run over from his house across the street to see how the work was pro-
gressing. But the man he was really interested in then was Tom, an elderly black man who did odd jobs for the Mathias family. Tom, who was in
his 90s when Mathias was growing up, had been a slave. It was one of
those things, the senator says, that made him understand how close he
was in time to the days when men, women, and children were the property of others in the United States.

"His name was Thomas Alexander Contee Hanson Howard Radford
Clark. He had been named for one of his owners and for the owner's five
sons. I used to go out and garden with him, to pull weeds. He would tell
me stories of slave life, about being whipped and having salt rubbed in
the welts. I must have been 7 or 8. Because he had terrible rheumatism,
he had these pads on his knees, so I said, 'If I'm going to help, you have
to make me some pads.' Tom was a wonderful person. He was a local
hero, one of the leaders of the black community. Every day on Emancipation Day—we don't celebrate it anymore, but we did in those days—
and every Emancipation Day, he'd sit in an open Ford car and drive in
the parade."[6] It was an idyllic scene, sweeter than the life Tom and other
black Frederick citizens were living.

Bill Lee and Mac Mathias recall the ways in which Jim Crow was an in-
trusive presence in daily life. Lee says white minders had to be present
when there were black gatherings, even on Emancipation Day. A "White
Only" sign greeted everyone at the amusement park in nearby Braddock

Heights. Black people were barred unless they were caring for white children. Mathias says his father would not put up with these discriminations. "He took Tom to vote one day, and the poll officials wanted to hassle him. One of them said, 'What's your name?' He told them, and they said, 'spell it.' My father objected to that. And one of the officials said, 'Let the n----- vote.' He was constantly looking out for some black man who was in some sort of difficulty. So I grew up in that atmosphere."[7]

Mathias, too, became one of Frederick's most important sons. He practiced law in the courthouse where the bust of Taney stands. As a young lawyer, Mathias participated in civil rights actions in Frederick, working with Baltimore's Juanita Jackson Mitchell to eliminate the Jim Crow movie house practices. Later, after he was elected to the U.S. Senate, he sponsored legislation on voting rights, traveling to the South to visit Martin Luther King Jr. in a Birmingham jail. He and Bill Lee lived their lives in opposition to the legacy of the man whose bust they passed in front of the Frederick courthouse.

Mathias attempted to understand the circumstances of Taney's life. "Over and over he was in court on behalf of some master . . . He must have been troubled by this whole [slavery] controversy."[8] But perhaps Mathias assigned a more enlightened view to Taney's thinking than Taney would have been capable of given his upbringing. Though Mathias knew that antiblack attitudes were strong in his community, his 1960s viewpoint grew from a profoundly different set of life circumstances.

Slavery was a part of Roger Brooke Taney's world from his earliest perceptions of life. Slaves helped raise him. Slave children were his playmates. He would not have questioned slavery any more than he would have questioned the love of his parents. He saw his mother intervene on behalf of adult slaves when they were about to be punished, and he seems to have inherited her generous and kindly manner. "There was a sweetness and benignity, a courtesy of the heart as well as of the manner and a simple kindness [in him]."[9]

Kind and gentle as they might have been, the Taneys helped sustain a violent system. Beyond the outrage of owning another human being, slavery involved cruel and even depraved punishment. The lash was a staple of slave management. At various points in the history of slavery, whipping became so ferocious that laws were passed to keep it within what were regarded as reasonable limits. The lash was, in effect, licensed by the state. "Violence," notes a historian, "was not only common in slave societies, it was systematic and relentless . . . planters understood that without a monopoly of firepower and a willingness to employ terror, plantation slavery would not long survive."[10] It would not survive because, despite the best efforts of their owners, many slaves were determined to be free, to escape, to have a life beyond the lash and the judgment that black people were merely property.

It is no surprise that growing up in this culture, Taney and other white Marylanders typically assumed the inferiority of black people. "The enslavement of most black people in the region—and more importantly the universal knowledge that people of African descent were enslaved throughout the Atlantic world—debased black people in the eyes of most whites."[11] In Taney, there was an essential conflict between his best instincts and the culture in which he was nurtured. In the course of his distinguished life, he would act in accord with both.

Taney was born on March 17, 1777, on Battle Creek in Calvert County. As an old man writing his memoirs, Taney recounted his birth on a "good landed estate," which included slaves. "The history of my life is necessarily associated with the manners, habits, pursuits and characters of those with whom I lived and acted."[12] Given the absence of any trace of remorse in this account, the assertion seems almost defiant, and he would defend this culture throughout his life. Taney and the young American nation were bound to slavery as grimly as slaves were bound to their masters. In such a culture, a kind man could lament an evil practice but make no effort—short of colonization—to end it.

His family history included a somewhat ironic illustration of how bondage, limited or lifelong, reached into the lives of some Americans. His earliest Maryland forebear, the first of five Michael Taneys, arrived from England as an indentured servant. By the time he died, he had escaped that identity entirely. He had opportunities denied blacks in similar circumstances of servitude and increasingly thereafter. Michael Taney "buried the record of his indenture in a position of unquestioned aristocracy, leaving to posterity all the prestige which any ancestor in such a locality could have handed him."[13] Slaves, money, land, and tobacco came down to his heirs in grand profusion. The quasi slave became a slaveholder. Roger Taney's biographers do not suggest that their subject found particular inspiration in the success of those who preceded him in Maryland—or that he had any wry reflections on that heritage. His forebear's success was woven into the fabric of his family's life over generations. He doesn't mention it in his own memoir. He was destined to prosper as a man of the planter class, raised to pursue a law career.

He did report that he and his sister walked three miles to school. His father taught him to hunt and fish. After attending Dickinson College, where he actively campaigned for valedictorian and was accorded that honor, he apprenticed in a prestigious law firm in Annapolis. He was a member of the Maryland elite, but he did not assume he would be hand-carried to fame and prosperity. He made severe demands on himself, studying twelve hours a day and setting aside any social life. He knew what he wanted.

But he did not have every attribute he needed. So timid was he, so stricken upon any call to speak in public, that friends made all his speeches when he ran for the state legislature. What he called "a morbid sensibility"—he feared it was cowardice—plagued him all his life. Yet he seemed always able to overcome it, sometimes propping his leg hard against a table to steady himself in court. Throughout his life, he declined speaking invitations on the Fourth of July, fearing he would be unable to acquit himself well. He knew he would not always be able to lean on his family.

As crippling as these tremors might have been, he proceeded in life with considerable confidence in his talents. Ambition and assurance of success seem to have been in his makeup from his first moments as a lawyer. "I looked with deep interest upon the array of talent and learning which I saw before me [in the Annapolis courts], and hoped (perhaps in candor I ought to say believed) that the day would come that I might occupy the like position in the profession . . . There certainly was about me at that time no want of ambition for legal eminence, not so much for the emoluments it would bring as of the high rank and social position which were in that day attached to it."[14]

When he finished his studies, he returned to Calvert County to be thrown by his father into a race for the Maryland General Assembly, its House of Delegates. The elder Taney had served there before him. Politics being politics, the younger man—just 22 at the time—won apparently on the basis of "foaming steins" and name recognition, on a voice vote of the townsfolk. After his victory, friends chaired him through the courthouse green.

His law practice necessarily involved slaves. As he moved toward a position of leadership in Maryland and in the nation, he would devote a considerable portion of his time to finding a solution to the problem of slavery, settling on the idea of colonization: returning slaves to their ancestral homes or to another supposed haven. Best for them, he concluded, and best for the nation. "He was never, at any state in his life, an abolitionist but in this there is no inconsistency," writes one of his biographers, Carl Brent Swisher. Slaves "were not legitimate objects of pity," Taney thought. "They were better off than many free Negroes who were trying to get along in a white man's economy and were no more to be envied indeed than some of the poor whites in the neighborhood . . . There is no state in the union where a Negro or mulatto can ever hope to be a member of congress, a judge, a militia officer, or even a justice of the peace: to sit down at the same table with the respectable whites or to mix freely in their society."[15] Perhaps it was no more than a statement of the facts as he saw them, and yet it was a cavalier if not callous dismissal of the rights of man. The arguments against slavery never overcame his view that outsiders had no right to tell him or his kin how to live, to suggest that he was, somehow, a creature of lower moral and ethical standing because he supported slavery.

That thinking was reinforced throughout his life. As a student at Dickinson College, for example, he was taught that "even in a Democratic society, aristocrats should rule." Slaves, he pointed out as if there were no possibility of denial, were "degraded." Perhaps this word refers not to the natural condition of black people, but to their transformation via slavery. His view of the innate differences in people went beyond slaves. "Men were essentially different in breeding and capacity," he believed, "and not just slaves but some whites as well."[16] And yet as a man who would help to shape the new state and national governments, he repeatedly stood up for democratic values.

Without the advantages of family, the public life he pursued might have seemed ill-advised. "He was a slender, flat-chested youngster, apparently impetuous and hot-tempered like his father, with a physique too frail to house a stormy disposition. His eyesight was so lamentably poor he worried later that he could never be a good politician because he was forever failing to recognize even close acquaintances or family members."[17] He said, "I sometimes pass my own children on the street without knowing them until they speak to me."[18] His sharply focused work ethic and his intellect—not to speak of connections in high places—enabled him throughout his life to overcome these disadvantages.

He took his seat in the state legislature in November 1799, one of four delegates from Calvert County, population 8,652, half of it black. Taney's introduction to politics and to law making came in the midst of the new nation's earliest development. He was born the year the Continental Congress approved the Articles of Confederation. In his first year of service in Annapolis, his assignments reflected the infant nation he would serve: one of his committees dealt with the matter of pensions for widows of Revolutionary War veterans. He watched tears roll down the cheeks of the Maryland patriarch Charles Carroll of Carrollton at news of George Washington's death.

During his brief legislative career, Taney voted against repeal of the state's ban on slave importation. Given his overall attitudes about "degraded" blacks, Taney's vote might have had more to do with controlling the number of blacks in Maryland than with hindering the slave trade. He also voted to abolish the property qualification for whites voting in Maryland and against a bill that would have eliminated state-provided daily expenses for legislators. Both measures won his support because he did not wish to see the state run solely by the rich. That thinking did not include blacks, nor did he think it should. He remained thoroughly committed to the authority of the elect and the wealthy, committing a political mistake fatal to his young electoral career in the process.

In the presidential election of 1800, he chose to back John Adams over Thomas Jefferson in a state that went for the man from Monticello. In Maryland, that election turned on the question of how presidents should be chosen—by legislatures or by voters at large. In this matter, Taney thought the assembly more qualified, and in keeping with his lessons at Dickinson, he was certain the privileged classes had an obligation to assert their prerogatives. When Adams lost, delegates running under his banner, including Taney, lost their assembly seats. The privileges of birth had limits. At this point, in March 1801, he and his father decided he should move to Frederick, where his father's connections once again put him at the head of the line. Noted members of the Frederick bar were retiring, the elder Taney had learned, so young Roger would have an opening in the Frederick courts. The Taney family network gave Roger advantages that must have been rarely matched by his young competitors.

Not long after his arrival in Frederick, Taney resumed his acquaintance with Francis Scott Key, who in 1814 would write "The Star-Spangled Banner." Key had been in Annapolis training for the bar at the time

Taney had studied there. In due course, Taney met and, in 1806, married Frank Key's sister, Anne Phoebe Charlton Key. He also quickly became a member of the social as well as the legal Establishment. He had been introduced and mentored at the Frederick bar by his father's friend Thomas Johnson, who had been governor of Maryland from 1777 to 1779 and then a U.S. Supreme Court justice, appointed by George Washington. Taney immersed himself in the politics of Frederick and of the state, most often as an adviser. His legal career shot forward. He became one of the men to see in western Maryland. And often those who needed his services were caught up in one way or another with slavery.

Such a person was the Reverend Jacob Gruber, an itinerant and somewhat eccentric abolitionist minister from Pennsylvania, whose peregrinations brought him to western Maryland. As a man of the Methodist Episcopal Church, which forbade slaveholding, he might have been expected to speak against it. So who had invited him? As it turned out, he wasn't expected to speak at all. Gruber was a fill-in for the scheduled headliner, who had been unable to appear at a camp meeting near Hagerstown. The audience of 2,600 whites and 400 slaves settled in for what turned out to be a stem winder. Gruber seemed determined to infuriate his audience.

Pennsylvanians, he suggested, were morally superior to Marylanders—his proof, a fictional newspaper advertisement he had prepared that enumerated the evils of slavery: "For sale, a plantation, a house and lot, horses, cows, sheep, and hogs; also a number of Negroes—men, women, and children—very valuable ones; also a pew in such and such a church."[19] Slaves, in other words, were property: like animals or wooden church benches. He mocked Maryland's carefully cultivated claims to a progressive and more kindly form of slaveholding. "We live in a free country and, that all men are created equal and have inalienable rights such as life, liberty and the pursuit of happiness, we hold as self-evident truths," the minister said. "The voice of our brother's blood crieth. Is it not a reproach to a man to hold articles of liberty and independence in one hand and a bloody whip in the other while a Negro stands and trembles before him with his back cut and bleeding?"[20]

Little is known of the slaves' reaction, if any. They seemed no more active in pursuing freedom than their owners were in freeing them, though silence could hardly be interpreted as acceptance. The white citizenry found the minister's remarks incendiary. The authorities had him incarcerated. Freedom of speech, like freedom itself in those times, had limits. Fear of insurrection—and of an economy shorn of its bonded labor force—led Marylanders to threaten sanctions against those who disturbed the peace of a society they were pleased to think of as more humane than the societies of other slave states.

The Reverend Gruber's remarks were bold. Daring to speak with such passion in front of 400 slaves, he found himself indicted almost instantly on charges of offending against the peace, the government, and the dignity of the state. Recognizing big trouble when they saw it, his friends went looking for a lawyer. They quickly engaged Roger Taney, who at 41 had become one of the most influential lawyers in Washington and Frederick Counties. The Gruber matter would not have seemed unusual to him. Once again, he was headed for court on a matter involving slaves but in this case standing on the other side of popular opinion: defending an abolitionist from out of state. He had been retained more often to pursue some matters of replevin: a legal term referring to property rights and, in many cases, a master's attempt to reclaim this or that runaway slave, this or that slave whose claim to the status of free black was challenged. In one such case, he tried to overturn a court verdict that granted emancipation to ten blacks who claimed they were freed by a will.[21]

In another case, a slave claimed his freedom on the basis of receiving a piece of land. Owning property was associated with citizenship and freedom. If he owned land, wasn't he entitled to his freedom? The claim was opposed by a man—represented by Taney—who wished to buy a farm and its slaves. Taney and his client lost. Much later in his life, he would consider a plea for freedom based on a slave's temporary move from a slave state to a free state.[22] In his Maryland practice, slavery and its attendant issues were routine affairs, staples of the bar much as drunk driving or personal injury, bankruptcy or drug possession would be for lawyers two hundred years later. Owners pursued their "property" in court because slaves were valuable, signs of a person's financial attainments—much the way a BMW or beach condo or country club membership would be later. If you had accumulated slaves, you had wealth. Thus, if you attacked an institution of importance to the state's economy and way of life—as Pastor Gruber had done—you were going to need good representation.

Such was the atmosphere of Maryland when Pastor Gruber stood before the bar in 1818 with Roger Taney at his side. The lawyer spoke "with abhorrence of those reptiles, who by trading in human flesh, enrich themselves by tearing husband from the wife, the infant from the bosom of the mother."[23] He spoke of this practice as if it were the deed only of professional slave sellers. Taney suggested that those who merely owned and worked slaves in the fields or in the master's house were morally superior to the professional buyers and sellers, the traffickers. Yet without their willing participation, slavery might well have collapsed. Though slavery was on the wane as a useful institution, many Marylanders were as agreeably addicted to it as the rest of the slaveholding states were. Taney suggested they were simply helpless before monstrous merchants who trafficked in human flesh, rendering otherwise right-minded Marylanders into helpless participants in a horrid practice. He blamed it on the British and suggested a less subservient American nation might act differently in time.

> A hard necessity, indeed, compels us to endure the evil of slavery for a time. It was imposed upon us by another nation while we were yet in a state of vassalage. It cannot be easily or suddenly removed. Yet while it continues, it is a blot on our national character; and every real lover of freedom confidently hopes that it will eventually, though it must be gradually, wiped away and earnestly looks for the means by which this necessary objective may be best attained. And until it shall be accomplished, until the time shall come when we can point without blush to the language held in the Declaration of Independence, every friend of humanity will seek to lighten the galling chain of slavery, and better, to the utmost of his power, the wretched condition of the slave.[24]

In the Gruber case, which he won, Taney could more freely undertake the defense of an abolitionist because, though belatedly, he had recently freed his own slaves. Eighteen years earlier, he had brought them with him from his father's plantation and then used them until they grew older. After setting them free, he saw to their well-being in an environment he regarded as hopelessly hostile to them. A slaveholding lawyer could represent an abolitionist, of course, but his arguments would have more weight coming from one officially unencumbered by the evil Reverend Gruber had come to decry. Taney proceeded to call slavery an abomination, leading some to conclude that he was an abolitionist. But even as he spoke that day, Taney was convinced—at a deep emotional level—that blacks were unsuited for citizenship. He had been generous and just in his care of the slaves left to him by his father, though the very act of manumission reeked of the evil of slaveholding. By what authority did one man have the right to own another?

Some Americans were eager to see the end of slavery, to be able to cite the Declaration of Independence without shame. Maryland remained as conflicted on the question as the rest of the nation. Baltimore stood as an example of black and white living productively together, but no one was looking for such a model. And yet Maryland was the home of a man, Frederick Douglass, who would slip the "galling chain" and show the world that a black American could become not only a citizen, but a transcendent statesman.

FREDDY BAILEY IN BALTIMORE: "ALMOST A FREE CITIZEN"

Freddy Bailey fell asleep one evening under the parlor table where Sophia Auld kept her Bible. He awoke to the "mellow, loud and sweet" sound of her voice, reading lamentations of Job.[25] "Wherefore then hast thou brought me forth out of the womb? . . . Why hast thou forsaken me?" The irony of the scene—a slave child of 8 overhearing his master's wife reading from Job—would no doubt mean more to him later, but the music, the poetry, the soothing pace of written and spoken language touched his soul. It was a moment that helped to shape the extraordinary life of a Marylander who would be known to the world as Frederick Douglass.

Sophia Auld's parents had taught her to revile slavery. She did what she could to resist: Freddy wanted to read, and she wanted to teach him. But she acceded to the stern objections of her husband, who feared for his family in the atmosphere of hostile opposition to teaching slaves and, he said, for Freddy as well: No good could come to a slave with high expectations and an ability to see beyond the work at hand. Better to be content with the blessing of a family that did not abuse him. Freddy regretted the loss of his sympathetic tutor, but he thought master Hugh Auld's arguments against teaching slaves were essentially right. "I instinctively assented to the proposition; and from that moment I understood the direct pathway from slavery to freedom. This was just what I needed; and I got it at a time, and from a source, whence I least expected it."[26]

Here was a hearthside tableau of the slavery conflict in Maryland and, perhaps, in the nation as a whole. Here were the Aulds in Baltimore's Fell's Point neighborhood—a relatively caring white family—and a gifted black slave child, living astride the deep divide between Marylanders who wanted slavery to end then and those who thought it was an unavoidable reality. Unlike some southern states, Maryland did not prohibit teaching black men and women to read, and many were taught, but the power of private sanction was as effective as law. Hugh Auld seemingly knew and feared the effects of such sanction. Thus in Baltimore whites and blacks, free and slave, were living together in relative harmony, but instead of building on the potential being demonstrated every day right in front of them, many Marylanders embraced the colonization movement, the idea that the "problem" could be handled by exporting it.

Throughout his life, Taney had seen black men and women as unfit for the role of citizen. That belief endured beyond Taney. Indeed, the modern civil rights movement would face, as one of its first objectives, winning acknowledgement that blacks in America were due as much respect as other citizens. In the nineteenth century, the reality that every institution in society would have to address the problems of newly freed slaves was hardly acknowledged. More than one hundred years would go by before the Swedish social scientist Gunnar Myrdal defined the problem in his book *An American Dilemma*.[27] Had the nation's leaders been more willing to consider the challenges of emerging from slavery—had they the foresight to recognize the "dilemma" in its fullest and, over time, increasingly complex dimensions—they might have addressed the importance of education and used the potential inherent in a slave like Douglass to the advantage of individuals and the nation.

The young Freddy Bailey (he did not change his name to Douglass until after he escaped) must have been unaware of any such controversy, but apparently he would have been undeterred. He found tutors in the ferment of Baltimore streets: his playmates, the carpenters he worked with, and Charles Lawson, a free black man. Lawson lived in a small shack on a street called Happy Alley. The two, slave child and free elder, read the Bible three or four hours on end, the younger man helping the older with the more difficult words. Young white boys helped Freddy, too. He would remember them in his writing later: Gustavus Dorgan, Joseph Bailey, Charles Farity, and the Cordery boys, Jim, Bill, and

George. "In the rough democracy of boyhood he was accepted as an equal."[28] He joined them in fights with rival groups and distinguished himself with his fists. Later, based on this experience, he decided that prejudice was learned, not inherent.

During this time, these helpmates led him to *The Columbian Orator,* a compilation of classical speeches from Socrates to the Englishman William Pitt, Napoleon, and many others. Included in one volume was a dialogue between master and slave. Freddy must have heard echoes of Hugh Auld in these stories. The slave ought to be grateful for good treatment, the master, Cato, says. The slave responds: "What can you do for me that will compensate me for the liberty you have taken away?" Cato says, "A day, an hour of liberty is worth a whole century in bondage." If reading was such a threat to slave masters, Freddy thought, he would take that path.

The young man who would become Frederick Douglass was born Frederick Augustus Washington Bailey in February 1818, the same year Roger Taney defended Jacob Gruber in Hagerstown. Douglass and Taney were further counterpoints illustrating the ambivalence of many in the matter of slavery.

The origins of these two extraordinary Marylanders could not have been more sharply different, nor could their lives have been more symbolic of Maryland's divergent attitudes about race. They were born in southern Maryland or Eastern Shore counties at a time when a slave culture prevailed. Douglass was born in a slave cabin—or was it a building on the plantation or an open field? The precise location was nine miles south of Easton.[29] Taney's relatively elegant birthplace lay slightly north and across the Chesapeake Bay from Easton. Descended from a five-generation line of successful businessmen and slave owners, Taney had every advantage of wealth and status.

Douglass did not know who his father was. He saw his mother fewer than a half-dozen times and only at night. He was raised by his grandmother. Until the end of his life, he could not say with certainty in what year he had been born and felt he could not safely ask. A slave's question, he said, signified to the master a restless and dangerous spirit. Owners were wary of an "impudent curiosity" in their slaves, regarding it as evidence of a restless and rebellious temperament. The goal was subservience and total absence of ambition. Of the first large wave of Caribbean Creole slaves, many had been successful at escaping bondage and constructing perfectly functioning lives. Slave masters determined to deny their African slaves any opportunity to see their Creole brothers: role models were not in the planters' self-interest. The idea was to make the slaves know how completely dependent they were on their masters.

Black families were often divided purposely to build instability into their lives, to keep them in place, productive and ignorant of any opportunity that might exist for them off the farms.[30] As a further attack on the personal identity of slaves, they were given names, often drawn from classical literature, and conferred, it seemed, with derisive intent. Wasn't it funny to call a black slave Augustus or Cicero? White Jewish slaves saw how this sort of dehumanization was employed in Nazi prison camps during World War II. "Nothing belongs to us any more," wrote Primo Levi, an Auschwitz survivor and writer. "They have taken away our clothes, our shoes, even our hair; if we speak, they will not listen to us, and if they listen, they will not understand. They will even take away our name; and if we want to keep it, we will have to find ourselves the strength to do so, to manage somehow so that behind the name something of us, of who we were, still remains."[31]

Some of these unhappy conventions were changing by the 1820s in Maryland because the tobacco economy was slipping. More and more Maryland slaves were leaving the land for Baltimore, which at one point had more free blacks than any other U.S. city. Baltimore became known as a freedom port, a place where black people could come and go with relative ease. They remained subject to Draconian penalties for minor infractions of local law or as a result of a small unpaid debt, but the city offered immense advantages. It was easier, for example, to escape from this city so near the free states of the North.

Yet the slave system continued unabated. Douglass heard shackled humanity struggling up from the ships to the slave pens located where the sparkling Inner Harbor markets and Oriole Park at Camden Yards would be built more than one hundred years later. If white and free black people were troubled by the traffic in human beings, they were obliged to face their anguished consciences every day. Many were able to resolve the conflict quite easily—the way generations of Baltimoreans would live in proximity to great poverty later in the city's life. Slaves were owned up and down the social and economic structure: merchants, ship captains, public officials, judges, and professionals owned slaves. Doctors, lawyers, and bankers owned them, as did craftsmen and owners of manufacturing concerns. Skilled slaves came into the city from the rural parts of Maryland, where three-fourths of blacks were slaves, the opposite of the ratio in the city.

In Baltimore the slave culture faced real opposition, much of it coming from Quakers, from men like Benjamin Lundy, who committed his life to opposing slavery. He brought a young newspaper editor, William Lloyd Garrison, to the city in 1829 to make the point Pastor Gruber had made more than ten years earlier in Hagerstown: slavery in any form is an abomination. Maryland continued to think of itself as the home of a more enlightened form of slavery. Indeed, the belief that an abolitionist sheet could survive in Baltimore at the time may be attributable to the city's more liberal outlook. Perhaps Lundy and his new editor thought Baltimore a place where the antislavery sentiment could be roused to action. They gave slavery no quarter. With Garrison in town, Baltimore felt the stinging rhetorical volleys of an uncompromising abolitionist. He had come to take over Lundy's magazine, the *Genius of Universal Emancipation.*

For a brief moment in 1829, three of the most important figures in the nation's struggle over slavery lived in Baltimore. Garrison had moved into a boarding house at 135 Market Street in 1829; Douglass and the Aulds lived on Aliceanna and Anne Streets in Fell's Point off and on between 1826 and 1838; and Roger Taney, having moved from Frederick in 1823, was settled with his family in a house on Lexington Street. The three men were separated by many city blocks, by their views of the U.S. Constitution, by wealth, and by age. Garrison was a firebrand. Taney was a political insider and policymaker in Maryland and, eventually, in the White House. He belonged to the state and national Establishment. Douglass was a child of about 11, a prodigy whose extraordinary talents were not obscured even on the less tolerant Eastern Shore. In the vibrancy of Baltimore, Garrison, Taney, and Douglass were encouraged to act on their beliefs by virtually every element of the urban landscape.

Lundy wanted Garrison to run his magazine so that he, Lundy, would be free to walk the new nation recruiting partisans in the struggle for abolition.[32] They had met in Boston, where Lundy had tried unsuccessfully to raise money. Garrison turned out to be the great consolation prize. He found himself in awe of Lundy's religious commitment, deeper and more emotional than Garrison's intellectual approach. Maryland thought of itself as a kinder and gentler venue for slaves, but Garrison saw only a glaring crime against humanity, an irresistible target.

The New Englander apparently spared no one his honest assessment of reality as he found it. He called Lundy's paper "a dingy little sheet." Lundy, the man, he praised. Though Lundy was slight and unexceptional in physical appearance, he had what Garrison called "the boldness of Luther."[33] Lundy's life had been a difficult one. His mother and father died when he was young, and he struck out on his own, settling in Wheeling. There he saw slaves hauled off in cages for sale in the South. He was jolted to the core of his being. He eventually left his wife and children to devote his life entirely to ending slavery. Lundy set out to change a culture. The job was not getting easier. Most Americans saw slavery as an inherited evil that they were powerless to change.

It was the argument Taney made in the Gruber case: slavery had been visited upon Maryland and the nation by the British. It should be abolished . . . in due time. Here, again, was the tension, the belief that slavery was evil but a "hard necessity." One could even wonder if the presence of Garrison did not harden the resistance of those in Baltimore who wanted blacks enslaved—or shipped to another country. But Garrison and Lundy were not the only opponents of slavery and not the only ones in the city to take a stand.

John Needles, a Quaker businessman who helped Friend Lundy set up his printing operation, concealed antislavery tracts in furniture he was shipping south and offered his warehouse for use as a school for free black children. By 1829, the year during which Garrison ran the *Genius*, Baltimore's free black population had risen from eight thousand to fifteen thousand, with most of the remaining five thousand slaves working as domestics. Though city officials were in some conflict with the slavery-preserving framers, Garrison thought slavery was sustained and defended chiefly by the City.

Its most powerful leaders, including Roger Taney, believed they had a duty to protect the state and the nation from integration of black people into the national life. Said U.S. senator Robert Goodloe Harper: "You can manumit the slave but you cannot make him a white man." Colonization was critically important, he thought, because blacks were "an idle, worthless, and thievish race."[34] Brave black men like Jacob Greener, an outspoken advocate of black freedom, rose in meetings of the colonizers to suggest washing the stain of slavery from the stars and stripes. The city was becoming "an island of freedom." Another Quaker businessman who had freed many of his slaves told of black children stolen and killed in Delaware and scolded newspapers for their insistence on printing "Slaves for sale" advertisements. Other editors, he said, were as guilty of "grasping avarice" as were the slave traders who bought the ads.[35]

For those who persisted in the belief that persons of color were degraded, there was an inconvenient fact on display daily in Baltimore. Many blacks prospered. By increasing numbers, they gained their freedom. They organized churches, schools, and community associations. Increasingly, masters allowed slaves to "hire their work"—to take jobs, to accept pay, but then to hand over most of the earnings to the master at the end of the week. Few slaves saw the farm/city contrast more dramatically than Douglass did.

"A city slave," he wrote, "is almost a free citizen."[36]

Free and even enslaved blacks were integrating themselves into the economy and the society before Taney's weak and unwilling eyes: weren't all these men and women a walking refutation of his view that blacks were incapable of surviving in the marketplace? Apparently they had the potential to overcome the disadvantages of their arrival in this country, just as Taney's indentured forebear had done.

Almost immediately, Garrison fell into conflict with prominent Maryland leaders. The *Genius* had made a special project of Austin Woolfolk, the most famous slave merchant in Baltimore. After a few broadsides about him appeared in the *Genius,* Woolfolk physically attacked Lundy on the street. He was convicted of the assault with a cynical wink and punished by imposition of a one-dollar fine, a sum so deliberately low as to license assault and to ally the court with Woolfolk, and slaveholders generally.

Garrison picked up Lundy's theme and expanded it. He challenged Taney's view that blacks were unfit for citizenship: "Could black people ever be on a level with the whites in this country? Not if we perpetuate their slavery, not if we deprive them of the benefits of instruction, not if they were denied the privileges of citizenship."[37] Garrison was honing the rapier. He skewered Americans determined to find justifications for slavery. In a different forum, Garrison recalled what Taney told the jury in the Gruber trial: Americans should hate slavery and help strike the "galling chain."

Surely, opportunity for the society was being squandered. The idea of a free black refuge in Baltimore apparently created fear in white Marylanders instead of inspiring them to build on black talent and ambition. Would blacks command too many jobs? Would they try to assume a role in community life? Would intermarriage become a threat? Would they lead murderous rebellions such as the one famously accomplished later in nearby Virginia by the slave Nat Turner? Increasingly, black people found themselves saddled with a series of discriminatory laws. They were struggling to escape the profound disadvantages of slavery, and the road was made harder. Their remarkable successes became proof that they should not be disregarded. Their very success at the arduous transition from bondage became a cruel impediment, since doing well undermined the assumption that only a ruinous existence was possible.

Garrison and Lundy—outsiders with nothing at stake socially or financially—were as embarrassing a presence as Gruber had been. Garrison invited Woolfolk to his house for a debate. Woolfolk did not appear. The young editor persisted. He ridiculed the idea that slavery could be benevolent in any guise. Slaveholders' silence—and their violence against those who illuminated their crimes—showed that they were under little pressure to change. The commerce was still profitable, widespread, and protected by authority: why change? But Garrison must have infuriated Taney and others with his rhetoric. Woolfolk and the slave traders, he wrote, were "no better than highway robbers and murderers."[38] His crusade was working splendidly at the humiliation level.

In 1830, the state of Maryland, through a grand jury, indicted Garrison and Lundy on charges that they had libeled a slave merchant operating out of Massachusetts, one Francis Todd. That Todd had done what they accused him of was not in dispute. He had sent seventy-five slaves to Woolfolk in a ship captained by Nicholas Brown, who made himself fabulously wealthy in the triangular trade. (Nicholas Brown was a forebear of the Brown family that endowed the Ivy League university of the same name. The slave trade was a matter of some friction in the family. Some members were profiting from it, and some were contemptuous of it.) In February 1830, Todd sued the *Genius* in civil court, probably at the behest of Woolfolk. Todd's lawyer, Jonathan Meredith, had been a law partner of Roger Taney, who may have been a silent partner in the legal proceedings.[39] Though Maryland law made truth a strong defense in libel actions, the *Genius* editors, Lundy and Garrison, were indicted by a grand jury for libel. The fact that slaves were shipped as Garrison reported had no impact on the judge—the same judge, Nicholas Brice, who had fined Woolfolk one dollar in the Lundy assault case. Slavery's opponents were driven out of business with the approbation of Baltimore's legal Establishment, which sat by while protections for press freedom were pushed aside. Since neither Garrison nor Lundy had the financial means to keep publishing, putting their magazine out of business may have been the lawsuit's objective.

Taney, by then, could have exerted his influence from the added prestige of a new position: attorney general of Maryland. If he was indirectly involved in this affair—and surely he was aware of it—the eloquent speech he had given twelve years earlier in defense of Reverend Gruber lost more of its luster: "Until the time shall come when we can point without blush to the language held in the Declaration of Independence, every friend of humanity will seek to lighten the galling chain of slavery, and better, to the utmost of his power, the wretched condition of the slave," he had said. Now, though, Baltimore's leading citizens and its courts drew the chain tighter, and the most strident voice raised in opposition fell silent. To be sure, efforts were made by eminent citizens such as Taney to solve the race problem by evicting black people entirely. The so-called colonization movement, of which Taney was a leading member, was more active in Maryland than it was in most other states.

Jurors in the criminal case epitomized the then-prevalent conflict between slavery and the marketplace. They reported revulsion at slavery and their hope that someday it would be abolished, reflecting the divided sentiments of Maryland as a whole. On the day at hand, they held that a man's property had to be protected even if that property were another human being. Garrison was convicted and sentenced to jail unless he could pay a fine far in excess of the one given to Austin Woolfolk for his assault on Lundy. The New Englander called the proceeding "a burlesque upon the Constitution."[40]

The outcome, though not ideal, had its advantages for Garrison. He had forced the authorities to show their colors and proved his willingness to take on any opponent in the cause of ending slavery. The cost was dear. The *Genius* went immediately out of business, with no one to carry on the public struggle. Garrison spent the next forty-nine days in jail, dining nightly with the warden, who delighted in the brilliant young editor's company at table. Later, Garrison wrote, "A few white victims must be sacrificed to open the eyes of the nation, and to show the tyranny of our laws. I am willing to be persecuted, imprisoned and bound for advocating African rights, and I should deserve to be a slave myself if I shrunk from that duty or danger."[41] (Garrison's sentiments, evoking the tactics of civil disobedience, would be echoed more than a century later in the declarations of Mahatma Gandhi and the Reverend Martin Luther King Jr.)

Judge Brice had his way: Garrison left Baltimore in the summer of 1830. The judge had written to Governor Joseph Kent the previous year, urging some attention to the troubling emergence of what he called "a sort of middle class" among black Baltimoreans. Their relative freedom, he warned, "menaced the institution of slavery . . . Leading them to think they had some rights in common with free men."[42] Indeed, this fear was precisely what had prompted slave owners to cut off slaves from contact with a freer outside world.

Racial tolerance was fading. Sophia Auld could not risk teaching Frederick Douglass to read, but a prison warden could entertain the uncompromising Garrison at his table without fear of being ostracized—or perhaps without much caring. It was a city, after all, a place where conventions could be disregarded without fear of the silent pillory. It was a place where, even when powerful lawyers ignored the law, a slave like Douglass could feel "almost free."

In Fell's Point, despite the unspoken ban on reading lessons, the Aulds were giving Freddy Bailey rare status. He was black, and yet, he was virtually a family member. He was getting in Baltimore the sort of nurturing a slave child might be denied in the course of a fractured life. Freddy did, of course, remain a slave. And in 1833 he was, unceremoniously, divorced from the advantages of Baltimore and the Aulds. His strong back was returned to its owners on the Shore. His foster family was unwilling to assume the care of a black child crippled in a childhood accident, so Freddy's owners somewhat spitefully pulled him away. He returned to the Shore with an invaluable gift, however: knowledge that freedom was not only possible but available to those determined to seize it. Baltimore had given him literacy and hope. It had shown him that not every soul on this earth was committed to perpetual bondage. It had shown him his own capabilities. He was ready to overcome his own trials of Job and to demand more than an hour of freedom, and not for himself alone.

Taney, meanwhile, was headed for Washington, where he would become attorney general of the United States.

"MERE PROPERTY": TANEY AND DOUGLASS ON
THE NATIONAL STAGE

As attorney general, Roger Taney was an influential member of Andrew Jackson's cabinet, and he found an early opportunity to express himself on the citizenship status of black Americans, slave or free. His predecessors as U.S. attorney general had chosen to avoid the question, but Taney seemed anxious to offer views that went beyond the cases at hand.

Black seamen were being jailed in some southern states lest they foment uprisings. Black sailors were deprived of their freedom under these state laws until their ships were ready to leave port. An 1832 case involving a version of that law in North Carolina drew Taney's attention. He found the practice acceptable, though it appeared to be a violation of a citizen's rights, because, he said, black people, even free blacks, were not citizens. Coming so soon after his move to Washington, Taney's holding seems an accurate reflection of convictions established in Maryland—on the Taney family's Calvert County plantation; in the courts of Baltimore and Frederick; as attorney general of Maryland; and in his colonization efforts. In 1832, twenty-five years before Dred Scott, he wrote:

> The African race in the United States even when free are everywhere a degraded class, and exercise no political influence. The privileges they are allowed to enjoy, are accorded to them as a matter of kindness and benevolence rather than of right. They are the only class of persons who can be held as mere property, as slaves . . . They were never regarded as a constituent portion of the sovereignty of any state . . . They were not looked upon as citizens by the contracting parties who formed the Constitution. They were evidently not supposed to be included in the term citizen. And they were not intended to be embraced in any of the provisions of that Constitution but those which point to them in terms not to be mistaken.[43]

The business at hand in the Jackson administration, however, was far different. Taney urged the president to dissolve the Bank of the United States, fearing that its directors would have the means to run the nation for their own ends without regard to democratic institutions. His thinking was rooted in the views he expressed while a legislator in Annapolis, voting then to retain state-paid living expenses lest only the wealthy could serve. Jackson was won over and agreed that the bank's U.S. funds should be deposited in independent, or "pet," banks. When the treasury secretary defied Jackson, the president sacked him and dispatched Taney to accomplish the task.

Here Taney's devotion to country collided with personal considerations. He wanted to be a Supreme Court justice, an ambition within reach given his talent and connections. Politics would be his path to that position—unless it derailed him. If he accepted the president's politically difficult chore, supporters of the bank would conspire against him. As then constituted, the Senate wanted to retain the bank, so it was a good bet its members would not have confirmed Jackson's appointment at Treasury. Taney was also certain to be denied a seat on the U.S. Supreme Court should he be appointed. Jackson dealt with the Senate's advice and consent duty by declining to ask for it. At the end of a year, the deposits having been handed over and the bank closed, Taney's appointment as treasury secretary did go to the Hill, whereupon the Senate unceremoniously said no. Taney returned to Maryland to great acclaim. A coach met him at the Baltimore city line. Dinners were held in the city and in Frederick, though a few supporters of the bank were conspicuously absent. All in all, the celebrators seemed to outnumber detractors.

President Jackson did not forget him. Within a year, he named Taney to the Supreme Court. Again the Senate said no. But in 1836, a new Congress more amenable to Jackson and less concerned about the now-departed bank was elected, and Chief Justice John Marshall, the Court's first shaping giant, had died. Now, Jackson could repay his loyal adviser even more handsomely. A Marylander would now exercise his authority and beliefs as head of the government's judicial branch. Taney would be not simply an associate justice of the Court, but its chief. He had, despite his "morbid" nervousness, navigated the political and judicial currents with great skill. His virtues were many. His experience, his scholarship, his involvement in crucial affairs of state made him an ideal steward of the nation's evolving system of laws.

While Taney was moving rapidly from attorney general to the U.S. Supreme Court, Freddy Bailey was looking for a way out of his bondage. He had been returned in 1834 to the Eastern Shore, where he worked for the brutal overseer Edward Covey, who had no regard for his talents. He tried to escape, triggering in the slaveholders of the Eastern Shore that just-below-the-surface fear that must have been a constant in the lives of slave masters. The stories of intermittent rebellion—Nat Turner's in Virginia and Denmark Vesey's abortive uprising in South Carolina, which led to the seaman's incarceration laws—brought even more fear into the hearts of white Maryland and restriction into the lives of black people. Thomas Auld, brother of Hugh, realized Freddy Bailey was too restless to be contained and sent him back to his brother in Fell's Point with the hope that Freddy would learn a craft.

The young black man began to work his way into the life of the city. He sang in the Sharp Street Church choir, then located near the Inner Harbor. The members of this Methodist congregation had worked with free blacks for years. In this part of the city, blacks and whites—sail makers, cooks, blacksmiths, seamstresses, teamsters, and others—lived jammed together in typically crowded urban conditions. But there was opportunity in this for a young man with ambition. During these days in Baltimore, his life lessons were profoundly affecting.

Hugh Auld could not stop what Freddy had begun. Later, Freddy would learn what the word "abolition" meant, from a *Baltimore American* story about John Quincy Adams's antislavery speech in Congress. The young black man learned more and more about his city and his world, aided indirectly by Auld, who sent him out to work at several Fell's Point shipyards, including Gardner Brothers, Butler and Lambdin, and Walter Price's yard, where Hugh Auld was the foreman. He allowed Freddy, a teenager at the time, to work for others, often taking the young man with him to the yard.

The family lived near the corner of Fleet and Durham Streets, scant blocks from the shipyards and Fell's Point's deep harbor. Both Auld and Freddy may have worked on ships later used in the slave trade: one of these ships later used in the trade was the Guatemala Packet, a schooner built in 1836.[44] The young man probably had no idea how the ships would be used. Auld might not have known either, but that seems less likely.

Young Freddy Bailey had escape on his mind. He needed money, but he was required to hand over most of what he earned in Baltimore's shipyards to his master. That Auld allowed him to work at all was a blessing. From the pennies he could keep, he built an escape fund of seventeen dollars. The Aulds had promised to release him eventually, but he could not wait—nor could a slave be certain that promises would be kept. Perhaps the old field hand's song of fear and determination described his thinking.

I thought I heard them say
There were lions in the way.
I don't expect to stay
Much longer here.
Run to Jesus—shun the danger—
I don't expect to stay
Much longer here.[45]

Finally, the moment came, in September 1838. He was 20 years old. He set out then for freedom, showing his considerable nerve and will. He slipped out of Baltimore by train, disguised as a sailor. More of the cash he needed to buy a ticket and for living in New York City came from his friend Anna, who sold one of her feather comforters to raise a few more dollars. He borrowed papers that asserted he was a seaman, though he hardly resembled the person described in the documents. Americans were anxious to honor men who were then engaging the British in nearly constant shipboard battles. Mother England insisted its men could legitimately board American ships and seize cargo at will. Patriotic fervor, Freddy must have hoped, would make a conductor less anxious to compare the descriptions to the person standing in front of him.

"I suppose you have your free papers," the trainman asked.

"No, sir," Freddy replied. "I never carry my free papers to sea with me."

"But you have something to show you are a free man, have you not?"

"Yes, sir!" the young slave said. "I have a paper with the American eagle on it that will carry me around the world." The conductor smiled, collected the fare, and moved on through the crowded car.[46]

The escape might have been thwarted at several other moments. Boarding a ferry across the Susquehanna River at Havre de Grace, he was spotted by a ferry hand he'd met in Fell's Point. Loudly, the man called out to him, asking what he was doing in a sailor get-up. Freddy muttered some reply and moved off quickly to find something like a hiding place.

Then boarding the train for Wilmington, Delaware, on the north side of the river, he saw a passenger, one Captain McGowan, for whom he had worked only days before. The man did not see him, but a Baltimore black-smith, Frederick Steen, did. Steen kept staring as if trying to place him. Freddy's Indianlike features, light color, and height surely made him a recognizable figure. Escape would now depend on a residue of human kindness, a revulsion over slavery—often there, but usually tamped down by money matters, by the political correctness of that time, or by one's own implication in the enterprise. White men and women might not join the abolitionists, but they might not wish to end anyone's reach for freedom.

"I really believe he knew me, but had no heart to betray me. At any rate, he saw me escaping and held his peace."[47] Humanity cries out for more affirmative expressions of goodness and courage on behalf of freedom, but measured against the ethos of the time, silence was sublime generosity. The Underground Railroad was not always underground. The "galling chain of slavery" came off not always by clamorous hammer blows but sometimes by absolute silence.

He made it to New York, moving on quickly to New Bedford, Massachussetts, hoping he could be employed there in his trade, ship caulker, the skill he had learned in Baltimore. He found that racism was not the exclusive province of southern or border states. He had trouble cracking the white worker's hold on jobs in his new hometown, but another vocation was soon manifest in his life.

Frederick Douglass gained some recognition after he spoke in churches, such as at New Bedford Zion chapel, and at meetings of antislavery organizations (Freddy Bailey having, in effect, been left in Baltimore). Some of his words found their way into the *Liberator,* the paper then being edited by Garrison in Boston. In 1841, Douglass spoke at an antislavery gathering on Nantucket. Garrison was in the audience.

"Have we been listening to a thing, a chattel person, or a man?" the editor asked.

"A man, a man!" the audience replied.

"Shall such a man be held a slave in a Christian land?" Garrison asked.

"No, No!" shouted the audience.

Douglass would later say with considerable understatement, "My association with the excellent men . . . helped to prepare me for the wider sphere of usefulness which I have since occupied."[48] He had found his purpose, his calling. It was miraculous. He became an instant luminary, a marquee attraction on the worldwide abolition stage. He saw the part he would be expected to play, and he had no hesitance, knowing his performance had every element of truth beneath it.

"People had to not only hear and see him but almost feel him; he had to make his wounds bleed: 'Yes, my blood has sprung out as the lash embedded itself in my flesh.' . . . And never could he appear less than totally noble."[49] He was 23 years old, standing in churches, often reciting words he had learned in Happy Alley with Charles Lawson.

Three years later, in 1845, the former slave published the first of his three autobiographies, *Narrative of the Life of Frederick Douglass, an American Slave, Written by Himself.* The book's publication drew wide acclaim and considerable controversy: surely, it was said, he had not written it himself. It was labeled a pack of lies by some, the fictional maundering of a writer who could not be trusted, whose bias was so overwhelming as to mark the whole enterprise fraudulent. And there were passages that, if not wholly inaccurate, were exaggerations that led some to think of Douglass as a propagandist. In time, he would acknowledge the role thrust upon him by his extraordinary life circumstance. Slavery could not have prepared him to pursue a public life—or a writing life. He would also acknowledge the debt he owed to Baltimore and even to those who had owned him in the city and in Easton. He was a sublime representative of the apparently inexhaustible black devotion to country, in spite of the country's aggressively malign attitudes. Maryland's Douglass was a progenitor of this remarkably generous response, and one of the historic antecedents of the nonviolent modern civil rights movement.

The *Narrative* propelled Douglass toward an extraordinary status in the world of 1845, a world in which he was a free man only as long as he eluded bounty hunters and stayed out of Maryland and the South. A.M., a correspondent for the *Liberator,* Garrison's newspaper, wrote: "I have wept over the pages of Dickens . . . but Douglass' history of the wrongs of the American Slave brought, not tears—no, tears refused me this comfort—it's horrible truths crowded in such quick succession, and entered so deep into the chambers of my soul, as to entirely close the relief valve."[50]

The early reactions of Marylanders to the *Narrative* boosted sales because they lent the work credibility, countering the belief that a slave could not have written it. For example, the editor of a Philadelphia newspaper, the *Elevator,* while reviewing Douglass's "exceedingly interesting autobiography," reported that on a trip to Maryland, he encountered several blacks who knew Douglass "by his assumed as well as by his real name and related to us many interesting incidents. More direct testimony validating the *Narrative* came from the pens of white Marylanders personally acquainted with slavery on the Eastern Shore and Douglass's owners."[51]

This valuable testimony—which might not have been offered in other slave states—began when a white resident of Baltimore reported in September 1845 that Douglass's *Narrative* "is now circulating and being read in this city, and five hundred copies are still wanted here. They would be read with avidity, and do much good." Signing his letter "A citizen of Maryland," the writer then assessed the credibility of Douglass's account. "I have made some inquiry and have reason to believe his statements are true. Col. Edward Lloyd's relatives are my relatives!"[52] This sort of endorsement spoke eloquently of tolerance for divergent, antislavery sentiment in Maryland.

Douglass was soon launched on an international speaking circuit, during which he laid out the horrors of his former life. "The slave has no rights," he declared during an 1846 visit to England. "He is a being with all the capacities of a man in the condition of a brute. Such is the slave in the American plantations. He can decide no question relative to his own actions; the slave-holder decides what he shall eat or drink, when and to whom he shall speak, when he shall work, and how long he shall work; when he shall marry, and how long the marriage shall be binding, and what shall be the cause of its dissolution—what is right and wrong, virtue or vice. The slave-holder becomes the sole disposer of the mind, soul and body of his slave, who has no rights."[53] More than his words, his presence was proof that the black man could not be thought of as "mere property," something to be bought and sold as any other commodity, unworthy of citizenship.

Roger Taney was a cloistered monk by comparison, removed from daily political commerce by his role on the high court. Douglass was becoming a marquee figure, putting himself and Maryland on the world map. What Douglass wrote and spoke of, he and Roger Taney had lived—Taney as slaveholder, Douglass as slave. During one of Douglass's speeches in England, he painted a grim picture of the slave's life:

The auctioneer's block in Maryland is the place to witness the heartrending cruelty of slavery, not merely in the infliction of the lash on the back of the slave, but there you see the iron of slavery enter the soul of the slave. There you see the husband torn from his wife, and the children torn from their parents. A case like this occurred not long since. A man and his wife, so far as such relations can exist in slavery, for there are no legal marriages among slaves, yet I am happy to say that among the slaves is to be found the purest morality and the strongest fidelity, especially amongst those who look upon themselves in the character of man and wife—unprotected by the law, virtue among the slaves is frequently regarded as a vice by their owners, and not a few female slaves have been made to feel the body lash in consequence of their adhesion to their own dignity as women.[54]

Taney was, no doubt, right when he wrote that free black men could count on no political influence. How could it have been otherwise? The power of the vote had been steadily stripped away since the days of the Revolution. From a distance, to be sure, these two Marylanders—Douglass and Taney—were about to stand among the nation's most important speakers on two sides of a deeply divisive question: how could a nation, founded on the bedrock of freedom, continue to accept slavery as an immutable "hard reality"?

A fugitive from the democracy of Baltimore streets—where slaves and the free black persons were virtually indistinguishable, where ambition and talent could flower—Douglass was showing what a black man could do in this life. If he noticed Douglass at all, Roger Taney must have thought him a dangerous aberration.

A SOUTHERN GENTLEMAN'S MANIFESTO: TANEY'S INFAMOUS DECISION

Eleven days short of his 80th birthday, on March 6, 1857, Chief Justice Roger Taney entered the U.S. Supreme Court's chambers, then still located in the U.S. Capitol, his robed brothers in procession behind him. "With firm and steady step . . . a tall, thin man slightly bent with the weight of years, of pale complexion and features somewhat attenuated and care worn but lighted up with that benignant expression which is indicative at once of a gentle temper and kindly heart," he read his decision in a low voice, making it difficult for listeners to hear him well.[55] Perhaps that "morbid sensibility" still clouded his ventures into any public arena, even one he commanded. The reading took two hours.

Despite various infirmities, including his compromised eyesight, he had impressed the world of politics and the law with his great talents, his stoic discipline, and his devotion to the law. He was said to be a most amiable fellow, kind to all, a considerate mentor and colleague. From the beginning of his career reading the law in Annapolis, he was determined to be a man of substance and standing. He more than accomplished his goals, serving at the pinnacle of the nation's executive and judicial branches. He was committed to interpreting the law with a faithful eye to the Constitution, but he was not blind to the political turmoil outside his chamber. There was combustible material in his own crucible of judgment: his life as a lawyer in Maryland, his concern about the nation's future, and his devotion to the southern way of life. Slaves and slavery were symbols of his determination to fend off federal interference in the affairs of the states, particularly the southern states. He was also convinced that the nation would not prosper if black people were accorded the rights of citizens.

In significant ways, racial hostility had grown in Maryland and in the nation over the course of Taney's long life. Something powerful—an affirmation of the rights of all or proof that these rights were limited to white Americans—would be needed to stabilize the nation. To serve as arbiter, the nation looked to the Taney Court, or so Taney thought. A case had been pending in Washington that might provide the needed guidance. Just what that guidance should be depended on one's point of view about slavery and the status of black people. Americans would look to one man's interpretation of the law, one man who would speak for the nation's highest court.

Political figures in Congress and in the White House awaited the Court's ruling in *Dred Scott v. Sandford* with undisguised eagerness. Taney would rule in that moment of high drama. His ambition, his passion for the law, had taken him to this point. He could not avoid making history. He seems to have relished the opportunity.

His home state, split neatly in half on the question of slavery and black rights, was a reasonably accurate mirror of the nation's posture on the so-called peculiar institution. There was little doubt where he fell on the question. "His sympathies with the South in the growing sectional struggle were beginning to [limit] the expression of his humane sympathies for the enslaved members of an unfortunate race. The conflict between these sympathies was one which he was never fully able to resolve," wrote one of his biographers, Carl Brent Swisher.[56]

The answer he gave was colonization—not abolition or manumission or integration, but deportation. He was much troubled by the increasing kinds of violent punishment directed at slaves. Better, he thought, if black people, slave and free, were sent to some other country. Frank Key was his ally in this, as were many others in Maryland. Colonization was a form of ethnic cleansing—and totally impractical, a further extension of the idea that black people could be owned or shipped out or whipped or freed at the whim of white people.

Douglass saw to the core of this idea, which was advanced by its advocates as benevolent. "The native land of the American Negro is America," he said. "His bones, his muscles, his sinews, are all American. His ancestors for two hundred and seventy years have lived, and labored, and died on American soil, and millions of his posterity have inherited Caucasian blood."[57] He challenged the conflict claimed by colonization supporters: "Let the nation try justice and the problem will be solved." Words, he said, can be dangerous things, and the idea of a "Negro problem" was pernicious and potentially ruinous for the nation.

For very different reasons, Taney agreed with this latter sentiment, but he thought the "problem" would submit to another solution if handed down by the high court, the nation's final and well-respected arbiter. And he may have seen himself as the last best hope for saving his sacred southern way of life.

In a letter to his son-in-law, he provided another take on his somewhat contradictory attitudes: as a "weak and credulous race," he said, blacks would fall to "absolute ruin" if freed en masse. He argued that nothing good would come of emancipation, though his own experience—and the example set by Douglass and others he saw coming and going in Baltimore—might have led to a different conclusion: "I am glad to say that none of those whom I manumitted disappointed my expectations, but have shown by their conduct that they were worthy of freedom and knew how to use it."[58] He was about to consider a matter of law that would allow a national testing of that experience.

Few cases in the history of American jurisprudence rival the importance of the case brought in the 1850s by a Missouri slave named Dred Scott. Scott argued that he should be free because his owner had taken him out of a slave state, Missouri, to live for a time in Illinois, a free state. These circumstances were well within the experience of a man like Taney, who had argued many such cases as a lawyer in Maryland. He must have seen the underlying matter as routine, no more than a variation on cases he had dealt with all his legal life. Questions about what constituted a freedom-granting event in a slave's life had been a constant in his law practice long before he argued Reverend Gruber's case in Hagerstown and afterward.

Taney was a man of great legal and political dexterity, talents honed to a fine edge by his life in Maryland politics and government. He had become a by-the-book student of the law, religious and secular. At one of the most difficult moments in his life, he followed the teachings of his church, which held that he could not be buried next to his beloved wife because she was not a Catholic. Was there a parallel between Taney's faithful adherence to canon law and to decisions he would make later about the words in the U.S. Constitution?

His overly rigid view of that document came into play at the penultimate moment of his life. The course he chose seemed the more remarkable because he was famously capable of thinking (as they would say a century later) outside the box—and outside the parameters of class. He thought about democracy—what threatened it, what might make it strong—and thus he had opposed the national bank, and he had opposed measures in the Maryland legislature that denied expense money for legislators and might have limited representation in the assembly to the wealthy.

Taney and his colleagues on the Court, not to speak of freshly inaugurated President James Buchanan, hoped the Court's decision might have some soothing effect on a brewing upheaval potentially as calamitous as any an abolitionist minister might have fomented. Sectional friction, the future of slavery, relations between the slaveholding South and the (relatively) abolitionist North had grown combustible. *Dred Scott* was an explosive mix.

It seems unlikely that Taney needed support for the conclusions he reached in the case, but virtually at his side in the deliberations stood another Marylander, Reverdy Johnson, who had been, like Taney, attorney general of the United States and a leading legal practitioner in Maryland. Johnson had served also as a U.S. senator from Maryland and as minister to Great Britain. In the *Scott* case, he buttressed Taney's view that Congress had no power to prohibit slavery in the territories. Slaves were property, and under the Constitution, property was to be controlled by the states, these two men insisted. Reverdy Johnson argued against Dred Scott and against Scott's lawyers, a team that included Montgomery Blair. Blair was the son of Francis Preston Blair, the newspaper editor and counselor to many presidents, beginning with Andrew Jackson. The Blairs lived on a farm called Silver Spring in Montgomery County. The family had been slaveholders, but later in life they were convinced that slavery was wrong. Thus were nominal Marylanders arrayed on both sides of this epochal case. The Blair family might be regarded as further evidence of Maryland's split view of slavery and black people, but they were not born-and-bred Marylanders as was Taney.

The chief justice made his political purpose clear in the letter to his son-in-law, where he wrote that the southern states would never have accepted the Constitution if free blacks had been embraced in the word "citizen." To allow blacks the same rights as whites, he wrote, would have produced "discontent and insubordination among them, and endangered the peace and safety of the state."[59] If that rupture was still likely despite or because of his decision, he seemed to think, so be it.

Once again, as he had in 1832, Taney asserted his view that the founders and their constituents saw blacks as inferior. He did not disagree with these views, having been conditioned initially by the prevalence of slavery and later by the sharp erosion of legal protections for blacks in Maryland. These protections had fallen away steadily during Taney's upbringing and legal training. His reading of the mood prevalent at the time of the nation's birth has been questioned, though, by many. "Racial prejudice in Maryland was strong then, but, with few exceptions, the law applicable to free blacks was color blind," writes David Bogen of the University of Maryland School of Law.[60] Over the next century and more, "racial legislation deprived freed blacks of many of the rights they possessed when the period opened around the time of the Declaration of Independence." That was true of the nation as a whole. "A list of the Negro's legal rights at that time [of the American Revolution] would be at least as long as a list of legal disabilities."[61]

Yet Taney ruled as if the black man had been virtually without rights from the beginning of the nation. A single line in his decision became one of the most famous, enduring, and injurious in American social and legal history: "They had for more than a century before been regarded as be-ings of an inferior order, and altogether unfit to associate with the white race, either in social or political relations, and so far inferior that they had no rights which the white man was bound to respect, and that the Negro might justly and lawfully be reduced to slavery for his benefit."[62]

This declaration lives in infamy, though it has been taken out of con-text from the day it was published. Taney offered it as a summation of public attitudes prevalent at the time the Constitution was written. Many, if not most, readers of Taney's decision interpret it as Taney's own view. He saw blacks as unfit for citizenship, virtually helpless in the mar-ketplace and ill-suited for many of the demands of citizenship. He thought slavery was an abomination, but he saw no way to abolish it quickly. His appeal for more time would be heard throughout America's struggle with slavery, Jim Crow, and racial attitudes. The reality of the black man's incapacities in Taney's eyes was upheld by his reading of the Constitution.

"He could turn a dead eye on the morality of the thing," wrote the Reverend Vincent Hopkins.

The law was the law and should be revered above even the judg-ments of humanity. Thus he never said a thing in his decision about the evil of the practice—notwithstanding his own views which, however kind and genteel, nevertheless arrogated the right first to own and then to free other human beings. Even as he was laying out the argument that the Framers regarded blacks as unworthy of citi-zenship, he offered no brief for a different view for, in truth, he agreed with them. He saw the slave as wholly and woefully incapable of caring for himself—and, in that, he may have been right, slavery having deprived men and women of their identity. Yet he knew also that this was not true of many blacks. How to decide which should remain free and which kept in some form of bondage? The ques-tions were not at hand in a decision that was to be largely political.[63]

The high court had been called upon to decide a citizenship question first: could black people, slave or free, ever be citizens and therefore enti-tled to have cases such as this decided in federal court? "We think they are not," Taney had written in his majority decision for the Court, "and that they are not included, and were not intended to be included, under the word 'citizens' in the Constitution."[64] A slave or former slave could be a citizen of one of the states, but that did not mean he was a citizen of the nation, Taney held. The chief judge said the Court could not presume to give the Constitution a more liberal interpretation than its authors had intended. "To do so," he added in a statement freighted with irony, "would abrogate the judicial character of this court, and make it the mere reflection of the popular opinion or passion of the day."[65]

That, of course, is precisely what Taney seemed to be doing, reflecting southern attitudes that were much like, if not identical, to his own. In this he was ignoring the split personality of his home state—and the ambivalence of the nation as a whole. He chose a side.

He might have stopped there since the noncitizen Scott was not entitled to a day in court, but Taney seemed determined to decide the more vexing questions, because, again, he thought the Court's authority might be accepted by the losing side. He found that Dred Scott had not gained his freedom by virtue of living in a free state. While he was at it, Taney found the Missouri Compromise of 1820 unconstitutional because it represented an improper interference by the federal government in a matter left by the Constitution to the states. Congress did not have power, under the Constitution, to deal with issues of persons and property. Taney sidestepped opportunities to advance the law beyond those political calculations made to achieve union a half century earlier. As long as he was so deeply immersed in interpreting the framers' intentions, he might well have observed that the aim then was union and continued in that vein to find flexibility in the founding document.

If the Constitution's language recognized a "right of property in slaves," argues the Dred Scott scholar Don E. Fehrenbacher, it also acknowledged the power of Congress "to extinguish that right." Suppose Taney had concluded that Congress might exercise this power? He might have chosen to recognize due process rights in black persons. Wasn't a slave a person who had been deprived of due process rights? Fehrenbacher asks. At this point in the decision, Taney speaks of "citizens"—not persons—because he has found already that black persons are not citizens and have no rights and were not meant by the framers to have rights.

Many southerners by then "had no significant economic stake in the institution of slavery, but they did have a vital stake in preservation of the southern social order and of southern self-respect."[66] Taney's colleague on the bench, Justice Peter V. Daniel, identified the issue in a letter to Martin

Van Buren, expressing the southern antipathy to interference and to abolitionists. They were saying to the South: "You are not my equal. And hence are to be excluded as carrying a moral taint with you. Here is at once the extinction of all fraternity, of all sympathy, of all endurance even; the creation of animosity fierce, implacable, undying."[67]

Fehrenbacher wrote of Taney's motivation, "His commitment was, not to slavery itself, for which he had no great affection, but rather to southern life and values, which seemed organically linked to the peculiar institution and unpreservable without it. He used the Dred Scott case to reinforce the institution of slavery at every possible point of attack, not because he had once been a slaveholder but because he remained, to the end of his life, a southern gentleman."[68] He addressed issues inherent in *Dred Scott* that might have been finessed—the Court's usual practice, but apparently he wanted to address them in defense of the South—as if he were the last man who could effectively do that.[69]

Many applauded, but many were apoplectic. Horace Greeley's *New York Tribune* called the decision "atrocious," "wicked," and an "abominable judgment." It was, said the *Tribune*, "detestable hypocrisy." In the South the decision was almost giddily hailed as "the supreme law of the land." Any further opposition to slavery, wrote the *Constitutionalist* of Augusta, Georgia, is "morally treason against the Government."[70]

Asked for his view of the decision, Douglass said Taney's objective was not attainable by any man. Speaking in New York to the American Abolitionist Society, he sought to minimize the decision's impact.

You will readily ask me how I am affected by this devilish decision— this judicial incarnation of wolfishness! My answer is, and no thanks to the slaveholding wing of the Supreme Court, my hopes were never brighter than now.

I have no fear that the National Conscience will be put to sleep by such an open, glaring, and scandalous tissue of lies as that decision is, and has been, over and over, shown to be . . . Judge Taney can do many things, but he cannot perform impossibilities. He cannot bale out the ocean, annihilate this firm old earth, or pluck the silvery star of liberty from our Northern sky. He may decide and decide again; but he cannot reverse the decision of the Most High. He cannot change the essential nature of things—making evil good, and good, evil.[71]

Douglass knew, perhaps, that Taney was not altogether wrong about the framers' intent. He addressed Taney's view that they had intended to exclude blacks from citizenship, cementing into their declaration of democratic ideals a wholly contradictory idea: that a nation proclaiming the glory of freedom and justice would find an entire race of people unworthy. "There was not a sentence, not a syllable in a sentence, of the Constitution that would lead any one to suppose there was any deceptive intent about it. If that Constitution had dropped down to us from the blue over-hanging sky, and we had read its contents, there was not a man who could reasonably suppose it was intended to sanction and support the slave system, but, on the contrary, that everything in it was intended to support justice and equality between man and man."[72]

Douglass's ally William Lloyd Garrison was less forgiving of the Founding Fathers. He and Douglass split over this and other interpretations of the Constitution. Douglass remained a believer in the goodwill of the American people because he thought his cause rested ultimately on the support of Americans who wanted a just society. But his reaction to *Dred Scott* contained its measure of spin. His insistence that the Constitution did, after all, make a promise to all Americans was the basis for his struggle. The Constitution and the Declaration of Independence were his best arguments for universal emancipation and universal freedom.

The decision certainly did more damage to the status of black people than Douglass could bring himself to concede, moving the nation toward civil war and diminishing the authority of the Court when this authority would be needed later (during Reconstruction) to right wrongs committed in the name of *Dred Scott* and its implications. The decision led some to speculate anew about the validity of the vote granted to free blacks in some states, and some suggested that slavery might be legalized nationally, a proposal that surfaced in Maryland more than once.

Douglass might well have been left to consider other ways of attaining his goal, a goal that seemed to be receding into the mists of fear. From his time forward, black freedom fighters had chosen appeals to conscience over violent confrontation. Alternatives were considered and in isolated instances adopted, usually with disastrous results.

Douglass had befriended John Brown, the revolutionary who would conduct the famous raid on Harpers Ferry. He and Brown had spent time together in Rochester, New York, where Douglass was publishing his newspaper, the *North Star*. Brown, as naïve in his pursuits as Taney was with the *Dred Scott* decision, believed he could spark a broad-based antislavery uprising. Douglass considered joining him.

In October 1859, they met at the Kennedy Farm in Washington County, west of Hagerstown, to discuss the raid and whether Douglass might participate. He chose not to. The Nat Turner rebellion in Virginia had shown that such uprisings would be quickly put down by overwhelming force and lead to further restrictions, not to freedom. Douglass left the farm—and the country. Knowledge of his discussions with Brown, he feared, would have been enough to bring recrimination and worse for him and others. He left on another speaking trip to Europe.

The Maryland he left was balanced precariously on the brink of secession. Governor Thomas Holliday Hicks, a Union-loving Eastern Shore man elected in 1857, the year of *Dred Scott,* would not allow the General Assembly to meet in the spring of 1861, when talk of Maryland secession—owing in part to memories of Brown's raid—ran highest. The public swung between pro-Unionist and pro-Southern sentiment. Federal troops moved into the state, and President Abraham Lincoln began to jail Marylanders who he feared would push the state into the secessionist ranks. After a skirmish on Pratt Street, in which the first Civil War blood was shed, the president incarcerated George William Brown, Baltimore's mayor, and held him for more than a year. Justice Taney, his authority damaged by the *Scott* decision, confronted Lincoln's peremptory suspension of the right of habeas corpus (the legal principle requiring that a person be charged with a crime before being jailed), but the wartime president prevailed. Baltimore's mayor was no friend of slavery, but he took the ambivalent and contradictory stance adopted by so many Marylanders in those days.

"Nowhere else," he wrote, "had the Negro slave been so well treated, on the whole, and advanced so far in civilization. They had learned the necessity as well as the habit of labor; the importance to some extent at least of thrift, the essential distinction between right-acting and wrong-acting. The duty of obedience to law; and—not least—some conception, dim though it may be, of the inspiring teachings of the Christian religion."[73] What if Roger Taney had found a way to recognize the changing reality of American life? What if he had acknowledged the political basis of the framers' decision to accommodate southern sentiment? Perhaps he was trapped, certain to offend one side or the other and launch the nation into war either way.

Within two years of *Dred Scott* and Harpers Ferry, Douglass was drawn to a much more powerful force. He had been skeptical of Lincoln's intentions, as were many Marylanders for a very different reason. Douglass thought Lincoln might not free the slaves. Most Marylanders apparently feared he would. In the presidential election of 1860, Lincoln attracted 2,294 votes in Maryland, losing the state to John C. Breckenridge, of the splinter Southern Democrats, who got 42,505 votes.[74] Douglass would have supported a more openly abolition-minded candidate in 1860, but Lincoln and his party had to suffice. No one in the Republican Party of that era sought Douglass's help: "I am not doing much in this presidential canvass for the reason that the Republican committees do not wish to expose themselves to the charge of being the 'N----r' party. The Negro is the deformed child which is put out of the room when company comes."[75]

Lincoln alternately gave Douglass hope and despair throughout the Civil War. Douglass became a major advocate of allowing black soldiers to serve in the Union Army. He had hoped black Union soldiers would supply another proof that black people were willing to fight for freedom and to die for it. The president apparently listened. By the time of Lincoln's second inaugural, black troops marched in the official parade.

From the dome of the capitol, a statue called Armed Liberty, an ironic symbol of freedom in the form of a freed slave, looked down on Lincoln as he took the oath. The president had issued his Emancipation Proclamation after the horrifically bloody battle of Antietam in Maryland, and Maryland was about to find itself at the center of another murderous moment in this history. Assassination plotters from nearby Clinton, Maryland, were in the crowd on inauguration day, as was Douglass.

He had visited the president in the White House before and was invited there again that day. Douglass had been deeply disappointed in Lincoln's first inaugural speech. Instead of calling for the outright abolition of slavery, Lincoln had focused on his primary objective: preserving the Union. He had avoided, for that moment, any declaration that would complicate his mission. Later, though, Douglass became one of Lincoln's advisers, talking with him on issues of slavery and race. The two men met on August 10, 1863, after Douglass was urged to put the mistreatment of black soldiers before the president. Douglass spoke of that meeting later: "I never met with a man, who, on the first blush, impressed me more entirely with his devotion to his country and with his determination to save it at all hazards."[76] The two men did not agree on many things—the pace of change foremost among their disagreements—but Douglass had as good and well-motivated an ally in the White House as he was likely to see. They met again in August 1864, at Lincoln's invitation, the president having heard that Douglass was distressed by his silence on the plight of slaves in the South. Lincoln said he wanted Douglass to encourage the escape of slaves still in Confederate territory.[77]

Here was a black Marylander, by then a man of distinction, offering counsel to the president of the United States—at the president's request. By then a political figure himself, Douglass may have been willing to tolerate some of the inhospitable, racially abusive language Lincoln used. Douglass overlooked it, choosing to embrace the man's overarching objectives. How he spoke, what may have been in his heart on questions of race, were less important to Douglass than how Lincoln acted and how he seemed when the two men met. What other leader had been willing to invite a black man to the White House, to hear him out and to adjust his policy accordingly?

With the war nearly won, Lincoln felt free to say publicly some of the things Douglass had looked for in the first inaugural speech. By then the war's proximate cause—slavery—was not in dispute. Even then, the institution of slavery gave pause: "It may seem strange that any men should dare to ask God's assistance in wringing their bread from the sweat of other men's faces, and yet one part of the nation was willing to tear it apart to preserve that right."[78]

Later that day, Douglass called at the White House but was about to be turned away by guards when a white friend of Lincoln's reported what was happening. "Here comes my friend Douglass," the president said. Taking him by the hand, Lincoln said, "I'm glad to see you. I saw you in the crowd today listening to my inaugural address; how did you like it?"

Douglass hesitated: "Mr. Lincoln, I must not detain you with my poor opinion when there are thousands waiting to shake hands with you."

"No, no," Lincoln answered, "you must stop a little, Douglass; there is no man in the country whose opinion I value more than yours. I want to know what you think of it."

"Mr. Lincoln, that was a sacred effort," Douglass then responded.[79] More a sermon, he would say later, than a state speech.

Lincoln was inaugurated on March 4, 1865. Forty days later, on April 14, he was shot by John Wilkes Booth, a Marylander. Lincoln, the Great

Emancipator, died the next day. The assassin had collaborated with other Marylanders then living in Prince George's County, a part of the state that felt itself far closer to the Confederacy than to Lincoln's Union. A deeply divided Maryland had stayed in the Union, but representatives of its Confederate faction acted in support of the secessionists' lost cause.

Booth fled into the Maryland countryside, where he was aided by a doctor outside Clinton, in Prince George's County. Another disaffected Marylander, an innkeeper named Mary Surratt, had conspired with Booth to kill the president. Lincoln could not have jailed all his enemies during the war or after, though he was certainly aware that many who bore him ill will lived in Maryland. There had been one suspected assassination plot in Maryland. There was no doubt about the second. The war's first blood had been shed in Maryland, and now the rending strife had claimed its most famous casualty.

A few days later, Douglass attended a memorial service in the Rochester City Hall. Urged to speak, he recited from memory two sentences from Lincoln's second inaugural address. "Fondly do we hope— fervently do we pray—that this mighty scourge of war may speedily pass away. Yet if God wills that it continue, until all the wealth piled by the bond-man's two hundred and fifty years of unrequited toil shall be sunk and until every drop of blood drawn with the lash, shall be paid by another drawn with the sword, as was said three thousand years ago, so still it must be said, the judgments of the Lord are righteous altogether."

Lincoln seemed to believe that God saw the war as necessary in the struggle to accord respect to black people, who had paid for it over 250 years. Less than a month after his second inauguration, he had written to a lawyer in Frankfort, Kentucky. "I am naturally anti-slavery. If slavery is not wrong, nothing is wrong. I cannot remember when I did not think so, and feel." No one can know if Lincoln would have been the friend of black people had he survived a second term. Douglass, at least, seems to have had no doubts. And where could black Americans have looked for a better leader?

TANEY'S LEGACY: WORDS THAT DON'T DIE

Roger Brooke Taney died on October 12, 1864, but his words lived for decades in the attitudes and actions of Maryland leaders. The assertion that black people had no rights their white neighbors were obliged to respect would be embraced in Maryland even more feverishly after the Civil War. In that same year, 1864, Maryland voters ratified, by a margin of better than two to one, a new constitution that freed the slaves but once again denied the vote to blacks and women. Maryland leaders, no doubt, reflected the attitudes of those who elected them. If there was promise for black Americans after the war, it was made illusive by an aggressive effort to place barriers in the path of the newly freed citizen. Ex-slaves and free blacks had a relatively easy time compared with their brothers and sisters in southern states, but a once forward-thinking Maryland had turned hostile toward blacks. Courts held that black children could be held in service by their former masters in near bondage as apprentices. A state law outlawed black testimony against whites, restricted the assembly of blacks unless whites were in attendance, and made having a job mandatory—or risk violating vagrancy laws apparently aimed at blacks. In Frederick, blacks could not celebrate Emancipation Day or any other holiday without white supervision. The constraints—which created and codified a second class of citizenship—continued until 1866, when the U.S. Congress passed a civil rights bill and federal courts began enforcing it.[80] These rights did not include the right to vote, and Maryland governor Thomas Swann found that prohibition appropriate and necessary.

I am utterly opposed to universal Negro suffrage and to the extreme radicalism of certain men in Congress and in our own state, who have been striving to shape the platform of the Union party in the interests of Negro suffrage . . . I look upon Negro suffrage and the recognition of the power in Congress to control suffrage within the states as the virtual subordination of the white race to the ultimate control and domination of the Negro in the state of Maryland . . . I consider the issue upon this subject of Negro suffrage as well made in the fall elections [congressional and state legislative elections, 1866] as the most important that has ever been brought to the attention of the people of the state of Maryland.[81]

On Swann-like platforms, Democrats dominated Maryland politics for more than a half century, relinquishing their hold only briefly in the 1890s. In 1870, the Maryland General Assembly voted unanimously to reject the Fifteenth Amendment to the U.S. Constitution, the amendment that gave blacks the vote without regard to "race, color, or previous condition of servitude." Several southern states had already agreed to extend the franchise to black people as a condition of returning to the Union after the Civil War. The Fifteenth Amendment was actually directed at border states like Maryland, where that leverage did not exist.

A sufficient number of other states saved some of the nation's honor by ratifying the amendment. But the issue did not die. The *Baltimore Sun* editors, among many Marylanders, questioned the amendment's constitutionality but dismissed it as having little practical significance. The political parties, including the Democrats, apparently thought otherwise and sought to win the support of this new constituency—or sought ways to bar it in the way suggested by Governor Swann. His party's determination to exclude blacks would grow over the next forty years.

With deepest irony, the enthusiasm with which new black citizens seized their prerogatives may have worked against them. They would compose a large percentage of Maryland's reconstituted black-white electorate, and if they showed themselves eager to vote, surely they were a force to be reckoned with. So it was their collective strength, not the weakness suggested by the *Sun,* that led a resourceful Democratic Party to war against them. They became a prize to be won—or devalued—in a forty-year struggle for political control of Maryland. The black vote became leverage for the Democrats, who called it a threat to whites.

Notwithstanding Swann's defiantly racist language, Democrats pretended to accept the federal amendment, hoping they could avoid whatever voting rights enforcement measures Congress might adopt.[82] This strategy fit perfectly in the approach adopted by party leaders for many years to come: assert white supremacy, but if obliged by law or circumstance to give ground, do it slowly; never allow a single victory by blacks to be applied across the board; regroup and overturn advances when possible; and never concede any overarching victory by champions of black equality.

All of this followed the gradual erosion of voting and other rights that had been granted at the time of the Declaration of Independence. With some property restrictions, free blacks had been eligible to vote in Maryland in 1776. The right was restricted in 1783 to those blacks who had voted in previous elections. The franchise was withdrawn entirely in 1802. Ever more Draconian efforts were to come over the next one hundred years.

Frederick Douglass walked directly and somewhat blithely into this storm of opposition. Before emancipation, through twenty-five years of abolitionist speaking and traveling, he had not dared visit his home state. Now, he thought he might return and make a new home. That idea made some of his friends nervous in the extreme, especially if the assassination of Lincoln by Marylanders was a reflection of racial attitudes in the state. Julia J. Crofts, a close white friend then living in England, urged him to reconsider. "Pray my dear old friend, stay in the northern states & leave Baltimore an untried field of labor—do not throw your valuable life away by venturing near the old home—think of realities and let those romantic visions remain in abeyance for the present . . . Dreadful murders are never anticipated by the sufferers."[83]

And the state's antiblack sentiments were clear enough. Douglass thought he might make a headquarters in Maryland for his new mission: winning the vote for a newly freed people. There was even a perfect spot for a headquarters. In September 1865, he spoke at the opening of the Douglass Institute in downtown Baltimore.

"When I left Maryland 27 years ago," he said during the institute's dedication, "I did so with the firm resolve never to forget my brothers and sisters in bondage. And to do whatever might be in my power to accomplish their emancipation. In whatever else I may have failed, in this I have not failed." He exulted in the promise of such an institution, a place in Baltimore "where we who have been long debarred of the privileges of culture may assemble and have our soul thrilled with heavenly music lifted to the skies on the wings of poetry and song. Here we can assemble and have our minds enlightened."[84] Douglass did what he could in those years to speak for a population that had few influential champions and little influence in politics. What had been lost in the killing of Abraham Lincoln was agonizingly clear. Lincoln had shown—in contrast with the attitudes of Governor Swann—that he would seek out and hear the counsel of a Frederick Douglass. Had black Americans been granted a second Lincoln term as president, with Maryland's Douglass as an adviser, how might the course of national events have been different? Instead of having a president to represent them, Douglass and the new black citizen were left alone to confront a hostile political environment. A great opportunity for the nation was lost.

Blacks were striving to integrate themselves into the life of Maryland. With the support of Quaker leaders in particular, black Marylanders displayed a fervent desire for basic education. More than one hundred schools were set up in Baltimore and on the Eastern Shore by men like Hugh Lennox Bond, a judge, and others who established the Baltimore Association for the Moral and Educational Improvement of Colored People. Once again, the energy of freedom had an unfortunate back-draft: among white Marylanders, it generated fear of revolution.

In these early postwar days, Douglass showed his grasp of political re-alities by advising that black people should not be special pleaders; he feared that legitimate, desperately needed, and enlightened policies would deepen prejudices. A leader in search of handouts would, in-evitably, validate the views of those like Robert Goodloe Harper and Roger Taney, who had asserted that the black man had no hope of sur-vival beyond the master's care. Thus, Douglass hailed mere opportunity, which, he hoped, would make special considerations unnecessary. He thought the reality of a new black voting power would persuade white leadership to grant the franchise. "They gave us the bullet to save them-selves; they will give us the ballot to save themselves," Douglass said.[85]

He was far too optimistic. White power did not believe it had to nego-tiate or deal with the black man—quite the contrary, perhaps. Both ma-jor political parties used the potential of black voting for their own ends by turns, decrying the threat and welcoming the new voting strength.

When the opportunity to vote did come in 1870 with adoption of the Fifteenth Amendment, black Marylanders responded with eager deter-mination, "despite the widespread white hostility and numerous dis-franchisement attempts."[86] The rate of black voter participation was, from the beginning, about the same as that of whites.[87] Perhaps this was because sixty-eight years earlier, blacks had voted in Maryland. There was something of a tradition of black voting, however truncated it may have been. Free black citizens were already participating in the life of the state, so the process was there to be observed, the franchise exercised— lost and then coveted. The white political parties, though, were anxious to use this new constituency or to avoid having it used against them. In some cases, new black voters were welcomed and educated. But quickly their votes were seen as a political problem, a prize to be won or a threat to be used as leverage. Too often, it was the latter.

Inspired by Douglass and by their own pent-up desire to participate, blacks voted eagerly, beginning in 1870, when a man named Elijah Quigley became the first black person to vote in Maryland since 1810. He cast his ballot in a local Towson election.[88] Quigley handed his ballot to the election clerk and departed without incident. A few white citizens were on hand to watch, but no protest was heard. The *Chestertown Transcript* observed the historic moment and reported it in the next day's edition. Quigley's vote and the votes of other black Marylanders personified a new political reality in Maryland. Quigley was one of the state's 39,120 voting-age black men. These new voting citizens increased the size of the electorate by about 30 percent. They were eager to become part of the system if not to join one of the two major parties. Black leaders formed "loyal leagues," "radical clubs," and "colored clubs" to instruct newcomers in the political process.[89]

But that spate of organizational fervor—that vibrant desire for citizenship—frightened some. The *Transcript* urged formation of "white men's clubs," and it urged the Democratic Party to make itself the official white man's party of Maryland: not a necessary adjuration, as it turned out. Black men voted Republican, the party of Lincoln. Democrats prevailed, but they saw the potential of the black vote for their opponents, and a campaign of opposition to black voting began in many quarters, not solely in political ones.

The *Transcript* repeated the view that the Fifteenth Amendment had been "forcibly and illegally obtained." On September 2, 1870, on the eve of a Congressional election, the Eastern Shore paper referred to the Republicans as "the Mongrel Party." The GOP and the Radicals, it said, had proceeded to register black voters "with zeal worthy of a better cause." That effort, it warned, "means Negro and carpet bag office holders in all our state and county offices. It means Negro equality in public conveyances, hotels, theaters, public schools, courts and juries. The Negro has the longest end of the Radical stick and he will learn to demand the best half of the loaf. The defeat of the blacks' party this fall will be its utter demoralization. The white expectants, who hoped to swim in this mixing of races, will slide off. Disappointed in their hope of living at the public crib, their love of the African will expire in a night."[90] Clearly it meant near hysteria in the *Transcript*'s editorial offices. One wonders how degraded blacks could have been if they were strong enough to take over the state. And, if they were degraded, why was it necessary to attack every aspect of black life, eventually via lynching, shredding families, attacking self-help associations like the Laboring Sons, denying education, making ballots complicated, eventually adopting southern-style voting rights resistance, and later attempting to circumvent the U.S. Constitution so that blacks could not vote? This was the work of Jim Crow, by now well under way.

Douglass continued to speak in Maryland, but the day-to-day welfare of black Marylanders, the ability to petition for their share of the public purse, fell to others, including a black Baltimore businessman, Isaac Myers, a churchman and unyielding advocate for black rights. His interests ranged from education to labor unions as well as to his Fell's Point business, the Chesapeake Marine Railway and Dry Dock Company. He wanted to demonstrate that Governor Swann was wrong, that blacks were not shiftless ne'er-do-wells, begging for funds. One should look, he said, at the tremendous advances made by blacks even before the Civil War "that long indicated blacks merited better public support for what they were made to do because of prejudice's hold on the public treasury." He pointed out that seven literary and debating societies were kept in operation by the black community's slender means, which were even more slender now with so many newly emancipated slaves coming to the city. Myers counted seventy-nine beneficial societies for the relief of the sick and poor, with an average membership of eighty and average contributions per month of forty cents per member. "We have the most extensive corporation that can be found with colored men in any part of this globe, and it has added to the influence and wealth of the state as much as any corporation of the same dimension."[91]

He wanted a public high school for black children and reinstatement of black teachers. The schooling of black children at the time was simply ignored. In June 1873, various black leaders sent what was called a "memorial" to the mayor, Joshua Van Sant, and city council, asking for a black high school and additional grade schools. The petition said, "For over a half century, indeed, ever since the establishment of the public school system have we been consciously paying into the treasury of our city government, annual assessments upon real and personal property for the support of the same, as well as performing all other duties and responsibilities applicable to other citizens, and that, too, without receiving the slightest benefits accruing there from, until within a very recent date when colored primary schools were established."[92]

Two years later, another group asked for establishment of a black high school on a site soon to be vacated by Baltimore City College, on St. Paul Street. That effort, too, was turned aside. H. J. Brown, who campaigned resolutely to get black teachers licensed, wondered how a city like Baltimore—a cultured place, he thought—would deny blacks an opportunity to teach when cities like New York, Washington, Richmond, Philadelphia, Boston, and St. Louis had black schoolteachers. Blacks were incompetent, it was said. They were unqualified. They had no desire to learn. White teachers had been unable to produce a single graduate in Baltimore who could be admitted to the schools, it was said. "No matter how the case may be turned over," wrote the Reverend James H. A. Johnson, a member of Bethel African Methodist Episcopal (AME) Church and a graduate of the Princeton Theological Seminary, "it will show but one spirit: that is, injustice to the Negro. It is this spirit today which the American people, like Pharaoh, will not confess and eliminate from their hearts that is now endangering the very existence of the nation."[93]

Isaac Myers wanted to expose the treachery. Since no law forbade the hiring of black teachers, he and others said, some other way had to be found to topple the education barrier. He was advised that such an effort would fail because no black petitioner could even get in the room with the school authorities. Others observed that blacks were denied jobs in the fire, police, and transit departments as well. Republicans were more welcoming, but Democrats—whose approach was openly and avowedly racist—would allow no blacks in the schools. Myers persisted as chairman of the Colored City Executive Committee, a Republican group. Groups like this one had marshaled support for the Fifteenth Amendment, so they became the natural enemies of the dominant Democrats, who denied them patronage and other emoluments that fell to the winners.

Blacks were shut out of the system at a time when they needed it most. As Douglass had done, and as the various self-help education organizations had done, Myers continued his efforts on behalf of black citizens, urging them to be depositors in savings banks, members of building associations, and holders of life insurance policies. Involve yourself in the system, he would say, echoing Douglass and foreshadowing the urgings of civil rights leaders in the coming years. A pillar of Bethel Church, Myers organized a trade organization, comprising black mechanics and tradesmen who met under Myers's leadership at the Douglass Institute. The group issued statements denouncing discriminatory white labor organizations and urged the formation of black unions throughout the country.[94] Lemeul Griffiths, a participant, called Myers's language injudicious, but Myers was adamant. The organization, he argued, would be an expression of great strength when the Fifteenth Amendment was adopted, allowing black men to enter the nation's workplace. Myers thought whites would want to accommodate the new reality and would be obliged to do so when confronted by an organized force of black workers. He, like Douglass, was overly optimistic.

Douglass was invited back to Baltimore to speak to the new organization. His talk was called "The Equal Rights of All Men to Labor," and he spoke as if the working man would soon be displaced if he were not educated. "Time was," he said, "when the man who could lift the barrel of cider and drink from the bung was the greatest man . . . Now the greatest was the man who could make the barrel of cider lift itself."[95] Speaking at Sharp Street Church, he urged the city's ministers not to discourage intellectual advancement.

Intellectual advancement, Douglass counseled, would be necessary to silence those who spoke vigorously in opposition to the participation of black people in politics. At the same time, Douglass thought, participation in the nation's political life could not wait for that advancement. Not for the first time, he reminded audiences of the black man's contributions to the Union effort during the Civil War. "When the colored man drops the bullet, he must have placed in his hands a ballot."[96]

Expectations remained high. During an Emancipation Day celebration, George A. Hackett, a friend of Myers, said, "The colored man now stands on the same platform in this country with the white man. He now has an equal chance in the race of life, and it will be his own fault if he does not show the world that he is entitled to all that our friends claim for us."[97] Hackett and Myers and Douglass could not have been less optimistic, perhaps, without dooming their prospects more rapidly. But the white world relentlessly dashed hopes, denying the black citizen many prerogatives of participation in American society.

As Douglass was speaking at the institute, white caulkers not far away on the docks of Baltimore were striking to protest employment of blacks in their trade. Though the protest was reported in local newspapers that day, Douglass apparently did not stay to stand in solidarity with the men who were practicing his one-time craft. Myers decided discrimination in the port could be addressed by forming a black company: the Chesapeake Marine Railway and Dry Dock Company. A stockholder in the company was John W. Locks, once a caulker himself and a childhood playmate of Douglass's.[98]

What the black community needed, in the absence of political power that should have proceeded from the ballot box, was help in obtaining adherence to the law. It needed lawyers and judges and support from writers to counter opposition from newspapers like the *Chestertown Transcript* and the *Baltimore Sun*. In what became a pattern, a few important white members of the bar stepped up to help.

And there was further irony in the early help. Former mayor George W. Brown, who had been jailed by Lincoln during the Civil War, was now a judge on the Supreme Bench of Baltimore City. He ruled that blacks could not be excluded from the state bar. The complexity of these matters was pungent: whether Blue or Gray in his thinking at the start of the war, Judge Brown addressed himself to the law when he ruled on the admission of black applicants to the bar: "It is a great injustice that no colored man can be admitted to the practice of the law. There is a large colored population in our state, and they ought to be allowed to enter any lawful occupation for which they may be fitted."[99] The Baltimore Supreme Bench held that excluding blacks from the practice of law was unconstitutional, and in 1885, Everett J. Waring became the first black man admitted to legal practice in Maryland. The court was assisted in its arrival at this decision, perhaps, by the active lobbying of the Reverend Harvey Johnson, pastor of Union Baptist Church, who had begun what would turn into a long tradition of civil rights activism within his congregation. Another black lawyer, Harry S. Cummings, became a prominent Republican, winning races for the city council in 1891, 1897, and 1907 through 1915. He was a delegate to the Republican National Convention in 1882 and in 1904, making a seconding speech for Theodore Roosevelt in 1904.

The aspirations of black citizens, already handicapped by an increasing array of barriers to participation, now faced a new challenge: bossism. Arthur Pue Gorman, one of the state's first and most effective boss leaders, invoked "the specter of black rule" to frighten white votes into his Democratic fold. Echoing Justice Taney and Governor Swann, he said, "We have determined that this government was made by white men and shall be ruled by white men as long as the republic lasts."[100] Taking their cue from Gorman and his ally Dean John Prentiss Poe, of the University of Maryland School of Law, law students signed a petition in 1891 demanding that blacks be excluded from the school. Medical students accomplished a similar statement of opposition to blacks. When a competing law school opened in Baltimore, Dean Poe and others said they were acting to prevent revenue losses, that is, students leaving for another school that did not admit blacks. Not only would this be the new policy of the school going forward, but two black students admitted the year before were dismissed.

Douglass watched this backsliding with alarm. He had spoken often in Maryland since he had been advised not to move back to his home state. He had been frustrated and essentially shunted aside by Republican leaders, who might have rewarded his service to the party with more substantial posts and positions of leadership. He was for a time minister to Haiti, but that post brought a variety of problems. The usual recompense was not likely to serve the party's political purposes in a time when black Americans were not prized members of any political team. Douglass had gone into the post–Civil War period full of hope in his public pronouncements, but he would be disappointed on many fronts.

Near the end of his life, some of the old abolitionist fire came back into his speeches. In an address he called "Lessons of the Hour," delivered in Washington, D.C., in 1894, a year before his death, he spoke of the atrocity of lynching, then plaguing black people in the South: "A white man has but to blacken his face and commit a crime, to have some Negro lynched in his stead. An abandoned woman has only to start the cry that she has been insulted by a black man, to have him arrested and summarily murdered by the mob. Frightened and tortured by his captors, confused into telling crooked stories about his whereabouts at the time when the alleged crime was committed and the death penalty is at once inflicted, though his story may be but the incoherency of ignorance or distraction caused by terror."[101] Douglass went on to describe the means by which black men and women were denied the vote. Echoes of Governor Swann could be heard in his denunciation: "That this is done is not only admitted, but openly defended, justified by so-called honorable men inside and outside of Congress." Lynching and obstacles to voting were of a piece with the South's effort to remove the Negro from the body politic. It was, he said, a conscious effort to further degrade the entire race—to justify the impending disenfranchisement. In all this, his words betrayed the loss of his lifelong confidence that the American nation was wise enough to see its monumental error and find a way to validate its ideals: "I cannot shut my eyes to the ugly facts before me . . . He is a wiser man than I am, who can tell how low the moral sentiment of this republic may yet fall."[102]

Douglass died on February 20, 1895. Supreme Court justice John Marshall Harlan, who would later express his views on the importance of Douglass's life, was among the dignitaries who attended a funeral service for Douglass in Washington. In a tribute written the day after word of his death reached her, Elizabeth Cady Stanton, Douglass's partner in the antislavery and women's rights alliance, wrote of their first meeting at an abolitionist rally in Boston in 1842, when Douglass was 25: "Around him sat the great antislavery orators of the day, earnestly watching the effect of his eloquence on that immense audience, that laughed and wept by turns, completely carried away by the wondrous gifts of his pathos and humor." The other speakers, she said, paled by comparison. He "stood there," she wrote, "like an African prince, majestic in his wrath."

Now he was gone, spared any further proof that the nation as a whole believed what Roger Taney had declared thirty-two years earlier. Fifty years later, another Marylander, Thurgood Marshall, would be the lead lawyer in a case that undid *Plessy* and unseated Jim Crow. Thus were Marylanders at either extreme of the national effort to end discrimination. Taney stood in history with *Dred Scott*, Marshall with a case to be known as *Brown v. Board*—but not before another 50 years of struggle.

CHAPTER 2

Suing Jim Crow

T he climate of race relations in Maryland and the nation worsened yet again at the dawning of the twentieth century and, once again, at the highest levels of the state and national governments. The U.S. Supreme Court's 1896 ruling in *Plessy v. Ferguson* was as damaging to black prospects as *Dred Scott* had been. Jim Crow rode taller in the saddle.

In *Plessy,* the high court affirmed the constitutionality of a Louisiana law requiring separate railway cars for black and white riders. As long as trains ran only in Louisiana, they could be segregated as the state wished, the Court held. Its language, referring to prevailing public attitudes, showed a willingness to base its judgment on factors beyond mere law. "The enslavement and debasement of the Negro had become the established usage, custom and tradition of the white people of Louisiana," it found, and government had no legitimate role in opposing the reflection of those feelings. A required separation of the races, the Court said, did not deny equal protection of the law guaranteed by the Fourteenth Amendment. The decision also addressed what it called "the [plaintiff's] assumption that the enforced separation of the two races stamps the colored race with a badge of inferiority. If this be so, it is not by reason of anything found in the act, but solely because the colored race chooses to put that construction upon it."[1] Here was a colossal case of blaming the victim. The Louisiana statute claimed equal treatment in rail transport on the basis that whites were being segregated as forcefully as were blacks.

"Legislation," the high court held in *Plessy,* "is powerless to eradicate racial instincts or to abolish distinctions based on physical differences." Though *Plessy* led to the idea of "separate but equal," the promise of fairer treatment was no more than a fig leaf. White officials would be under no compulsion to believe that the law had really been intended to protect the rights of black people. The deception was sanitized by a call for equality to which white authorities would be all but deaf. Separate and equal facilities for black Americans would rarely exist, and often there was no effort to provide anything approaching equal accommodations. Here was a demonstration of the nation's pattern of dissimulation, a tendency to grant or affirm rights to black people in theory but to ignore the reality of deprivation.

Only one of the justices dissented in *Plessy,* but it was a powerful and foresighted disagreement. Just as Taney's decision had not soothed regional hostilities, *Plessy* would not result in any improvement in race relations—if indeed that was the intention. Quite the contrary, said Justice John Marshall Harlan: "The present decision . . . will not only stimulate aggressions, more or less brutal and irritating, upon the admitted rights of colored citizens, but will encourage the belief that it is possible, by means of state enactments, to defeat the beneficent purposes which the people of the United States had in view when they adopted the recent amendments of the Constitution."[2] Why wouldn't this decision lead to any number of arbitrary separations, he wondered: blacks on one side of the street, whites on another, for example?

Discrimination of this odious sort, sanctioned by the highest court in the land, became commonplace and endured. "You were supposed to walk out in the gutter when you saw white folks walking down the street," said Walter Carr, who published a black community journal in Baltimore decades later. "My grandmother knocked me in the gutter a half dozen times."[3]

Justice Harlan had looked prophetically to the future rules enforced by Carr's grandmother: "The destinies of the two races, in this country, are indissolubly linked together and the interests of both require that the common government of all shall not permit the seeds of race hate to be planted under the sanction of law."[4] Planted they were, however, and antiblack attitudes intensified. Some Democrats later called these attitudes "progressive." In that context, progressive meant actions that kept unworthy people, most of them black, from voting, from participating in the democracy. Roger Taney was thirty-two years dead when *Plessy* was decided, but his views seemed full of life. In *Plessy,* the high court acted as if racial animosities had to be accommodated. Antagonisms were licensed.

As it turns out, the Court's mechanism—separate but equal facilities—had already been tried without encouraging results for black citizens in Maryland. In 1872, Governor Oden Bowie had ordered separate but equal schools. Anyone who thought the justices were on the right course twenty-four years later might have been disabused of that idea by looking at the results. Schools for black students in Maryland were anything but equal. Buildings were inferior. Hand-me-down books were good enough for black students. Black teachers were paid less than their white counterparts. Black students were required to attend school many fewer days than whites. In Maryland at least, separate but equal had been a scrim to obscure discrimination.

Black Americans had no way to resist. They had virtually no political influence. And whatever they did have was coming under attack.

In Maryland, Governor Swann's 1864 declaration that the Democratic Party in Maryland was the party of the white people set the black citizen on a steep post-emancipation climb. The slope grew steeper in the new century as generations of political leaders echoed and redoubled Swann's determination. In 1903, the Democratic Party's election platform once again affirmed that "the political destinies of Maryland should be shaped and controlled by the white people of the State." In 1904, the first of three extraordinary efforts was made to bar blacks from voting. Democrats said they were acting because the black voter was "ignorant, corrupt, the blind instrument of unscrupulous and selfish leaders," posing "a perpetual menace to the prosperity and peace of Maryland."[5]

At the request of the reigning political powerhouse Arthur Pue Gorman, a boss with considerable skill and connections, a bold new disenfranchisement scheme was devised. Gorman's motivation seemed quite personal: he wanted to win back his seat in the U.S. Senate, lost in 1898. He thought the road would be smoother without the largely Republican black voters opposing him.

Marylanders in and out of public life continued to reject the vote-granting Fifteenth Amendment, calling it an evil device visited illegitimately upon opposing states such as Maryland. By this argument, Maryland could proceed to violate the Constitution and hope to be vindicated. The official rationale was to rid the process of voters who could not read or write and were easily manipulated. But there was a partisan element too: denying Republicans the potential black voting power. In a 1901 effort preliminary to the more ambitious gambits, the legislature put the illiterate black voter into the realm of ballot-box guesswork: symbols denoting the candidate's party were outlawed, and ballots without the precise marking demanded by the law would be thrown out.

The Great Emancipator had given Republicans a leg up, so Democrats did what they had so often done since the Civil War. They played the race card. They said the GOP was manipulating ignorant blacks. Democrats had been stymied just before and just after the turn of the century in pursuit of the same goal, and they were dealt decisive setbacks at the polls.

Blacks became scapegoats. "As a voter, the Negro was both hated and cajoled, both intimidated and courted, but he could never be ignored so long as he voted."[6] Here was the deepest irony: a group of new citizens, barred from advancement in life by law and custom, became a political shuttlecock, denigrated and knocked back and forth by the dominant political parties even as they sought a footing in the terrain of freedom. Race and political chicanery were stirred into a toxic brew. "Until very late in this period, Democratic politics in Baltimore was almost entirely the politics of white people. In the city, as in the counties, Negroes voted almost invariably for Republican candidates until the Roosevelt Era, and played no part in Democratic primary elections."[7]

Fear of the black "menace" underlay much of what occurred in the election arena. Fear of race mingling, not just by marriage but in daily life, had grown to a high pitch of emotional anxiety. "The possibility that one fireman, or one policeman or one schoolteacher should have a black face sets all their nerves on edge and makes them ready to sanction any absurdity or injustice which promises relief from this enormity,"[8] one leading citizen wrote to an associate.

Boss Gorman continued then with his breathtaking challenge to the Constitution. He asked John Prentiss Poe, dean of the University of Maryland School of Law, to propose a disenfranchisement tool. A man who might have been expected to be a zealous defender of the law would now work overtime to frustrate it. The whole enterprise seems to have gone forth, winning approval by the General Assembly at various stages, as if it were wholly appropriate.

Poe would push three bills through the General Assembly. One ruled that the vote would be granted to

> (5) a person who, in the presence of the officers of registration, shall in his own handwriting, with pen and ink, without any aid, suggestion or memorandum whatsoever and without any question of direction addressed to him by any of the officers of registration, make application to register correctly, stating in such application his name, age, date and place of birth, residence and occupation, at the time and for two years next preceding, the name or names of his employer or employers and whether he has previously voted and if so, the State, county or city and district or precinct in which he voted last, and also the name in full of the President of the United States, of the Governor of Maryland, of one of the Justices of the Supreme Court of the United States, of one of the Judges of the Court of Appeals of Maryland and the Mayor of Baltimore City, if the applicant resides in Baltimore City, or of one of the County Commissioners of the county in which the applicant resides; or (6) a person or the husband of a person, who owned and was assessed on the tax books for $500.00 at real or personal property, and had owned, paid taxes on, and had tax receipts for his property for the preceding two years.[9]

The Poe maneuver was both an antiblack and an anti-Republican scheme, since blacks voted overwhelmingly for the party of Lincoln. That tendency continued for decades. Victorine Quille Adams, a Baltimore councilwoman in the 1970s, remembered the way it was into the 1930s and earlier: "My whole family were Republicans. Practically all black people were Republicans. They were trained to put their X under Lincoln's nose. And then for Lincoln's candidates under him."[10] The symbols were eliminated and replaced by names that might or might not be known to new black voters. In 1890, a survey suggested that almost 50 percent of black adults were illiterate as compared with 8 percent of whites.[11] Another way of looking at the matter was that half of black Marylanders had overcome immense obstacles and were literate.

The antiblack campaign was a perfect example of what Justice Harlan, in his dissent from *Plessy*, had called the contagious nature of segregation. If blacks could be banned legally from schools or train cars, why not find a way to ban them from polling places? The Poe campaign went on at virtually every level, from high official to average voter. State senator Blair Lee of Montgomery County—otherwise a good government reformer—called the Fifteenth Amendment a "stain" on the Constitution.[12]

The so-called 15th Amendment to the Federal Constitution has been the source and cause of untold calamity to our country. It has not benefited the race for whose benefit it is presumed to have been enacted; and it has greatly injured our Aryan race and seriously threatened the stability of our Aryan institutions. The reason of this is that it is based upon radically erroneous principles. Conceived as it was in iniquity and begotten to sub-serve grossly partisan purposes, it has served as a boomerang to those who originated it. It has taxed the ingenuity of those most intimately affected by its operation to evade its provisions; and the other section of the country has looked with complacence upon the effort to nullify its efficacy. And yet there has been little or no movement for its formal repeal. The majority of our people are wisely averse to any tampering with the organic law of the federal union; and deeming this amendment to be part of that law, they prefer to see it evaded in its operation than to appeal again to the dangerous process of constitutional amendment.[13]

In his observations about evasion of the constitutional guarantees made by the Fifteenth Amendment, the senator is apparently commenting on Dean Poe's extraordinary efforts to bar black voters by imposing conditions on voting that would be difficult if not impossible for blacks to meet.

As for the iniquities visited upon black Marylanders by the Poe-Gorman maneuvers, Senator Lee was, no doubt, correct. Black voters were pawns in Maryland politics for decades after the Civil War, shunned and demonized, largely by Democrats. Senator Lee and his party seem to have taken little notice of the many voter education efforts made in the black communities of Baltimore and some other parts of the state or of the enthusiasm with which blacks went to the polls in those days. Surely it was true that many black voters were illiterate and easily steered in one direction or another, but political leaders with a more fully developed sense of the term "progressive" might have attempted to capitalize on the civic excitement of the nation's newest citizens.

The senator's use of the terms "Aryan" and "our race" also suggest a usage—and bias—amply expressed during those days. William Cabell Bruce, a Pulitzer Prize–winning author and later a U.S. senator, wrote far more scurrilous denunciations of the black man. The attitudes were part of the political tenor in those days, from Taney to turn-of-century political bosses. Discriminating practices were apt to arise anywhere. Black Baltimore city councilman Harry Sythe Cummings, a Republican, was ushered off to a segregated, blacks-only gallery during a Republican Party function. Black districts of the city had sufficient strength to elect Cummings but insufficient status to gain him a seat among his own party's members.

Increasingly, color was at the root of this ferocious effort to keep blacks on the sideline of the system, reckons David Bogen, a University of Maryland School of Law professor and student of the law and discriminatory practice. Through the Revolutionary War, free blacks were almost always mulatto, and they had rights, including the right to vote. When the Quaker movement took hold on the Eastern Shore, and Methodists freed slaves who were totally African—distinctly black—the rights issue changed.[14]

In post–Civil War Maryland politics, Republicans had seen black votes as a way to compete with the stronger Democrats. Democrats responded by trying overtly to solidify a white party base, emphasizing that Republican was the party of blacks. The strategic restraint and self-help urgings of Frederick Douglass—unreciprocated, if they were even recognized by the white world—had been replaced at the end of Douglass's life by frustration and anger.

In 1895, however, Republicans won control of both Baltimore City Hall and the state house. A year later, Republicans won all the congressional races in Maryland. But Democrats quickly regained their grip. Rather than try to recruit black voters to their side—not a popular enterprise, they calculated—they teamed with powerful forces to move blacks out of the process entirely.

Poe and others asserted white supremacy as if it could become not only dominant but legal in Maryland, as if a state could pick and choose among the laws it would obey. Perhaps there was a belief that the high court, given the exertions of *Plessy,* might find for Maryland and its School of Law dean. When he drafted what came to be known as the Poe Amendment, he borrowed ideas from the southern states: a literacy test and the notorious grandfather clause among them. White males, whether they could read or not, automatically qualified if their fathers or grandfathers had voted. All other males (females were excluded of course) could qualify by demonstrating their literacy.

This amendment was meant to institutionalize the wink and the nod. Election officials would know they were meant to flunk blacks and pass illiterate white immigrants. This expectation must surely have been based on the view that many Marylanders, serving as election judges, would be as antiblack as Dean Poe and his associates. Nor was it just voting that occupied Maryland's leadership class.

The specter of a "Negro menace" so infused the white world's consciousness that several other racial segregation laws were put into effect. Schools and prisons had always been segregated, but new laws were passed segregating steamships and railroads. After *Plessy,* the Maryland legislature moved to mandate segregation in areas previously untouched by Jim Crow. In 1904, Howard University professor William H. H. Hart protested a railroad conductor's order to sit in a blacks-only car. Maryland's Court of Appeals held that Professor Hart had to move in keeping with *Plessy* as long as the train traveled only in Maryland and did not run afoul of federal law. The case was quite similar to the *Plessy* case in Louisiana.

Professor Hart thereupon became a Maryland version of Alabama's Rosa Parks, fifty years before Parks's refusal to move to the rear of a bus triggered a bus boycott and the official start of what has been called the modern civil rights movement. Though he would later participate in the founding of the National Association for the Advancement of Colored People (NAACP), Hart did not, like Parks, become a household word. Such moments of defiance got little attention, and probably not by accident: news of black people resisting humiliation might have brought more protestors into the field. Just as Maryland leaders had feared a wide circulation of Lundy's *Genius of Universal Emancipation,* white authorities were anxious to stifle reports of black protest. There was no national leader, no muscular civil rights organization, no galvanizing successes—and no television to put the sometimes brutal discrimination in America's living rooms.

In the absence of national scrutiny or any countervailing force, disenfranchisement worked in some southern states. In 1896, 130,334 blacks in Louisiana were registered to vote. By 1904, the total was barely 1 percent of the figure from eight years earlier, 1,342. In the annals of Jim Crow, the disenfranchisement effort ranks among the most infamous. One scholar called these proposals "ruthlessly destructive . . . of an all-absorbing autocracy of race, an animus of aggrandizement which makes, in the imagination of the white man, an absolute identification of the stronger race with the very being of the state."[15]

Yet, as heavily supported as it was by powerful men in Maryland, the disenfranchisement movement failed. It was defeated in large measure because new immigrants voted no, fearing they too would lose the vote. Isaac Freeman Rasin, a Baltimore boss, appears to have been conflicted: though he was not opposed to barring black voters, he worried that the good offices of the registrars—upon whom the proposal's effectiveness depended—could not be trusted to turn away blacks while licensing illiterate white voters, of whom there were many.

Disenfranchisement, to be sure, had considerable support. The first Poe Amendment went down in 1905 in a vote of 104,286 to 70,227. Two more attempts were made to find a proposal that could surgically remove blacks without damage to whites or to the rule of law. Reformers opposed the form of the Poe proposal, but not because they wanted to assist black voters. They wanted a more legitimate way of removing the "menace." Another version of the disenfranchisement effort arose in 1908 with the same result, though the margin was closer, 106,069 to 98,808. On a third try in 1910, with the voters fatigued if not annoyed by the insistence of their leaders, the vote was roughly 84,000 to 46,000. The margin of defeat was almost two-to-one—not a sign, however, that Maryland was growing more tolerant. In each of these cases, the black vote was preserved, and the reservoir of antiblack feeling was measured anew.

Lest anyone think defeat of these efforts was a victory for the emerging black citizen, the effort to restrict the lives of black Baltimoreans drew city leaders into action on another front. This time, in 1910, they sought to prevent blacks from buying property and moving into white city neighborhoods. Until then, blacks had lived throughout Baltimore in no particular pattern. Blacks who tried to move into largely white neighborhoods were set upon by thugs, apparently paid to keep them out.[16] A more systematic tactic was deemed necessary.

When the black lawyer George W. F. McMechen moved to a house on 1834 McCulloh Street in the fashionable Eutaw Place neighborhood, the city council went to work. The nearby Mount Royal neighborhood didn't want him. Police were called—and, notably, responded—to protect the house from thugs.

The main mischief was to be accomplished by law. The new, discriminatory housing ordinance did not bar McMechen, who was moved in before the law was passed. But other blacks could not live on blocks that were more than 50 percent white. The city solicitor said the ordinance was within the state's police power: because of "irrefutable facts, well known conditions, inherent personal characteristics and ineradicable trains of character peculiar to the races, close association on a foot of absolute equality is utterly impossible between the races, wherever Negroes exist in large numbers in a white community and invariably leads to irritation, friction, disorder and strife."[17]

Drafters of the ordinance held their rule was evenhanded because it imposed the same restriction on whites who might want to move into black neighborhoods. It was, says Professor Garrett Power of the University of Maryland School of Law, apartheid Baltimore style, a reference to the system of separation later employed by white South Africa. This Baltimore-born idea was copied by more than twenty U.S. cities, an illustration of Jim Crow's wide appeal.

As in the matter of voting, the involvement of Progressives raised troubling questions, which ultimately submitted to overly easy, wrongheaded, and damaging answers. Power says Progressives accepted the idea that poor blacks should be "quarantined" in the slums to reduce outbreaks of rioting and to fend off the spread of disease. This solution was justified partly on incorrect census data showing that the black population was in decline numerically. He quotes historian George M. Fredrickson, who wrote, "if blacks were a degenerating race with no future, the problem ceased to be one of how to prepare them for citizenship or even now to make them more productive and useful members of the community."[18] Why educate if the group was about to disappear?

As frosting on the Jim Crow, segregationist cake, the council decreed that "neither black schools nor black churches could be established in white blocks and vice versa."[19] That addition sent the city of Baltimore careering down a path toward surgically segregated neighborhoods. And toward near rampant communicable disease. There was so much tuberculosis that one concentration of poor black Baltimoreans was known as the "lung block": "The law," wrote *Baltimore Evening Sun* columnist and literary eminence H. L. Mencken, "practically insists that [blacks] keep on incubating typhoid and tuberculosis—and that he keep these infections alive . . . for the delight and benefit of the whole town."[20]

Though widely praised in theory, the ordinance encountered opposition in practice and underwent various emendations. Some of these changes were accomplished by the prominent lawyer William L. Marbury. Marbury had been a participant in the disenfranchisement movement as well. The political bosses led the assault on black citizens, but they had help from society's leading citizens. The success of Jim Crow housing ordinances—originating in Baltimore—was midwife to the NAACP. Local branches across the nation in cities that adopted the Baltimore model fought back with the legal leadership of Maryland's W. Ashbie Hawkins, among others.

In 1917, the U.S. Supreme Court ruled that separate but equal had not been violated by these ordinances because they called for equal treatment of the races. Bound apparently by *Plessy*'s transparent flimflam, the high court found the housing ordinances unconstitutional, not because they denied blacks equal protection of the law, but because they deprived white property owners of the right to sell to a black purchaser. With the high court's decision in a 1917 Louisville restrictive covenant case as precedent, Ashbie Hawkins's Maryland case went forward.

Hawkins handled the appeal of a man found guilty of violating the fourth version of Baltimore's separatist ordinance. Marbury represented the City. The Maryland Court of Appeals handed a victory to Hawkins and the NAACP. "The right of the individual citizen to acquire or use property can not be validly restricted by State or municipality, on the ground of his color."[21]

The decision, potentially helpful in eliminating barriers to blacks seeking housing, also demonstrated the limitations of law as a force for social change. Civil rights lawyers warned at many points along the way that change ordered in any given case would be but a step. There would be no umbrella ruling, no universal concession based on principle no matter how obvious application elsewhere might be. Nor would resistance in court be sufficient to topple the structure of discrimination because public attitudes would still govern much of the behavior of people in their everyday lives. It would not be the last time this limitation was made manifest.

Following the pattern of stubborn, spiteful resistance, "Baltimore's white leadership was undaunted. They borrowed from Chicago a plan to keep Negroes in their place. City building inspectors and health department officials were directed to charge landlords with housing code violations—costly to repair—if they were selling or renting to African Americans in white neighborhoods," Power explains.[22] City hall, in other words, was using its power to help private entities maintain segregated housing.

Here was Dean Poe's idea expressed anew: instead of election judges enforcing discriminatory practices against black voters, the burden of enforcing segregation fell to real estate agents. With no little irony, they were to be charged with immorality if they failed to enforce the Jim Crow exclusions. This formulation apparently was consistent with the use of "progressive" to describe people who worked to keep black people out of the voting booth.

Among the participants in this private enforcement of restrictive covenants was the Home Protective Association, an association of homeowners who had property within a twenty-four-square-block area. When first developed, the area was occupied only by whites. The association members agreed that their houses would not be occupied by blacks. In keeping with that agreement, the title holder of 2227 Barclay Street agreed to exclude blacks, but a black man, Edward Meade, purchased the property and prepared to move in—a violation of the covenant.

An injunction was sought to keep Meade out, and the circuit court in Baltimore held that he could not move in because a private covenant barred him legally. Courts said as long as the covenants were not enforced by government, they were acceptable. Meade's appeal also failed. In *Meade v. Denniston,* the Maryland Court of Appeals ruled, in 1938, that private discrimination was not illegal. The ruling was a setback not only for equal rights but for practical problem solving. A growing black population needed space, but the white majority fought to deny it. Horrendous overcrowding resulted.

A story of attempted integration of city neighborhoods further illustrates white resistance. The story emerges from the strange career of Phillip Perlman, a newspaperman who worked for the *News Post* and the *Sun* while becoming a lawyer. In those employments, he met Mencken and others of social and professional import in the city. In 1923, Mayor Howard Jackson made him chairman of a committee to study segregation in the city. The committee might well have been called the Committee to Protect our Segregated Way of Life.

As city solicitor in 1925, Perlman and his committee worked to keep blacks from moving into various parts of the city, again by means of restrictive covenants: bans on certain people owning or living in certain houses. Perlman would be a fixture in the civil rights struggle for a quarter century—on both sides of the issue, opposing as well as advocating for the dismantling of Jim Crow.

More than twenty years later, having been named solicitor general of the United States by President Harry Truman, Perlman argued that restricting sales to white buyers was "not in the national interest." Whether it was legal or not under various court rulings, he seemed to be saying, it was bad policy. This observation recalled the observations of Justice John Marshall Harlan when he found *Plessy v. Ferguson* not in the national interest.

Power wonders if Perlman's conversion wasn't merely political: in 1925, black voters were Republican—and so weak as to warrant no consideration. The powers that be could get away with segregation, in other words. By 1947, when the restrictive covenant case was finally settled, many blacks had become Democrats, a trend of importance to Democrats like Perlman. They had the ballot potential Douglass had envisioned after the Civil War. Since the days of Franklin Delano Roosevelt, the Democratic Party could see the potential too.

"Perhaps his change of heart was symptomatic of a metamorphosis in the body politic; a national consensus in support of greater racial equality may have been growing," Power says. In his last years, Perlman's transformation seemed complete. Always active in Democratic Party politics, he was appointed to the Democratic Advisory Council, and in 1960, he wrote the party's civil rights plank.[23]

Power points out that an associate of Perlman thought the man did not change his mind about integration much at all. He was, says Philip Elman, who worked with Perlman in the solicitor general's office, implacably opposed to it. Thus, one of Perlman's greatest contributions to the civil rights cause was his decision to resign from the solicitor general's post just as the most important school desegregation case, *Brown v. Board of Education of Topeka*, was about to be argued in 1954.[24]

As shabby and damaging as Perlman's maneuvers had been in service to Mayor Jackson, there was no physical violence. But violence had not been removed from the Jim Crow arsenal of enforcement. In the early 1930s, with the Great Depression exacerbating racial tensions, a few Marylanders were about to resume a dalliance with lynching.

"BLOOD AT THE ROOTS": THE MOB HELPS RAISE A MOVEMENT

Lucretia Harris went home from work early while there was still light. The Princess Anne family she cooked for insisted. Schoolchildren were being sent home early as well. One of them, Lloyd "Hotdog" Simpkins, says there was a rumor: someone had been lynched, hanged from a lamppost. It wasn't true. No one was dead yet. But everyone knew what was coming.[25]

On the evening of October 18, 1933, a mob of several thousand assembled in front of the town's gray stone jail. Twenty-five or so policemen, backed by state troopers, stood before them. The town sheriff, Luther Daugherty, was there, too, along with Somerset County judge Robert F. Duer, who made an effort to deflect the crowd. "My friends, why don't you disperse and go home quietly. The grand jury will be convened promptly and this man will have a speedy trial."[26]

But the people did not listen. They swarmed past the assembled authorities and into the building. A black man named George Armwood was hauled from his cell, and before he hit the street, a young man jumped on him with a knife, apparently slicing off one of his ears. They dragged him through the streets of this lovely Eastern Shore town, past the courthouse, with its portrait of Marylander Samuel P. Chase, a U.S. Supreme Court justice and signer of the Declaration of Independence, who was born in Princess Anne. Chase's devotion to the law would not be honored on this day.

A householder pled with the vigilantes to move on lest the grisly deed be performed in front of his children. The mob complied. A suitable tree was found in front of a judge's house, and Armwood was hanged. Then his body was burned. Then he was dragged further through the town. Armwood got what he deserved—that was the consensus, according to Simpkins, who grew up to be state legislator, a high-ranking state official in the administration of Governor J. Millard Tawes, as well as secretary of state and a judge.[27] Innocent until proven guilty (Armwood had been charged with assaulting an elderly woman) was a lofty principle of no consequence to a lynch mob. It would decide what George Armwood deserved.

Clarence M. Mitchell Jr., then a young reporter for the *Afro-American* newspaper in Baltimore, described what Armwood got:

> [His] skin was scorched and blackened while his face had suffered many blows from sharp and heavy instruments. A cursory glance revealed that one ear was missing and his tongue, between his clenched teeth, gave evidence of his great agony before death. There is no adequate description of the mute evidence of gloating on the part of whites who gathered to watch the effect upon our people.
>
> After the crime, a civil officer called John M. Dennis, a prominent Princess Anne undertaker, and asked him to take care of the muti-lated body of Armwood. The request was met with a refusal on the grounds that it was the city's duty to remove the murdered man. The final way of meeting the issue was to toss the body into a lumber yard . . . Silent groups of our people on their way to work or with nothing in particular in view, solemnly gazed at the horribly-mangled corpse which had been stripped of all clothing and was covered with two sacks.[28]

Mitchell and two other *Afro-American* reporters had driven to Princess Anne the day after Armwood's murder. They made the trip in *Afro* publisher Carl Murphy's car, traveling north to Cecil County and then south down the Eastern Shore. (There were no bay bridges then.) Rolling through white Maryland, they had a moment of panic when smoke began to pour from beneath the vehicle—the result, it turned out, of their failure to release the emergency brake. They carried a handgun. Surely they were nervous. They were headed for a community that had two reasons for resenting their presence: they were black, and they were reporters.

Mitchell walked through the town without incident, interviewing townspeople and police and writing an account for Murphy's newspaper. The *Afro* covered news of interest to black readers in Baltimore far better than the mainstream, white press, which in too many cases did not cover the black community at all. In this case, though, the *Sun* and other white papers made clear the depravity of this act, called it atrocious and shameful, and demanded action.

In his *Evening Sun* column, Mencken wrote, "At least since the World War the lower shore has been going downhill mentally and morally. It has been sliding out of Maryland and into the orbit of Arkansas and Tennessee, Mississippi and the more flea-bitten half of Virginia. Time and again the whole state has been menaced by the peculiar sinishness of its boozing dry politics, and now it holds us all up to the contempt of the nation and the world by staging a public obscenity worthy of cannibals." Indulging himself in lavish language as always, he called the lynchers "prehensile town boomers, ignorant hedge preachers. That a community so debauched is in a mood to restore the orderly processes of civilized government is certainly hard to believe. Inflamed to frenzy by the very men who ought to calm it, it is bound to proceed to other outrages. Unless the decent people of the region regain the upper hand, such outrages will undoubtedly follow." To that end, he praised the editorials of the *Salisbury Advertiser,* which, though blaming Communists, denounced "an ugly blot upon the name and reputation of our peace-loving Christian community which it will take generations to live down, and which cannot ever be erased."[29] If there was more than the usual determination by local officials to have the matter in their hands, recent criminal justice proceedings were blamed. The Shore was inflamed by the case of Euel Lee, a black man who had killed an entire family, confessed to the crime, and was convicted in a Baltimore County courtroom. Then, through his lawyer, Bernard Ades, a member of the Communist Party, Lee managed to win a series of reprieves. He was not hanged quickly enough for many.

And those feelings may have been driven higher by a number of circumstances. Federal policy had begun to have an even greater impact on race relations and civil rights. In 1932, the year before the Armwood lynching, 89 families in the Eastern Shore's Somerset County sought welfare relief. A year later, with the Great Depression deepening, the number had grown seven-fold to 625. Franklin D. Roosevelt's National Recovery Administration (NRA) had begun to move in with help, but its arrival had been delayed by Governor Albert R. Ritchie's opposition to federal involvement in state or local affairs. Ritchie had made his political reputation as a proponent of self-help, with a deep skepticism about federal money. People were hungry, but Ritchie clung to principle. In listings of federal assistance to the states, Maryland ranked near the bottom as a result of the governor's concerns.

That policy spared Maryland one sin at least. In states where government jobs were handed out, black recipients were paid less by local authorities. Eleanor Roosevelt, after touring in the South, reported this short shrift to her husband. On the Eastern Shore, the NRA came to be called the Nigger Relief Act. After Governor Ritchie sent National Guard troops into action against the Armwood lynching mob suspects, some said the letters stood for Never Ritchie Again.

The atmosphere of racial hostility made changes of venue and precautionary removal of defendants an almost automatic step in cases involving blacks. In the matter of George Armwood, however, Ritchie allowed Princess Anne officials to have their way, as if to remain consistent with his idea of federalism. He and his staff attempted to stay in touch with local officials, who were promising to safeguard their prisoner, but the matter was soon out of control. Armwood had, in effect, been delivered to his executioners. The situation raised serious questions about the decisions of Governor Ritchie, then in the fourth term of a distinguished political career in which he had made a strong run for president.

Ades would charge later that lynching was an official policy of the state—tolerated at least. Ades's opponents said he deliberately inflamed racial passions, hoping to win support for his Communist cause. He had strong evidence: habitual, all-but-official disregard for the rights and living conditions of black Marylanders. Ades became a well-known and, in some quarters, reviled figure in Maryland, a resourceful advocate whose interventions made him anathema to white authority. A graduate of the Johns Hopkins University and the University of Maryland School of Law, Ades was another outsider challenging the system. He was threatened with lynching several times, but he seems to have been absolutely fearless in the face of mobs and the Maryland legal Establishment.[30]

A day after the lynching, the president of the United States came to Washington College, in Chestertown, north of Princess Anne, where he was given an honorary doctor of laws. The school's namesake had been the first to receive the honorary degree. When it was his turn to speak, Roosevelt said, "I cannot help but feel a very close relationship with the early days of the Republic as I stand here." He urged his audience to remember its youthful ideals. The newly minted doctor of law was silent on the atrocity of the previous day.[31]

Antilynching legislation was pending in Congress, but Roosevelt was not one of its vocal supporters. He had resisted efforts from many, including his wife and the NAACP, to convince him to take a stand on the issue. "I did not choose the tools with which I must work," the president told Walter White of the NAACP. "Had I been permitted to choose them I would have selected quite different ones. But I've got to get legislation passed by the Congress to save America. The southerners by reason of the seniority rule in Congress are chairmen or occupy strategic places on most of the Senate and House committees. If I come out for the antilynching bill, they will block every bill I ask Congress to pass to keep America from collapsing. I just can't take the risk."[32]

But the proximity of the nation's capital gave the event more prominence—and potential for corrective action—than a similar event would have had in Georgia. The prevailing animus on the Shore was illustrated by local witnesses who told a congressional committee they had no knowledge of the event. A local druggist, William Thompson, later named to a coroner's jury that would investigate the matter, may have been a participant in the event. He and his wife told senators they had been at the pictures in Salisbury on the night of the lynching. Clearly not believing him, Senator Patrick McCarran asked them for the name of the movie they saw. They hadn't bothered to prepare that part of their alibi. "I don't recall the name," the druggist replied. "I have had too much on my mind to remember." "You never looked that up to familiarize yourself with the name of the picture?" the senator asked. "I hadn't thought it necessary. No sir." Senator McCarran turned then to Thompson's wife with the same question. "I don't remember," she said. "You do not remember the name of the picture?" "No, I do not." "Did you go that night to see a particular picture?" "Yes." "What was the picture?" "I don't remember."[33]

Proponents of an antilynching law used Maryland as Exhibit One in hearings they hoped would lead to a national antilynching law. This was an opportunity for Ades and the Communist Party as well. Testifying before the Wagner Committee, Ades said lynching was designed to keep the lower classes at each other's throats to spare the throats of the wealthy. The congressional committee regarded Ades as a provocateur and may have given less attention to those aspects of his testimony that were or should have been deeply troubling. It was more difficult to set aside the testimony of others. Louis Azrael, a columnist for the *Baltimore News-Post,* took the committee through a damning history of recent lynchings on the Shore. He made the same points advanced by Ades, though he attributed them not to policy but to lapses or to apathy. And, he suggested, Governor Ritchie was constrained from acting by some of the same factors that kept President Franklin Roosevelt on the sidelines: fear of alienating forces he needed for the passage of his bills.[34]

Clarence Mitchell told his biographer much later that many Americans did want an antilynching law, but Ritchie and Roosevelt weren't willing to take the political consequences of calling lynchers criminals and outlaws. Unfortunately, there was an equally strong group in the country that saw lynching as a means of keeping blacks in their place— that if whites did not have such a weapon, blacks would take over, particularly in areas where they were numerically strong. The sensitivities of white Americans, once again, weighed more heavily than due process for black Americans.[35]

The committee also heard from Simon Sobeloff, then the U.S. attorney for Maryland. Sobeloff addressed the complex legal and constitutional aspects of the antilynching bill. He said the measure merited serious consideration because the Fourteenth Amendment to the Constitution, guaranteeing equal protection of the law and due process, was essentially neutralized by the conflict between state and federal rights. If states or counties refused to indict in such matters—a usual if not uniform occurrence in lynchings—federal authorities could not intervene without at least theoretically usurping powers left to the states. What he said about the complexities of the law were translated by Mitchell, who gave the committee a hint of the atmosphere in Princess Anne and the willingness of law enforcement to let matters take their murderous course. Commenting on the mild resistance mounted against the lynch mob, a state policeman told Mitchell: "We weren't going to kill anyone for the carelessness of state officials who permitted Armwood to be brought here." This was a reference to the decision by Governor Ritchie not to intervene more forcefully. Elmer A. Carter of the National Urban League told the committee that black leaders had counseled faith in what he called the better class of white citizens. Their silence in the face of outrage gave sanction to the mob.[36]

Sanction had been written into the laws. No one approved of murder, to be sure. But a different word was used to describe the punishment meted out by the mob-appointed posses that turned lynching into community affairs. The lynch mob as enforcer of community values—

particularly when no specific law was passed to stop it—was seen as an enforcer of Jim Crow laws. *Dred Scott* was the best example of that enduring view. As a matter of strict legality, the decision and its offensive language had been nullified by constitutional amendments. But the words did not die. And as Howard University Law School dean Charles Hamilton Houston would point out, there was more to obtaining redress in society than a court decision, no matter how lofty the tribunal. Marylanders and other Americans behaved for decades as if Taney's words could quite properly guide their behavior. Clarence Mitchell thought Armwood's body had been left in the street at Princess Anne as a warning.

The cook Lucretia Harris says silence reigned in the days and years after that night. "Of course it affects you knowing that anybody was being killed, but I can't say how it affected me. I don't think you can put it in words when you know something like that is going on. I don't think people thought it would be so bad until there was such a gathering. I went to work and then went back home. It was something people didn't talk about too much. People you worked for didn't say anything. It went along. It happened. It was just something that happened." Just the way it was. Was it done to frighten people? "I can't say much about that." Did it frighten you? "I think to a certain extent, everyone was frightened."[37]

The fear of violence on the Eastern Shore was chronicled by many, including the writer Adele Holden. Like Douglass, she loved the Shore and clung to a conviction that things could change, that life could yield opportunities for everyone. In the 1930s and 1940s, her father, Snow Henry Holden, became a one-man movement for better black schools. He put his relatively good mechanic's livelihood at risk in an effort to remedy deprivations no one bothered to deny. The *Worcester Democrat* had done some reporting, showing how bad the area's black schools were. As always when black people challenged white people, Holden's effort was met with concern from his black neighbors: "Let well enough alone," his friends said. "Don't need to turn the world upside down." But, if getting a high school for black kids meant turning the world upside down, he knew he had to try.

His daughter says the prospect of lynching loomed in the minds of those who counseled utmost care. Parents tried to insulate their children, but children overheard. "I haven't forgotten any of it either," Adele

Holden said years later. Parents were trying to raise them so that they wouldn't have the "full weight of racism on their little shoulders." In the days before television, a child could be effectively quarantined—a good thing in some ways, but a practice that may have minimized outrage and incorporated a "just the way it is" outlook on life.

But the message got through eventually. Something bad could happen at any time. "If anyone asked why lynching might happen, [black] people said, 'It's just in 'em,' "[38] Holden said. Murderous rages were "just in" white people, part of their makeup, something you had to live with. Just the way it was. This view was a deplorable by-product of the violence committed by a lawless few, but then, for those who were willing to countenance lynching, this sort of thinking was the objective. And, for whatever reason, there was no law against vigilante violence.

As George Armwood burned, the mob sang "John Brown's Body" and "Something to Remember You By." A few years later, there came a countering song, "Strange Fruit," the dirge sung famously by Billie Holiday, the drug-and-sadness-addicted jazz singer who grew up in Baltimore. The song was written by a Communist schoolteacher, Abel Meeropol, of Brooklyn, New York, and performed by Holiday in jazz clubs around the nation. Camay Murphy, the daughter of Cab Calloway, another of the Pennsylvania Avenue stars, says the song was unmistakably part of the awakening civil rights movement.

"People thought, 'At last we're getting something into the music so people knew what was going on in the country.' It came at a time when people just didn't say anything about injustice," she says.[39] Leonard Feather, the late jazz writer, called it "the first significant protest in words and music, the first unmuted cry against racism."[40] Unmuted, untempered, the enormity of it was laid bare. You could have a lynching with impunity. No one would talk about it. You didn't say anything about injustice and race-generated murder, but maybe you could sing about it.

"She took a chance with the song. Even though when you see her singing it, she seems kind of out of it. It almost added to the drama and pathos of it. You put yourself in a frame so you could get through it." Murphy thinks these performances were often in white clubs. "I don't think many blacks saw her sing it in that kind of intimate club setting, except the activists." Holiday, she says, "had a bit of an image issue: she was considered an unsavory type. Parents, black and white, didn't want their kids to hear her." But the song was heard. It got into the air supply. Lynching did not instantly stop, but it lost some of its proud, church-picnic, picture-taking festive atmosphere.

Efforts to find and prosecute the Princess Anne lynchers were unsuccessful. Governor Ritchie sent in the national guard to help, all to no avail. At the same time, a disbarment proceeding was mounted against Bernard Ades, the Communist lawyer who had intervened to provide legal defense for black defendants. As adjudicator of this disciplinary procedure, U.S. District Court judge Morris Soper praised Ades for insisting on full representation for black men like George Armwood, Euel Lee, and others whose rights were compromised and whose lives were clearly in danger. Ades, he pointed out, got Euel Lee's case removed from "the excited and hostile community of the Eastern Shore." Lee had been beaten into confessing by police, but local authorities refused to investigate the abuse. Contrary to the public anger over procedural delay, Judge Soper pointed out, authorities had ignored the law in their determination to quickly convict and hang Lee.

In the disbarment proceedings, Ades was represented by Houston, the Howard University School of Law dean and a man who was about to begin a Maryland-based, NAACP assault on the Jim Crow statutes, an assault fueled by growing anger in the black community over the lynching of Armwood and others. Soper declined to disbar Ades, finding him innocent of most of the charges. "This phase of his activities," the judge wrote, "led one of the counsel opposed to him in the matter to say frankly in argument that the respondent [Ades] had rendered a public service which, without him, would have been left undone."[41] Soper's ruling was a rebuke to the bar and to the courts of Maryland. But it did not lead, in the short run at least, to any adjustment—a conclusion amply supported by the Armwood case, which came shortly afterward. On the contrary, the lynching fever and the unwillingness of high officials to stop it gave license to those who stormed past the law enforcement of Princess Anne to drag George Armwood to his death.

But important and far-reaching change did come from the fires of Princess Anne, Maryland. Armwood was Maryland's last lynching victim. No one paid for his murder, but his death stoked the fires of a revolution. Clarence Mitchell's life, and the life of the nation, changed profoundly. A lifetime of impassioned service to the nation was forged by the mob.

A NEW VISION: ECONOMIC LEVERAGE

One of the emerging change agents in Maryland was the *Afro-American* reporter Clarence Mitchell, a young man of elegant profile, partial to blue serge jackets and white pants. He had wanted to be a doctor, but the Depression and what he saw in Princess Anne changed all that. People noticed him, how he held his head proudly high, how he spoke with self-assurance and competitive fire. He won debate contests, exhibiting in high school what Juanita Jackson, a young woman who was a year or so behind him in school, called "handsome oratory."[42]

Handsome and elegant as he seemed, he was well grounded in home truths. Discipline came from his father, Clarence Mitchell Sr., a musician, and his mother, Elsie Davis Mitchell, whose life was her seven children. "She believed in neatness, honesty, and . . . keeping your word. I would say that my mother and father always felt that if you gave your word, you ought to keep it," Mitchell Jr. said.[43]

One of his mother's religious or social memberships had a children's branch called Lilies of the Valley, "a membership that got us into a lot of trouble with boys in the neighborhood who didn't think so kindly of boys who were members of anything called Lilies of the Valley. Be that as it may, we were members, and my mother and father always encouraged us in activities of a civic nature."[44] Perhaps he was making up for this childhood embarrassment when he became, for a short time, a professional prize fighter known as the Shamrock Kid.

The family lived on Stockton Street, near Presstman in northwest Baltimore, when he was born. That neighborhood's amenities included a lumber yard "with a lot of wonderful mules that I thought made real assets." Mitchell Jr. had many jobs, often two or more at a time, at one point in a bakery and at a soda fountain. He worked until midnight, walking home along Pennsylvania Avenue from North Avenue. When he reached Gold Street, he would start whistling. "My mother would be sitting by the window waiting for me. I just liked to let her know I was on the way." On into their 20s, his brothers and sisters pooled their wages, turned them over to their mother. Nevertheless, the family moved several times, losing a large house during the Depression when they were unable to make the mortgage payments. "We put up a battle, and I guess if it left me with any feeling, it left one with more knowledge of how to deal with adversity than I had before, and a whole lot less fear about things that might be troublesome. I think I learned then that whatever is bad, you can either overcome or endure, and I'm much less intimidated by adversity now than I perhaps would have been if I hadn't had that experience."

He and his sisters went to the Pitcher Street branch of the Enoch Pratt Free Library. "We spent a tremendous amount of time there because the library was free and you could get books there that were very interesting."[45] Frederick Douglass's skill as a writer and orator had sprung from the eastside streets of Fell's Point and the pages of *The Columbian Orator*; Mitchell's talents were burnished and his horizons broadened on the other side of the city, at the Pitcher Street branch of the Pratt.

Like many black mothers and fathers, the Mitchells tried to shield their children from a world organized to frustrate them. What Clarence saw in Princess Anne must have been even more dispiriting than Jim Crow. When he returned, he said little about what he had seen, but his family could see he had been profoundly changed. He was sickened, emotionally drained, and devastated, according to his brother Parren.[46]

He was not immobilized, as his bold reporting foray made clear, but his life and the course of it had changed fundamentally. If Clarence had been somewhat accepting of the life he knew in Baltimore, Princess Anne gave him a new consciousness, clear to all his family. He saw discrimination and race hatred in its raw form, with none of the protections of family or dulling mitigation that over time inured one to the way things were.

When Clarence returned to Baltimore, settling into his job with the *Afro,* he and the rest of the city beheld a mysterious young outsider, Kiawah Costonie, introducing himself as a prophet. Mitchell and his boss, Carl Murphy, watched with some excitement as the prophet told his story. Costonie began most famously with the idea, haltingly adopted by a list of black civic and fraternal groups, that white merchants along the 1700 block of Pennsylvania Avenue ought to employ black workers.

Though the overwhelming majority of their customers were black, few if any store owners put black faces behind the counters or in any other jobs. If that didn't change, Costonie said, black shoppers should buy what they needed elsewhere. This was a revolutionary thought—revolutionary to make the observation so publicly and to propose doing something financially harmful to the white community in retaliation for grievances of any sort. Such declarations in southern states would have been met with violence almost certainly.

And, to be sure, some Baltimore blacks were wary of such a confrontational tactic. Lynchings were committed, in part, to make people think twice before stepping forward on any issue. Still, the Costonie campaign attracted a substantial group of recognizable black leaders in Baltimore. After first rejecting the idea, a number of women, including Lillie May Jackson, signed on. Jackson pointed out that all the city's officials, from time to time, had urged people to fight for their rights, and because of this, she suggested, they could hardly object if black Baltimoreans seized "the opportunity when it presented itself."[47] Jackson was already thinking strategically, crafting the pretexts for direct action.

This was one of Jackson's earliest forays into an arena not yet fitted with the name "civil rights movement." Her daughters say she was drawn toward activism when they were denied an adequate education in Maryland. In a sense, her view of how things were had been altered in a fashion similar to the shock that had changed the thinking of young Clarence Mitchell. She and her husband, Keiffer "Jack" Jackson, had returned to Baltimore when it was time for their children to start school. They had been itinerant church entertainers, traveling in the West and the South: she sang and she spoke.

"My first recollections of my mother is lying asleep on a church bench and waking up hearing her sing," her daughter Juanita said.[48] What she also remembered was a telepathy game she and her mother played in church. She was three years old at the time. A prodigy? A medium? Neither. "My mother developed a code. She said 'Juanita, when I call the number, first you will tell what I'm pointing at. When I cough, it will be a bench. Number two, the second thing I do, and so on . . . There were about ten things that she taught me . . . She would blindfold me, and then she said, 'Juanita, what is this?' I would give the [predetermined] answer, whatever it was. And at the end, she said, 'Juanita, what am I touching?' I said, that's a bald-headed man. And that was always the end of the performance.' "[49]

The church entertainment touring ended when the Jackson children needed schooling, and when Lillie May tired of traveling. "She wanted to come back to Baltimore so that we would be able to get the education we should," Juanita said. Juanita's father continued to travel in Virginia, Delaware, and other states. He made his own movies often, showing black people in churches, doing business, "in order to show the constructive side of Negroes in his films, because usually in the theaters, the only black people you saw on the screen were people like Stepin Fetchit, who were buffoons and the like, and he thought that was terrible."[50]

At one point, he had owned a theater called Dreamland in Little Rock, Arkansas, but it didn't work out because a white competitor who opened across the street could get pictures unavailable to her father. The family kept the Dreamland sign in their basement on Druid Hill Avenue.

When she was about 30, Lillie May Jackson's life changed—for ill and for good. A misdiagnosed case of mastoiditis required a major operation, a botched job, apparently. Her grandson, Michael Mitchell, says she was wheeled out in the corridor and left for dead. Another physician saw signs of life and saved her. The surgeon told her afterward that God had saved her. "Yes, Doctor, I know, because I told God if he would just bring me out of this hospital so that I could rear my three daughters, three little girls, I would give Him a life of service. I know He saved me because He wants me to rear my children."[51]

When she got home, she realized something had changed. She called out to her husband. "Jack, come here. I can't smile." A facial nerve had been severed, permanently disfiguring one side of her face. A very handsome woman, she was in no way deterred from the service she had promised. She usually turned to keep the paralyzed side of her face out of photographs. But she never turned away from a challenge. If anything, she grew more determined.

In her new role as an activist, Jackson offered herself as the offspring of a founding family. Her slave father, Charles Carroll, was a descendant of Charles Carroll of Carrollton, a signer of the Declaration of Independence and a member of the Maryland legislature. Jackson's grandmother Amanda Bowen Carroll was the granddaughter of an African chief. (Her great-grandson, councilman Keiffer Mitchell of Baltimore, and David Carroll, a white descendant of the founding Carrolls, would delight in the irony. They enjoyed greeting each other decades later as "cousin.") For Lillie May Jackson, making her ancestry clear was poignant and powerful. She came to the struggle for equal rights as the offspring of men and women on both sides of the racial divide in America—slaves and slaveholders.

Jackson was a more successful apostle of justice than her famous forebear. Charles Carroll of Carrollton, who owned many slaves, attempted to have slavery outlawed by the General Assembly but failed. Jackson came to her role with an illustrious family tree, but she came as did many with nothing like fame. She was a Baltimore mother anxious to find the best possible education for her children. In this regard, she was like many Marylanders who were drawn into the civil rights fray. These moments of opposition helped to create a strong underpinning for the movement.

As the Pennsylvania Avenue "Shop Where You Can Work" campaign proceeded, a committee was formed to work on other objectives. Its members included Thurgood Marshall, in his first years as a Baltimore lawyer, working for Jackson; Marshall's wife, Buster; the Reverend A. J. Payne, pastor of Enon Baptist Church in West Baltimore for fifty years; the black lawyer William Alfred Carroll Hughes; and Jackson. Her daughters Juanita and Virginia had already formed an organization of great potential. They called it the City-Wide Young People's Forum.

Clarence Mitchell joined the NAACP and eagerly attended meetings of the forum. Its speakers attracted him, but so did Juanita Jackson. She remembered his oratory. He remembered her beauty. Lillie May Jackson had prohibited dating for her daughters until they were finished with college.

"In a way, the city-wide forum was all my sister and I had. Because my mother wouldn't let us go to dances. But we set it up because life in general for blacks was so unbearable. There was so much deprivation."[52] Juanita and her sister had been denied admission to Maryland universities: Juanita was turned away by the University of Maryland, and Virginia by the Maryland Institute College of Art. Juanita, and eventually her sister, left for the University of Pennsylvania.

Juanita remembered coming back to Baltimore from Philadelphia. She and her sister saw the city as if for the first time. Their shock made them good allies of Prophet Costonie. The prophet attended some of the forum meetings, and young people became an important regiment in the new army of resistance. As the movement slowly accelerated, the idealism and the outrage of youth—and their relative lack of concern about economic loss—became an important part of the struggle.

The forum hosted important speakers, including W. E. B. Du Bois, who was living in Baltimore at the time. Clarence Mitchell's son Michael says his father spoke with Du Bois often. The older Mitchell told his son that Du Bois was not reluctant to be critical of the black community when he thought criticism was deserved. "You know the problem with black people is they don't read," Du Bois said one night during a forum event.[53]

The ministers read, of course, and some of them were uncomfortable with the young people's forum. Juanita and the other leaders were asked to take their group away from the Sharp Street AME Church, where it had begun. The minister then was unwilling to risk angering city officials. The forum found a new base at Bethel AME Church, just around the corner. They relocated with no diminution of momentum. Similar organizations had buoyed and inspired black self-help in Baltimore for at least one hundred years. The forum's founders might have looked back to the Baltimore Benevolent Society of the Young Men of Color, the African Friendship Benevolent Society for Social Relief, the Free African Civilization Society, or the Star in the East Society, groups devoted to the social, economic, or spiritual needs of the black community.[54]

At about the same time, Costonie, Jackson, and Marshall were pushing their dramatic public statement on Pennsylvania Avenue to a conclusion.[55] Some of the merchants cooperated. Others resorted to violence in the way property owners had when trying to keep blacks out of white neighborhoods: hiring thugs to roust the picketers. Buster Marshall came home bruised and upset after one day's marching. Thurgood Marshall responded in kind: he hired Scrappy Brown, one of his clients, to protect him and his wife. "Scrappy was one of them nice, peaceful fellows. He carried an ax up the back of his coat," Marshall said.[56]

Pennsylvania Avenue was main street for Baltimore's black community. It had just about everything. Its most famous edifice was the Royal Theater, built in 1921, a stop on the Chitlin Circuit, a string of nightclubs, from the Howard Theater in Washington, D.C., to the Apollo in Harlem, where every celebrated black performer could be seen. Billie Holiday, Count Basie, Duke Ellington, and Fats Waller were among the regulars. A distinct black culture flourished along Baltimore's twelve-block strip of the circuit. The pulse of the street beat steadily for decades. "Loud and cantankerous, pulsating with honking horns, droning voices, and raucous laughter, and smelling of cigars, perfume, and roasted peanuts—this was city life," wrote Kweisi Mfume, later a congressman and head of the NAACP, in his autobiography *No Free Ride*. "I was mesmerized by its fast, brazen rhythms, its neon lights and fancy cars . . . The black people here were as classy as any whites I'd seen . . . They drove up in fancy fish-tail Cadillacs and handed them over to red-capped valets. The men stepped out sporting black Stetson hats, tailored sharkskin suits, bright silk ties and shoes so shiny you could see your face in them."[57]

The picketers who began to march on the avenue were no less elegant. They carried signs in front of the Tommy Tucker and the Goodman five-and-tens, the Max Myers shoe store, and the A&P. Costonie's plan had the desired effect: receipts dipped sharply. Here was an object lesson for Baltimoreans, black and white, a glimpse of coming days in which conflict would be rife with consternation and pain and hope of success. One victory led to another. The day of black acquiescence had been set aside by the dawn of a new refusal to accept things as they were. The *Afro-American* put it this way: "Unhampered by the inhibitions, obligations and fears of retribution which cause many of our older residents and leaders to refrain from taking these forward steps, Costonie is entitled to our encouragement and support. May his work continue." The editorial appeared under the headline "Costonie Strikes Again" in the September 30, 1933, *Afro*. Carl Murphy was remonstrating with his black readers, urging them to be more involved. Some had resisted joining the fight because they had no confidence that direct action could do much for them—and it might hurt. That feeling was often reinforced by the fears of retribution mentioned in Murphy's editorial. Manners and courtesy were used against black citizens. To speak out was rude and out of keeping with accepted norms, an assault on the accepted order and an offense to civilized behavior, so that blacks, anxious to be accepted, were doubly put off. You couldn't confront someone without being called uppity or rude. You wanted to avoid anything that suggested the charge had validity. Yet even if you voiced unhappiness at clear injustices, the white opponent seldom gave up anything beyond palliatives, tokens, and half-measures.

"Shop Where You Can Work" was different. Within days, the merchants were announcing new hires; young black men and young black women would be serving black customers. But even as businesses were acknowledging that black shoppers had a point, even as businesses were giving in to the demands, lawyers for the Pennsylvania Avenue merchants were asking the courts to find the pickets illegal. It didn't take long for the usual discouraging response from white authority. Judge Albert S. E. Owens ruled for the merchants. He said the picketers should have been arrested for disorderly conduct. They were, he declared, engaged in a "common conspiracy." Mitchell, writing in the *Afro*, said the judge had "stepped back into the stone age of economics." Others began to raise money for an appeal, and Jackson brought in the largest sums. The appeal was argued by one of Baltimore's leading black lawyers, W. A. C. Hughes.

The appeals court endorsed Judge Owens, holding that "a race, in this case a group of Negroes, [could not] impose its will on a white merchant and compel him to employ colored instead of white clerks." The appeals court found much merit in the picketers' cause, asserting that the merchants had planted themselves in a black community with a clear purpose—"exploitation of the community for profit"—but, the court said, it could not endorse an unlawful remedy. Reverend Payne and others worried that cautious attitudes among blacks would be, once again, affirmed by this result. "The prevailing feeling here then," he said, "was that segregation was segregation and it was going to stay that way until kingdom come. The Negro's place was fixed and few had the nerve to try to change it."[58]

More challenges would come, and these days on Pennsylvania Avenue would be recalled proudly as a time when Baltimore blacks moved assertively beyond the boundaries imposed on them and observed for so many years. They were, in this respect, far ahead of many other communities in the North and South. The accepted belief that people were living in a hopeless world of discrimination began to give way. Murphy's appeals for more joint action gained traction.

White people of distinct social standing entered the lists, not in great numbers, but dramatically. On August 25, 1934, the *Afro* reported that Mrs. Broadus Mitchell, wife of the Socialist candidate for governor, had been arrested for picketing a local Depression relief agency, demanding that it offer more relief. Broadus Mitchell was joined under the Socialist banner by Elisabeth Coit Gilman, wife of Daniel Coit Gilman, the first president of the Johns Hopkins University. As fearless and fiery as Lillie May Jackson, Elisabeth Gilman had scandalized many in Baltimore and in the nation when, in 1928, she volunteered her house for a dinner party to be attended by blacks and whites. One of the downtown hotels, adhering to the dictates of Jim Crow, had turned them away.

Encouraged by Gilman, Clarence Mitchell ran in 1934 for the Maryland House of Delegates. He was not a Socialist, but the Republicans and Democrats were not reaching out to black candidates. He did not win but proved again that he was a determined and restless soul, eager to be involved.

By now, Carl Murphy had enlisted Jackson to revive the NAACP branch in Baltimore. It was all but dead, with one hundred members of whom only a handful were active (and that apparently was a generous description). Black Baltimoreans would have had no chance at joining the mainstream if some organization like the NAACP were not making the case persistently. Murphy chose Jackson, a woman whose prepossessing temerity was becoming well known, to lead the Baltimore branch.

She and Murphy were motivators, and under their direction, the Baltimore NAACP went from those one hundred members to many thousand in short order. The *Afro-American* became the *North Star* of Baltimore, Carl Murphy, the Frederick Douglass. He put his newspaper at the service of Jackson, and she used it well—not that any of those with power were at all moved by the editor and publisher's diatribes. Nor were those guardians of "the way it was" his target.

"God opened my mouth and no man can shut it," she said. That signature declaration gave Lillie May Jackson a place in Baltimore lore with the "Ain't I a woman?" leadership ranks of Sojourner Truth and the Eastern Shore's Harriet Tubman, the most famous of the Underground Railroad engineers, who had threatened to shoot a man if he did not stop quailing and follow her to freedom. Jackson began to confront the Establishment of Maryland with a withering insistence.

She would have more than the sound of her own voice. She had Carl Murphy and the *Afro*. She had Du Bois, who admired her pluck. She had the NAACP, the organizational rock upon which equality for black Americans would be built. She had Clarence Mitchell, the Shamrock Kid, who would become her son-in-law and the NAACP's eloquent representative in Washington.

EUGENE O'DUNNE: COURT OF JUSTICE

In the early 1930s, the University of Maryland School of Law's registrar, W. M. Hillegeist, following orders, warned his superiors that trouble was coming. News stories in the *Afro-American* suggested that a black student would be applying to the school, which had, since the 1890s, barred black students. Hillegeist dutifully sent the clippings to his superiors. Harold Arthur Seaborne proved him right in the summer of 1933. When the application arrived, Hillegeist quickly wrote to the school's dean, Roger Howell. "The 'nigger' has applied for admission. Please formulate a reply for me that is 'Bernard Ades' proof. Do you suggest that I talk to the President [Raymond Pearson] before I send the official reply to the applicant?"[59]

The registrar's correspondence, using offensive language common in pre–civil rights United States, certified the arrival of a new day. That day was dawning in Maryland on the strength of many forces.

Registrar Hillegeist's request for a "Bernard Ades proof" reply was a reference to the Johns Hopkins University graduate and Communist lawyer who had been a courageous if somewhat flamboyant tormenter of state officials, particularly in the case of Euel Lee, the black man convicted of murdering an Eastern Shore family. Seaborne's application was quickly rejected. In a letter to him, Hillegeist wrote, "I am in receipt of your application for admission to the school of law. The University of Maryland does not admit Negro students and your application is accordingly rejected. I direct your attention, however to Art. 77, Sec. 214 A, Code of Public General Laws of Maryland (Acts 1933, Chapter 234)."[60]

The assault against the maze of official resistance had begun. As it turned out, Bernard Ades was not the real threat to university policy. His efforts on behalf of black people, later applauded by some in the Maryland bar who saw some principle in it, were undermined by his association with the Communists. While black leaders welcomed it, they were as wary of Ades's involvement as were the School of Law officials. There was no advantage in alliances with people who wanted to tear down the structure black people were struggling to be a part of.

Registrar Hillegeist, Dean Howell, and President Pearson probably had little real appreciation of the challenge in front of them. They would soon enough be dealing with unprecedentedly determined opponents, ready to meet them on their home turf, the courts. Their track record was not particularly good—School of Law dean John Prentiss Poe had failed in his effort to disenfranchise black voters—and it was about to get worse.

Perhaps the law school leaders were encouraged to know they would be opposed by the young and inexperienced Thurgood Marshall of Baltimore and his mentor, Howard University's School of Law dean, Charles Hamilton Houston. Marshall knew the ethos of Baltimore and of Maryland. He had grown up in the city, and he had worked for some of its elite citizens. He surely knew his adversaries better than they knew him. Rail thin and wearing wire-rimmed glasses, he had become a careful student of the law and of people.

As a college student, Marshall had worked at the aggressively exclusive gated community of Gibson Island, south of Baltimore in Anne Arundel County. Its members would not have seen themselves as positive social irritants, but at least one of them was precisely that, His abusive treatment of young Marshall helped motivate him toward an extraordinary career in the law. Another club member—Hugh Young, a prominent physician and Democratic Party activist—was a more benevolent force in young Marshall's life.

Shaped over the centuries into a ray-shaped mass, Gibson Island was a secluded preserve of the wealthy who sought open water for sailing, a private golf course, and other dimensions of privilege. The place was founded by a member of the Symington family who was annoyed about his inability to get tee times at exclusive Baltimore area clubs. He moved to Gibson Island, where an even more exclusive course was built among the dense forests, hills, and inland ponds.

As in Baltimore and in many parts of the nation in the 1930s, buyers were obliged to sign antiblack restrictive covenants if they were admitted to residence. "At no time," the island deeds ordered, "shall the land included in said tract or any part thereof or any building erected thereon be occupied by any Negro or person of Negro extraction. This prohibition, however, is not intended to include the occupancy by a Negro or person of Negro extraction while employed as a domestic servant or otherwise."[61]

Young Marshall worked at the club under his father, William, who was the club's steward. The members were by all accounts quite fond of the older man they called Marshall. An old island resident, in an article called "I Remember" in the *Sun*, wrote of a fire in which the elder Marshall was credited with saving much of the club's silver among other things: "The club steward, Marshall, made sure everyone had enough to eat. One of Marshall's sons, incidentally, was a law student who worked as assistant head waiter at the club in the summer. This son, Thurgood Marshall, is now an associate justice of the U.S. Supreme Court." Quite an "incidentally." The article moved quickly on without further detail about the Marshalls, or how the club had helped nurture the future justice who had served them.[62]

Marshall apparently had a number of jobs there, caddying and waiting tables among them. As a waiter, he said later, he was volubly abused by a club member, who hailed him with the N word. Marshall made no protest, attending to the man's wishes without noticeable reaction. When his father scolded him later for his silence, Marshall said he would tolerate offensive language as long as the old man kept favoring him with twenty-dollar tips. If the twenties stopped coming, he said, he would express himself.

It is part of Gibson Island lore today that one of the founding members and one of its most famous residents, Hugh Young, a noted Johns Hopkins University urologist, helped Marshall pay his tuition at Howard University School of Law. Young was active in Maryland politics during the 1920s. He lent the hospital important prestige—and financial treasure—when he operated successfully on Diamond Jim Brady, the famous railroad tycoon and Olympian eater. Young's grandson William Rienhoff, later a surgeon at Johns Hopkins Hospital, says his grandfather mentioned his help for Thurgood Marshall occasionally without giving any details. Young does not mention Marshall in his rambling biography, but the tuition assistance story has noteworthy backing and seems consistent with the physician's reputation for generosity. Thurgood Marshall and his father were recalled also by Sally Henderson, whose uncle was a founding member of the club and whose father-in-law, William Henderson, was chief judge of the Maryland Court of Appeals. "I think a lot of people helped him along the way. They had the greatest respect for his father," she said.[63]

The story of white-black relations was not always a story of strife, of fights between boorish whites happy to taunt young blacks. Gestures of humanity do not expunge the sorry record of white society in general, but they show that, in the hearts of some men and women, there was a more benevolent impulse, and sometimes the generous spirit led to profound change far beyond Gibson Island.

Not everyone moved from being a waiter accepting twenty-dollar tips to being lead lawyer in epochal civil rights cases, but the young Marshall found himself on a path strewn with personal and institutional motivations. He found himself pitted against the University of Maryland School of Law, the university president, and the state's political Establishment.

Two years after the School of Law rejected Arthur Seaborne's application, the team of Marshall and Houston appeared in Baltimore Circuit

Court on June 18, 1935, along with another black Baltimore attorney, William I. Gosnell, to plead the case of applicant Donald Gaines Murray. Murray had graduated from Amherst College in 1934. He was perfect for the groundbreaking chore. He was personally beyond reproach. He had a solid academic record achieved at one of the nation's best private schools. He was not a Communist. Here was the illustration of the NAACP's approach: find a sharply focused issue like separate but equal and go hard after it in court. Present no extraneous excuses for dismissing a case.

Maryland had no separate school of law for blacks, so the case seemed open and shut. Houston did not assume victory, however. "How could he have?" asks J. Clay Smith in the *Harvard Law Review*. "He litigated in the era of *Plessy*, an era in which the courts were as much the pillars of American apartheid as they were parties to its ultimate dismantling."[64]

"We cannot depend upon the judges to fight," Houston said in a speech to the National Bar Association, an organization of black lawyers.[65]

Houston had been born in 1895, a year before *Plessy* and the same year Frederick Douglass died. Like Murphy, Houston had attended Amherst College and, after service in World War I, enrolled at Harvard School of Law. He had seen hurtful discrimination during his military service and determined to spend his life making the law a more powerful tool of democracy. He became the first black member of the *Harvard Law Review*, a testament to his exemplary scholarship.

After they had a test case, Marshall and Houston went judge shopping: they settled on the fiercely independent Eugene O'Dunne of Baltimore, a judge who had taken on several powerful forces during his years on the bench. The NAACP knew he was sympathetic to its cause. Shortly before the Murray trial, members of the black National Bar Association met in Baltimore. At one point they were received in Judge O'Dunne's chambers, a remarkable courtesy for the time. In many parts of Baltimore, the races were forbidden to convene in virtually any forum. At one downtown theater, blacks could be on the stage as actors but not in the audience. At another, the rule was reversed: blacks could see the show, but they could not be in it. Blacks and whites were carefully segregated in courtrooms, but they were not barred from the chambers of Eugene O'Dunne.

In slight alterations of attitude, in observations by commentators, and in others who slowly emerged from self-imposed silence, the collective decision to remain oblivious in the face of injustice was changing. The *Evening Sun*'s Mencken wrote one of his most famous columns, characteristically acerbic and skewering, about the Murray case.

Nevertheless, he counseled against "mixing the races. In the present state of public opinion in Maryland it would probably be most unwise, no matter what may be said for it in the abstract."[66] This was the *Plessy* reasoning: fairness and equality could not be enforced over racial animosities. The secondary schools would surely have been a flash point, but they were but one institution built to exclude black citizens—not just from service but from common decency. Few protested. That's the way it was. Or had been. Change was coming: after George Armwood was lynched, after Clarence Mitchell's life changed, after Governor Ritchie's dilatory response to Armwood's perilous situation, after Lillie May Jackson became head of the NAACP in Baltimore—and after Eugene O'Dunne got the Murray case.

The patrician O'Dunne was one of Baltimore's most colorful characters, legendary in the courts, a man whose admirers included prostitutes, governors, distinguished lawyers (black and white), and Mencken. "From the days of his arrival in this Pompeii of America, he has been the honest workman and the good citizen—always hard on the job, always bold and original, always jealous of the rights of the poor and the friendless . . . always against the law's delay," Mencken said of him.[67]

When he ran out of enemies, O'Dunne made new ones among his colleagues on the bench. Given his determination to apply the law with an even hand, favoring neither rich nor poor, O'Dunne may well have run afoul of other judges, many of whom were of the silk-stocking variety, according to his former student Robert Cohen.[68] He was clearly a maverick, determined to apply the law as he read it, whatever recriminations might come his way from displeased colleagues on the bench. He ran three times for state's attorney of Baltimore—and lost each time. Why wouldn't he have lost? He was running against the Democratic machines, against the henchmen of those who had declared the Democratic Party a sentinel for racism in Maryland.

The city's Democratic boss in those days, John S. "Frank" Kelly, was, O'Dunne declared, King of the Underworld. O'Dunne urged an end to political patronage in the courts, calling it a way "to pension the politically lame, halt and blind in a species of prostitution which debases and debauches the political conscience." He had a long public argument with the local court's chief judge, Samuel K. Davis. After another of their colleagues died, O'Dunne asked if he could take his place, to which Davis replied, "I'm not an undertaker, but I'd be perfectly happy if you did."[69]

He ran against corruption, against inhuman conditions in the penitentiary and in the asylums. He made people pay attention with his courage and his teasing wit. A judge who had prosecuted prostitutes and represented them as a lawyer would quite solemnly ask his young students to join him at a bawdy house: "We'll spend the night there and we'll talk about it in the morning."[70] In these times, it took a man such as this to reach the right result in a case like Murray's.

The NAACP and its lawyers filed their suit when they knew O'Dunne would be likely to hear it. Murray was asking the court to find the state of Maryland guilty of violating the 1896 *Plessy v. Ferguson* separate but equal ruling. He wished to become a lawyer in Maryland, and he thought it best to study for the bar in Maryland. There was no black school of law: not separate, not equal—nonexistent. Here was a case that Marshall and Houston thought might result in a watershed breakthrough. How could the state sustain its policy?

Perhaps it was not surprising that the state's lawyer, Charles LeViness III, began his defense by asking for a postponement. At first, Marshall said nothing in response. Whether he was too inexperienced to realize he should protest or he had chosen to be overly deferential, Marshall hung back.

Judge O'Dunne nudged him from the bench.

"Excuse me, Mr. Marshall, do you wish to proceed with this case?" he asked.

"Oh, yes, your honor."

"Well act like it. Say no [to the postponement]!"[71] O'Dunne spoke like that to white lawyers, too, particularly new practitioners, according to Cohen, who at 88 remembered practicing in O'Dunne's court and studying under him at the University of Maryland.[72] The judge promptly ruled for Marshall and the trial began the next day.

Marshall stood in court as heir to the work of Maryland's first black lawyers: Everett J. Waring, followed by Warner T. McGuinn and W. Ashbie Hawkins. McGuinn and Hawkins struggled against the Baltimore City Council's apartheid legislation, four versions of which were introduced between 1910 and 1913, including the one that barred black buyers from blocks that were more than 50 percent white. That idea, imported by various other U.S. cities, was eventually overturned by the U.S. Supreme Court.

The McGuinn and Hawkins legacy went beyond a single court decision. They "created the tradition of legal struggle for equal rights in Maryland," according to Larry S. Gibson, a black lawyer and civil rights activist.[73] That approach was the underpinning of virtually everything that followed in the movement: boycotts, marches, sit-ins, and increasingly open discussions of segregation. These lawsuits were not always successful in the short run. White authority had too many resources for delay and deflection. Freedom fighters and lawyers had to soldier on for many years, long after they had achieved victories that should have applied across the board. Marshall and Houston were about to see that pattern arise all over again in the university system of Maryland.

University officials defended themselves first by saying black students were to be given scholarships to study out of Maryland. They acknowledged there was no money in a fund newly created to relieve pressure from those who would penetrate the barriers of restriction. They seemed to justify the failure to appropriate funds, suggesting that few black people wanted to be lawyers or to study at universities.

Judge O'Dunne had a question that went directly to the issue of separate but equal and to the mendacity that accompanied racist public policy: Would the dean argue, O'Dunne asked, that colored people should not be given separate cars in states where Jim Crow railway transportation was upheld? "How would you let them ride? In ox carts?" The courtroom audience laughed. "Well," replied Dean Howell, "if the ox cart were about as good as the cars, I think I would."[74] O'Dunne was happy to skewer such assertions. Gerald W. Johnson, Mencken's counterpart on the *Sun,* said O'Dunne ran "a court of justice not a court of law."[75] Actually, his court respected law as the mechanism of justice. And he was willing to enforce it for black Americans too.

Judge O'Dunne thought it mildly humorous as the trial began that Marshall would be in the position of introducing his teacher, Houston, to the court. Usually it was the mentor who introduced the younger man, the judge observed, but that was merely a momentary digression. Houston's presence had immediate impact. The university's president, Raymond Pearson, insisted that Princess Anne Academy, located a few blocks north of the spot where George Armwood had been lynched, offered facilities equivalent to those at College Park, the main campus. Was it true, then, Houston asked, that the University of Maryland faculty had only one member with a master's degree and none with a doctorate as was the case at Princess Anne? No, said Pearson. Did he believe, Houston asked, that the single table, small batch of test tubes, and glass butterfly case that made up the chemistry and biology laboratory equipment *in toto* at Princess Anne was adequate? Yes, he did. Pearson went on to acknowledge that just about every other nationality would be admitted to the university and that, while he had offered Murray a scholarship to study at Howard, there was no money to give him. Houston went on to demolish the assertion that the education offered black children was equal to that of whites. Black students were in school for a shorter period of time; black teachers were paid less; there were far more one-room schools for blacks than for whites.[76]

Marshall then handled that part of the case that would be important if *Murray v. Pearson* were appealed to the U.S. Supreme Court, an eventuality Houston and Marshall were hoping for. "The separate part of the 'separate but equal' doctrine of segregation had been legitimized by the court on several occasions, Marshall was arguing, but its position on cases where the facilities were inarguably not equal—as in the absence of a school of law open to Negroes in the state of Maryland—had never been directly tested."[77] Until then and there.

Judge O'Dunne turned quickly to grilling the state's lawyer, assistant attorney general LeViness. "Does the state of Maryland establish the reason of race as a cause for barring Mr. Murray from the University?" he asked.

"Yes," said LeViness promptly, "it is the public policy of this state to exclude colored from schools attended by whites and to maintain a separate system of education."[78]

Marshall and Clarence Mitchell heard LeViness attempt to explain further. There was no demand by blacks for education, intoned the state's lawyer as if on cue. Clarence Mitchell, in court to cover the case for the *Afro-American*, knew the truth. Many Marylanders, possibly Marshall himself, did not bother to apply, knowing they would be rejected.[79]

Baltimore's white Establishment would later think of Marshall as a bitter, querulous man who never got over his anger, as if he might easily have forgiven those who denied him full citizenship. His father taught him never to accept indignities, and he seldom did unless he thought tactical acquiescence gave him advantages, opportunities for greater victories: when he worked for a hat maker in Baltimore, he dropped the lids when he was hassled on a city street car.[80] He believed in the law, but he did not think he was required to accept the ambient insults of Jim Crow Maryland.

Houston argued that a Baltimorean anxious to practice law in Maryland needed to study the laws of Maryland in a Maryland school. Mencken had written that black students sent to Howard were being done an obvious injustice: "The regents might just as well advise him to go to Addis Ababa or Timbuctoo."[81] Further argument seemed unnecessary.

O'Dunne ordered the state to admit Murray forthwith. A stunned Mitchell ran twelve blocks to write a story he had never thought he or anyone else would write in Baltimore.[82] LeViness asked for a stay until the state's appeal could be heard. O'Dunne said no. An American citizen was being denied his constitutional rights. How could a stay be granted?

The *Murray* win was a major breakthrough, but it did not mean the university would, accepting the principle asserted by Judge O'Dunne, dismantle the discrimination then flourishing in its other professional schools or at the undergraduate school. It was not even an end of Maryland's attempts to keep blacks out of its School of Law.

In the summer of 1935, Harry C. "Curley" Byrd, the university's former football coach, was taking over from Raymond Pearson as president of the university. Rumor held that Byrd went on to bargain with state legislators for construction money, promising in return to keep the school free of black students. He started on that enterprise immediately.

On July 15, he wrote to Registrar Hillegeist, "This is a very serious matter." By hand, he wrote on the left corner of the letter, "Don't register any Negro students until I talk with you. CB." On September 18, Hillegeist wrote, "Registration is on over here. What shall I do about the Negroes? Unless the Court of Appeals intervenes, we will have to admit Donald Gaines Murray should he show up on registration day . . . (You know what Judge O'Dunne would do to me if I 'thumb my nose' at the writ of mandamus granted to Murray. The writ ordered Murray admitted.) Help is needed. Give it to me—promptly."[83]

After the *Murray* decision, Mencken wrote another memorable column, mocking the controversy: at the Maryland school of law, there would now be "an Ethiop among the Aryans." He ridiculed the idea that white students would resist having black classmates. "To think [of the white students] as crackers hugging idiotically to their more fortuitous whiteness is to say at once that they are unfit to be admitted to the bar of any civilized state."[84]

At least one School of Law professor was arguably unfit. Garrett Power, a student at the university not long after Murray attended and later a professor there, described how this man of the law refused to call on the student Murray until the Court of Appeals ruled on the state's appeal, seeking to have Judge O'Dunne's ruling overturned. Mencken was almost certainly right when he attributed the state's resistance to a fear that black students would want to enter the undergraduate school at College Park. He did not think that was a good idea, he said, but he also questioned why anyone would be so protective of what he called "a fifth-rate pedagogical dump patronized largely by the children of Washingtonians." It would be easy, he wrote, "to bring the academy at Princess Anne, which is for colored students, up to equality with it."[85] Perhaps so, but that would not happen for decades—not fully until the U.S. Office of Civil Rights Compliance ordered the upgrading in the 1990s.

Murray proceeded through school easily enough. Chairs were left vacant on either side of him on the first day of class, but by the second day, students were welcoming him, offering to help, and demonstrating that they were not, as Mencken said, "hugging idiotically to their whiteness." Murray's biggest problem? He had no money for the tuition. Carl Murphy, who later raised and dispensed thousands to bail demonstrators out of southern jails, loaned it to him, and then kept after him doggedly to get the loan repaid. He knew he was going to need it.

Carl Murphy's importance in the struggle was immense. He goaded black people into a movement. He helped to choose the movement's leaders. He bankrolled the movement's work. He helped to shape strategy in Baltimore and in the nation as an editor and a member of NAACP councils. At a time when Baltimore's major newspaper was virtually silent on black community news, the *Afro* filled the gap. Its leader was a dignified and passionate crusader, as committed and courageous as Lundy and Garrison had been with their *Genius of Universal Emancipation*. He was as persistent as Frederick Douglass and the *North Star*. And he made money: the *Afro* was one of the nation's largest black businesses. He not only gave focus to the effort, he helped to choose its leaders, Lillie May Jackson, in particular. There were rumors of a love affair, says Michael Mitchell, Jackson's grandson. True or not, the movement was helped by the relationship.[86]

The chemistry of the movement continued to develop. Jackson's street demonstrations, Communist Party agitation, and a new and broader willingness to take risks based on a growing sense that action might succeed began to bring change. Calamity and insult, privation and anger provoked people, but a feeling that success could be achieved was part of the movement-building chemistry as well. Dramatic victories, though, were needed to sustain the emerging confidence. In the case of *Murray*, the state appealed—and lost.

Over time, the Marshall-Houston-Gosnell win, the win achieved for the local NAACP and its president, Lillie May Jackson, found its place in the annals of progress toward more sweeping victories. Nothing quite like it had been achieved before in America. More victories were coming—and, of course, more setbacks. But Marshall and Houston and Jackson had begun to show that Houston's assertion—"Mrs. Jackson, we can sue Jim Crow right out of Maryland"—might be more than bravado.[87] He and other NAACP officials believed Maryland was, relatively speaking, "less hostile" to equal rights for black people.[88] Houston certainly saw Maryland as so replete with illegal antiblack sanctions that the courts would be hard pressed not to concede the presence of separate and unequal facilities from one end of the spectrum to the other.

Houston was also a realist: he quickly wrote an article for the *Crisis,* the NAACP magazine, entitled "Don't Shout Too Soon." "Law suits mean little unless supported by public opinion. Nobody needs to explain to a Negro the difference between the law on books and the law in action. In theory the cases are simple; the state cannot tax the entire population for the exclusive benefit of a single class. The really baffling problem is how to create the proper kind of public opinion. The truth is there are millions of white people who have no real knowledge of the Negro's problems and who never give the Negro a serious thought. They take him for granted and spend their time and energy on their own affairs."[89]

Houston needed patience from the oppressed—the more so because he insisted on an approach to equal rights based on the nation's court system. Success, he thought, had to be constructed painstakingly so as to give it permanence and to insulate it from those who would be inclined to ignore it. In this insistence, Houston opposed more radical elements in the nascent movement who wanted a more aggressive—even separatist—approach. His strength of intellect, and his prodigious appetite for work, gave the NAACP a coherent and lasting support system. The fight against Jim Crow, though urged toward more radical approaches over time, stayed in the mold built by Houston and perfected by his students, including Thurgood Marshall.

The Houston approach was validated in dramatic fashion before Judge Eugene O'Dunne in Baltimore. O'Dunne was, to be sure, an ideal sounding board. He had the cranky, iconoclastic belief in following the law as he read it. Just how far outside the mainstream he was might have been glimpsed when he retired. More than four hundred luminaries, including governors and attorneys general, gathered to toast and roast him.

He had been the conscience of the court, one of the guests said. He had "kept the offices of the law conscious of their obligations under the law."[90] There were references to O'Dunne's jealous defense of the poor, his cantankerous relationships with other judges, and his campaigns against corruption. Not a word was uttered, though, according to the event's official record, about the *Murray* case. Unless it was in the unspoken subtext of this praise, the encomiums included no reference to O'Dunne's most important witness for justice.

Here was validation of Houston's warning after O'Dunne's verdict and Marshall's extraordinary victory. The verdict and the victory were treated as if they did not merit mentioning in the list of the maverick judge's accomplishments, but the nation was about to meet a Maryland champion for justice as courageous and cranky as the more or less anonymous judge who thought the law was a sacred trust, to be used for the protection of everyone.

LILLIE MAY AND TED: GOD OPENED THEIR MOUTHS

In Baltimore, neither Thurgood Marshall nor Clarence Mitchell was the most important civil rights leader. Mitchell came home to Druid Hill Avenue almost every night from his job as NAACP lobbyist on Capitol Hill, but he was soon more a Washington than a Baltimore figure. Marshall's departure was even more decisive when he became the point man for many national NAACP initiatives.

There were many local leaders, of course, but two in particular became icons of the period. They were a remarkable twosome, a man and a woman, one white, one black. They were products of Baltimore's loving, salt-of-the-earth culture. They were churchgoing optimists, patient and grittily determined, not easily turned around.

In what may have seemed to some a curious partnership, Theodore Roosevelt McKeldin joined Lillie May Jackson to speechify, hector, cajole, and sue Baltimore into living up to the more tolerant and progressive posture it had been pleased to claim for itself in spite of its commitment to impose second-class status on black citizens. The tools they had—courage, strong voices, and no capacity for embarrassment—would have been, for less prepossessing people, wholly insufficient and unremarkable. And yet these were the qualities most in demand, the elements of character that Charles Houston had been looking for when he warned that lawsuits had to be supported by more understanding of blacks by whites—and more action by blacks.

Civil rights leaders were young and fearless or they were outsiders—newcomers or Marylanders who had lived outside the state, where they saw a different way. They were people who saw the restrictive, stultifying system without the blinders donned over time by people who adjusted to the life imposed on them. Lillie May Jackson had, in fact, been away from Baltimore for some years, but Ted McKeldin was as Baltimore as marble steps, as welcoming and open and generous as the white-gloved women ushers in black churches. He and Jackson were remarkable because they resisted being absorbed by the worst aspects of Baltimore's race relations.

James Crockett, a black McKeldin partisan who as a high school student met McKeldin and later drove him to work every day for years when the latter became mayor, says McKeldin, in the beginning of his career, occasionally recited the idea that blacks were "not ready" for citizenship. Jackson "pushed him off that position," Crockett says. "She tore into him. After that, they would come to a function, and they would immediately go into a little caucus, just the two of them, and get their presentation together."[91]

Crockett was one of McKeldin's many "firsts"—blacks appointed to this or that commission by the breakthrough mayor. With McKeldin's blessing, Crockett worked at the city's board of elections and later as one of the city's first black firemen. He was also the first black member of the Maryland real estate board. McKeldin himself may have been the most important first. He was the first major Maryland politician to break entirely with the politics of Governor Swann, Dean Poe, and all the others in the pantheon of discrimination.

McKeldin was elected mayor of Baltimore in 1943, in the middle of World War II, a Republican mayor in a Democratic city. He became a regular in the pulpit of black churches. He was the equivalent of a rock-star politician, who had crossed over from politics to religion, from white to black. "McKeldin was a preacher. He knew scripture. And he enjoyed being around black people. He became lyrical in our idiom. And we were all Republicans then," says the Reverend Vernon Dobson, pastor of Union Baptist Church. "He was a decent Christian person. He wasn't a fraud."[92] He must surely have been a startling figure for his time.

With a cadre of loyalists and clever fixers, one of whom was Bill Adelson, a Duke University–educated lawyer nicknamed "Sweetie Pie," McKeldin became a force. In 1950, he ran for governor and won with the help of the Democratic bosses. He unseated William Preston Lane, who had been attorney general in 1933 when George Armwood was lynched. Lane had been a witness for honest and decent government, but he had passed a penny sales tax, which some business and political leaders despised. Lane also committed a mortal political sin: he fired one of Jack Pollack's loyalists. The fabled Baltimore leader became an instant McKeldin man, helping him to win 17,346 to 9,282 over Lane in Pollack's home district. A few weeks earlier, in the Democratic primary, Lane had beaten his opponent, with Pollack's help, by a similar margin. Pollack could move the vote.

Republican McKeldin kept his footing in an overwhelmingly Democratic state by being more small "d" democratic, more connected with Democratic leaders who had their reasons for siding with him. He made himself worthy by locking up the black vote. When Republican leaders were choosing candidates, he brought something to the table.

Eugene O'Dunne's ruling in *Murray* seven years before McKeldin's election as mayor may have made McKeldin's arrival less startling, less an occasion for fear that such a man had appeared on the Maryland scene, a political scene dominated theretofore by men who acted as if Marylanders would always be loutish enemies of their black neighbors. Change occurred in the interstices of social and legal intercourse.

Perhaps it was McKeldin's own experience with privation that made him sympathetic to the cry of his black brother. There were those who

saw his public life as the barely submerged evocations of his earliest vocational dream. For McKeldin, the politician's bully pulpit was a perch
from which to address his flock. Someone was ready, finally, to put the
majesty of public office behind the nation's guarantee of equal justice.

His son, Theodore R. McKeldin Jr., wonders if his father's motivation
could be traced to tent meetings conducted in Baltimore by Billy Sunday, the evangelist. McKeldin Jr. thought his father had seen the power
of redemption, of sobriety, and of striving against the vicissitudes of human nature. "He was very poor, the last of eleven children. They all slept
in one bedroom. His father was a policeman—and a raging alcoholic.
He and his mother would go around on Saturday nights in the saloons,
searching for and then dragging the old man home.

"He followed his father into revivals to hear Sunday, and his father
swore off alcohol, and for the rest of his life, his father never had another
drink. He said his father must have converted a thousand drunks in
South Baltimore." McKeldin's relationship with Mayor William Broening in the early 1920s also influenced his politics. McKeldin had gone to
work for him as a secretary. "Mayor Broening was an incredible liberal,
and he got a lot of liberal philosophy from Mayor Broening. So some of
his ideas were germinating in those times."[93]

McKeldin's decision to be a racial bridge builder had undeniable importance for him politically, but that, too, was a breakthrough. As generations of Republicans had done unsuccessfully before him, he sought the
black vote; but he found a way to win it—at a time when black voters
were swinging sharply away from the GOP to the Democrats and
Franklin Roosevelt's life-saving New Deal.

Promoting racial justice as a way of winning votes made him as remarkable as his partner, Jackson. She had to prod her people. He, on the
other hand, might have been reaching past his, rejecting the prejudices
he had grown up with, challenging his neighbors to see the injustice in
their city. He came from a part of Baltimore where political leaders had
proclaimed proudly the absence of even one black voter. Yet, he had a
conviction that the people he knew, black and white, could get along.
His primary contribution to the quality of justice was to speak out for it.

And he was, first and foremost, a speaker. As mayor, McKeldin de-
claimed on every conceivable subject as if the citizens of Baltimore could
not begin a day without knowing what their mayor was thinking. No
issue escaped his scrutiny: the evils of automation; the menace of

communism; the quality of John F. Kennedy's cabinet appointments; the Cuban dictator, Fidel Castro; and civil defense. Long before another Marylander, Spiro T. Agnew, turned alliteration into a liberal-bashing rhetorical weapon, McKeldin reveled in it. With retired *Sun* columnist Gerald Johnson as one of his writers, he decried "Hydrogen hysteria" and "nuclear neurosis."[94] Harry Truman, he said, was a "fountain of fiction from Independence." Adlai Stevenson, the Democratic former governor of Illinois who ran for president against Eisenhower, was a "huckster of horror." In the midst of a fallout shelter–building panic in the mid-1950s, there was a plan to record his voice and use it in the event of attack. "Any Marylander, even in a time of terror, might find some comfort in the knowledge that since McKeldin is making a speech, things are not completely abnormal."[95]

Because he was such a showman, some people found him "ridiculous"—but courageous on the subject of race. He was, they said, ahead of his time. Jackson and others thought he and his white society were way behind, but they saw the political risks he was taking. He stood at what would have been called the tolerance end of the race spectrum as compared with Governor Swann and Dean Poe, who held down the other extreme. Swann and Poe almost certainly reflected the views of Marylanders in general. They had chosen to reinforce the worst in people: their fears, their prejudices, and their uninformed judgments.

McKeldin adopted a persona that stirred emotions in some and invited ridicule from others. If he took offense, he hardly moderated his style. He was offering bombastic bread and circuses along with an unsettling message. He made no apologies.

He knew, of course, that black voters were important to his political success in general and particularly for the leader of the Republican Party, a distinct minority in Maryland. "There are two Democratic Parties in Maryland," he would tell his aide Sam Culotta, a former member of the House of Delegates, a Baltimore lawyer, and a perennial GOP candidate who worked as McKeldin's secretary for years. "One in and one out. If you're a Republican, you have to join the outs." But if you were McKeldin, you could win with black support, a fact some GOP leaders didn't see or didn't want to see. At a meeting of party leaders in the Belvedere Hotel to decide who would be the nominee for governor in 1950, McKeldin was not on the short list of potential candidates. One member of the group "went up there and told them he was going with McKeldin. He starts out with sixty thousand votes, black votes."[96]

A tall man with a prominent chin, a blond forelock, and a greeting of "My brother!" for almost everyone, he reversed the usual flow of politician-to-voter communication: he put demands on voters. He invited them, in a sense, to oppose him. They did not. He was no purveyor of wedge issues—of using prejudice to win support—to use the terminology of a later era. And he put these urgings behind the needs of black people. In 1953, he was given the Hollander Foundation Award for his leadership. It was conferred specifically for his high-level help in integrating Ford's Theater in Baltimore after a struggle of almost a decade.

McKeldin deserved the ceremonial accolade, but once again, no-name workers had done the heavy lifting. The inexhaustible gadfly A. Robert Kaufman says people worked for seven years to force Ford's away from a Jim Crow admissions policy that pushed blacks into the balcony. Jackson and the Mitchell family worked on that project along with the NAACP. Kaufman had devised a letter-writing scheme in which he urged visiting Broadway stars to honor the local picket lines. Baltimore is an apartheid city, he told them: don't endorse discrimination. Many did not. And the black opera star Paul Robeson marched with Kaufman and other Baltimoreans, white and black.[97] Robeson spent some time in Baltimore during these protests, and some in the city recalled hearing him sing through an open window in the house where he was staying.

The English actor Rex Harrison refused to perform in Baltimore. Tallulah Bankhead, the flamboyant actress, and Canada Lee, an African American who had been a band leader, boxer, and jockey before moving onto the stage, walked the line in costume. Some prominent Baltimoreans would sympathize with the protesters—and then walk inside for the show. But the campaign was having an impact.

In the end, the theater's owners agreed to change their policy, as long as Lillie May Jackson did not get credit. The *Sun*—which, Kaufman says, called the picketing a private matter and did not cover it—hailed the breakthrough in an editorial: not because loathsome discrimination had ended, but because, it said, some decent shows might now be allowed into town.

Lillie May Jackson's daughter Juanita marched in the Ford's picket line while she was a student at the University of Maryland law school and an editor of the school's law review. She would have been the top editor, her son Michael insisted later, if she hadn't been demonstrating at Ford's.

As often happens in such matters, a political figure—McKeldin—got credit for the work of Kaufman and Juanita Jackson and others who marched for years. The Ford's victory McKeldin said, "shows that there is nothing inherent or permanent in these evil practices but that progress can be made if the proper effort is exerted." His words were strong and uncompromising. "Injustice, which the fainthearted and the indolent accept without challenge . . . is not inevitable."[98] It had been until then, and that was the point McKeldin, Kaufman, and others were making.

Here was uncommon leadership that Maryland and the nation desperately needed. McKeldin's tone and ethical standard—beyond any specific civil rights action he took—were his greatest civil rights contributions. People around the country began to notice that Baltimore had a colorful and outspoken advocate for black people and for justice. Still, McKeldin found himself under attack—from both sides. He was not moving fast enough. He was moving too fast. He handled it all with that hearty "My brother" greeting and pressed on.

Lane Berk knew the McKeldin lore as well as any in Baltimore. McKeldin was the grandson of a Union soldier killed at the Battle of Monocacy. His father was a stone cutter turned city cop. McKeldin helped to heat the family home by "encouraging" coal to fall from rail cars on tracks near his South Baltimore home. He left school after the eighth grade to find work that would put food on the family table. All very fine politically, but Berk didn't find his public style to her taste. At the same time, she marvels at his leadership, calling it "a magnificent tribute to the fact that human beings can be fully human. I don't rob McKeldin for one moment. But I think he began and ended with a Brotherhood Week mentality, and I think civil rights goes much deeper than that. I think that the concept of brotherhood in terms of liking a person or being nice to a person is one thing, but that's something I bestow on you. I [can] give you pleasantness, decency, but I think that the black movement is what you are and, therefore, what you have a right to demand of me, and it isn't my gift to give you."[99]

Berk identifies a propensity for whites who thought themselves enlightened to assume that they could grant rights to people who had those rights already under the Constitution. People who struggled to overcome the barriers imposed by society, by custom, by parents, and by their upbringing wanted to think of themselves as enlightened, unbiased, and anxious for justice. "Some of my best friends are black," they would say, offering grist for mockery. Such a declaration became proof that the speaker was in the early stages of enlightenment. Lane Berk put Ted McKeldin in that category. "I thought if I ever heard him tell me again that he had just had breakfast with a black leader . . . I began to wonder if he ate them!"[100]

Still, she knew, McKeldin was as steadfast and consistent as Jackson. He took the "best friend" declaration and made it real. "The very fact that he never deviated from his attitude, that he was so persistent in that attitude, gave a certain habit and respectability and unavoidability to being human . . . And therefore I think many whites in his day couldn't have escaped the fact that here is a man who's up front, who can't fail to be noticed because his position is such that he is noticeable, and who will never deviate from his goodwill. The kind of standards that he set and example he set that could not be missed, was incredibly important."[101] McKeldin's sincerity, his determination to act on his Christian beliefs, she thought, was beyond question. He gave nonconformity a high-level sanction, a nobility even.

Jim Crockett and McKeldin's black chief political aide, Marse Calloway, took him to the churches. Like the illegal numbers king and Democratic fixer Tom Smith, Calloway became the black community's entrée to the mayor's office. "He was in there anytime McKeldin was meeting people in Baltimore," says Culotta. "Marse had total respect. Total. He was a character. Quaint. He was charming. Had a nice smile. Had a little shuffle. And he had a way of talking that you felt like you wanted to talk with him. His big thing was the way he was involved with all the black churches. He went to all of them." So did McKeldin and McKeldin's son, who winces to think of how many Sundays he spent hearing the same McKeldin sermon three or four times. Culotta remembers those Sundays, too. "We'd make a contribution and McKeldin would speak. He would say something like, 'Of one blood hath God made all nations. When the black man's blood runs, it's red too.'"[102]

What he said and the way he said it had an effect on some parishioners, stirring in them the same sort of religious fervor McKeldin felt so deeply. On occasion, he would say, "Sam, I have to hold back sometimes."[103] Lane Berk wondered how he could get away with such over-the-top histrionics. "I always felt as though he was going to take off his voice and his face and say, 'I was only kidding.' I feel that way, of course, toward zebras. I am sure that when they take off their skin, they show themselves to be normal horses."[104] She was not the only one. Sam Culotta says the new black assertiveness kept McKeldin on the defensive because he was, relative to other white political leaders and the campaign bankrollers, a freedom fighter. A few black successes at the ballot box had the effect of putting even more pressure on McKeldin.

In 1954, Harry Cole defeated Pollack's man to become Maryland's first and only black state senator, but that victory did not translate for the GOP the way it would have in the past. Cole had an agenda that went beyond party loyalty. "There was a feeling," says Culotta, "that we could never get Harry Cole supportive of all our programs because he wanted more. We could understand why we didn't have his vote. He was more demanding. He was among those who thought not enough was being done for black people. People said, 'Harry Cole is not a Republican senator, he's a black senator.' "[105]

Judge John R. Hargrove, one of the first black judges in Maryland, thought McKeldin had never escaped the slow-it-down ethic of white Maryland. He made beautiful speeches and gave just enough in the way of appointments to cool passions, Hargrove thought. "McKeldin was a flashy governor and a first-class con artist. He did lots of things, but he was the kind of a person who would come to Lillie May Jackson's church and make beautiful speeches, conning everybody and giving just enough to keep you happy. He appointed blacks, but the time had arrived, the pressure was so strong, that change would have happened whoever had been there." It was easy to say, but there had been no real progress before McKeldin. "Blacks of that time wanted to hear good words, good promises, and token types of stuff, and that's what they got. Today, they wouldn't be satisfied with this."[106] But many black Marylanders were more realistic. They were won over by McKeldin's alliance with Jackson.

Judge Hargrove was unforgiving. "He never made her happy. She stayed on him even though they were good friends. He was well paid for what he did—returned to office with strong black endorsement each time." Hargrove thought McKeldin "rode our backs." And he said McKeldin was a lot more passionate in condemning things at Jackson's Sharp Street Church than he was when he spoke to the chamber of commerce. "Mrs. Jackson always forgave McKeldin" because she understood that he had a white constituency to think about, knowing that many were not similarly invested in brotherhood. She understood that she and McKeldin were in a dance. They were mutually dependent and reinforcing.

Lillie May Jackson, the judge said, was all there was of black leadership in Baltimore for a time. Judge Hargrove could be as tough on black leaders as he was on McKeldin: "We had no black leaders of any strength. We had leeches, guys interested in lining their own pockets." There were exceptions. Walter Carter, the head of the Congress for Racial Equality (CORE) during its most effective moments, was "very unselfish"—a leader of integrity, Hargrove said. In the end, the judge said, McKeldin "preached more than he practiced."[107]

The judge's verdict on McKeldin is understandable but unfair. No one else was taking the risks McKeldin took—or making the progress he made. His incrementalism was revolutionary. He did what he did affirmatively, without prodding by the courts. And he did not slip back into old hateful practices. He was guided by politics, of course, but the Bible was as important to him as the law. What mattered here was the spiritual bond between these two leaders, Jackson and McKeldin. Leon Sachs, head of the Baltimore Jewish Council for decades, said McKeldin was not an impressive lawyer—nor was Jackson a penetrating strategist or thinker. Both observations were, he told an interviewer, irrelevant. "I was with McKeldin many times with Lillie May Jackson. They consulted many times on policy. They were intimately bonded. Each one responded to the other."[108]

Not everyone was impressed. On the contrary, many were derisive.

"When we went to Annapolis," Sachs said, "Mrs. Jackson—we all—had a hostile audience in the legislature. What hurt her, she had a manner of delivery—these fellows, you know, were laughing up their sleeves. Nobody, at least the yokels from the Eastern Shore and elsewhere, never took her seriously, because she had a manner of delivery of—she could really put on an act. So that I looked upon Lillie May Jackson as an elderly woman who had done whatever she could almost alone in her day, and she had my respect and my admiration as a person. But, as I say, I didn't think she had too much savvy in the field."[109]

A fair-employment-practices bill Sachs drafted and pushed finally passed in 1956, while McKeldin was governor. The Baltimore struggle went on for almost fifteen years after a similar action had been taken in 1941 by President Roosevelt with Executive Order 8802, banning discrimination in war industry hiring. Denton Watson, biographer of

Clarence Mitchell, says this order was nothing short of a second Emancipation Proclamation. Many saw it as the most important piece of governmental action for black people since the Civil War. As Baltimore's experience in this matter demonstrated, what looked like progress was not always complete or permanent.

In the final hours of the city council's debate on this bill, Sachs agreed to have penalties for violation removed, though it retained language that made discrimination illegal. "These guys in the council were sleepier than I was, and all they were interested in was striking out the penalties," he says. They were willing to pass the bill finally because they were beginning to realize the dimensions of discrimination. In another council proceeding, Sachs testified against George R. Moore, a property owner who discriminated against Jews as well as blacks and other ethnic groups. Joseph Bertorelli, an East Baltimore legislator, spoke to Sachs while the two men were standing next to each other in the bathroom. "I don't think they like Italians much either," Bertorelli said. "That's what I've been trying to tell you," said Sachs.[110]

"So we got that ordinance through, and as the ordinance came out, it made this conduct not just contrary to public policy but beyond that. They said it was illegal to [discriminate in hiring and the like]." Penalties or not, passage of the ordinance was a watershed moment. "It's one thing to tell a company or anybody that discrimination is against public policy. It carries more punch when you say, 'It's illegal, it's against the law.'"[111] The significance was profound for the message it sent in the wider community—as profound as the higher expectations of Theodore McKeldin and the shouting of Lillie May Jackson.

What Sachs was doing with the city council, he thought, took the form of public education. It was, he said, "a great educational experience in a community."[112] Education was needed, even with a man like McKeldin affirming things like fair employment. The *Sun*'s editors were skeptical, for example. Morals cannot be legislated, they said. In the end, though, they said the challenge to Baltimore was severe but important to meet.

Some Baltimoreans who were well disposed to the elimination of discrimination in hiring, promotion, and pay were not willing to discuss their views in public. Raymond V. Haysbert, a black political and business leader, remembers walking somewhat furtively into the Belvedere Hotel and up to a second-floor meeting room, where discussions were held in secret.[113]

Jackson never took the back stairs. For that alone, she had many admirers. This was at a time in America when six million Ku Klux Klansmen drew relatively little condemnation. This silence reflected the tenor of the time—an atmosphere of fear surrounded everything black Americans did. It was almost a miracle that a man like W. E. B. Du Bois would posit the idea of twoness or doubleness: the psychological demand that black Americans find a way to live comfortably in their black skin while trying to be part of a society that condemned them for their color. "It is a peculiar sensation, this double-consciousness, this sense of always looking at one's self through the eyes of others, of measuring one's soul by the tape of a world that looks on in amused contempt and pity. One even feels his two-ness—an American, a Negro, two souls, two thoughts, two unreconciled strivings, two warring ideals in one dark body, whose dogged strength alone keeps it from being torn asunder."[114]

Lillie May Jackson seemed to have had less trouble with that duality than Du Bois did. Like Martin Luther King Jr. and other black ministers, she urged black and white to "live together as brothers." Jackson's declaration "God opened my mouth and no man can shut it," in an era of murderous Klan activity, makes clear why she was revered. She was risking her life.

She came along at a time when stepping up made you not a leader, but a kook. "I had the greatest respect for her because she was pleading a dangerous cause, an unpopular cause, and in many instances a disrespected cause and still had the courage to proceed," says Lane Berk. In a more inclusive civil rights hall of fame, she said, room would have to be provided for Jackson alongside Rosa Parks, Malcolm X, and James Farmer. For some in the movement, Berk thought, being popular was more important than the cause. Jackson was never prey to that failing. "She showed unswerving goal direction, and therefore, unlike the necessarily always-moving advocacy of national leaders, Mrs. Jackson never moved, never left the eye of the local storm. She had what it took. She was very tough."[115]

Little Willie Adams, the businessman and former numbers king, found Jackson little more than a screamer. "We said 'holler,'" Adams said. But, he conceded, screaming (or hollering) was about all a black leader could do in the 1930s, and many—most—didn't do that.[116] There was not much to lose for most of them, but it was more than they were prepared to lose. Much of Baltimore and much of the South had determined that the implied threat—carried out often enough on the lynching trees—would relieve a man of his fortune and his life. People made their accommodations at every level of society. They trusted in divine providence to show a way some day. But the day was almost never at hand, particularly for anyone who wanted to take a more assertive approach to the denial of civil rights.

Jackson had a kind of incendiary focus that put her in the chain of connection with Douglass; Benjamin Banneker, the Maryland-born scientist; and Tubman. If Berk had a criticism of Jackson and the civil rights movement in Baltimore—and for thirty-five years, the movement and Jackson were almost the same—it was "that black folks and those among us who are Caucasian black folk, but who have fought the battle, spend too much time being sensitive to the differences among us than to consolidating the similarities."[117] It was that consolidating that gave the epochal pairing of Lillie May Jackson and Theodore Roosevelt McKeldin such synergy. The street leader and her ally in a high place were a remarkable, possibly unique team. Her lineage, as a descendant of slaves and of a signer of the Declaration of Independence, distilled the American experience in a deeply ironic sense. McKeldin, the grandson of a Union soldier killed at Antietam during a war fought over slavery and the son of policeman, was a man who understood what it meant to be poor in America. He and Jackson had similar beginnings, but he knew his own extraordinary success had been unimpeded by race.

CHAPTER 3

Different Drummers

William L. "Little Willie" Adams made a Horatio Alger character look like a son of privilege. He went from rags to riches several times over. An early traveler in the great northern migration of black Americans, he came to Baltimore in the 1930s from a farm in Zebulon, North Carolina. Arriving in the midst of the Great Depression, he went to work in a rag factory. Then he repaired bicycles. Then he became a runner for the illegal street lottery, commonly known as the policy, or numbers, game.

His first city role models were these entrepreneurs of gambling. He joined them at the age of 16. Within two years he had his own runners—route salesmen, in effect. In two years, he'd made—and lost—a small fortune. He was among those Americans ruined in FDR's bank holiday, losing three thousand dollars he had collected virtually penny by penny. In that era "Depression pennies," or half-cent bets, were welcomed by the numbers men. A thirty-dollar win was big in those days. Adams built his business by paying players promptly, to the penny or half-penny, and in person.

He had learned how to manage money as a youngster figuring what cotton would sell for when taken to market from the farm in North Carolina. Getting up early was nothing new for him, and he did so every day. He saved. He remarked later how many of his colleagues spent whatever they made as soon as they had it in hand.

He could not cope with the Depression, though, and was back working again for the guys who got him started. None of them worried much about the law: black gamblers operated as if numbers were legal, and the police, who seldom came into the black community, left them alone. Not until organized crime attempted to muscle the black operators out of their games, not until Congress held hearings, not until outsiders bombed Adams's place on Druid Hill Avenue, did law enforcement show much interest in his game. Over the next twenty years, Adams prospered. At some point he became known as Little Willie, a slightly gangsterish sobriquet borrowed from the movie *Little Caesar,* starring Edward G. Robinson. He opened bars and became an unofficial banker for black businesspeople unable to get credit from Baltimore banks.

In the early 1950s a study of long-standing real estate and banking practices in the city found that almost 50 percent of the city's substandard housing was occupied by black families. Only 38 percent of black households were owner occupied, far below the rate of ownership among white families. But authors of the city's self-survey said the black ownership figures were misleadingly high. "The status of this ownership appears highly tentative in a large number of cases" because so many had purchased their homes with contracts, a fragile form of ownership not nearly as stable as a mortgage. A form of buy-like-rent contract sales were used by aspiring black buyers because banks and other lenders seldom gave mortgages to black borrowers.[1]

Eighty-two percent of the firms surveyed would not sell to blacks or limited the areas of the city where they would make housing loans. Lillie May Jackson had occasionally used an intermediary to buy the housing units she owned. Rentals were restricted as well. Eighty-four percent of landlords would rent to blacks only if the unit was in a black neighborhood. What would later be called black inner city ghettos began to form in the early 1900s, after the last flurry of Jim Crow laws flew out of Annapolis. But by the 1940s and 1950s, the patterns were well settled, save for the few adventurous souls who tried to settle in white enclaves.

In this context, the gambling enterprises run by Willie Adams and, before him, the politically powerful Tom Smith had the importance of mainstream businesses. Smith and Adams became iconic figures. They were preying on people, but they were offering something people wanted, and they exhibited more than a ward heeler's level of generosity. They were entrepreneurs—and managers of an informal United Way at a time when the city's official helping institutions often did not pay much attention to the black neighborhoods.

Adams in particular became something of a legend, joining or quietly challenging the white Establishment in a number of areas, from the city's segregated golf courses to the savings institutions, real estate development, and the criminal justice system. It was not surprising that, in time, he became a political power center, joining forces with one of the most influential of the old political fixers, Irvin Kovens, a furniture dealer located on West Baltimore Street. Together, Kovens and Adams could make or break careers.

Adams had helped families in the way old bosses had helped: with a load of coal, a holiday turkey, a helping hand in the boss-controlled courthouse. Some said he helped teachers with home mortgages. In turn, the beneficiaries felt they owed him, because he had been generous. It was, after all, a classic pathway to involvement in the American mainstream.

And Adams had another powerful ally, his wife, Victorine. As demure as Lillie May Jackson was fierce, Victorine Adams became a role model for black women in Baltimore. After her teaching career, she turned to both politics and business. She opened a dress shop on Pennsylvania Avenue, a place where black women could actually try on clothing. She helped young women with styles and colors and a sort of finishing school etiquette. Delegate Salima Siler Marriott says her eighth-grade class at Cherry Hill High School bought their graduation dresses from Adams. By the 1990s, Delegate Marriott observes, Maryland had more black women state legislators than any other state.[2] Adams's leadership must be credited, Marriott says.

Adams's style and quiet charisma carried over into political life. She formed various voter registration and issue-related clubs at a time when politics was frowned on as dirty, unbecoming of proper women. But she thought the interests of her community were damaged by attitudes that may have sprung from generations of being used—and seldom heard or helped—by office seekers willing to take black votes and willing to risk the displeasure of people who had few, if any, elected officials to stand up for them. As quietly elegant as she was, Adams threw her frilly hat into the ring and, with the help of her husband and others, launched a quiet revolution in Baltimore. It started while she was teaching.

"There was an election coming. Mayor Jackson was running for re-election. He was having tough opposition. So he called teachers together and said if they voted for him, he would not cut their salaries. He wouldn't be able to give the yearly increment, but he wouldn't cut their salaries," Adams remembers.[3] She knew there were things you couldn't get unless you were connected, but here was an even more meaningful benefit of participation and the vote.

She remembered going to a Mrs. Minor, "who had the registration machine in her house. I said I'd be Republican. She said, 'Oh, Victorine, you don't want to be Republican. All of us are Democrat.' So she wrote me up. When I got home, my mother was standing in the door crying. 'You've disgraced the family. Your grandfather was a ward leader. Go up there and change.' I said no. Over the years, I changed everyone but my aunt Julia Lee, who died at 98—never changed her registration." All through the years that Adams ran for office, she kept after her Republican aunt. "I said 'Look, if I'm in a primary, your vote could help me.' She didn't say anything, but she wouldn't change."

Adams's decision to seek public office, she thought, came directly from her grandfather Mungo Tate. There was a pattern scrupulously followed. "Somebody in the community would be a political leader. They would open their houses when the candidates were coming. They'd put chairs in the living room. Candidates would come and talk. Alliances, clubs, and tickets would form. People would become part of the process. One of the early leaders in Baltimore was Lloyal Randolph, tavern owner and member of the House of Delegates, who would hold rallies at the Elks Hall at Madison and McMechen. Adam Clayton Powell [the New York congressman from Harlem] and other black elected officials from other sections of the country would come and talk to us and tell us we should be the power on our turf. We shouldn't have to depend on other people to do things for us. We should do for ourselves."

So she talked to Randolph. "How can I help?" she asked him. "What would you like to do?" he said. "I felt the women were not active enough. I didn't think the men were doing much, but the women were nonexistent . . . I thought everything in the city was politics. If you wanted a light at the corner, political power had to get it. I tried to organize women to teach the political process, get out the vote, register our people, elect qualified individuals, qualified black or white, but emphasize black because we didn't have much representation." She formed several groups of women who she could put at the service of candidates endorsed by her group, her husband's, and Irv Kovens's. Mostly, her group supported Democrats who seemed "more liberal and willing to change."

Adams's knowledge of human nature—an essential tool for political leaders—made her an effective political organizer. Her groups met regularly. Members were encouraged to dress up, and they were often brought to the meetings in what amounted to chauffeured cars. They were made to feel important, and they were important, Adams and future generations of Baltimore politicians said. "The grassroots women had some good brains. They could sit down and work on things. It was surprising when a lady in the corner saying nothing said, 'try this' or 'try that,' and many times it worked out."

To some it seemed that such a soft-spoken, diminutive person could not possibly have been very effective outside her neighborhood, but they were wrong. Over time, political observers would say that the profile of a Baltimore voter looked something like this: a black woman over 40 who goes to church, belongs to sororities, and knows the issues. If that was so—and many candidates thought it was—the profile had been etched into the political landscape by Victorine Adams.

She had plenty of help from her husband, of course. His stature in the black community and hers were on the same level, for different reasons. A bit of folklore developed around Willie Adams. He could add long columns of figures in his head, accurately and quickly, a skill of some importance to a man in his business. He was an unassuming man, often smiling behind his glasses. He wore a short-sleeved white shirt every day, never carried more than seven dollars in cash, and drove relatively modest cars—Buicks not Cadillacs—to avoid airs of success he feared would draw unwanted attention to his activities. He saved his money and frowned on others who spent what they had immediately. He had access to large sums of cash that would be needed to start black businesses or to bail young civil rights workers out of jail. He became something of a mythic figure, viewed as corrupt in the outside world but as the man to see in black Baltimore.

He was not the first such entrepreneur in Baltimore. The first and possibly more powerful figure was Tom Smith, whose life in politics tracks the early development of black voters' political involvement in the city. In the beginning, Smith worked for Democrats. They paid him to suppress the vote, because until the 1930s, blacks were almost entirely Republican, owing to the Republican president Abraham Lincoln, the Great Emancipator to whom Victorine Adams's aunt would be loyal all her life.

Thomas R. Smith, born at about the time of the Civil War, had no schooling but possessed unusual intelligence and leadership qualities. He opened a saloon and became wealthy and influential in the black community. Because of his status, white politicians paid him for every registered black voter who did *not* vote in an election. Smith was faithful to the Democrats, once carrying off ballot boxes and serving time in prison for the stunt. He was obliged to leave his lottery business in the hands of friends, who may have fleeced him of one hundred thousand dollars. Since the money had been accumulated illegally, the story goes, he could say nothing. His legend holds that he was hardly inconvenienced. He reconstituted his balances, political and financial, in short order. At his death in 1933, three thousand people came to his funeral, including many members of the Democratic Establishment.

Toward the end of his life, as Democratic candidates stopped campaigning on white supremacy, and local Republicans alienated blacks, Smith executed a political pirouette, scouring for Democratic votes in black precincts where he had once worked to suppress votes. He was on close personal terms with Mayor Howard Jackson and Governor Ritchie and is said to have been sufficiently influential to "make" black police lieutenants and captains. Many white firemen owed their jobs to him as well, according to James Crockett, one of the city's first black firemen.[4]

Tom Smith represented a kind of change, a new strength in numbers—recognition that the black vote mattered and had to be accommodated. Political leaders conferred status on a black man because they needed representation in a constituency of growing importance, a constituency that would not remain quiescent. They gave Smith a piece of the action, bought him off in a sense. That status, and the cash from his numbers accounts, made him a powerful man. The numbers game in Baltimore enjoyed a loose, almost enforcement-free existence for some years, and city police were said to enjoy the cash benefits of looking the other way along Pennsylvania Avenue.[5]

Smith showed himself to be quite a good learner, adopting the tactics of the bosses—passing out small but gratefully accepted favors. "In the summertime, he would come up Park Heights Avenue and Reisterstown Road, and he'd have his chauffeur drop five pounds of sugar, lemons, and ice at 29 Engine and other firehouses," Crockett says. "He wanted to make sure they were well taken care of." If there was a problem of any kind with city or state—permits and the like—Tom Smith could take care of it.

Smith's ability to find jobs for loyalists in the police and fire departments pushed the black community somewhat furtively but significantly into the political system. Crockett says Smith helped Thurgood Marshall's mother get a job as a teacher. She put that money toward her son's law school education at Howard University in Washington. Small favors enabled people to make enormous gains. Crockett knew Norma Marshall. "She used to come to my confectionary store at Lexington and Carrollton to smoke. Women didn't smoke or wear pants in those days, but she would come in with friends, have coffee and a sandwich, and talk about events. Mrs. Marshall talked about Thurgood and his accomplishments five days a week."[6] In time, whole generations of Baltimoreans—of Americans—would be talking about her son.

By most accounts, Willie Adams did as well as Smith, perhaps better. He was regarded by black Baltimoreans as a man of scrupulous honesty, another important trait for a numbers man. His image beyond Pennsylvania Avenue was the reverse: shady, inscrutable, immersed in an illegal activity in a dark corner of the city unknown to white Baltimoreans, with the possible exception of jazz lovers. For decades, he stood at the top of what was considered a criminal enterprise. His image softened a bit after time as he transitioned into more mainstream activities, and as the state stepped into the lottery game itself.

He was another of the influential outsiders. He came to the city with ability and a determination to prevail. He would move through the lowest to the highest of enterprises: rag, or garment, tradesman; numbers runner; bar owner; unofficial banker; real estate man; property developer; and political leader. His unofficial United Way operation got little if any attention. He liked it that way.

In the course of all this, he became a golfer. In the South, blacks weren't allowed to play golf at all for the most part. In North Carolina, where Adams grew up, the caste system often meant that whites had the golf-course maintenance jobs and blacks were caddies.[7] Up from North Carolina, Adams wanted to play golf in Baltimore, and so did many other blacks. The Monumental Golf Association sprang up, and many social events were held with golf as a centerpiece.

When Adams began to learn the game of golf, there was almost no place to play in Baltimore if you were black. Hardly a surprise. You couldn't get a cab from Pennsylvania Station if you were black. (The Urban League under Furman L. Templeton solved the cab problem.) Adams and his friends could play at Carroll Park but nowhere else in the city's system of segregated courses. He and other black players were taxpayers in the city, helping to cover the costs of operating the courses, but they were not allowed to play on any of them save Carroll Park, which had sand greens and only nine holes, half as many as the standard layout.

Though sand greens were not unusual when the game began, they were regarded as particularly blatant proof of discrimination, proof along with the nine holes of something separate, surely, and far short of equal. That *Plessy v. Ferguson* was a sham and a delusion was well illustrated by golf courses.

Adams and others decided to take the issue to court. He asked Lillie May Jackson if she would help. She said no, of course not. "If you fellows are wealthy enough to play golf, you're wealthy enough to pay your lawyers yourself," she said. There were too many other things of greater importance, she said.

Jackson was asked, more than once, how she could deal with a numbers man. "The devil has had this money long enough. Time for the lord to have it for a while," she said.[8] Adams was, after all, a generous benefactor of the NAACP. He loaned CORE money to set up an office. Larry S. Gibson, then a young lawyer starting a practice, handled some of the legal documents. Adams occasionally ribbed him about getting the money back but clearly looked at the transaction as a gift and was shocked when a loan was repaid.

While he surely wanted to play on better courses, Adams's cracking barriers on the golf course carried a high level of significance in the battle for access to public accommodations. He and the businessmen who played with him knew their task—in the courts or in the councils of city government, where exclusionary policies were defended—would be anything but simple. Would it be possible, then, Adams asked Jackson, to hire the services of Charles Hamilton Houston, the NAACP lawyer? That, she said, would be between Adams and his friends and Houston. The famous barrister agreed, turning at least some of his attention to the links. A decade-long battle began.

Adams's case had considerable local and national support. A handful of black businessmen anted up several thousand to pay Houston's fee. They had an interesting national, even international, supporter: the heavyweight champion of the world, Joe Louis, a frequent playing partner of Willie Adams, who apparently met Louis when the fighter was in the army and stationed at nearby Fort Meade. Louis wanted to play on the best courses, and he knew which cities would make them available to him. William B. Dixon, an insurance broker, and Arnett Murphy, Carl Murphy's brother, joined Adams in the suit. "Really what brought this [legal action] about," Adams said, "was Joe Louis, a good friend of mine."[9] The Louis-Adams foursome would have breakfast at Adams's Club Casino at 1516–1519 Pennsylvania Avenue before they went out to play.

The champ had come to Baltimore in 1940 for the Chick Webb Memorial, a benefit on behalf of the jazz drummer at the Fifth Regiment Armory. Louis and Adams met there, started a friendship, and played golf in Baltimore, Las Vegas, and other cities over the years. Louis's son, Joe Louis Barrow Jr., says his father always protested the exclusions he encountered in the cities he visited.[10] In Baltimore, at least, the friendship drew some attention.

Roger Pippen, a white writer at the *News-American*, played with Adams and Louis at Carroll Park, at a time when it was against the law for whites and blacks to play golf together or even to eat together. A day or so later, Pippen's account of the round appeared in the newspaper.

Louis, he wrote, was a pretty fair golfer. "Pretty fair" would be an understatement. Louis played well enough to be invited to a professional tournament in California. Pippen apparently got quite an education: "Among his own people, Louis is well-behaved, mannerly. He doesn't strut. Nor boast. Or act superior." In these days, to declare a black man polite and modest was apparently a daring departure from the stereotype. His column had its nice touches. "Two youngsters, hearing that Joe was at the park, came on the run to get his autograph. They looked over the five men on the tee and picked Askew Gatewood as the object of their search. From then on, Gatewood did the strutting for the golf party."[11]

Roger Pippen's story included no appeal for blacks to have citywide golf-course privileges. He said the city park board might think about installing grass greens at Carroll Park, but he didn't mention, except obliquely, the ban on black players at the other city courses—nor did he say anything about the fact that Carroll Park was then a nine-hole layout, not eighteen as were all the other city courses.

The park board tried in every way possible to avoid integration of the courses, offering various all-black days and holiday schedules—keeping white players off the courses on days they would have been playing in droves—all of which were met with great unhappiness by white and black players, as Mencken wrote:

Of equal, and maybe even worse, irrationality is the rule regarding golf-playing on the public links, whereby colored players can play on certain links only on certain days, and white players only on certain other days. It would be hard to imagine anything more ridiculous. Why should a man of one race, playing in forma pauperis at the tax-payers' expense, be permitted to exclude men of another? Why should beggars be turned into such peculiarly obnoxious choosers? I speak of playing in forma pauperis and that is precisely what I mean. Golf is an expensive game, and should be played only by persons who can afford it. It is as absurd for a poor man to deck himself in its togs and engage in its witless gyrations as it would be for him to ar-ray himself as a general in the army. If he can't afford it he should avoid it, as self-respecting people always avoid what they can't af-ford. The doctrine that the taxpayer should foot the bills which make a bogus prince of pelf of him is New Dealism at its worst.

I am really astonished that the public golf links attract any appre-ciable colored patronage. The colored people, despite the continued efforts of white frauds to make fools of them, generally keep their heads and retain their sense of humor. If there are any appreciable number of them who can actually afford golf, then they should buy some convenient cow-pasture and set up grounds of their own. And the whites who posture at the taxpayers' expense should do the same.[12]

Though he was well aware of the white man's phobia about being around black people, Adams laughed at the resistance in the matter of golf, where players had plenty of room to keep their distance. It was this deeply ingrained near hysteria at the thought of "mingling" that civil rights and open accommodations proponents were up against. The Rev-erend Marion C. Bascom says that much of the overall struggle had to do with proving to white people that living with blacks on the same side-walk or restaurant or swimming pool or golf course was not the equiva-lent of having a terminal disease.[13]

The golf suit was filed in 1938 by Dallas Nicholas and William I. Gos-nell, who had worked with Marshall and Houston on the Donald Murray law school admission case. The courses were finally opened to blacks in 1951. It had taken thirteen years.

At about this time, another Baltimorean was exerting pressure on professional sports. The *Afro-American* sports writer Sam Lacy thought he would prevail, though others thought Sam would see little progress even if he lived to be 100. He did live that long, and he never stopped writing about the injustices heaped on black ballplayers. Sam Lacy went to bat for golfers as well. The case was without ambiguity in the world of golf. Black players were kept out of tournaments by rules of the Professional Golf Association (PGA). Article 3, section 1 of the PGA constitution read "Professional golfers of the Caucasian race . . . Over 18 years of age, residing in North and South America who can qualify under the terms and conditions specified, shall be eligible."

Lacy used Carl Murphy's newspaper to campaign for fairness. He was an unapologetic, unremitting advocate for black players—as unaffected by pressure to ignore the discrimination as Lillie May Jackson had been with judges and politicians. Lacy wrote about a club maker who was asked to sponsor Charlie Sifford, one of the great black players. The company said it couldn't because Sifford played in only ten or so tournaments a year and didn't give the company enough exposure. This was akin to asserting that black Americans wouldn't be allowed to vote because their voting record was poor.

Without being recruited or challenged the way Houston had challenged young black lawyers—calling them parasites if they did not work on civil rights—Lacy gave over much of his life to the struggle. He confronted the big men of professional sports, cajoling and pushing them to see the talent they were missing and shaming them for accepting the nation's caste system. Adams's life on the verge of criminal prosecution made his personal story illustrative of that history. Golf was one thing, but the racial aspects of staying out of jail were quite another.

A bar he owned was firebombed in what was believed to be an effort by organized crime to force him out of the Baltimore street lottery. In 1947, he testified before a U.S. Senate committee investigating organized crime. Though he had been promised immunity from prosecution, he was immediately besieged by Maryland law enforcement officials who wanted to put him away. His subsequent conviction, based on this immunized testimony, was overturned after seven years by the Maryland Court of Appeals.

The black lawyer George L. Russell represented Adams through many of his legal battles. Their professional relationship offered yet another perspective on race relations in the daily life of Marylanders. Adams had been urged by many associates, black and white, to hire Arnold Weiner, a skilled advocate who would have an edge over Russell, many thought, because he was a white man in a white system.

Russell says lawyers and judges in various courthouses sent penniless clients his way, telling them Russell's services were free. Beyond that, if you were going on trial in a courthouse dominated by white judges and prosecutors, you might well decide a white lawyer would be your best bet. This bit of courthouse lore may have been a reflection of racial attitudes, and it didn't hurt the white lawyers' pocketbooks either.

So, though it looked like he might go to jail, Willie Adams was conflicted. He was inclined to retain Weiner, but he wanted to do business with a black lawyer. It looked like it might be a choice between his freedom and loyalty to his community. Russell says Adams asked if he'd be co-counsel with Weiner. Russell said no. "You choose the lawyer you think is best for you," Russell told him.[14] In at least one earlier case, the "hire white" ethic had not helped at all: Adams had walked out of court with a conviction. For his later cases, he chose Russell, who enjoyed reminding his client of his hesitation.

In one important case, wiretap information offered in evidence purported to show Adams in an incriminating conversation. Robert Mack Bell was the judge, having decided not to recuse himself, though he might well have walked away based on his political connections with Adams. Bell was certain Adams and Adams's wife, Victorine, had helped him win appointment to the district court. She had been impressed with Bell's courtly manners and, while she did not adopt a drug program he was recommending to the city, she recommended Bell to her husband; Little Willie had close connections with the governor, William Donald Schaefer, who would make the appointment.

When Russell and Adams finally had a chance to hear the tape, Russell came to a stunning conclusion. "I said, 'Willie that's not you.' " Adams agreed. Russell looked at his client and said, "Weiner would have known that, wouldn't he?" The intonations of the black voice—Willie's voice and another man's voice—might understandably have escaped Weiner. (Bell had taken the tape home, listened to it repeatedly, and reached the same conclusion Russell had.) Moreover, Russell was convinced that the police had manipulated evidence in such cases, and he was less trusting than another lawyer might have been.

A voice expert, a southerner by the sound of his voice, certified Russell's assertion in court. "He said, 'That is the voice of a southern negro.' " Judge Bell called Russell to the bench to ask how long the expert witness would be on the stand and what he would say. As the conference ended, he said, "I'm tired of listening to this cracker."[15]

"Any time after that," Russell says, "when [Adams] had something important to him personally, he hired me. My star really rose after that."

In the matter of golf, Adams went to federal court twice; even though real greens had been installed at Carroll Park, there were still only nine holes there. Nicholas and Houston argued the case, and once again, the federal judge ruled for Adams and his associates: until the city gave Carroll Park grass greens, it had to allow black players on the other city courses. The Baltimore case was used to open courses in other states.

Over the next twenty years, Willie Adams prospered. He put up $150,000 to help his friend Henry G. Parks Jr. found Parks Sausage Company.[16] Parks and one of his partners, Raymond V. Haysbert, say the company's start-up money came from the numbers. There were few other ways to raise capital if you were black. Gibson handled some of Adams's business loans as well. In time, Adams had some power to make demands. He saw that there were no black drivers on trucks delivering beer to his bars and restaurants. He negotiated with the suppliers and others in the chain to insist on jobs for black workers. Like the picketers on Pennsylvania Avenue, he found economic leverage, and he began to use it.

HEALING ARTS: BLUE BABIES, BLACK GENIUS

The baby girl was so small it was difficult to tell, peering into the deep folds of sterile linen, if there was a patient on the operating table at all. One of the attending physicians finished arranging the surgical drapes as Johns Hopkins Hospital's chief of surgery, Alfred Blalock, entered the room.

Blalock looked searchingly toward the theater's observation gallery and found the man he was looking for. Earlier he had sent Clara Belle Puryear, a chemistry technician at the hospital, to get him. "Vivian," he said, "you'd better come down here." Vivien Thomas made his way into the room. He had decided to stay away initially because he was afraid he would make Blalock, whom he called "the professor," nervous.

A Johns Hopkins Medical School graduate, Blalock had been brought back from Vanderbilt University to resuscitate the hospital's surgical service. On this day, November 29, 1944, he was about to lift its profile more than he might have imagined. He would not proceed alone in that enterprise. The man he summoned from the gallery, Vivien Thomas, had mastered the "blue baby" operation Blalock was about to perform. Thomas had perfected the surgery during more than a year's careful practice, study, and preparation in the hospital's laboratories. In the operating theater, they worked as one, the closest of partners.

But they could not sit together in the hospital lunchroom. Blalock was white. Thomas, the indispensable man on this historic day, was black. The life-saving operation they would perform gave hundreds of suffering infants a chance at life—and put Baltimore and Hopkins on the medical world's map. The patient, Eileen Saxon, was restored to a healthy pink color but did not thrive immediately. The surgery prolonged her life for only two months, but it was pioneering pediatric heart surgery.

Blalock and Thomas were separated outside the laboratories and surgical venues by the racial ethic of the day. Hospitals and other large institutions tended to adopt the attitudes of the people they served. They were not alone in their policy. Government at every level, Bethlehem Steel, Baltimore department stores and restaurants behaved as if defying Jim Crow would bring ruinous problems with their customers or voters.

Yet, as in the case of Vivien Thomas, these fears subsided, if slowly, when others saw that black people could perform perfectly well and on occasion with distinction when they had an opportunity. What a more open society could accomplish for mankind was demonstrated in the 1940s at Hopkins and the University of Maryland School of Nursing. The glacial movement toward equality was accelerated by individuals of skill and determination, people who earned a chance to show their ability and their courage.

Daring to proceed against the norm, Georgia-born Blalock challenged the mores of a hospital that religiously guarded the lines of separation between blacks and whites. Black patients, restricted to blacks-only wards, were referred to by their first names only, as if somewhere in the official manual, whites were instructed to deny the honorific Mr. or Mrs. Something revolutionary, something almost beyond the imagining in those times would be necessary to break through these impermeable walls.

Thus, an objective of the civil rights movement was attained inadvertently at Hopkins, where the ultimate value of science and medicine trumped the conventions of social separation. During that November day in 1944, a black man's "voice could be heard guiding Dr. Blalock through the operation." William P. Longmire, the resident who had arranged the drapes, wrote later that "Vivien Thomas stood in back of Dr. Blalock and offered a number of helpful suggestions in regard to the actual technique of the procedure."[17] In his autobiography *Partners of the Heart,* Thomas recalled, "I watched closely as each suture was placed. If he began a suture in the wrong direction (which he did on several occasions . . .) I would say, 'the other direction.' On occasion, he would ask if I thought a particular suture was being placed near enough to the preceding one."[18]

Preparation for the surgery had begun a year earlier, when Helen Taussig came to Blalock and Thomas with a challenge. The so-called blue baby operation, later credited largely to Taussig, was conceived by the three of them according to Thomas and other Hopkins doctors who worked on the project. The babies afflicted with this deadly congenital condition, called blue baby syndrome, were not getting sufficient blood flow to the lungs. Taussig said she thought "it might be possible to get more blood to the lungs, as a plumber changes pipes around, but [she] gave us no hint as to how this could be accomplished—what pipes to put where. She left us with the problem."[19]

Thomas invented the tools as well as the procedures. A finer gauge of suture and various pieces of hardware were needed to accomplish the work. Thomas, whose vocational training had been in carpentry, had no education beyond high school, but he would become the teacher of men like Blalock and a generation of skilled and eventually famous surgeons. Thomas burnished the hospital's image by hand. What he and Blalock accomplished in those days saved the lives of many infants and eased the anguish of their parents.

"He was a master technician," says William Rienhoff, a chest surgeon at Hopkins, one of many who learned the technique from Thomas.[20] "Even if you'd never seen surgery before, you could do it because Vivien made it look so simple," said the renowned heart surgeon Denton Cooley, who had a role in the early blue baby procedures. "There wasn't a false move, not a wasted motion, when he operated." At one point in the operation's development, Blalock saw Thomas's work on a laboratory animal and said, "Well, this looks like something the Lord made."[21]

Blalock, Taussig, and Cooley became household words in the world of medicine. Thomas's status hardly changed at all for many years. He made so little money at Hopkins that he was obliged to seek outside work. This man of surgical genius worked as a bartender, pouring drinks for the doctors he trained or worked with, including Blalock. Blalock eventually intervened to make him the highest-paid technician at Hopkins by 1946, and by far the highest paid African American on the institution's rolls. But, from 1943 to 1947, hospital records show that Blalock earned roughly ten times as much as Thomas.

Blalock's relationship with Thomas was, to put it politely, complicated. He would not proceed without Thomas's assistance in the operating room, but there were limits to his generosity. A party to celebrate Blalock's 60th birthday was held at the Southern Hotel in downtown Baltimore. Vivien Thomas was not invited, but Mark Ravitch, one of the party's organizers, secreted Thomas into the segregated hotel so that he could observe from a screened room. Later, Ravitch encouraged Thomas to write a book, which he did. *Partners of the Heart* recounts Thomas's work with Blalock. Thomas apparently accepted his treatment in Baltimore as another fact of life in those times. Just the way it was.

Ruby Glover, the black club singer who worked in the Hopkins emergency room when Thomas was there, insists Alfred Blalock followed his assistant home after the retirement party. She says they sat on the back porch of Thomas's home for a time and talked. Blalock could not have done otherwise on the evening of his party, Glover says. He could not have had Vivien with him at the head table. He was as trapped in the dehumanizing system as Thomas was. The story is at odds with the report by Ravitch, and it demonstrates the hope for black-white fraternity in some minds. Cruel and unjust separations were not always what people wanted. Life-saving surgeries and monumental court victories were not enough to close the wounds. That work would have to be done over and over, not just by grand movements, but by individuals finding ways to demonstrate their skills and their humanity.

Alfred Blalock died in 1964 at the age of 65. Thomas remained at Hopkins for fifteen more years, imparting his skills to many, including a number of African American lab technicians as well as Hopkins's first black cardiac resident, Levi Watkins Jr., whom Thomas assisted with Watkins's groundbreaking work in the use of the automatic implantable defibrillator.

Blalock knew he had happened upon genius in Vivien Thomas. Here was a black man with only a high school education showing generations of physicians, including Blalock himself, how to proceed in various procedures. Thomas's autobiography, which includes detailed passages illustrating his masterly approach to the most vexing surgical problems, is remarkable. His accomplishment in medicine rivals Frederick Douglass's in letters. One had emerged from slavery. One had lived with Jim Crow. Both prevailed.

The blue baby operation was a step into the frontier of medical science, a step into a part of the human body surrounded in myth and mystery. The heart was thought to be the realm of God. An intrusion by man had been regarded as almost blasphemous. And yet the events of that day in 1944 might have broken through even more fearsomely high barriers. The involvement of a black man in this operation should have challenged the deepest fears and convictions revolving around race in America, convictions that the black man was inferior, certainly not up to the work of scientists and healers. Had more people known of Thomas's work, barriers in society might have been moved as well, but it would be more than a half century before this extraordinary black man's role would be known in the wider world. Taussig got the acclaim. Thomas toiled on in obscurity. Just the way it was.

In later years, after his surgical genius was recognized, second glances still followed Vivien Thomas as he walked through the sprawling Hopkins campus: a black man in a white physician's jacket? With more luck and a less hostile white world, Thomas might have gone to medical school. He had saved enough to begin, but the Depression robbed him and many other Americans of their money and their dreams. When he met Blalock, he was a janitor in the Vanderbilt hospital. Their earliest days there had not gone well. Blalock grew impatient with him and swore. Thomas said he was quitting. Blalock immediately apologized, not a predictable gesture of white officials in those days.

When the doctor's work at Vanderbilt earned him an invitation back to Hopkins, he asked Thomas to join him. In some ways, the young man found, Baltimore was a less hospitable place for black people than the Deep South city of Nashville, Tennessee. In Baltimore, where the Depression's impact was still visible and where "Whites Only" signs remained, Vivien Thomas would have difficulty finding housing for his family.

Schools and libraries had been closed to him, says Watkins, whose own path to Hopkins was littered with obstacles. Watkins had grown up in Montgomery, Alabama, where his family attended Dexter Avenue Baptist Church. Martin Luther King Jr. was the pastor there. Watkins went to Tennessee State University, and then to Vanderbilt Medical School, where Thomas and Blalock had begun their extraordinary partnership. "I was able to do what Vivien wasn't able to do," Watkins says.

Their lives, separated by three decades, illustrated the price and the agonizingly slow progress of the movement. "What awaited Vivien at Hopkins was absolute segregation, absolute boundaries of who you are and where you will ever go. In spite of real changes, what you see in Baltimore today in terms of physical conditions for black citizens is what Vivien saw. It reminds me of what Steve Biko, the South African freedom fighter, said: 'You're born in the ghetto, and you die there.' "[22]

"When I came to Hopkins," Watkins says, "public discrimination was on its way out. There were three bathrooms then: male, female, and colored. There were separate morgues, separate cafeterias, separate blood banks." Change came as a shock to blacks as well as to whites. One of Watkins's first patients in the Hopkins emergency room was the son of Homer Favor, a professor at Morgan State University and a civil rights activist, who told him "I've never seen a black doctor here."

"You're seeing one now," Watkins replied. Blacks had to adjust to dealing with blacks, wondering if they were getting the same level of care. It happened with lawyers as well. Blacks headed to court wondering if they had the best or the most influential representatives. One patron of a formerly segregated city theater always had a white friend buy her tickets because she was certain she'd get better seats than a black patron would, even after the Jim Crow barriers had fallen. Homer Favor himself was one of the first patients admitted to the until-then whites-only Marburg Service of the hospital. Before this, black patients were treated on Halstead.

In a television documentary of the Thomas-Blalock partnership, several doctors spoke of their personal debt to Thomas—and their remorse over his treatment. "They cried in the context of his being their bartender. They knew how the man was actually treated. They knew it was not right, and they tolerated it. They were part of it," Watkins says. "None of these men and women had the courage to protest at the time." Thomas had been an unrelenting hair shirt for those who would forget the ease with which they accepted the status quo.

And Watkins holds himself to the same standard. "I didn't do anything either at first. You always need a catalyst." Growing up in Montgomery, he says, no one thought much about the places that were off limits. "We couldn't go to the Dairy Queen. We'd go around the back like we were supposed to. We couldn't go to Oak Park [Montgomery's version of Gwynn Oak Park]. We knew which restaurants not to go to. It seemed the natural way—until consciousness was raised." As a teenager, after attending Sunday school and a youth group called the Crusader's Club, he became one of the church drivers. Station wagons purchased during the famous Montgomery Bus Boycott triggered by Rosa Parks ferried parishioners to church, and Levi Watkins drove Martin Luther King Jr. home after the services.

At Vanderbilt, he chose to make his position on the issues of race very clear. Soon after he arrived, Watkins put a poster of King on his dormitory room door. After King was assassinated, someone scrawled a message: "We finally got the coon." Things did change eventually at Vanderbilt, and the change from his introduction was stark. Years after Watkins's graduation, a professorship was endowed in his name. "We went from literally throwing shit in my face to establishing a professorship in my honor. When they called to tell me about it, I thought they were calling to ask for a donation."

Rowena Spencer, a student of Thomas's who went on to do important research on conjoined twins, said later that any time she returned to Hopkins, it was Vivien she most wanted to see. He had watched her fight battles not unlike his own as she encountered the bias against women.

Thomas eventually received an honorary doctorate from Hopkins. He was made a professor. A portrait was done and hung near Blalock's. But his colleagues, reflecting on his life and their own, felt it was not enough—not enough because they had done too little themselves to make things right.

Watkins continues the struggle. He attempts to keep Hopkins focused on the still-disadvantaged black kids who need advocates to keep expectations high: "I want the 8-year-olds to see the 22-year-old students here," he says. Every year, Hopkins brings a major national black figure to speak on Martin Luther King's birthday. "My task," he says, "is to tell the truth. I try to leave kids with more hope than I sometimes feel."

And he tries to move the massive Hopkins institution—an institution that gained significant prominence on the strength of a black genius—

toward increasingly concrete recognition of the remaining obstacles to overcome. The lessons were learned. Levi Watkins learned them.

And a waifish East Baltimore girl named Esther McCready learned them. Without an exact model to follow, she proceeded on her own, refusing to accept the belief that applying for a place in the University of Maryland School of Nursing would be a futile exercise for a black girl. McCready decided to assume she would be given a fair chance. The courage of individuals, proceeding as if the world would welcome their talent, forged a better world. It helped that, over time, the prospects for success improved.

ESTHER McCREADY: A LOVER OF SOLITUDE

Change agents were often young people still in touch with youthful ideals and a belief that right was might. Like Donald Murray, Esther Mc-Cready wanted to study in her home city, though she knew nursing schools were not admitting black students. She decided to dare the university to turn her away. Thurgood Marshall did not apply to the University of Maryland School of Law, perhaps because he knew it would be useless.[23] Twenty years later, a quiet black girl from East Baltimore, emboldened by Marshall's successes elsewhere, decided not to do the school's cruel mischief. She would not exclude herself. She sent applications to every hospital nursing school in Baltimore.

"You know what's going to happen," said a friend who was applying to nursing schools with her. McCready didn't care what other people thought would happen. There was more to her determination. "I'm sure I was assigned a mission. I knew at age 8 what I wanted to do when I grew up. When I went for my yearly physical examination, I saw nurses, and I decided I'd like to do what they were doing."[24]

Esther's friend adopted her approach. The two young women made a list of all the schools in Baltimore, dividing the list in half. They wrote for the necessary applications and course catalogs, and they took care to say they were black. Esther McCready's list included the University of Maryland School of Nursing, which had never had a black student. The responses were not surprising. No black students were to be admitted, most of the hospitals wrote back. The University of Maryland's response was less definitive, though. It may not have welcomed her application, but it did not reject her out of hand. She completed the application and mailed it. Then she waited. While she waited, a representative of the NAACP in Baltimore called. Her doctor had told a friend in the civil rights organization that his patient, Esther McCready, was engaged in an interesting exercise. He had told her she would never succeed without the NAACP. But her mother encouraged her. "He's from the old school," she told her daughter. "You can do it on your own."

Then McCready got a phone call from Charles Houston, the Howard University School of Law dean and NAACP lawyer who, with Marshall, had succeeded in getting Donald Murray into the law school fourteen years earlier. He knew that the other professional schools operated under the policy enunciated in court before Judge O'Dunne by the State of Maryland's lawyer Charles LeViness. Maryland authorities had allowed this agonizing process to continue long after the illegality of Jim Crow practices had been well established.

"He gave me the third degree: 'Who put you up to this?' " he demanded when they met later.

"Nobody," Esther said. Houston listened more and then said, "Okay you started on your own. We'll let you continue alone." Then he looked at her and said, "You're very brave."

She had wanted to enroll in the fall of 1949, so she knew she couldn't wait forever. She wrote to the school and was informed, "We're reviewing your credits." Weeks passed without a response, so she wrote again. Again she was told: "We're reviewing your credits."

Then she called the NAACP. "They have no intention of admitting you," she was told. Houston, Marshall, and the precedent-setting lawyer Donald Murray then took her case to court. The state sent the hospital's chief of medicine to testify. He told the court he'd recently been to Metairie Medical School, a black institution in Tennessee. A fine school, he said. How long, Houston asked, had he been there? Six hours, he said. And did he think Metairie was on a par with the University of Maryland's school? The doctor didn't answer. Then the dean of the School of Nursing came to the stand. She testified that the school had never denied admission to a black student. Houston asked if the school required applicants to say if they were black or white. No, she answered. Then how, he wondered, would anyone know if blacks had been denied?

Still, the case was lost at the trial stage. Houston, who said they would appeal, soon thereafter suffered a heart attack and could not continue. Marshall and Murray stepped up. Esther McCready, quick to smile and laugh, found Marshall to be "laid back and very funny." The appeals court found in McCready's favor.

All she had to do then was persevere against those at the school who would be unable to accept her. One of the supervisors told her, "If you don't pray to God, you won't get out of here, because no one is for you." But, she replied, "If God does want me to get out of here, no one can stop me."

She and the other incoming students that year were told there was no room for them in the dormitories. When space became available, some of the white students were moved in. McCready wasn't told. Later, she was given a room on a different floor—with no roommate. Roommates had all been assigned, she was told. Later, years after they had graduated, one of her classmates asked how she'd been lucky enough to have a room of her own. McCready wondered if her classmate was really so unaware.

Looking back, she thought she had survived the "coldness" because she was a person who had loved being alone from childhood. She had fashioned contentment in a world of solitude, a world populated then with her dolls and her imagination. She had spent hours quietly playing alone. Sometimes her mother would assume she'd gone outside because she had not made a sound for so long. That propensity for getting along without human companionship helped in nursing school.

Donald Murray was available, at least, to let her know what she was about to face. He told her of the empty chairs on either side of him in early classes, and the professor who refused to call on him until the appeal was heard in Annapolis. Other students whistled Dixie or some other Confederate tune whenever they saw Murray. Later, white students decided this treatment was not something they wanted to continue and offered their help.

When things like this happened to McCready—a professor took pains to show he was looking away from her in class—she counseled herself: "I'd better not speak at this particular moment." She was not allowed to attend the class dinner dance at the Emerson Hotel, still segregated in 1953. She called to ask the hotel for its policy. "Your school knows full well what our policy is," she was told.

McCready's defensive arsenal included her mother's voice. Just hearing her mother speak eased her anxiety and heartache. "You don't have to stay if you don't want to," her mother told her. "Don't let anyone tell you they're better than you are. You're not better than anyone else, but you're just as good." That advice and assurance was given to many black young men and women.

During McCready's senior year, a priest at Bon Secours Hospital offered her a scholarship to continue studying. The award was to have been printed along with others on the graduation program, but somehow it had been omitted. She graduated in the spring of 1953 at College Park. Governor McKeldin officiated. Photographers recorded her march across the stage and her diploma, proof that Esther McCready had withstood the hurtful glances, remarks, and isolation—she had, as a lover of solitude, almost reveled in it. She had overcome the effects of centuries of exclusion to put herself in the ranks of caregivers.

Today, she speaks at graduation ceremonies with other nurses. She sits on the stage as a kind of unknown Rosa Parks, someone who refused to accept the dictates of Jim Crow. When the graduates walk past her holding their diplomas, they silently mouth the words "thank you." She says that someone else would surely have done what she did. Perhaps she is correct in her modesty, but the inescapable truth is that she was the one who did.

WALKERS AND THINKERS: OPINION LEADERS

Dean Houston's warning after the *Murray* law school victory might have been written across the façade of America's civil rights struggle. If one immense barrier had been cleared, if separate but equal had been repudiated in court, some might expect others of the same unlawful weight to fall almost automatically. Houston knew better. It was not going to be that easy. "Lawsuits mean little unless supported by public opinion. The really baffling problem is how to create the proper kind of public opinion."[25]

Many argued that morals and ethics could not be legislated. Houston did not entirely disagree. Changing the law was a way into the abstract realm of attitude and thought. But there was no substitute, Houston was saying, for changes of heart and mind—and not just white hearts and minds. Black Americans, who had the most to lose, would need to join in the struggle. Who would be the opinion leaders outside the courtroom? What tactics would they use? There was Carl Murphy's newspaper, the

Afro-American, which white readers did not see for the most part, and there were white papers that did not cover the black community, black life, black thought, or anything black beyond black crime. So for many decades, there stood the press, uninvolved, rejecting its role as a spur to conscience and to justice.

But there was a process under way, an essentially unseen process of change in which the community's opinion leaders began to say and do things that altered outlooks. Four of those who would help were important leaders in Baltimore during the 1930s and 1940s—two black and two white. They looked for answers during daily walks in their neighborhoods on opposite sides of the city. They and others like them were, in a sense, reshaping the infrastructure of their community's governing thought. Their conversations were not the only ones in which race and justice and business were kicked around among friends. But they were among the most important.

They were men of the city and of the world, successful in business, in the world of letters, and in the lives of their communities. They were classic "can do" Americans, people who were confident of their ability to fix a broken society. They were communicators, acutely attuned to the concerns of their neighbors. They walked for the exercise, for the companionship, for the measured pace—and for the conversation that helped them refine their ideas.

They relished intellectual combat carried on in the comfort of friendship. Each pair knew the other pair's names, but they probably wouldn't have thought of walking together. In their isolation they represented the social and racial divide in their city. In their focus on that separation, they were in the vanguard of men and women who, with one exception, would never get much attention outside Baltimore. But they were part of that glacial process by which public opinion is shaped. They represented a new subtext of life, a tectonic shifting of attitude. They were wrestling with what one of them had properly identified as the problem of the twentieth century, "the problem of the color line."

The white walkers were Sidney Hollander, a wealthy businessman who had devoted his life in retirement to civil rights, and his friend Albert Hutzler, a department store owner who thought Hollander was moving too fast. One of the black walkers was *Afro-American* publisher Carl Murphy. His partner was W. E. B. Du Bois, the intellectual firebrand, scholar, and cofounder of the NAACP, who lived in Baltimore for more than a decade without acknowledgement by either of the city's major newspapers. The famous and controversial author of many books, including *The Souls of Black Folk,* was out and about in Baltimore when he was in town. But the white press did not notice or chose not to recognize the important figure in the midst of the city.

A chance to inform readers was missed—not to mention a splendid political and human interest story. Du Bois and his family lived in Baltimore off and on from 1939 to 1957. Even the *Afro-American* offered only bits and pieces. Perhaps the great and famously haughty man would not deign to be interviewed by a Baltimore paper.

There were plenty of opportunities: his autobiography *Dusk of Dawn* was published in 1940, while he and his family were living in Baltimore; *Color and Democracy* in 1945; and *The World and Africa* in 1946. Some comment from the great man might well have been sought during those years, but they were years in which many important events in the black community went unacknowledged and un-covered by the white newspapers. The lapse was unprofessional, at least: had newspapers been doing their job—informing readers of important events—different cultures would have had an opportunity to learn of each other. "An old newspaperman will wince," wrote *Evening Sun* editorial writer James H. Bready in 1970, "on being referred to Baltimore telephone directories that list Du Bois, W.E.B. from 1940 to 1960, and being reminded that no newspaper interview was ever printed."[26]

The *Sun* in those days was an enforcer—or an endorser—of Baltimore's apartheid, its carefully tended discriminatory practices. As a result, it failed to recognize the presence in its midst of the black intellectual whose passionate brilliance gave enduring force to a nation-altering movement. Du Bois's son-in-law Arnette Williams told Baltimore historian Gilbert Sandler that Du Bois's reputation as a man who didn't suffer fools gladly was appropriate. At the same time, he had his human side, "a terrific sense of humor," Williams said. "Believe it or not the irascible and notoriously serious-minded W. E. B. Du Bois, first black ever to receive a doctorate from Harvard, loved to read the funnies . . . I used to call him our very own autocrat of the breakfast table." There he was, at his address on Montebello Terrace, chuckling over *Mutt and Jeff, The Katzenjammer Kids,* and *Barney Google.*[27]

Diversion must have been welcome. He almost had the weight of the world on his shoulders—and wanted it there. Du Bois and Murphy had become colleagues when Du Bois was editor of the *Crisis,* the NAACP magazine. Du Bois had come to Baltimore with his family in 1938, after being forced out as editor and teaching for a time in Atlanta. He settled his wife and children in a house down the hill from the Murphy family, in Morgan Park. Du Bois was the nation's pre-eminent black intellectual, living anonymously in Baltimore, ignored as was so much of black life in Baltimore. What he thought about his adopted city; who, if anyone, welcomed him here; and what observations he might have on the progress or lack of it in race relations were all ignored.

Carl Murphy, though he owned one of the largest black businesses in America, got scarcely more attention. More than sixty years later, leading members of the black community are surprised to learn that Du Bois once lived in their city. He could have added much to the conversation about race.

In *The Souls of Black Folk,* he had written of Jim Crow's corrosive psychic damage: "The facing of so vast a prejudice could not but bring the inevitable self-questioning, self-disparagement, and lowering of ideals which ever accompany repression and breed in an atmosphere of contempt and hate. Whisperings and portents came borne on the four winds: Lo! We are diseased and dying, cried the dark hosts; we cannot write, our voting is in vain; what need of education, since we must always cook and serve?" The nation eagerly reinforced this indictment, he said: "Be content to be servants, and nothing more; what need of higher culture for half-men? Away with the black man's ballot, by force or fraud,—and behold the suicide of a race!"[28]

Notwithstanding his eloquent analysis of the American black man's plight, Du Bois was a global theorist. His grasp of the world's dilemma may have led him to think less immediately about the problems he so deeply understood on home ground. Carl Murphy had been a member of the NAACP board that decided, after some considerable tension and debate, that Du Bois had overstayed his editorship and was advocating positions of separateness the board could not accept. Murphy did not disagree with the conclusion that it was time for Du Bois to go.

Jake Oliver, a later publisher of the *Afro,* says Carl Murphy campaigned against the acceptance of indignities however understandable that acceptance might have been. His black readers needed an awakening, a call to meet their own increasingly achievable needs in American society. They needed a challenge to stop living with discrimination as if it were beyond their control—to get past the idea that Jim Crow was entitled to define their lives. "Negroes really weren't interested in having their world changed that much," Oliver says. "At least they had jobs. At least they weren't as bad off as they had been a hundred years before. So this thing called integration or being able to sit on the first floor of the Hippodrome may not have resonated that much with them. At least they could get in the place to see the movie or get into the Lyric on the top floor, but it was Carl and the *Afro* who really worked at conditioning the black population as to what they were missing as a result of the continued implementation of separate but equal and segregation."[29]

Carl Murphy felt he wasn't safe in his own house. He slept with a gun near his bed. His daughter Frankie says keeping a weapon seemed prudent. It was something he did to give himself a little confidence, she said, a little protection "against what you knew you were going to run into."[30] What you were going to run into in the course of your daily life, she meant. You never knew exactly when something might happen, but you knew it could be any time or any place.

"I can see my dad on this lawn," she said pointing out the window of her family's house in Morgan Park fifty years later, "right out here, and the police came up and arrested him."

No one in the family saw it happen. The phone rang later, and Frankie Murphy's mother answered.

"You're where?" she said.

"In jail," he said again.

"You are where? I thought you were in the yard. What did they arrest you for?"

"Trespassing."

In 2005 they would call it standing in front of your own home while black. It was that sort of obstacle that Carl Murphy resisted and campaigned against in the pages of his newspaper and with his bank account. He had inherited the *Afro* from his father, John H. Murphy Sr., a former slave, who had developed the paper from a church publication. The younger man earned a degree in German from Harvard and then studied in Europe. As editor and publisher of the newspaper, he became one of Baltimore's—and the nation's—most important black opinion leaders.

Du Bois's biographer David Levering Lewis says the newspaperman and the scholar probably met when Du Bois was editor of the *Crisis*, when their differences on national civil rights strategy were being debated by Du Bois and NAACP leaders.[31] In that job, he had occasionally asked black editors around the country to comment on various positions he had taken in his magazine. Then and thereafter, black leaders debated whether integration had to be part of the quest for equal justice. Du Bois thought it not essential; some of his NAACP colleagues thought it was a fundamental reason for their existence. In 1932, Du Bois convened a symposium of black editors.[32]

In the middle of the Great Depression, they contemplated the interplay of racial prejudice and a Communist Party anxious to win black converts. "No white group is openly advocating the economic, political and social equality of Negroes except Communists," Murphy said then. He was not advocating communism or affiliation with the Communists even in the face of economic catastrophe, but the point, made in frustration, was a further discouraging perspective on the lack of help from others. "With the Depression," says Lewis, "the NAACP was lucky to stay afloat. Massive retrenchment was under way. Du Bois thought crisis called upon you to be bold. Economy moves—office savings in the teeth of a recession—were quailing, he thought, and irrelevant to the big picture challenge. He wanted the organization to adopt a bolder strategy for the rest of the century. It was an intellectual conceit, but the board was unhappy. He wanted a separate, socialist philosophy. He was saying, 'We must segregate ourselves.'

"Carl and White [the NAACP head] thought, 'My God, the whole reason for the NAACP was to be part of the mainstream.' So they told him, 'one more editorial column to that end and you're out.' Soon, then, he was out. Du Bois thought, or said, 'good riddance.' Carl was not in agreement with him, but that did not end their friendship. There was great friction then between Du Bois's uncompromising intellectual orientation and the real world concerns of men like Carl Murphy."[33]

In Baltimore, the famous thinker and the *Afro* publisher could be seen touring the hilly neighborhood behind Morgan College, two of black America's most important leaders walking in total obscurity in a Baltimore neighborhood. "We children walked along with them," Frankie Murphy remembers. "We'd walk around the circle. And in those days— we laugh about it today—it looked like these men were out walking with all their children. Dad and Dr. Du Bois would talk and talk and talk. They didn't always agree. Dr. Du Bois and Dad were in—we would call it—friendly combat." Friendly, but deeply consequential: whether, for example, black voters should finally divorce the GOP, and just what direction should be taken by leaders of the NAACP.

Meanwhile, Jim Crow perched on every limb of life, implacable, sneering. White neighbors farther east of the Murphys and Morgan Park, which was an enclave of Morgan College's black faculty east of the campus and just off Cold Spring Lane, jeered and shouted racial epithets. The black leaders counseled their children to ignore the "ignorant" prattle. Nor did they bother with the humiliating treatment they knew awaited them at Albert Hutzler's store—and at many other white-owned establishments in downtown Baltimore. Frankie Murphy says her family traveled to Philadelphia to shop at Strawbridge and Clothier and other emporiums.

Murphy's next door neighbor, Morgan professor Richard McKinney, says Du Bois would occasionally show up in front of the publisher's home and send his driver to the front door. "Dr. Du Bois would like to speak with you," the driver would report when Murphy appeared. Du Bois apparently felt it was beneath his dignity to knock on the door himself. McKinney had encountered similar treatment from the great man when, as president of Storer College in Harpers Ferry, West Virginia, he got Du Bois to be his graduation speaker. The great man spoke not on U.S. race relations, as McKinney had hoped, but on social conditions in Japan. Though Du Bois did not explain his choice of subject, McKinney believes his guest was being hounded by U.S. authorities (who accused him of Communist sympathies) and chose not to aggravate them with anything controversial.

McKinney later managed to secure an interview with Du Bois but was unable to learn much. Du Bois did not like a question McKinney asked about the role of the church in higher education for black Americans. What should the role be, McKinney asked. "None at all," Du Bois said and abruptly ended the interview.[34]

In these Baltimore years, Du Bois was finishing the autobiographical *Dusk of Dawn*. It was published in 1940. While he was in the city, he was scheduled to make a graduation speech at Morgan, but Martin D. Jenkins, the school's president, asked him not to come. This followed remarks Du Bois had made in Paris in defense of Paul Robeson, who said black men would not reject the Soviet Union. Du Bois was becoming even more defiant. "On a grand scale," Lewis says, "Du Bois saw the struggle as part of a worldwide effort for equality of the downtrodden. Carl Murphy did not disagree, but he wanted a more practical approach, one with some prospect of success in the United States—and soon."[35]

"Dad wrote all the editorials for the *Afro*," Frankie remembers. "He would use Dr. Du Bois as a sounding board. [And vice versa.] They had a lot in common. They read a lot. They could really talk. They would get here in this room [a large enclosed porch in the Murphy home where his daughter lived after her parents died]. We'd sit down and listen to them talk. The NAACP was at a turning point in those days. Dad and them were fussing about separate but equal: dad saw no reason why [black and white] policemen weren't paid the same. He wanted to win those battles. The local NAACP went ahead with the beaches, the golf courses, the schools. Those were Dad's priorities as head of the *Afro-American* newspaper." He was chronicling the victories, laying out the next challenge, keeping his readers informed—and focused.

Du Bois did not reject the local initiatives. He was impressed with the work of Lillie May Jackson and spoke at meetings of the City-Wide Young People's Forum, which had adopted an agenda and some rhetoric that apparently made black church leaders uncomfortable, leading to its move from Sharp Street to Bethel AME Church. Remarks by Du Bois may actually have been the proximate cause of their move. He seems to have questioned the necessity of the church's involvement.

"Dr. Du Bois, you may think this is difficult, but we know God can make victory possible," one of the church elders said.

"Is there a God?" Du Bois asked.[36]

Michael Mitchell says his father and Du Bois met during youth forum meetings. Before Du Bois moved to Baltimore, the NAACP, Thurgood Marshall, and Charles Hamilton Houston had won the *Murray* law school case. Then they won a teacher pay-equalization case. Murphy had been critical in his newspaper of Maryland teachers for not coming forward with a plaintiff for the equal pay case. His call to arms was appropriate, but the reluctance of many blacks to enlist was understandable. Jim Crow was a vindictive opponent.

In 1935, Howard Pindell, then living in Baltimore but teaching in Anne Arundel County, stepped forward. As vice president of the Maryland Colored Teachers Association, he might have been the ideal plaintiff. His experience in that role further illuminated the lengths to which practitioners of Jim Crow would go to maintain discriminatory practices. "I served on the Strategy Committee, the objective of which was the removal of the salary differential between the races," Pindell told the Frederick County Historical Society years later. In accordance with state law, Maryland paid black teachers and administrators less than whites. The statutory minimum for whites in the late 1930s was $1,250 per year; $765 for blacks.

Marshall won a partial victory: a year later, the Court of Appeals ordered the cessation of salary discrimination based on race but refused to specifically require school boards to pay black teachers the same as whites. The law apparently could not be violated under *Plessy,* but the practice of differential payments could continue if schools found a plausible maneuver to achieve that end.

Pindell had been an ideal plaintiff. But he withdrew before the case went forward because authorities in Frederick offered to make him principal of Lincoln High School there. He told Marshall what was happening. Marshall suggested he accept the "kick upstairs." "We'll find another plaintiff," the lawyer said. The case went forward with Walter Mills, a black teacher in Anne Arundel County. Two years later, Pindell was removed from his post at Lincoln High. He felt he had been promoted only to get him out of the court case and dismissed when he was of no further use.[37] In May 1942, the NAACP gave him a silver loving cup in appreciation of his service.

Frederick's Bill Lee says he discovered ten years later, in 1952, that his salary was about 25 percent less than that of his white colleagues. A mistake in the distribution of checks one week showed the discrepancy for teachers of the same experience and training. The uncovered mistake led to raises for black teachers—a considerable one for Lee and his family. Justice came in fits and starts, by risk and reward, and by everyday mistakes.[38]

The victories were spectacular. Funds for out-of-state scholarships promised but not delivered by the legislature were tripled. At one point, Carl Murphy was chairman of the board managing that money. His daughter Frankie proudly took advantage of it. Schools out of state were better, she says. And the idea all along was not solely integration but fairness and equality. If the state wanted to pay tuition out of state, there were many who would take advantage of it. Many looked back at the plan with dismay, though, since it tended to take the most talented and motivated young black people out of Maryland. The *Murray* law school dividend—money made available by the state—included $100,000 for a new gymnasium at Morgan and $250,000 for new buildings at Bowie State. These appropriations helped with NAACP membership. People saw progress and wanted to be part of it. NAACP membership jumped from a few dozen in 1934 to fifteen hundred by the end of 1936.[39] Black Marylanders were sensing opportunity for change, but it would take more struggle.

Discussions similar to those in Morgan Park between Du Bois and Murphy were going on in the same period between two white Baltimoreans who differed on how to confront the forces of fear and bigotry that led to racial discrimination. The two Jewish leaders disagreed sharply on the right path to equality in their city. They walked and talked every day in Windsor Hills, on the city's west side. One was Sidney Hollander, who had made a fortune with a cough remedy before becoming the conscience of the city in the 1930s; the other was Albert Hutzler, who owned one of the city's major downtown department stores. Hutzler wanted to go a lot slower than his friend—not on their walks but in integrating city life. They walked and they talked of Hollander's controversial—if not radical—civil rights agenda for Baltimore. He was a single-minded man thought by many in the city to be altogether too heavily invested in civil rights.

The Hollander family home in Windsor Hills had become a venue for interracial conversation and action. The famous black opera star Marian Anderson was a guest. She had been barred from singing at the DAR Constitution Hall in Washington six years earlier and at the Lyric Opera House in Baltimore. In 1945, the Lyric dropped its ban, and Anderson performed. Before the event, a reception was given in her honor in the Hollander home on Talbot Road. Sidney Hollander Jr. remembers the hubbub and, in particular, the weight of the singer's mink coat, which he fetched for her from the hall closet. The coat—and the cause—stayed with young Sidney all his life. He demonstrated for civil rights and for peace well into his 90s.

His father was a founder and leader of the Urban League in Baltimore, an organization devoted to removing barriers to black progress, particularly in employment. Except for wartime steel making at Bethlehem Steel's Sparrows Point, businesses were often unwilling to hire black workers. As Hollander and others pushed for change, he would occasionally find himself in conflict, not only with his friend Hutzler and others in the white community, but with black leaders as well, notably

Lillie May Jackson. Jackson felt that Hollander, whatever he said or did, was ultimately obligated to serve the interests of business—and therefore moved too slowly. It was the classic bind for the white progressive, politician or citizen: his white constituency was none too eager for change; his black friends were impatient and sometimes angry. He could never quite satisfy either group. Hollander felt that Jackson was too rigid, unwilling to compromise. But he tried to understand. Hutzler had to deal with the sit-in and other tactics as pressure rose for him and other merchants to drop their "final sale" policy for black shoppers, a policy allowing no returns of purchased items.

In December 1961, Sidney Hollander's family and friends threw a gala 80th birthday party for him. Hutzler, by then a member of the Johns Hopkins University board of trustees, was one of the guests. When it was his turn to speak, he observed that the honored guest had recently undergone neck surgery. "You know, Sidney," he said, "there are many people in Baltimore who would have cut your throat for nothing." The guests howled.

Then Broadus Mitchell, the former Hopkins faculty member who had spoken out for civil rights dramatically in the 1930s, rose to speak. Mitchell had been a scourge to Hopkins, a persistent critic. And he was even more troublesome for the wider community, attacking racist Jim Crow, class divisions, and political corruption. Mitchell was asked to leave Hopkins for remarks he made about the Supreme Court that were thought to be unacceptable, even under the broad free speech latitude afforded on college campuses. The times had ended unhappily for Mitchell, but by all accounts he had put those days of pain behind him. He was happy to be back among old friends. When he stood, he addressed Hutzler's throat-cutting observation. "You know," Mitchell said, "that's the first time I ever heard a Hopkins trustee be funny on purpose."[40] Sidney Hollander Jr. told that story often over the years.

Young Hollander had his own run-ins with Hopkins officialdom. He and his sister had wanted to honor their father's work in civil rights, and they thought a scholarship named for him would be a fine way to do that. The scholarship, they thought, should go to an African American student, and they presented their idea to the Hopkins president, who promptly thanked them and turned them down.

They pressed their case, but Hopkins was not interested. Sidney Hollander made one final attempt to convince the man, who cut him off by saying, "Mr. Hollander, now you're becoming disputatious." (That moment and that word were recalled by members of the Hollander family in later years whenever a participant in dinner table conversations verged toward disagreement. "You are becoming disputatious," someone would say to great gales of laughter.) Years later, the university inaugurated a scholarship program for Baltimore students who graduated from city high schools with at least a B average.

Perhaps the Hopkins refusal was for the best. The family inaugurated a series of annual Hollander Awards to the individual or institution that made a significant contribution to improved race relations. The first recipient, in 1946, was the *Baltimore Sun*, which had finally agreed to end the practice of designating what race was desired in help wanted advertisements. Sidney Hollander Jr. says he and others on the committee were reluctant endorsers of awarding anything to the *Sun*. They thought the newspaper had been a notorious offender for too long. It had not been much help as their father and others sought, over seven years, to desegregate Ford's Theater.

But, the young Hollander discovered, the award served an unanticipated purpose. Once it had been recognized for doing something admirable in civil rights, the *Sun* began to change its attitude in other areas, apparently so it might seem deserving. To the extent that the city's major newspaper began to cover the black community, to schedule interviews with important black figures like Du Bois, and to purge its pages of unnecessarily derogatory designations, the award made a statement to the rest of the city and state.

MALCONTENTS: INSIDE AGITATORS

The University of Maryland School of Law was integrated in 1935, but Jim Crow was allowed to circle above the state's other professional schools for more than a decade longer. Doors had to be opened one at a time and then held open, as if the same discrimination could be successfully defended in these other schools. After the law school victory, university officials tried to intimidate black students who applied to study there. Why don't you go where you're welcome? students were told. We'll pay you to leave the state. Some, like Frankie Murphy, daughter of the *Afro* publisher, accepted the offer, imagining they would go to better schools for less money.

William H. Murphy Sr., the third black law school student at Maryland, refused the out-of-state scholarship from university president Harry C. "Curley" Byrd, who had tried to keep Donald Murray out of the school. When the *Murray* case was tried, state officials pointed to a fund they had created as if that would stand in for separate but equal. No money had been appropriated for the fund at first. That bald deficiency was remedied, and Byrd offered Murphy tuition and travel money to Harvard if he would attend that school instead of Maryland. Murphy's father told him if he went to Harvard, he'd have to *walk* back and forth to Boston. That threat might not have been necessary. Young Murphy told Byrd, "You've just made up my mind. I'll be coming to your school in the fall."[41] That sort of brave individual resistance was part of the movement's subterranean momentum.

Fifteen years after Marshall and Houston got him admitted to the law school, Donald Gaines Murray was one of the lawyers on a team that got Esther McCready admitted to the university's School of Nursing. There was a lovely symmetry there, Murray helping in a case nearly identical to his own, but the underlying message remained the same: Maryland was holding out to the end, giving ground grudgingly and only under pressure.

Some of the workaday revolutionaries were on the scene for mere minutes. Others gave a lifetime to the struggle. Among the second group were two World War II veterans: Harry Cole, a black lawyer who saw how to beat a mighty political machine, and Milton Bates, a Jewish businessman with a passion for citizenship and justice. The Cole-Bates tandem forced Baltimore's pre-eminent boss, Jack Pollack, to "take"—endorse for his powerful ticket—black candidates, something he'd refused to do until then.

And there was Chester "Chet the Jet" Wickwire, the Johns Hopkins University chaplain who advanced the revolutionary ideas that a university should be open to the surrounding community, that students were eager to work for a freer society, and that black and white Baltimoreans could sit together in the same auditoriums without rioting. Wickwire was perfect for the part. If he'd been wearing white linen slacks and a navy blue blazer, standing on the porch of the Elkridge Club, the city's upper-crustiest country club, the bespectacled young man on crutches could not have seemed less a threat to Baltimore's Establishment. The Reverend Chester Wickwire was sublimely camouflaged. He was one of the most earnest and charismatic marchers for equal justice. From within, Wickwire confronted Establishment bastions in the city for thirty years.

He worked at two Baltimore institutions that would not have knowingly hired a revolutionary, but his protective colorations were perfect: he had a crew cut and he had a PhD from Yale Divinity School. After his bout with polio, he'd been a seller of children's toys, a case worker for the Traveler's Aid Society in New Haven, Connecticut, and a graduate assistant in the Divinity School's Old Testament Department.

He came to Baltimore in 1953, at the age of 40, having been hired by both Johns Hopkins University and the Baltimore YMCA. He would serve these two masters from Levering Hall, then owned by the Y but located on the university campus. Because of some difficulty with his predecessor, the people who hired him were eager to know if he was a drinker. Wrong question. What should they have asked? Will you be a disturber of the peace? The university's and the city's intransigence would be challenged by a man who preached and practiced the social gospel. Jackson, the Mitchells, and A. Robert Kaufman would now have a white minister fighting with them from within the citadel of privilege. Together they would demand access to hotels, to bars, to graduate professional schools, to undergraduate studies, to labor unions, to the councils of government. The religious man on campus would begin to bring black students onto the Hopkins campus for tutoring.

Wickwire arrived at the university in north-central Baltimore aflame with the urgency of academic freedom—the right of learned people to voice their opinions no matter how offensive to authority—but that concern was to broaden considerably. He would be a trusted intermediary in negotiations between local police and the sixties revolutionaries known as the Black Panthers. The university and the Christian association had hired a decidedly sober man whose life had shaped him to act on the dictates of his conscience, to put himself in the service of young minds, to speak for minority groups whose life he had shared as one of the earth's afflicted. Hampered but not crippled by polio, he seemed to regard his affliction as a blessing, a vehicle that took him to levels of insight unknown to many in his adopted city. The city had not begun to grasp the reality that was upon it: an insistent appeal—a demand, to use the word of the movement—for an end to discrimination. Thus did Chester Wickwire walk through what he called Baltimore's "open door," a city so afflicted with discrimination and injustice that no one with an outsider's unclouded eyes could fail to see it.

He was born in 1913 in Colorado. His mother, he says, was a religious zealot, his father a man of racial insensitivity in a world that thrived on it. "Mother was a Seventh-Day Adventist. She was waiting for the second coming. My father wanted nothing to do with that. But my mother would ask, 'Papa, are you saved?' "[42] And apparently he needed a little saving. Wickwire says his father was part of an unquestioning racist culture. The Klan was in full and open operation, burning crosses on Lookout Mountain on Monday nights. Its members had controlled the state legislature in the twenties. The Klan was mainly Republican, but it was eventually driven out of business by ridicule directed at its costumes. As a young man, Wickwire worked in the Seventh-Day Adventist Church, but knew he didn't belong in that faith. He went off to Yale Divinity School at 23. Then, in 1948, he found himself swept up in the polio epidemic then ravaging the country. He was hospitalized for thirteen months, half in a pauper's ward. He had no money. "Sometimes I'd go to sleep at night and there'd be somebody next to me when I woke up. There'd be people dying. I shouldn't have been in there, and yet it was a good thing for me in terms of education."

He was desperate to get out—and he was learning every day how those without resources were treated. The experience was exacerbated by the mystery of the disease. "They didn't know what to do about polio. So I was being warehoused. It was so obvious I was not getting care. A nurse brought me in a book on polio for the layman, and it was taken away from me. They didn't want me to have it. I was told by a doctor to stop asking questions. They were talking about sending me to Rocky Point, a nearby veteran's hospital, [but] I wasn't a veteran. I was going to get more warehousing."

But birth and circumstance made his case different from those near him in the wards. He had an unparalleled connection, someone who could get him the best available care—in Warm Springs, Georgia, where President Roosevelt had been treated for polio. One of Wickwire's friends, with a church near Yale in Hampden, Connecticut, had a wealthy Republican parishioner who was an acquaintance of Eleanor Roosevelt's. "She got Eleanor interested in me. Eleanor got me into Warm Springs. When I was there, she came to visit me. I introduced her to the rest of the patients." He knew his good fortune was based on status and class and color.

The Klan was "very active in Georgia when I went down there. It was operating right on the grounds of the Warm Springs Foundation. Blacks were not treated. They were sent to Tuskegee [and he knew Tuskegee wouldn't know what to do with them if Yale Hospital hadn't known]. And the black persons that worked there were treated badly by the whites. If we wanted to go to a black church on Sundays, we were always followed by white segregationists in their cars. There was a Klavern within a mile of there. So that was part of the picture. So when I came to Baltimore in '53, I came with the social gospel, a belief that ministers should be engaged in the pursuit of justice, not just in the pulpit but in the streets. Christianity, according to this idea, had deep obligations to address the excesses of capitalism, the problems of workers, and discrimination against black people. All this should occur from within the system. The work might seem revolutionary, but it would include the belief that the system, however distorted, could be redeemed. I came with the door open to try to do something. Immediately what you ran into was the 'red scare.' "

Wickwire wanted to arrange a speech for Owen Lattimore, an unorthodox academic and expert on China who was unwilling to trim his sails under pressure from right wing demagogues. Hopkins administrators said no. They "were supportive in the sense that they paid his salary, but they didn't want him speaking around," Wickwire remembers. The red scare, "a cloud of poison gas spreading over the country had not yet smothered the faculty of the Johns Hopkins University who remained faithful to their university's motto, 'The truth will set you free.' " In July, a congressional report cleared Lattimore: "We find no evidence to support the charge that Owen Lattimore is the 'top Russian spy' or, for that matter, any other sort of spy." Maryland senator Joseph Tydings labeled Senator Joseph McCarthy's case "a fraud and a hoax."[43]

Wickwire found the Lattimore case emblematic of the atmosphere on the Hopkins campus: "It was a very segregated place at the undergraduate level. There were [virtually] no blacks, no women, and a quota for Jews. The Y itself was segregated. They had a seaman's branch. They had a black branch." Wickwire could work against this segregation because he enjoyed a certain immunity from criticism: "If the Y didn't like what I was doing, they could blame Hopkins. If Hopkins didn't like it, they could blame the Y." There would be plenty for them to dislike in those days.

Imagining that the campus leadership would reject their initiative, students encouraged by Wickwire "went to the newspapers with a complaint that landlords in the university neighborhood would not rent to blacks or Jews." That charge was indisputable, affirmed by some university officials, according to Ross Jones, a longtime assistant to Hopkins presidents. Günther Werthheimer and his wife, Joan, who later became chairman of the CORE chapter in Baltimore, lost an apartment when the landlord asked if they were Jewish.

Hopkins president Milton Eisenhower, brother of President Dwight D. Eisenhower, was livid when students went to the newspaper to unmask the policy. They went public without consulting first or negotiating with Eisenhower, but they worked out a deal in which Eisenhower wrote a letter telling landlords they'd have to open their properties to all. "We also demanded that they begin to recruit black students. And employ more blacks. So that was it. And Milton did put out a directive to the landlords that said if you're going to be listed by the university, you have to rent to everyone," Jones says. Wickwire had more support than he realized: "I always thought it was important to have someone like Chester, a burr under the saddle." Jones agreed that before Wickwire, Hopkins had been "in the community, but not of it."[44] Here, then, the students and their chaplain were dramatically changing the university, as Esther McCready had changed the University of Maryland's nursing school.

Encounters of this sort earned Wickwire an unusual status in Baltimore. Whites in authority and others thought him a rabble-rouser at best, a Communist at worst. Black activists found him almost unreal as a white ally. He served a term as president of the all-black Interdenominational Ministerial Alliance, a group of activist black ministers.

What he wanted was almost laughably simple: he wanted to make Baltimore safe for intergroup activities. "My feeling was try to relate the campus to the city, and the students to the city, and to bring the city to the campus. So we were often accused of being Communists . . . We did juvenile delinquency, courses allowed in the social relations department, and I got students to run them. It was amazing what the students could and did do in terms of relating to the city. They wanted to do it. We gave them a chance."

Wickwire became a clergyman impresario. Music, he thought, could promote racial harmony. He found allies in the performers. Dave Brubeck was particularly anxious to perform in these adventurous concerts. As

Bob Kaufman discovered in the Ford's Theater demonstrations, actors and other performers were unwilling to endorse discrimination and Jim Crow by participating in segregated theaters. "We began concerts all over the city," Wickwire recalls. "You were not supposed to have them before mixed audiences. We had the first one at the Fifth Regiment Armory in 1959."

Brubeck said years later that he was surprised to learn that the armory gig had been a first: the first integrated concert in Baltimore. It was not a first for him. He refused to play segregated halls anywhere, including universities. "If they wouldn't integrate the halls, I wouldn't play . . . We lost many concerts, because in those days, schools were afraid they would lose state support if they integrated, and so we just would cancel, and the students wanted us and the teachers wanted us and the president of the college wanted us, but there was that law. So finally one governor said—because I wouldn't go onstage; they wouldn't allow my bass player to go on stage with me, so I wouldn't go—so the university president called the governor and said the kids are about to riot. 'Put him on. We don't want another Little Rock.' " Brubeck said, at 85, that he still couldn't quite understand how someone like Louis Armstrong could have been so beloved and yet black people were treated "in such a strange way."[45]

Wickwire put Baltimoreans up against this contradiction. "We had Brubeck, Maynard Ferguson, Chico Hamilton, Chris Connor; Lambert, Hendricks, and Ross; Leonard Feather was the MC. Lawyers for the university and the Y were writing letters absolving themselves for the race riot we were going to have," he said. "People had a fantastic time. So we began doing the concerts all over the city in high schools. Along with other programs, we were doing this. We brought Duke Ellington twice. We had Joan Baez, Odetta, Flatt and Scruggs, Simon and Garfunkel, Charlie Mingus, Thelonious Monk, Ravi Shankar."

Breakthroughs were occurring at every turn in these days. When the bassist Charlie Mingus saw what looked like an all-white audience, he ripped off his white ministerial collar, which he wore as a symbolic protest, and went back to New York without playing. Years later, after one concert, Ruth Fegley, the director of the interracial Fellowship House, who ran a kind of refuge for the civil rights armies, led a group over to get a cup of coffee at the Blue Jay, a Hopkins haunt on St. Paul Street. It was a hangout, a headquarters for strategy discussion and a symbol of the civil rights–era solidarity felt by many of the activists. Someone wanted Ellington to ride over in a sports car. Too damn small, said the bandleader. So Fegley drove him in her car. Alerted somehow to the imminent arrival of a mixed black and white party, the Blue Jay turned its lights out. Ellington left immediately with a shake of the head.

On the night of the Ellington concert, Frank Somerville, a reporter for the *Sun,* offered a story on the snubbing of Ellington, but the *Sun,* as it often did in matters of public racial protest, said it wasn't interested.[46] Its frequent response: it's a private matter. The way to deal with racial unrest, many papers concluded, was to ignore it.

Later that evening, the Blue Jay burned. Wickwire absorbed some of the blame. "When we finally got a public accommodations law, I took Reverend Neubold [who was black] to the Blue Jay for lunch. They were very slow in serving us. And when we got ready to pay, I went up to the counter to give them the money. The cashier threw the change so it flew off the counter, and he said to me, 'You get the hell out of here and never come back.' 'You're welcome,' he said to Neubold, 'you can come back anytime.' " Just the way it was.

In the white world, Wickwire was seen as someone who wouldn't listen to reason, someone you couldn't talk to—a little like Eleanor Roosevelt and Lillie May Jackson. "It helps to be civil," said Samuel Hopkins, a descendant of the university's founder, "no matter what the situation is."[47] Wickwire and the students thought they had been very civil.

People like Wickwire—or Douglass, or Tubman, or Friend Lundy, or Eugene O'Dunne, or Eleanor Roosevelt—would not look the other way. Roosevelt brought her observations to Baltimore in 1944. Peggy Waxter, the wife of lawyer and social welfare champion Jake Waxter, met her at the train station. Peggy Waxter's long record of involvement in such matters brought her scorn, too, and the charge, frequently leveled at such people, that she was a Communist. "I wasn't a Communist," she said. "I didn't know what a Communist was." She and her husband met Roosevelt at the train. "She was traveling alone, I think. No Secret Service or anything."[48] The speech was to be given at the Sharp Street Church—the larger auditoriums refused to make their space available to the first lady of the nation because a mixed audience was expected.

The agitators suddenly had an ally in the White House.

At Sharp Street, Roosevelt addressed a packed building. Seven hundred people sat in the church basement, and another crowd, an estimated one thousand, was outside. When she spoke of human rights, she was speaking most particularly about black Americans. They were entitled to fundamental rights, she said repeatedly. They had the rights, in theory, but they were not allowed to exercise them. She did not say "black Americans," but everyone took her meaning. "No group can remain a discriminated group without doing harm to other groups," she said. The audience applauded.

She was scolding white Baltimoreans, asking them to consider certain practical realities that might incline them to act with some commitment to fairness. Black Baltimoreans were being denied inalienable rights conferred on American citizens from the dawn of the republic. These rights were withheld by law and by custom. Neither Governor Herbert O'Conor nor Mayor McKeldin was in the church, though both had been expected. Governor O'Conor was to have welcomed Eleanor Roosevelt. He had been so committed by the printed program. The mayor was represented by Linwood Koger, "Negro assistant city solicitor, who extended the city's greetings to Mrs. Roosevelt." Yet Governor O'Conor and Mayor McKeldin had spoken earlier that day in Patterson Park, on the east side of the city, at the annual "I Am an American" Day parade.

Roosevelt told her audience that Americans had to prepare for a special postwar responsibility. "We've been fighting a war against fascism," she said, "set up by a man who taught his people that they were supermen ordained to rule the world, and eventually we had to say to him, 'your people are not supermen,' and we have been saying it effectively while our people have fought together. Never again," she said, "will it be possible to say the Chinese are inferior or to say that any race is inferior to any other." She did not address the issue at hand, the issue illustrated by her nearly all-black audience, by the absence of the governor and the mayor, and by the unwillingness of the city to welcome her properly, to allow her speech in one of the grand assembly halls. The German people, she said, will require reeducation—and they must be taught by people who practice the equality they claim to live by. "We must go forward together," she said. "We cannot be separate."

Roosevelt also spoke at the annual meeting of the Baltimore NAACP. She was welcomed by Lillie May Jackson, who said, "this gracious lady has shown us democracy can work, and with the help of God, we intend to show it can work forty miles from Washington."[49] On this occasion, Roosevelt spoke at the Sharp Street Methodist Church at Dolphin and

Etting Streets, the church—though not the location—in which Frederick Douglass had sung briefly in the choir more than one hundred years earlier. The church was then located near the Inner Harbor on Sharp Street. As before, Roosevelt had been turned away as a speaker at the Lyric and Ford's Theaters. All groups might be entitled to an array of basic rights and freedoms, but in 1944, these did not include the right to assemble freely in a private theater. Again, she was barred because these establishments knew she would be speaking to mixed black and white audiences. Eleanor Roosevelt was among the other famous people treated rudely in Baltimore, people thought of as cranks, idiosyncratic, nonconformists, people who wouldn't go along.

Change would depend on law and policy but also on the quiet courage of individuals doing what they felt was right. Some sort of major breakthrough was necessary in virtually every corner of society, from housing to politics. A veteran of the Korean War, Harry Cole had seen much of the world. Like Juanita Jackson back from college in Philadelphia, he returned from Korea with new eyes, new confidence, and a new sense of entitlement. He'd learned poker from a Mississippi boy. He'd seen how the game was played. He knew he could compete and win—after he learned how the game was played. He got his law degree and, in 1954, he decided to run for public office. He would be a Republican because he knew he would get no attention from Democrats.

His campaign drew talented and equally impassioned allies. Like many Baltimoreans returning from the war, Milton Bates had a deeper understanding of the city's apartheid. He had seen Hitler's one-thousand-year Reich thriving and growing stronger before the Allies intervened. As a Jewish American, he was both angry and fearful about racism. In 1954, he was not only a worker in Harry Cole's campaign but a candidate for the U.S. Congress in Maryland's Third Congressional District, as well as the owner of a new home-improvement business. He was also a full-time law student and a leader in the state's Progressive Party. Bates was a partisan, impressed with the power of evil.

He and Harry Cole were determined to crack through the battlements of race, one of which protected the ultimate Baltimore political boss, Jack Pollack. Neither Cole nor Bates was a Republican, but Cole switched parties. The Democrat Pollack never took black candidates. Once on the ballot with the GOP endorsement, Cole accomplished a spectacular victory. He managed it by outthinking and by outworking Pollack, the master.

And in men like Bates, he found allies with the courage to run against powerful forces, to challenge even broader societal norms governing who could aspire to any position in society, including public office. If you were poor and afflicted with polio, you could be warehoused. If you were a young black girl from East Baltimore, you were expected to take yourself out of the race by not applying to nursing school. If you wanted to be included, you might be told you were "not ready" or "not qualified." No one was going to give them a chance to prove their mettle.

But none of what Cole and Bates knew, none of their logistical work or brainstorming of issue papers or debates, would mean much if the faithful didn't vote, so Bates started making his election day rounds early. He deployed his squads of poll workers to push sample ballots through mail slots and to watch the polls for electoral hanky panky. When he arrived at one polling place, a private home in the Eleventh Precinct, Thirteenth Ward, he found a long line of impatient voters. The line wasn't moving at 7:20 a.m., twenty minutes after voting was to have started. Doors to the voting booths were still closed. This virtually all-black precinct was electoral gold for Harry Cole. A few Jewish families still lived in the area, but many had moved out of the city in the push for suburban living even then. Bates found his precinct captain, who didn't know why the poll was not open. Inside, officials told him the required Democratic poll judge had not arrived. Milton Bates thought, "I guess she overslept on someone's instruction." This group of black citizens was middle class: shopkeepers, professional people, and others—people with jobs and businesses and offices to go to. They would not stay in line forever. It was 1954, and the value of taking black voters out of the picture remained as strong as in the days of Tom Smith and his diversion excursions on the bay, the ones that ended after the polls closed.

Bates acted on impulse.

"I'm a registered Democrat; let's get the doors open," he said.[50] He would become the necessary Democratic judge. He was also, of course, one of Harry Cole's campaign aides. Not likely he would have been acceptable as a judge had anyone known who he was. Nevertheless, Cole appeared to have lost on election day by a mere handful of votes, a number that would have been larger had voters in this precinct in particular been unable to cast their ballots. In the end, Cole won by managing to disqualify many voters who had voted in the district though they no longer lived there. Pollack knew all the tricks, but so did Harry Cole and his team. They knew certain polling places might not open on time. They knew certain ineligible voters would vote if allowed. They knew they had to counter all these dirty tricks. The recount would have had a much higher hill to climb had Bates not imposed himself on the process.

Harry Cole won, becoming the first black state senator in Maryland history. In Annapolis, he established useful relationships with liberals and segregationists. He became not a Republican or a Democratic senator, but a black senator, working for the interests of black Marylanders. Four years later, he was defeated—by another black candidate, taken this time by a newly enlightened Boss Pollack. Here was real institutional change: Pollack had to take black candidates or lose. Harry Cole had integrated the boss's clubhouse.

FINAL SALE: HATS, TENNIS, AND WHITE COFFEE POTS

We couldn't sit at the counter of the white establishments, the beautiful White Coffee Pot, just about four blocks from us. You could go in and order a cup of coffee, but you couldn't sit down, you had to stand outside to drink it. And the place was beautiful. I mean it was immaculate and for a boy, for a child, it was just a dream world. So I saw my mother and other church women fighting that issue at an early age, and I think they were my heroines.[51]

The Reverend Vernon Dobson, pastor of Union Baptist Church

If you were black, there were so many places you couldn't go and things you couldn't do in Jim Crow America. Baltimore's famous White Coffee Pot chain was just one of them.

Mitzi Swann remembers watching black women looking at hats in a downtown Baltimore department store—just looking and looking.

"Aren't you going to try them on?" she asked.

"We can't," one of them said. Black people were not allowed to have physical contact with hats or other clothing a white person might want to buy.

What a hurtful thing, the young girl thought. Her mother's stories about growing up Jewish in Russia came to mind immediately. "She told me what she had to endure. There were the pogroms, eradication or ethnic-cleansing campaigns. I heard the stories of discrimination." Her mother's point was clear to her. "If one group of people could be treated this way, then another and another."[52]

Stories of that sort had somber resonance in the 1940s. This was the era of World War II and the racist effort of Germany under Adolf Hitler to purify the Aryan race with a Final Solution, a reference to the gas chambers in which six million Jews were murdered. In Maryland, the "final sale" rule signaled a different sort of cleansing. If you were black and you bought certain articles of clothing at certain stores, you owned them. You couldn't return them, receipt or not. Here was the policy of Governor Swann and his successors, institutionalized by department store owners who felt they were merely responding to the demands of their customers, declaring their stores to be for the comfort and convenience of white shoppers, just as Swann and others declared the Democratic Party the exclusive preserve of white people. In those days, a white householder could call a store to arrange for some purchase or other to be returned. The service was not available for blacks who bought under the final sale rule.

Afro-American publisher Carl Murphy would never let his daughters shop in Baltimore.[53] In addition to shopping at Strawbridge and Clothier in Philadelphia, they went to other major stores in the north. The out-of-town stores were better, after all. And he and his family weren't about to endure the humiliations of the final sale rule that governed in Baltimore's department stores, stores that held so much romance and fantasy for young children, who might hope for a soda or a sundae at Hutzler's tearoom, called the Colonial Restaurant or the Quixie, or a ride on an escalator, moving slowly over a perfume counter, past all the heady displays of neckties and luggage and clothing. Department stores, like amusement parks, were a forbidden dream world for black Baltimoreans. Other Baltimore shoppers could try clothing on for size. Blacks could not. Department stores accepted all the stereotypes and enforced them over the counter. At various points, they hired watchers who could spot light-skinned black people who might try to break through the barriers.

These forms of discrimination had deep roots in Baltimore and in wider Southern sensibilities and practices. Barring blacks from 'white collar' department store jobs allowed employers to reserve jobs for white friends and associates in times of job scarcity, especially during the Depression. Within the context of department store managerial culture, job discrimination drew on widespread racist assumptions about black intelligence, competence, honesty and decorum. A kind of racist aesthetic also likely played a role: department stores were places where dreams of class mobility and endless material prosperity glowed from racks of elegant clothing and wafted from perfume counters.

In complex ways, this particular dream-world was an exclusively white utopia, tied to notions of racial order and purity . . . Managers assumed, rightly or wrongly, that white customers would find their fantasies upset by a black sales presence.[54]

Bill Lee's family in Frederick coped with similar shopping rules, regarding them as inconveniences, setting aside the insult. "There were four of us, two boys, two girls. The boys would be first. It was kind of easy for boys. My grandmother just put a shirt up in front of us. But with the two girls it was a little more difficult. You couldn't try anything on in most of the stores. Sure it made you angry. But what could you do? It's just the way it was."[55]

When an attempt was made to end these practices in 1943, the reform measure was sent to the General Assembly's Hygiene Committee, not to the Judiciary Committee, where it probably should have landed as a matter relating to state law. The Reverend Marion Bascom, pastor of Douglas Memorial Community Church, says the fear manifested by such behavior was a function of separation, a set of unflatteringly exotic notions endorsed by public officials and pushed to the extreme of fear by Jim Crow and his henchmen.[56]

Not every Baltimorean was willing to abide by these restrictions in silence: Madeleine Murphy, wife of judge William Murphy Sr. and later a TV personality in Baltimore, set out her views in a letter to Hochschild-Kohn, one of the most prominent of the big stores: "I am sure also that you know that there are certain gentiles and Jews commonly known as trash who are infinitely dirtier, more unkempt and repulsive than those with whom you may come in contact from day to day. And yet some of these are your customers and are allowed to use every facility of your store—white skin and straight hair being their only prerequisite—even though lice are generally a malady of straight-haired people and not Negroes."[57] Not everyone could summon up the rhetorical cannons as quickly as Madeleine Murphy.

Others, like Mitzi Swann, made their statement in different ways, at least as eloquent. Her mother's daughter politically, she joined Baltimore's branch of the Progressive Party, an anti–Joseph McCarthy movement. She became an adherent of Henry Wallace, the populist Progressive Party candidate. She met with other young party members in Baltimore to discuss and endorse the Wallace platform and to observe many issues in their society: for example, black soldiers, just home from another war to make the world safe for democracy, faced the same antidemocratic society they had left.

They all wanted to do something to express their opposition to the prevailing ethic of separation and discrimination. Why not make an issue of the segregated tennis courts, someone suggested? The courts were across the street from Mitzi Swann's house on Whittier Avenue, a street that bisected a neighborhood that included Eutaw Place, heavily Jewish but increasingly black. The Mitchells and other black middle-class families lived at the northern end of Druid Hill Avenue, and many of them belonged to the city's Black Baltimore Tennis Club. Some of its members agreed to participate in the protest, which was more remarkable in a way than the decision by white Baltimoreans to challenge the systematic exclusion of blacks from amenities they were, after all, paying for as taxpayers. The tennis courts were not segregated by law, but regulations passed by the park board—a powerful body because it governed places where the races might meet—kept black people out. The police enforced the board's separate but equal rules.

"Separate," Swann says, "but never equal."

On July 11, 1948, some years after Mahatma Gandhi first used the nonviolent civil disobedience tactic of Henry David Thoreau—and years before the tactic was used in the civil rights movement—eight tennis players, black and white, walked onto the courts at Druid Hill Park. Black players were not allowed there. And they certainly weren't allowed there with white players. Some five hundred people were on hand to watch because the Progressives had alerted everyone, including the police, to their plans. The white-shirted cops, uniformed then in natty hats and dark neckties, stood by with billy clubs at the ready. The players were arrested before a single serve or volley.

"The Gestapo!" someone in the crowd shouted.

"Storm troopers!" shouted another. As the police moved in, the crowd began to sing "America the Beautiful." Others were not at all sympathetic. A Baltimore woman of some standing in the community took a dim view of it: "I thought they should just play on their courts," she said, recalling her attitude then. "A lot of the players on those courts were Jewish. They lived on Auchentoroly Terrace and Eutaw Place, which some of us called Jew-taw Place."[58] Observations of that sort were acceptable in many quarters then.

These were the days of Joe McCarthy and the red scares, days in which McCarthy, a man of power as a U.S. senator, made lists of "known Communists" in the U.S. State Department or the movie industry. If you were for social justice—for programs designed to help the poor—you were moving into dangerous territory. You began to look like a Socialist at best. It was a time also in which authority faced no challenge save from cartoonists or writers such as H. L. Mencken, the *Evening Sun's* acerbic scold. Demonstrations—a too vigorous questioning of authority—were subversive, grounds for labeling and ostracism. One is reminded of the slave's fear of asking questions; one was meant to go along. Conformity was a virtue. "Shop Where You Can Work" had run fully counter to that ethos, but it had happened in the black community. The ongoing protest at Ford's Theater was ignored by the management and the patrons for years as a conspiracy against business. It was impolite to point out injustice. Injustice was institutionalized. Unwilling to endure the anger of friends and family, white Baltimore went along for the most part.

In all, twenty-eight people were arrested on the tennis courts and taken to the North Baltimore Police Station, a gothic brick structure not far away on Keswick Road in Hampden. They were immediately brought before Reuben Caplan, a magistrate and member of the city's Pollack political faction, dominant in northwest Baltimore. Police had charged them with unlawful assembly, violation of park rules (refusing to leave), and conspiracy to disturb the peace.

An otherwise decent and reasonable man, Caplan nevertheless found them guilty and sentenced them to an astonishing forty-five months in jail—suspended—$150 fines, and fourteen years on probation—a stark warning designed no doubt to fend off any further outbreaks of conscience. Caplan's sentencing reflected the political realities of the time. "It wasn't a law," Swann says. "It was policy—but no one spoke up. No one wanted to buck the system." Permits to play tennis were like the papers needed by South African blacks during apartheid because of the pass laws. You had to have a permit if you were black to pass onto the tennis courts of Baltimore.

Mitzi Swann hardly knew her black partners, and their acquaintance lasted less than an hour. "I never saw them again," she says. "They all went to Morgan. Our lives went different ways." It was still Baltimore. Her witness for equality, however brief, was a brave one. Later, she walked the picket line at Ford's Theater and served on the boards of directors at some neighborhood foundations.

The tennis match with city authorities exposed Baltimore's aggressive opposition to equal opportunity—a fierce and angry manning of the barricades. Opposition to Jim Crow lay tightly coiled and ready to strike anything that opposed it. The ferocity of feeling was breathtaking. It flared instantly, as if any breach in the wall of exclusion would lead to grievous loss—of what? A way of life, Taney would have said; not simply his beloved southern way, but a way of life based on exclusion and separateness, which conferred something intangible but profoundly important to those who had been brought up to worship and defend it with the religious conviction with which one defended family and personal honor. To challenge it set off sharp emotional responses.

Businessmen testifying against open accommodations laws in Baltimore said their businesses would be destroyed if they were forced to serve American blacks. So lunch counters, tennis courts, golf courses, and swimming pools became the first lines of defense against incursions that might reveal to whites (more than to blacks) that eating and playing would change almost nothing.[59] The restrictions were, after a while, laughable to many blacks. So what if I can't eat in your greasy spoon? I can live without it. But there was symbolism and principle: a matter of financial equity when it came to public amenities.

In theory the cases were simple, Houston had said: the state cannot tax the entire population for the exclusive benefit of a single class. Mencken weighed in with a column on November 9, 1948.

Has the Park Board any right in law to forbid white and black citizens, if they are so inclined, to join in harmless games together on public playgrounds? Again: Is such a prohibition, even supposing that it is lawful, supported by anything to be found in common sense and common decency? I do not undertake to answer the first

Maverick: Political and social reformer Judge Eugene O'Dunne said the University of Maryland School of Law could not lawfully bar Donald Gaines Murray simply because he was black. O'Dunne's ruling was seen later as an important step on the road to *Brown v. Board of Education of Topeka, KS.* Circa 1930. Courtesy of the Maryland State Archives, Special Collections (Baltimore City Circuit Court Art Collection). MSA SC 5590-4-70.

Youth Power: Juanita Jackson, later the wife of NAACP Washington lobbyist Clarence M. Mitchell Jr., helped found the City-Wide Young People's Forum, which here she addresses in about 1935. Students and young people often led their elders in the struggle for civil rights. Photo from a private collection.

Rehearsal: Thurgood Marshall (*left*) works on his presentation of the landmark Maryland law school case *Murray v. Pearson.* His client, Donald Gaines Murray, sits to Marshall's left, along with Marshall's co-counsel and mentor, Howard Law School dean Charles Hamilton Houston. Circa 1935. Courtesy of the Maryland State Archives, Special Collections (Maryland History Slide Collection). MSA SC 1260-129.

Crusader: Carl Murphy (*right*), editor and publisher of the *Afro-American,* used his newspaper—one of the most successful black businesses in the country—to urge fearful black readers to push for racial justice in many spheres. Here, Murphy meets with Jackie Robinson (*center*), the baseball player, and Sam Lacy (left), longtime *Afro-American* sportswriter who campaigned for black athletes. The portrait in the background is of Martha Howard Murphy, wife of *Afro* founder, John Murphy. From her own savings, she provided two hundred dollars to help get the paper started in 1892. *Baltimore Afro-American,* 1949. Courtesy of the AFRO-American Newspapers Archives and Research Center.

Student Leader: Morgan State student Clarence Logan, head of the Civic Interest Group, led students in sit-ins, campaigning for open accommodations in Maryland long before the more famous sit-ins began in the South. *From left:* George Mesologities, president of the Restaurant Association of Maryland; William Fulton, vice president of the association; the Rev. Logan Kearse, pastor of Cornerstone Baptist Church, and Logan. *Baltimore Sun,* November 21, 1961. Courtesy of the Baltimore Sun Company, Inc. All Rights Reserved.

Uncivil: The owner of a segregated Cambridge lunchroom, Robert Fahsenfeldt, douses a kneeling student protester, Edward Dickerson. Demonstrators in Cambridge were regularly assaulted and beaten as the demonstrations continued. *Baltimore News-American*, July 8, 1963. University of Maryland, Hornbake Library, Maryland Room, Box 130, Folder 28, Photograph 4. Courtesy Hearst Corporation, Inc.

Excuse Me: Cambridge Nonviolent Action leader Gloria Richardson brushes aside a Maryland National Guardsman's bayonet during the tense summer of 1963. Baltimore *News-American*, July 21, 1963. University of Maryland, Hornbake Library, Maryland Room, Box 130, Folder 27, Photograph 9. Courtesy Hearst Corporation, Inc.

Resistance: Hundreds of Morgan State College students went to jail after demonstrating to open the theater at Northwood Shopping Center in North Baltimore. The student arrests during an election season ended discriminatory practices at the theater and set the stage for other successes, principally at Gwynn Oak Amusement Park. *Baltimore Sun,* February 19, 1963. Courtesy of the Baltimore Sun Company, Inc. All Rights Reserved.

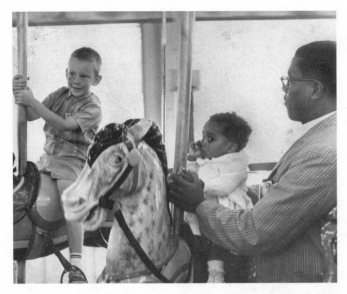

The Dream: Sharon Langley, age 11 months, with her father, Charles, riding the carousel at Gwynn Oak Park on the same day Martin Luther King Jr. made his "I Have a Dream" speech. She rides with a young white boy. King said he dreamed of a world in which black children would be judged by the content of their character, not by the color of their skin.

Before His Time: Theodore R. McKeldin, Baltimore mayor and then governor of Maryland, defined himself as a civil rights proponent long before many political leaders in his state or elsewhere in the nation. In the spring of 1967, he greeted Tyrone Yarborough during a tour of the Lafayette-Douglass housing project. *Baltimore Sun,* October 23, 1967.

Community Action: Mayor McKeldin swears in Parren J. Mitchell as director of Baltimore's antipoverty program. Mitchell was later elected to the U.S. Congress from Maryland's Seventh District. Profile in background is James Calhoun, first mayor of Baltimore (1794–1804), who owned eleven slaves according to his 1798 direct federal tax return. *Baltimore News-American,* September 19, 1967. University of Maryland, Hornbake Library, Maryland Room, Box 1316, Folder 16, Photograph 4. Courtesy Hearst Corporation, Inc.

Genius: Vivien Thomas, the black lab technician who invented complicated medical devices for the so-called blue baby operation and who perfected the actual operation; Levi Watkins Jr., Johns Hopkins University's first black cardiac resident; Reginald Davis, a Johns Hopkins University medical student, and his son. July 1979. Photograph courtesy of Dr. Levi Watkins Jr.

Jim Crow Golf: In the fall of 1964—with the support of boxing champion Joe Louis—black Baltimore businessmen sued to end one of the most blatant illustrations of life under Jim Crow, restricting black players to a nine- and later a fourteen-hole golf course. *From left:* Johnny Bass, Joe Louis, Vernon Terry, Clyde Martin, and Willie Adams. *Baltimore News-American,* September 8, 1964. University of Maryland, Hornbake Library, Maryland Room, Box 1022, Folder 28, Photograph 47. Courtesy Hearst Corporation, Inc.

Voice of Change: The NAACP's Lillie May Jackson in 1971, with pictures and plaques commemorating her resolute civil rights campaign; she once declared, "God opened my mouth and no man can shut it." *Baltimore News-American,* January 21, 1971. University of Maryland, Hornbake Library, Maryland Room, Box 1613, Folder 12, Photograph 12. Courtesy Hearst Corporation, Inc.

Another View: George L. Russell, Baltimore's first black city solicitor, thought Jim Crow was pernicious beyond its discriminatory evil, diverting the energies of leaders who might otherwise have contributed to the black community as doctors, lawyers, and businesspeople. Here he is shown with Mayor William Donald Schaefer. *Baltimore News-American,* October 19, 1971. University of Maryland, Hornbake Library, Maryland Room, Box 1451, Folder 7, Photograph 1. Courtesy Hearst Corporation, Inc.

Breakthrough: The Reverend Marion C. Bascom (*pointing*) became the first black member of the Baltimore Fire Board. Here he examines a firefighters' contract along with (*from the left*) Mayor Thomas J. D'Alesandro III, Edward J. Guttmann, and George L. Russell. *Baltimore Sun,* December 2, 1971. Courtesy of the Baltimore Sun Company, Inc. All Rights Reserved.

Another First: Judge Joseph Howard's study on sentencing disparities between blacks and whites convicted of the same crime embarrassed the bench and almost derailed his career. Instead, civil rights advocates helped him become a judge of the U.S. District Court. *Baltimore News-American,* August 19, 1973. University of Maryland, Hornbake Library, Maryland Room, Box 1451, Folder 5, Photograph 1. Courtesy Hearst Corporation, Inc.

Ballot Power: Larry S. Gibson, the black political strategist and University of Maryland School of Law professor, wore sharp, lawyerly business suits, but people remembered him attired in militant-seeming dashikis. Here he consults with Kurt L. Schmoke, the first elected black mayor of Baltimore. July 1986. Courtesy of the Schmoke for Mayor campaign.

Walter Sondheim Jr.: He engineered immediate compliance with *Brown v. Board of Education*. Much of the rest of the state and nation resisted. *Baltimore Sun,* May 13, 1954. Courtesy of the Baltimore Sun Company, Inc. All Rights Reserved.

Profile of Justice: Thurgood Marshall, standing near the sculpture by Balti-
more's Reuben Kramer, harbored bitter memories of his early years in Baltimore.
Later, the University of Maryland law school library was named for him, as was
Baltimore Washington International Airport. *Baltimore Sun*, May 17, 1980.
Courtesy of the Baltimore Sun Company, Inc. All Rights Reserved.

Lion: After covering the aftermath of a lynching on the Eastern Shore, Clarence M. Mitchell Jr., the NAACP's chief lobbyist in Washington, presided over passage of landmark public accommodations and voting rights cases. President Lyndon B. Johnson called him the "101st senator." *Baltimore News-American,* August 15, 1983. University of Maryland, Hornbake Library, Maryland Room, Box 305, Folder 1, Photograph 1. Courtesy Hearst Corporation, Inc.

The Man to See: Once a bicycle repairman and illegal numbers operator, William L. "Little Willie" Adams gave money to the NAACP, made loans to schoolteachers so that they could buy houses, and supported black entrepreneurs who were unable to get credit at white banks. *Left to right:* former mayor Clarence H. "Du" Burns, Marie Henderson, Victorine Adams, and Willie Adams. *Baltimore Sun,* June 6, 1997. Courtesy of the Baltimore Sun Company, Inc. All Rights Reserved.

Chet the Jet: The Reverend Chester Wickwire, chaplain at the Johns Hopkins University and an official of the YMCA in Baltimore, got his nickname from students who saw him relentlessly challenging discrimination at the university and in Baltimore. Here, in 1998, he returns to Gwynn Oak Park, where thirty-five years before he helped end a whites-only admission policy. *Baltimore Sun,* July 30, 1998. Courtesy of the Baltimore Sun Company, Inc. All Rights Reserved.

RIP, finally: William O. Lee Jr., educator and former Frederick alderman, speaks during the dedication of the city's Laboring Sons Memorial Ground. Once a black cemetery, it had been bulldozed to make a whites-only playground in 1949. The city neglected to record all the names of the deceased. *Baltimore Sun,* January 15, 2003. Courtesy of the Baltimore Sun Company, Inc. All Rights Reserved.

question, for I am too ignorant of law, but my answer to the second is a loud and unequivocal No. A free citizen in a free state, it seems to me, has an inalienable right to play with whomsoever he will, so long as he does not disturb the general peace.

If any other citizen, offended by the spectacle, makes a pother, then that other citizen, and not the man exercising his inalienable right, should be put down by the police. Certainly it is astounding to find so much of the spirit of the Georgia Cracker surviving in the Maryland Free State, and under official auspices. The public parks are supported by the taxpayer, including the colored taxpayer, for the health and pleasure of the whole people. Why should cops be sent into them to separate those people against their will into separate herds? Why should the law set up distinctions and discriminations which the persons directly affected themselves reject?

It is high time that all such relics of Ku Kluxry be wiped out in Maryland. The position of the colored people, since the political revolution of 1895, has been gradually improving in the State, and it has already reached a point surpassed by few other states. But there is still plenty of room for further advances, and it is irritating indeed to see one of them blocked by silly Dogberrys. The Park Board rule is irrational and nefarious. It should be got rid of forthwith.

In answer to all the foregoing, I expect confidently to hear the argument that the late mixed tennis matches were not on the level but were arranged by Communists to make trouble. So far as I am aware this may be true but it seems to me to be irrelevant. What gave the Communists their chance was the existence of the Park Board's rule. If it had carried on its business with more sense, they would have been baffled. The way to dispose of their chicaneries is not to fight them when they are right.[60]

This turned out to be Mencken's last newspaper column. It seems to have been an accurate reflection of his growing desire to see the discriminatory practices end. Some department store customers were canceling their accounts, and the stores began to see some erosion of their profits. The old Pennsylvania Avenue picketing dynamic was working. And while segregated tennis—or golf or baseball or swimming—was less important than discrimination practiced in employment or housing or hotels, equal opportunity in sports was symbolically powerful. Black taxpayers were asserting their entitlements. They had paid for the courts and the pools and the golf courses, but they were barred from using them. Whites were literally fearful of having to share amenities with black people. Challenging these exclusionary practices was a way of forcing the majority community to face the coming change and ultimately to see how silly it was.

Emboldened by their mounting victories, Jackson and various groups—led increasingly by students—accelerated their campaigns. Jackson called frequently on Walter Sondheim Jr., then an officer at Hochschild's. "Mrs. Jackson, she was tough. I knew her quite well. She would come in and really give me hell." Often, as it turned out, the more sympathetic white citizens, those who wanted the policy changed, got most of Jackson's outrage because they were willing to see her.

She asserted that Jewish store owners in particular were guilty of discrimination. Until then, her campaign had been supported by men like Sidney Hollander, the successful businessman who had made civil rights his life work. Leon Sachs, the labor negotiator and longtime head of the Baltimore Jewish Council, clashed with Jackson, too. Both took umbrage at her remarks. Her daughter Juanita once told Sachs, "We're more critical of Jewish owners because we expect more of them." Sachs feared another explanation: one downtrodden and vilified group was turning on another in a perverse bit of minority scapegoating.[61]

The effort to win shopping equality was reinforced—taken over eventually—by CORE and the Civic Interest Group (CIG), an organization largely comprising Morgan State College students. Some Johns Hopkins University students were involved as well, and various others volunteered for the citywide assault on whites-only restaurants. Larry Gibson, then a student at Howard University in Washington, was one of these leaders.

Teams of students would be assigned their targets. They would expect to be arrested for violating the trespass laws, but they would try to avoid the police until they had hit every restaurant on their list. Gibson recalls an evening when he and his team moved past other diners at the Oriole Cafeteria on York Road in Baltimore. He remembers the ad hoc menu, the dishes he happened to choose from the steam tables: baked fish and a carrot and raisin salad. "I remember because fish in my house was fried. And I'd never had that salad. I think there's a name for it, but I've always thought of it as my sit-in-salad."[62]

Then a surprise. The students were not asked to leave. The police did not arrive. Instead, cashiers began ringing up the purchases. The students, not expecting to be served, had little money. "We pieced together enough to pay," Gibson says.

Here was the appearance of victory, but in short order, the restaurant was resegregated, a typical dodge in those years. The campaigns would begin anew and run on for months. Efforts to open theaters and restaurants, drugstore soda fountains and the like, typically took years.

In April 1960, years after negotiations had begun—after Jackson's many meetings with Walter Sondheim and others—the Jim Crow barrier fell unexpectedly one day for a group of Morgan students who arrived for a sit-in. Usually, a mannered dance would ensue: the students would be polite and quiet. The stores would allow them to sit but would not serve them. A few of the restaurants would close when the students appeared.

They were, therefore, stunned when without notice, Hochschild-Kohn invited them in and took their orders. The shock included a by-now-familiar question: who was going to pay the bill? Once again, no one in the group had enough money for a tuna fish sandwich. There are differing stories about how the bill was covered. Mildred Atkinson, one of the adult advisers, provided some of the money. And a frantic message went to Sidney Hollander, who, according to his son, sent money via his driver.

The other downtown stores quickly followed suit. The more famous Greensboro, North Carolina, lunch counter sit-ins began at about the same time and drew more attention, perhaps because they were in the South and therefore more daring. The Baltimore crusade drew considerable praise for the students and demonstrated, once again, how long it took for change to come. In the official announcement of their changed policy, the stores' managers said, "Oh, well, we were just about to act on our own."

The importance of the victory may not have been fully appreciated outside the black community and may seem almost inconsequential in retrospect. But it had great resonance for Reverend Dobson and others who remembered their mothers fighting a fight deemed too dangerous for men. Men did get involved, of course, and some of them were white.

One of these was Peter Angelos, later principal owner of the Baltimore Orioles, a lawyer, and a young member of the Baltimore City Council. One of his colleagues on the council was Walter Dixon, a black man from northwest Baltimore. Angelos would go out occasionally to buy lunch for himself and for Dixon and bring it back to the council chambers since they couldn't sit with each other in any downtown restaurant.

"I used to go to Horn and Horn to pick up carry-out. I used to say to Walter. 'What would you like me to bring back?' He'd tell me what he wanted. Then he'd say, 'Wouldn't it be nice if I could walk down there with you? Then you wouldn't have to bring it to me.' He said that, and it was likely suddenly right there on the spot when I said, 'I'm going to do that open accommodations ordinance, and I'm going to put that in.'

"We couldn't get it through completely, and Henry Parks picked it up but got it improved again. All those bars on Belair Road in my district, they were blowing their minds. They were going crazy. You traitor, you son of a bitch. We got no help from [Mayor Harold] Grady. He was sort of for it, but we had to do it in the council. The Jewish guys were for it. The problem was in my district. We got no one from the Sixth or First District. Clem Prucha was with me because the district was getting blacker. Don Schaefer [later mayor, governor, and comptroller] was for it, and he came from a very white district, very much like the Third, and very apprehensive about that thing. But he was always very politically astute."[63]

In that same period, Henry Parks, the black councilman and business partner of Willie Adams, introduced an open accommodations bill year after year. Each time, the bill was amended to take away much of its value. It passed at one point because restaurants that made more than half their money selling beer and other alcoholic beverages were not required to serve blacks. The rationale—beyond holding back change—was difficult to discern. It was another contortion reminiscent of other open accommodations half measures: in some theaters, performers could be black, but blacks could not sit in the audience. In others, blacks could be in the audience but not in the performance. It would take a state law in 1964, ten years after *Brown v. Board of Education,* to open Baltimore restaurants.

GEORGE RUSSELL: THE ENDURANCE OF JIM CROW

When George Russell graduated from the University Maryland School of Law in 1954, eighteen years after it was integrated, Jim Crow was waiting for him. He was denied a seat in one of the state's private bar review courses, the refresher almost every law school graduate wants to take before the bar exam.

"No problem with you," the course manager told Russell, "but if you're in the class, white students won't enroll." The same argument had been used sixty-three years earlier to justify closing the state's law school to black students in 1891: white students would be drawn to a school that did not admit blacks. But the review course owner may have misread the mood of the changing times. At least one of the 1954 graduates was offended and angry.

"I didn't like people telling me what I thought," says James J. Doyle, president of the law school's class of 1954 and, later, the dean of lobbyists in Annapolis, a man whose conduct in the hurly-burly of lobbying reflected the principles he expressed in 1954.[64] Doyle wanted to make what would have amounted to a federal case of Russell's circumstance. He took the matter to the other graduates.

"George had been our classmate for three years, I said. I thought, 'Who was going to refuse to be in a law review course because he was in it?' I didn't think we should step away from him. It was wrong," Doyle said fifty years later.[65] Doyle was older than many of the students, having served in World War II before enrolling. Many veterans, black and white, came home with new eyes for their society.

But George Russell said no. He did not want the controversy. He worried that a big protest would make practicing law in the racially divided city even more difficult for a black lawyer. He'd be labeled a troublemaker, a malcontent, a radical. Things weren't changing that fast.

It was 1954, the Korean War was winding down, and Russell's name was on the draft list. A member of the local draft board, whose son was in the army, had warned Russell that he was going to Korea, lawyer or not, as soon as he was out of school. "When you drop the pen, you'll be in the army," she said.[66] Was it because he was black that this woman resented Russell's temporary exemption from the draft? He couldn't be sure, but he wanted to stay focused on the real task for him: passing the bar exam. He figured any demonstration on his behalf would be a distraction. He would face persistent criticism over the years for deciding against a dramatic, public protest.

He chose to follow a less confrontational path throughout his life, a choice that brought him many successes—and bitter criticism. Why hadn't he protested this gross discrimination? Why hadn't he been part of the many legal battles against lingering discrimination in Baltimore and Maryland? The system of discrimination needed to be fought on many fronts, and George Russell would fight, but he would fight his way.

Within days after he took the bar examination, Russell was on his way to Camp Gordon, Georgia. All the way, he thought about how his future was being decided back in Baltimore. If he hadn't passed, all his studying would have been wasted, lost entirely, because by the end of his two-year tour, he'd have forgotten much of what he had learned. Several weeks after he arrived at the camp, Russell's mother wrote to tell him he'd passed.

But he was still not home free. In those days, he and others believed, there was a final obstacle, an unofficial quota: no more than two blacks a year were admitted to the Maryland bar. In time, once again, Russell learned he had been admitted. He had made it on his own, by his own rules, without causing any disruption.

He had wanted to be a lawyer from the third grade onward. At Public School 103, on Division Street between Lanvale and Lafayette in Upton, students were required to state their ambition. What did they want to be when they grew up? The teacher, Victorine Adams—wife of Little Willie Adams and later a member of the Baltimore City Council—demanded an answer. One of Russell's classmates listed "bartender" as his dream and was almost thrown out of the building.

Adams and her colleagues were strict disciplinarians. One day Russell pretended not to hear an instruction from one of the administrators, Ada Watts. She called his parents. "I had to take two years of lipreading as a result, to make certain I never missed an instruction again."[67] He had no excuse: if in fact he didn't hear, he would be expected to read lips. This story—Russell had many—was a way of explaining how strict the elders were in those days.

Russell went on to Frederick Douglass High School and then to Lincoln University, the college years paid for by Maryland's out-of-state scholarship fund for black students. That program helped him, but he thinks it contributed to a decline in the quality of black education in the state. Many outward bound black students were, by definition, the best black students in the state. They were educated elsewhere, and many did not return, resulting in a state-sponsored brain drain that diminished the community, black and white.

Russell graduated shortly before the U.S. Supreme Court struck down the separate but equal ruling of *Plessy v. Ferguson*. This monumental victory, enshrined as *Brown v. Board of Education of Topeka, KS,* had its roots in the school where he studied. But, as Houston had warned in 1935, decisions in a court do not necessarily signal progress or change in the society. How well George Russell understood.

Many of Russell's friends and law partners—Robert B. Watts, among others—were front-line warriors in the legal battles that had to be waged. Bob Watts was an NAACP lawyer, one of the successors to Thurgood Marshall. Watts traveled the state for Lillie May Jackson, urging local school boards to follow the dictates of *Brown*. Russell meanwhile worked hard at building a law practice, a goal he thought was erroneously relegated to second rank behind fighting Jim Crow. His was not a popular position in the black community.

He thought Jim Crow was white reactionary genius, a way of suffocating talent and draining off energy, reaching beyond its devisers' original intentions. It was not just the patchwork of laws and customs thrown up to deflect and defer black progress. Talent that might have developed in the professions was diverted to fight unjust law and custom. There were so many battles, all the creative and entrepreneurial energy of the best black achievers would be shattered against the barriers of discrimination.

Education was the way to enter the mainstream, he thought, and that education needed to be used for economic progress one person at a time. He understood very well that barriers in the law and custom needed to come down, but he was not convinced that many of those people he regarded as self-serving civil rights warriors stayed involved in anything but the professionalization of the effort. He thought, upon occasion, that freedom fighters would be unhappy if freedom ever came. They depended on discrimination for their status and livelihood. That attitude did not endear him to those who toiled on the streets or in the courts for equal rights. His detractors found discrimination in everything.

In the 1960s, Russell wrote an essay laying out his views and sent it to one of the most sympathetic editorial writers at the *Sun,* Edgar Jones. He says Jones told him it was too negative and pessimistic. Beyond that, the newspaper had only recently been persuaded that its own attitudes on race needed to change radically, that it needed to focus on its role in the perpetuation of Jim Crow's life.

Russell's essay would have been confusing, no doubt, since it contained criticism of those who were fighting what looked like the good fight. With institutions like the *Sun* not fully converted to the civil rights point of view, criticizing those who were so committed might have baffled some. But, agree or not, the point should have been considered. The fight against Jim Crow, Russell argued, could never end. Whatever anyone does to fight it will reduce the personal or group effort to succeed at the business of life. The fights, however necessary, reinforced differences. And every win or loss demanded another corrective action. Russell concluded that racial separation was pretty much a done deal. Blacks had to accept a split society. The twoness of America posited by W. E. B. Du Bois was institutionalized.

"Until we put race aside and pursue excellence we're not going to win," Russell wrote. It was not an argument for giving in. It was an argument for recognizing reality, for insisting on change but not imagining the system could be defeated. His approach was to develop and prosper on his own, penetrating the white preserves when possible and convenient, but not counting on that or making it the ultimate prize. All this is not to say that Russell made no sacrifice for black progress. Shortly after moving to a downtown office with his partners, Joseph Allen and Bob Watts, he was offered a judgeship, the first for an African American in Maryland. He accepted—at some personal cost.

He'd gotten space in a prime new building downtown, breaking through a practice of withholding office space from black lawyers. Nothing personal, of course. Just the way things were. In this case, the owner had no choice because the building had gone up with federal funds, and therefore discrimination was against the law. Russell was on his way. His firm was flourishing. He and his partners had many cases. They were into all-white domains of many kinds. He became one of the first black members of the Center Club, an elegant new businessmen's meeting place, one of the first in Baltimore to be open to blacks and Jews.

William Boucher, then head of the city's major business development organization, said the new club was unencumbered by racist membership rules because one of the development project's financial backers, the fabulously successful real estate magnate Joseph Meyerhoff, would not agree to help unless the club was opened to blacks and Jews. Russell says Joe Meyerhoff was a benefactor and an ally in things like redevelopment of Provident Hospital, a black hospital in West Baltimore. But there were limits. Russell asked Meyerhoff if he would sign Russell's application for membership. Apparently not wishing to have anything supporting black aspirations on the public record, Meyerhoff said, "No, but I'll vote for you." People were willing to say things privately, but they were reluctant to have their names attached publicly to the movement of individual black people into white society.

Meyerhoff was not alone in his caution. The club's first president, Clarence B. Miles, warily set aside the objective of an integrated club until he was sure he had enough members to make it financially viable.[68] Russell got William Boucher, executive director of the Greater Baltimore Committee, to sign the application.

Then, in 1966, Russell was appointed to the circuit court by Governor J. Millard Tawes. A group of Catholics protested. They urged Tawes to remember that he had promised to name a Catholic to the bench. "George is a Catholic," Tawes said. "Well, we didn't mean that kind," they said. "Oh," Tawes said, "I didn't know you had two kinds."[69]

Catholics in Maryland had otherwise demonstrated courageous leadership on matters of race. There was an unhappy history of slaveholding among the state's church leaders, but in 1908, when various efforts were made to disenfranchise blacks, James Cardinal Gibbons offered one of the most astringently pro-freedom declarations of that time: "I do not believe the Negro should be disfranchised solely on the ground of his color." Various qualifications—property ownership and education—might be permissible, he said, but only if applied fairly. If the black man were a menace to democracy, he said, "educate him; if he be corrupt and venal, punish him for his corrupt practices and his venality; but above all things, let us not condemn the righteous for the sins of the unrighteous."[70]

Russell saw life in Baltimore through many lenses. He was one of eight children. His grandfather was a Piscataway Indian, the tribe that was concentrated in southern Maryland. His mother and his aunt Rebecca worked for the Finney family, long associated with the Gilman School. His mother cooked for them. They took exceptionally good care of the Russells. When his aunt died, she had an estate of $875,000, a sum built over the years with the expertise of Finney advisers. Russell was appointed executor of the estate, affording him a fee much appreciated by a young lawyer. In one of Russell's first cases as a circuit court judge years later, William H. M. Finney, a noted brain surgeon at Johns Hopkins Hospital, appeared in his court as an expert witness. Judge and witness came together as family. "Tears came down, and we had to recess the court," Russell recalled. Later, Finney and ten other Hopkins physicians volunteered to work at Provident Hospital. They worked there at Russell's request during a strike. The black patients and the white doctors found the exchange both gratifying and eye opening.

Russell's personal connections made this possible, but he had an increasingly bankable stature in the white community. For black lawyers, his judgeship was far more important than many may have realized. He was able to make certain that they were among the lawyers appointed routinely by the court to represent indigent defendants, which was not something black practitioners could rely on when the bench was all white. Russell's viewpoint was now important in the judicial policy making, in councils of the bar, and in the general thinking about criminal justice. He had become an expert on search and seizure as a lawyer—an important skill for practitioners in a city where the courts were overwhelmed with drug cases and where the police were always needing new lessons in constitutionally acceptable procedure. His ability in this sphere attracted national attention and acclaim.

Lawyers competing with Russell and others would occasionally suggest that they were better able to defend black defendants in a white system. That claim was undercut as more black judges were named over time. Russell's skill and professionalism were always necessary, as he knew they would be even after getting the judgeship. He worried that his race would make him a target for the least indiscretion. Once, when he released a prisoner in keeping with U.S. Supreme Court rulings, the city bar challenged the propriety of his action. William L. Marbury Jr., one of the city's most prominent lawyers, came to his defense: "George Russell has been willing to stick his neck out and risk the censure of his own race for statements which he has been making, all of which are designed to establish the fact that the law protects the poor as well as the rich and the Negro as well as the white."[71] The suggestion that Russell should be censured quickly evaporated.

Notwithstanding this success and many others, Russell left the bench at Mayor Thomas D'Alesandro's urging to become city solicitor in 1967. He was thus a member of the city's board of estimates, one of five men and women who did all the important city business: he became one of the city fathers, officially. No black man or woman had held a post of similar rank in city history. One of the lawyers he would now supervise was Charles LeViness, the assistant state attorney general who had argued against admission of Donald Gaines Murray to the law school. Russell did not think LeViness was sympathetic to the aspirations of blacks, but, Russell said, "He was my friend." Nor was this the only such ironic twist in the black-white history of Baltimore. Thurgood Marshall says LeViness had hired Donald Gaines Murray as an assistant attorney general.

At one point, Russell thought he could succeed as a politician. He decided to run for mayor against then-councilman William Donald Schaefer in 1971—shortly after the riots of the 1960s and the insistent demands of black activists for access to public office. Many Baltimore businesspeople seemed ready to endorse Russell. Lumberman Louis I. Grasmick was one of the first. It was time for Baltimore to have a black mayor, Grasmick and others thought, time to do something to ease tensions. Russell was ready, but he might not have been right for politics.

"I was a bad candidate," Russell says. He reacted to some of the shenanigans too personally. Clarence M. Mitchell III, a son of the NAACP lobbyist, entered the race at the urging of political forces who wanted to dilute the black vote. "When they put Clarence in the race, I should have ignored him," Russell said. Hyman Pressman, the crafty comptroller whose doggerel for every occasion entertained many—and annoyed many others—went after Russell with borderline rhetoric. He called Russell a peacock, a reference to Russell's reputation for dressing well. This was code: good suits were a sign of a black person getting ahead of himself, beyond his place. Russell responded in kind: some people, he said, couldn't abide the sight of a black person in a city car that wasn't headed for jail.[72]

Willie Adams said later that he thought Russell had made a mistake: "George is one of our best lawyers, one of the best brains we had, and I didn't ever think he was cut out politically to run for office."[73] Adams was also an ally of the 1960s and 1970s political kingmaker Irvin Kovens, who supported Schaefer—who won easily and proceeded to have a spectacular career. "The best thing for George is that he lost. He's a millionaire now. He was a lot better lawyer than I was. The best thing for Baltimore is that I won," Schaefer said.[74] A year or so later, Russell ran again against another Mitchell—Parren—and lost again. He would concede it had been a race to get even with the Mitchells. Schaefer kept Russell as city solicitor and would always think of him as a friend.

Russell says black Americans had to rely on the largesse of people like Willie Adams, who found ways to succeed—in his case, running numbers and then anonymously supporting hundreds of small projects. Or they were helped secretly by fraternal organizations, groups like the Laboring Sons in Frederick but sometimes significantly more influential. One of the most august of these was the Boulé, a group spawned by the Niagara Movement and W. E. B. Du Bois's idea of the black talented tenth. Doctors, lawyers, educators, and others were chosen to sit in these secret councils. They were benefactors. They were anonymous in part to preserve their ability to discuss and deliberate and to act in ways that could not be restricted by forces inside or outside the black community.

Just as Frederick Douglass and Thurgood Marshall thought change had to be rooted in law—and feared a backlash from whites angered by the civil rights movement—Russell put great stock in the power that would grow from a cadre of successful black men and women in the professions. He did not relent in his views. He affiliated with a number of important firms, and he became, among other things, a member and then chairman of the Federal Reserve Board. At the same time, he knew that Jim Crow still tormented Baltimore's black community.

In his 70s, he became the shepherd of an ambitious project, a museum of African American history. At the lower end of Pennsylvania Avenue, Baltimore's richly textured black history echoes through a fake marquee—something like the Royal Theater, represented by a few columns opening onto a vacant lot. The feeble effort is rescued partially by a fine statue of Billie Holiday, the blues and torch singer, but her bronze likeness is an unhappy reminder of the inner city's continuing battle with drug addiction and drug-related violence. Holiday, in her classic head-thrown-back singing pose, illustrates this poor community's trajectory—down and down since the King assassination riots of 1968.

A better sense of the avenue's past, its vibrant strength and panache, comes from the Baltimore club singer Ruby Glover, who gives occasional tours of the avenue, hailing the past and lamenting the present. "Drugs ravaged a weakened community," she says. How different it might have been without heroin and crack, drugs that sap the community the way they sapped Billie Holiday. Glover used to sing on the avenue, too, at places like Buck's, the Comedy Club, Tijuana, and the Club Casino, Willie Adams's old place. Most of them were torched in the King riots of 1968.

Some of the Chitlin Circuit entertainers would swing by Frederick's Pythian Castle, an entertainment venue available to blacks in the city. Bill Lee wouldn't always wait for those performances, driving to Baltimore when groups he liked were playing on Pennsylvania Avenue. He remembers seeing the Sweethearts of Rhythm, an all girls band. He caught other headliners who performed for a night or two at the Royal and then headed on to New York.[75]

The vibrancy of that era died, though, with the riots. There was barely an echo of the Avenue at its peak. Only faint traces of the glory years remained. Years later, after the King assassination disturbances have ravaged Pennsylvania Avenue, Glover stops by the Holiday statue to pick up the trash. "Someone should cut the grass," she says. She salutes whatever anonymous admirer left a floral tribute to Holiday, faded but touching. Then she speaks softly to the weathered image as if meeting an old friend. As a young girl, she had visited Holiday backstage at the Royal and had seen her from time to time in other clubs as drugs and alcohol ravaged Holiday's body.

Glover is joined one summer afternoon by three neighborhood children: Nattie Gunther, who at 12 is about the same age as Ruby Glover had been when she met Lady Day. With Nattie are Styriane Talent, 11, and Styriane's brother, William Donald Talent, 10, who gives his entire name just as his namesake, former Baltimore mayor William Donald Schaefer, has always done.

Do they know who Billie Holiday was? Glover asks.

"Yes," says Nattie. "She was a wonderful black person who made a difference in history by singing and making the way for other black singers. She sang jazz and the blues, slow songs."

Nattie learned this and more from Miss Moore, her teacher at Furman L. Templeton Elementary, a school just down the street named for where the late Baltimore Urban League president had lived.

"Do you sing?" Glover asks Nattie.

"In the shower and at school," she says.

"You've got beautiful dimples," Glover says.

"I know," says Nattie.

"I want to go to Harvard," Nattie says without being asked. "Probably law school. You have to argue with people, and I'm very good at that. I'm always right."[76]

Nattie Gunther seems unfazed by the turmoil that grips her community, the murders, the generational addiction and poverty. She faces life with the optimism of a young girl thrilled by the world she sees in school through her own bright eyes and the eyes of her teachers. She looks beyond the tattered streets, the ponderous public housing. She and her friends are the energy, the heart, and the potential of these windblown urban plains.

And there are those, like Russell, who want to help.

Just as Lillie May Jackson hoped to rescue an earlier generation from Jim Crow, George Russell and his partner, Louis Grasmick, hope they can intervene for Nattie, Styriane, and William Donald. They know it is possible because they know Ruby Glover and Pete Rawlings—and Richard McKinney, who made it out of privation and prejudice ninety years ago. The retired Morgan State University professor was nearing his 100th birthday that summer day when Ruby Glover and a writer met Nattie Gunther on Pennsylvania Avenue. McKinney remembered his history, the years when "we were still catching hell," when black travelers had to drive "straight through," when they were never sure they could find a place to eat, use the bathroom, or spend the night.

Richard McKinney and the NAACP were born in the first decade of the twentieth century. The NAACP built an organization to make life better, just as he and George Russell and others hope to make it better for Nattie Gunther. Past and present, united in hope, coming together. McKinney was born in Georgia, during the worst days of Jim Crow segregation, North and South. But he never forgot the injunction of a college choir director at Morehouse College in Atlanta. At the start of a singing tour, the director cautioned his idealistic young charges: "Don't try to solve the race problem in a single trip."[77]

He complied, but he remained determined, and his determination led to opportunity. McKinney got a scholarship to the Yale Divinity School—by having the nerve to ask for it and the ability to use it— during a summer camp run by a man from Yale. Later, he became president of the small Storer College near Harpers Ferry, West Virginia, the "holy ground" of John Brown's brave but doomed raid. Frederick Douglass had been a Storer College trustee. The NAACP's founding fathers, the Niagara Movement, had held their second meeting on the campus. Holy ground indeed.

In Baltimore, where McKinney came later to teach philosophy at Morgan State College, he wrote a citation commemorating Martin Luther King's visit there in 1964. He applauded King and the movement. But he didn't hesitate to arm himself against black revolutionaries of the 1960s who resented his achievements, saw him as an enemy of his people, and threatened to burn down his house. He borrowed his son's pistol just in case. In time he was taken into the Boulé.

In his 98th year, having given up driving only months before, he made his way almost every day to Pratt Street near Baltimore's Inner Harbor, where he watched an imposing building take shape in the midst of what had been a harsh and alien environment: the Reginald F. Lewis Museum of Maryland African American Culture and History, named for an East Baltimore–born man with a dream like Nattie Gunther's. Lewis had become CEO of a major multinational corporation.

McKinney was on the museum's board of directors as well as being its unofficial clerk of the works. Like Clarence Mitchell, who could not have attended the segregated University of Maryland and who lived to become a member of the university system's board of regents, Richard McKinney would preside over a tribute to Marylanders who started their lives in the Free State as slaves.[78]

Recognition had come, though not in a single day.

CHAPTER 4

Roadblocks and Resistance

I t was 1:20 p.m. The wire services proclaimed the news to the nation . . . In the United States, school children could no longer be segregated by race . . . Jim Crow was on his way to the burial ground."[1] The forecast of Justice John Marshall Harlan in the 1896 case of *Plessy v. Ferguson* had been validated and the decision reversed—after more than fifty years. The burden laid on black Americans by the nation's high court had been, as a matter of law, lifted at last. Or so it seemed.

Almost two decades after Judge Eugene O'Dunne ordered a black student into the University of Maryland School of Law, striking an early blow at separate but equal, the Supreme Court caught up. A long struggle, with roots deep in Maryland, had been won by a team of lawyers led by a Baltimorean, Thurgood Marshall. Many thought the high court ruling flowed inexorably from the Maryland victory won by Houston and Marshall in 1935. The establishment of a second-class citizenry—rooted in slavery, essentially sanctioned by Roger B. Taney in *Dred Scott,* and reinforced by Jim Crow—had been reversed. The Court's opinion addressed the profound damage done by state-supported discrimination against black children. "To separate them from others of similar age and qualification solely because of their race generates a feeling of inferiority as to their status in the community that may affect their hearts and minds in a way unlikely ever to be undone," the Court held.[2]

This judgment had far broader application, directing the entire society toward openness and equal justice. No wonder there was celebration.

Clarence Mitchell's son Michael remembers that day, May 17, 1954, a day of joy—yet a day leavened by the decision's consequences in the real world. Church bells rang along Druid Hill Avenue, but Michael Mitchell remembers an ironic chore falling immediately to his father: an architect of the grueling landmark victory, the NAACP's chief lobbyist, Clarence M. Mitchell Jr., had to convince black teachers and black parents in his home city to accept the decision that would be, many expected, the most liberating decision in the history of American jurisprudence.

The feverish back-home lobbying demand grew out of the disjointed progress made over that same nineteen years since Judge O'Dunne's ruling in Baltimore. Black school teachers and administrators were reluctant to embrace the uncertainties and dislocations that people knew would come somewhat perversely with the new freedom. A great victory in Washington was a problem in Baltimore—not just for whites fearful of integration but for blacks fearing immediate career setbacks.

Black administrators who had labored in the old segregated system, men and women who had moved up, were suddenly going to be thrown in to compete for their jobs with whites. Black educators might have to give up hard-won salaries and status. Black parents might have to send their children into the teeth of angry crowds to be taught by hostile white teachers. Blacks, in other words, would bear the brunt of the new day, however glorious and essential it was in the annals of history and law. *Brown v. Board of Education* would impose more sacrifice on those it would free from the constraints of Jim Crow. Beyond that, the value of education administered to black kids by black teachers was undermined by the tolling bell of freedom.

In spite of these worries, what mattered most to many was the breakthrough and the possibility that black children would go to school in better buildings, with better equipment. Separate but equal was branded a hoax by the nation's highest court. In Frederick, says Bill Lee, NAACP leaders like U. S. Bourne, a pioneering black physician, and Donald Bayton (father of Lee's wife, Cynthia) were urging compliance with Brown. "I can remember when Mr. Donald was president of the Lincoln School PTA. He was promoting integration of schools, emphasizing that we ought to be going to the other schools. Our schools were inferior. He was not afraid. He was a strong man. He was ready to fight for it. His daughter [Bill's wife] was the same way."[3]

Nevertheless, there was a price to be paid. Professor Alvin Thornton, a Howard University educator who in the 1990s headed a commission on public education funding in Maryland, recalled his arrival in Prince

George's County. He had moved north from Alabama, where he'd attended the Randolph County Training School. That southern, black-run school "produced better students than we have today. There was Du Boisian scholarship and Booker Washington type teachers, a rich combination. I wish some aspect of that could come back."[4] There was in this wish a certain nostalgia voiced by many in the years after *Brown*. It was a reflection of the toll taken by Jim Crow.

Against the broad civil rights implications of *Brown*, black teachers became expendable. Community-oriented, personal concern for black students got lost in the merger of black and white people and institutions. Moreover, as the *Brown* cases (there were five of them) made their way to the Supreme Court, American society had actually been changing, if only in isolated cases involving individual black students. This progress, too, was being made by courageous black families.[5] Ken Montague, who would have an exemplary political career, and his father integrated Loyola High School, one of Baltimore's most prestigious preparatory academies. Montague's family lived in a relatively remote corner of Howard County; Ken's father, the son of a bricklayer, thought his son could handle the challenge. Young Montague would, for the next few years, commute several hours a day, walking three miles to a bus stop before riding into the city. On at least one occasion, he missed his bus home and walked the entire distance—twenty miles or so—while his parents fretted about what might have happened to him.

Loyola was located then next door to St. Ignatius Church on Calvert Street, just up the street from the *Baltimore Sun*. (The school later moved to the more sylvan climes of lower Towson.) Dave Kennedy, the admissions director, got Montague's application.

"He panicked," says Ralph Moore, one of Montague's black classmates. Moore and Montague recall the seismic tremors loosed by Montague's application.

"Oh my god, there's a colored boy who's applied," Kennedy said, according to a widely repeated rendition of his reaction. With an important difference, the reaction was not unlike the one at the University of Maryland School of Law eighteen years earlier, when Registrar Hillegeist opened an application from a black student. The difference was that Loyola was not run by Curley Byrd—and not committed to barring blacks. It was not 1935.

"What should I do?" Kennedy asked the headmaster, Tony Zeits.

"Process it," said Zeits.

Montague had also applied to Mount St. Joseph and Calvert Hall. Moore says the word was that you didn't apply to Calvert Hall. "They didn't deal with blacks until they discovered basketball," he says.

Montague passed the Loyola admissions test.

"Oh my god, he passed," the registrar said. "What should I do?"

"Ad-mit him," said Zeits. The questions were being asked for the usual reasons, but also because Loyola had gotten a $1 million gift from the Blake family with a no-black-students stipulation.

"Who's going to tell Mrs. Blake?"

"You are," said Zeits.

In time there was a meeting with Mrs. Blake, and someone offhand-edly said, "Oh, by the way, we admitted a colored boy." And Mrs. Blake said, "I thought you'd tell me that some day." Here again was the difference between fear of change and change itself. The world did not come to an end. People could adjust and, often, to their distinct advantage. Mrs. Blake made no protest.

And yet it was a big deal. Ralph Moore, a social activist later, remembers his own first days at the school. "Everybody stood up and said what their parents did. My father's a lawyer. My father's an insurance man. My friend Eric said, 'my father's an undertaker.' I said, 'My father's a maintenance man.' " So much conflict in the heart of a young man, faced on the one hand with the exalted professions of his classmates' fathers and the humble work done by his dad. Nor did the confusion and embarrassment end with that. "They wanted to know what we did that summer. My family had taken a trip out to Timonium to the state fair. I had a hotdog with relish. This was a big deal to me. These guys *lived* in Timonium."

Moore was one of eight kids growing up in a two-bedroom apartment in West Baltimore. His father worked for the city recreation department. He was "a card-carrying Republican," Moore recalled years later, smiling and shaking his head.

He laughed when he told the story about Mrs. Blake, but there was an enduring reality to the underlying tension of desegregation, which seemed to settle over Maryland in waves as one group after another settled into a more open society. During holiday masses in the gym, the faculty would arrive formally, followed by a gathering of school benefactors, old ladies with fur stoles. "Faculty members would say to me, 'Get down, Ralph,' so the old ladies wouldn't know there was a black kid in the school." Were they serious? Did it matter? They said it.

Families dealt with the new world opening to their children in different ways. Ken Montague says his father created something of a stir when he came to school cookouts, events for parents and supporters of school activities. The movie *Guess Who's Coming to Dinner*, with Sidney Poitier and Spencer Tracy, was not quite out, but at Loyola, it was a discomfiting reality. Montague looks back on the school events with pride in his father's determination to be a part of his son's experience, his refusal to segregate himself or to let his son bear the burden of integration alone.

Montague was elected and reelected to the Maryland House of Delegates, and he became secretary of juvenile services under Governor Robert L. Ehrlich Jr. But other young people whose names would never be as well-known as his—let alone Thurgood Marshall's or Clarence Mitchell's or Lillie May Jackson's—had to walk through gauntlets to achieve the promise of *Brown v. Board of Education of Topeka.*

In Baltimore at least, the moral challenge would be seen and accepted instantly at the highest level. Walter Sondheim, then president of the city school board, determined that city public schools would integrate immediately. Sondheim said the *Afro-American* reporter was late for the meeting, and the board's vote had to be restaged for the reporter's benefit.

A day or so later, Sondheim paid a visit to the mayor, Thomas D'Alesandro (Old Tommy, father of the mayor who would serve later in the 1960s), who was recuperating from some indisposition at Good Samaritan Hospital.

"I don't know if you did the right thing, Walter," Old Tommy said, "but the priests say you did, so I guess you did."[6]

Fifty years later, the mayor's son, Thomas J. D'Alesandro III, chuckled at the story. His father, he says, was old school, a way of saying he was not a daring advocate of integrated schools. But, the younger D'Alesandro says, no one should conclude from the Sondheim story that his father was unaware of the school board's action.[7] Even though boards of education always felt free to act on their own and held that decision-making authority as a cherished, sacred, and separate-from-politics duty, Old Tommy was in close contact with everything and everyone in his city. He was old school, but he was also smart, a devotee of FDR, and shrewd enough to see—as his progressive son did years later—that times were changing. He made no move to undo what Sondheim had done. Others did. The state superintendent of schools, Tom Pullen, was furious and wanted the action rescinded. Other school systems in Maryland were not nearly so well disposed to desegregation as Baltimore was in those days. The state's education chief, as political as most people in charge of big school systems were, did not wish to be a leader in this field. Sondheim and his board invited the superintendent to "come in and unscramble the eggs" if he wished.[8] But the ruling was going to stand. Richard Shifter, a member of the state board, says "there was a constant battle with the superintendent over desegregation.

"When I first got on the state board, Pullen made a point of taking me to the Eastern Shore. We went school to school. Choirs would get together and sing for us. We were supposed to see these beautiful schools, kids singing, all happy. I remember looking out and saying to Pullen, 'All the faces are black. That's wrong.' " Pullen and, Shifter remembers, a board member would not relent. "It's the law of the land," the member said.[9] The Supreme Court had debated for a year about how to proceed, whether swift action was better than a drawn-out process. As Kluger notes, "One thing that stands out in the [Brown case] is the frequency with which those who have had the experience with integration— professional educators and laymen alike—have steeled themselves for a far more severe public reaction than they actually encountered."[10] The integration of Loyola and Mrs. Blake's reaction to it was an example. The high court ordered lower courts to implement Brown with "all deliberate speed," a somewhat contradictory phrase blamed later for years of dilatory compliance.

In Maryland, Ted McKeldin, running for governor once again, this time against Curley Byrd in 1954, was asked during a stop on the Eastern Shore for his reaction to *Brown*. "I represent the law," he said. Fifty years later, Sondheim and others—board members and several students who had been volunteered by their parents to integrate the schools—reflected on the days of desegregation. In his 90s by then, Sondheim joked about the many interviews he'd done about the city's uncharacteristic decision to comply instantly with the Court's ruling. "People thought it should have been done more slowly, that people could have been eased into the new world of integration. We thought that made no sense." He thought the board had made a big departure from what segregated Baltimore had done historically. "Maryland is a border state with real southern tendencies," he observed.[11] A cross was burned on his lawn and extinguished by Edgar Jones, an editorial writer at the *Sun* who was Sondheim's neighbor in Windsor Hills, on the west side of the city. Sondheim thought it a "puny little cross." He said, "Edgar didn't want my children to see the cross." Walter saw its embers but did not see it burning. He recalled eloquently racist letters from a former judge; unhappiness from a carpenter who had two kids in the schools and other unhappy people, many in South Baltimore.

Sondheim, 46 years old at the time, was well on his way to becoming Baltimore's longest-serving city father, a man who went from his job at Hochschild-Kohn's Department Store to overseer of major redevelopment projects, counselor to city leaders, and a paragon of thoughtful, stabilizing common sense. Baltimore, then near its peak population in 1950, with just under a million souls, had a big enough school system to set the tone for the entire state. It could easily have put up Deep South–style resistance, but there was no sentiment for that. Other issues were equally challenging, he says.

He urged Clarence Mitchell not to engage in counter picketing—to suggest, more or less, that the other side did not have a right to demonstrate in this way. Mitchell was angry about commotion near the school where his son Keiffer was a fourth-grade student. "He was very agitated," Sondheim recalls. It was one thing to argue these things in the abstract, but another to deal with them when your own family was involved. The Mitchell children, Keiffer especially, loved their father for his lone defense of them. "I am an American, too," his picket sign said. Keiffer suffered a beating but regarded the experience as character building and something that stimulated his artistic side.[12] He later became a physician, practicing in an office on Druid Hill Avenue not far from the family home. He is also a skilled photographer and avid watercolorist.

Looking back, Sondheim is struck by the makeup of the board. "Most members lived above North Avenue in the wealthier parts of the city—not in South Baltimore or on the east side, in the ethnic enclaves where opposition was most fierce," he says. The board did have one black member, Bernard Harris, for whom an elementary school is named. At one point, Harris called Baltimore superintendent John H. Fischer to ask if he would avoid appointing a white principal at Frederick Douglass High School, where the incumbent was retiring. Sondheim says he told

Harris as he had Clarence Mitchell, "You can't have it both ways." Harris, a surgeon, was a bit abashed later upon reflection, Sondheim thought.[13] But the instinct was to protect those who had persevered against discrimination, had progressed and prospered—and were now to have their life's work undercut ironically by a law designed to level the playing field. It was not the first time that victims of progress included achievers who were called upon to sacrifice their own interests for progress.

Relatively speaking, Baltimore schools integrated without much fuss: no water cannons, no dogs, no sheriffs with names like Bull enforcing racism. Yet, there was so much more to it, so much no one ever saw. University of Maryland School of Law professor Sherrilyn Ifill says the nation must see *Brown* "as a process which doesn't end once a great decision is rendered . . . *Brown* was not self-executing. It required the commitment of a nation sadly never there in some places," Ifill says.

President Eisenhower sent troops to enforce the integration of Central High School in Little Rock. There was massive resistance in Prince Edward County, Virginia, where officials closed the public schools for five years rather than integrate. "We're proud of Walter," Professor Ifill said, "but we also know the decision to integrate was only part of the story. The issue was not solved by admission of young black boys to one high school."[14]

Brown would force the issue toward the broader impact Marshall, Mitchell, and Jackson had labored for all their lives, but the toll on young people was appreciable. Alfreda Hughes, for example, probably had no choice about being a pioneer. She was the daughter of William Alfred Carroll Hughes, who had preceded Marshall as chief NAACP lawyer in Maryland. She left Frederick Douglass High. "After *Brown,* my father announced to me that he wanted me to go to Western, an all-girl, soon-to-be-integrated school. I didn't like the idea, so my father and mother enticed me. They said 'It's like a private school, and we don't have to pay.' I had a lot of friends whose parents had sent them away, so I said, maybe. My father said 'Tell your friends. Bring your friends with you.' I only got two or three to go with me."[15]

She had heard that Western's principal had made it clear that "before a colored girl came to her school, it would be over her dead body. She set the tone for the school, so a lot of people were not very receptive to us. A lot of the teachers weren't. The first class I went to was my English class.

I remember I was happy-go-lucky coming down the steps, walking into the classroom, and I said to the teacher, 'Hi. Good morning.' I greeted her with a smile. And I never will forget the look in her eyes. It was so cold and so mean. She told me to go and sit over there. I went and sat somewhere, and she said that day in front of the whole class, 'I don't see why some people don't stay where they're wanted. I don't know why some people won't stay where they belong.' I never will forget that.

"Miss Diggs, our French teacher, had all the colored girls sit in the back row. She would call the white girls Mademoiselle so and so, and she would look at us and say Alfreda, Margorie, or Ann.

"Then it was time to grade us. She had no idea my mother was a French teacher. She gave me a bad grade on a paper. My mother came up and confronted her. Miss Diggs resigned or retired that February. She did not stay. And the principal who said no colored girl will come into this school except over my dead body left, and she got very, very ill, and she was dead.

"There were mobs that came around our building. The mobs came, and a lot of them had baseball bats, and they wanted to get to us. They wanted to hurt us. Of course, the doors were locked. We were called down to the cafeteria. The principal said she wouldn't stand for that. But the crowd was yelling, 'Let them out of there!' I cried. And I remember some of the white girls cried, and some came over and patted me and said they were sorry it happened. Everybody there was not hostile toward us. Some white teachers fought for us in the faculty meetings. They were complaining about the unfairness shown to us by the white teachers who were sitting us in the back of the room and who were hostile to us.

"We had a police chief and mayor who stood up against them and said you're not doing that here . . . I remember this teacher gathering us together and taking us to the counter and demanded that they seat us at the counter and they did. So we had a lot of interesting things at Western. We definitely were trailblazers. I think our experiences were pretty much the same as in the South, only not so prolonged. I have pictures of the first graduating class. We were young; we were naïve. I don't think we were prepared for the way teachers treated us. But we got through it. It wasn't all bad. I learned. And I was never afraid of white people. I found out that people are people."

Her father and the fathers of other black students had a special burden. "Daddy drove me every day, and he had a gun in his pocket."[16]

Clarence Mitchell had mounted his one-man picket line at his son's school. Mitchell and Hughes felt obligated to offer their children for the integrated schools they had fought to achieve. It meant offering them to the mercies of unpredictable forces in an alien world.

Baltimore lawyer Dwight Petit's father lost his job as a result of his determination to integrate Aberdeen High School. "My daddy said, 'Son, I'm being transferred to a place called Aberdeen.' I had never felt such a disaster. We went up to Aberdeen, and there was nothing there but the deer and the skunks. And a military base. We rode over to Aberdeen High School. I did notice that they had a goal post, so they had a football team there. We pulled up to the school, where we heard the chants, 'Nigger, go home.' The only difference was I was by myself. We went in to register, and they told us basically, 'No sir.' We went to Juanita Mitchell, who took my case along with Jack Greenberg [an NAACP lawyer, who worked in consultation with Thurgood Marshall].

"The judge was Rozel C. Thomsen. Outside the city, there was a stair-step, year-by-year desegregation plan [a plan in force outside Baltimore in which one grade was to be integrated each year until all were integrated]. They looked at your record and then went to the school you were going to. That principal wanted to keep the school segregated. But Havre de Grace admitted four African American females; the two males were denied on the conglomerate test on which the decision was made. They were maintaining a segregated system years after 1954. This was in '57, '58, '59, and '60. The irony was that Thomsen did not strike down the stair-step plan. He argued that I should have been admitted, smart or not, that I had the right to succeed or fail."[17]

Football helped. "One of the greatest bridges was athletics. I played football. James Brown was our coach. I give him accolades. First thing I did was knock a kid out. He called everybody together. 'If you want to play, I tell you right now, the young man, the Negro kid, is going to play. If he makes the team, he'll play.' " Things worked out. "I had the opportunity on my 16th birthday to catch the winning touchdown while the game was running out, and the kids actually carried me on their shoulders and sang happy birthday to me."

His real hero was his father. "I can't talk about myself without my father. My father had come to Aberdeen as an electrical engineer from Fort Holabird. They told him in no uncertain terms that he would never be promoted again as long as he was at Aberdeen Proving Grounds. And they put a big Confederate flag on the wall, so when he came in every morning, they'd come push a button and it would play Dixie. They told him the decision was not appreciated, and they reminded him every day. He went on to be vice president of the NAACP . . . The Nixon administration gave me an exclusion so I could work on the case with Juanita in the U.S. Court of Claims. We won 4–3. The court declared that my father had been illegally and wrongfully discriminated against. He got $100,000 in back pay, and he was promoted several pay grades." Petit says he personally got a special thrill when the decision carried his name as well as Mitchell's and Greenberg's. All were referred to as "learned counsel."[18]

No county in the state, it seemed, escaped these years without some tension. Richard Shifter, on the state school board from Montgomery County, found himself dealing with school authorities who demanded sensitive handling. When the board was pushing for action in Prince George's County, Congresswoman Gladys Spellman warned him about the man he would be dealing with, the superintendent there: " 'I just want to warn you, don't be too hard on him because if you ask him tough questions, he'll resign on the spot.' So I didn't push at him during the hearings. I just filed a strong dissent. The board hadn't come to grips with the issue, so I took it on."[19]

After he filed his dissent, his phone started to ring late at night. "I'd pick it up, and no one was there." John Anderson, a reporter for the *Washington Post,* wrote a story about it. "Tom Pullen hated me for everything I was doing. I was really the bane of his existence. This was his point of view. This was the way he did things. He was really committed to keeping things the way they had been. And he was not the only one."

Shifter says a state senator from Prince George's County, Winship Wheatly, went to see J. Millard Tawes, and Governor Tawes promised that Shifter would be replaced. A law school classmate of Shifter's, Burke Marshall, was Robert Kennedy's assistant for civil rights matters. Marshall talked to Kennedy, and Kennedy talked to Tom Finan (Maryland's attorney general), and Finan talked to Tawes. Shifter stayed on the school board.

Not that he was out of the woods. Shifter was coping simultaneously with pockets of resistance in Montgomery. Though regarded as liberal and fully amenable to the change ordered by *Brown,* some of the same issues arose there. In Montgomery, the board encountered some of the same resistance encountered in Baltimore. Not every black parent or black administrator applauded *Brown.* One Montgomery principal, Shifter said, "had been head of the School of Education at Howard University, and as Maryland saw the situation developing, we recognized we had to live up to *Plessy v. Ferguson,* separate but equal, there was a comprehensive construction program: brand new black schools, so it was the graduates of the Howard School who were the teachers and the principals. They were caught in a bind. We said, think of the kids. They agreed with us." At some expense to themselves and their careers.

Montgomery desegregated after locating all the black kids and drawing districts to achieve racial balance. Along with this beneficent gerrymandering, they adopted one firm rule: Principals were told, if you can identify any troublemakers, put them in the white class. But once you have assigned a white kid to a black teacher's class, there will be no transfers. Then she [the principal] made a mistake in one case, and the father came to see her.

" 'I know it's wrong,' he said. 'I am prejudiced, and I passed it on to my daughter.' He came close to crying." Shifter said the rule stood. Then he said to the principal: keep an eye on this girl. The report? "This girl is having her best year yet." Her father may simply have wanted his daughter out of an integrated school, but apparently he did not pass on his prejudices to his daughter.

There was real pain in the process, but the mixing of black and white kids—and their parents—did not create the kind of upheaval many had expected. The law had not transformed society. It had not changed attitudes, but it had established a boundary within which people could see that they were bigger than they thought. They had Jim Crow, if not caged, at least back on his heels.

ALL NATIONS DAY: THE CIVIL RIGHTS MERRY-GO-ROUND

If you were a black kid, you couldn't ride the roller coaster at Gwynn Oak Amusement Park in Baltimore County. You couldn't get into the place.[20] Your presence, it was said, would drive white patrons away. Just the way it was—still was—long after the barrier-busting promise of *Brown.* You couldn't have the all-American recreational apple pie of summer: no bumper cars, no ice cream, no cotton candy, none of these staples of summer life in America. Kids with good grades could get in free one day a year, All Nations Day, July 4th—unless they were black. All nations could participate in the celebration—unless they were African nations. But then another tradition took root. Every year, beginning in 1956, protesters marched outside the park, asking the owners to change this policy, and failing each time.

Inside and outside the classroom, the *Brown* decision made little immediate difference in the lives of black Americans. Just as the decision to allow a single black student into the University of Maryland School of Law did not desegregate the rest of the university, more action would be necessary to enforce the dictates of *Brown*. The rulings of a court were important but not conclusive. Some parts of the nation would erect "massive resistance" to the school desegregation dictates of *Brown*. Other regions, cities, and towns continued their exclusionary practices as if *Brown* did not apply to them. More legislation would be needed, eventually in the area of public accommodations of many varieties. The All Nations Day outrage drew angry demonstrations before Selma and Montgomery, before Rosa Parks, before the Reverend Martin Luther King Jr. and other leaders of protests that marked the official start of this nation's most dramatic desegregation effort. Television, with its coverage of violent protests in the South, increased the momentum. Brutality, transported to the nation's living rooms, enabled King and his army to make the movement national and compelling. In Maryland, the drive for equal rights had been under way for some time with indifferent results: a seemingly big win here, a limited win there, a loss.

But on this day in July 1963, an impressive contingent of protestors would push the Gwynn Oak exercise beyond its symbolic protest-and-go-home cycle of defeat. National stars of the religious and entertainment world came to the front gates of Gwynn Oak Park to renew the eight-year effort to force it open for black families. The park's nearly comical adherence to a whites-only admissions policy on something billed as All Nations Day drew the highest-ranking official in the United Presbyterian Church, Eugene Carson Blake. "The churches in this country have for a long time been saying a great deal about discrimination," said Blake, "but we can no longer let the burden of winning freedom for the Negro or any other oppressed people be the burden of the oppressed people themselves."[21] Black leaders would point at Gwynn Oak later as a watershed.

William Sloan Coffin, the antiwar chaplain at Yale, was there. Michael Schwerner, who would be murdered a year later during Freedom Summer in Mississippi, was there with hundreds of others, including a chronicler of the tumultuous sixties, Todd Gitlin. Demonstrators used local churches as staging areas. "It was my first taste of the Southern movement," Gitlin wrote. "We launched ourselves with freedom songs from a Negro church, where the good citizens in their Sunday finest smiled upon us as if we were visiting diplomats."[22] Having heard King speak of the "the beloved community," Gitlin found it in Baltimore. Local black clergy were moving their involvement to a higher level. The Reverend Marion C. Bascom of Douglas Memorial Community Church, adjacent to the relatively posh Bolton Hill enclave, was there at Gwynn Oak with Chester Wickwire, Hopkins chaplain. All of them marched up to the gates, threatening to surge through. Police were called, and 283 men and women were arrested, ten by ten. For years, Gwynn Oak Park owners had taken refuge against picketing behind the trespass laws, just as merchants along Pennsylvania Avenue had done almost thirty years earlier. Often this defense was upheld by the courts. The rights of private property trumped *other* constitutional rights. Law students could be barred from the state's law school and then from the law review course and then, it was thought, from admission to the bar if the number of black applicants exceeded the unspoken quotas—because white law students would be offended or turn away. Ford's Theater in Baltimore withstood the picketing for seven years.

Northwood Theater in northeast Baltimore resisted successfully, too, until overwhelmed by students from Morgan State College and the CIG, a critically important student organization led by Clarence "Skip" Logan and its faculty adviser, August Meier, a white scholar who had studied several protest campaigns originating on campuses around the country. Lunch counter sit-ins first gained national attention in Greensboro, North Carolina, but they had been under way in Baltimore for at least five years. The CIG effort at Northwood had begun a year after *Brown*, in 1955. Its objective was to integrate the movie theater, and as with virtually every other assault on the bastions of discrimination in Baltimore, protestors were denied their objective for years.

In the winter and spring of 1960, the campaign grew more intense, with its soldiers moving to the center of the city. On June 17, 1960, a group of twelve students demonstrated along Baltimore Street. They were looking for an open restaurant and found Hooper's. One of their leaders was Robert Mack Bell, then 16, the newly elected president of the rising senior class at Dunbar High School. Six years after *Brown,* Dunbar had no white students and only one white teacher. And black people were still denied the right to have a hamburger in downtown restaurants.

Bell says the picketing and sitting in always drew counter pickets, shouting and menacing crowds coming to support the restaurant owners. This group of picketers was unusually young, having been recruited by the sit-in organizers to expand the forces and, possibly, to test aspects of Maryland law that would have allowed the students to be tried as adults.

The students were told to conduct themselves civilly—and to have enough money to pay for whatever they ordered in the unlikely event they were served. The demonstration was anything but peaceful on the other side, as Bell recalls: "It was the most frightening thing I ever experienced. If you ever wanted to see hate, there it was. We had been told the last thing we could do was respond. It would have undermined the [nonviolent ethic] of the movement. When we got there, everyone took a different table to maximize our strength. We walked in, and we were told they wouldn't serve us, that their policy prohibited it."[23] In short order, police arrested the twelve and charged them with violating the antitrespass ordinance.

But by 1963, demonstrations were conducted with increased sophistication. One tactician, reasoning that progress could not be made against a single restaurant or store, counseled the Morgan students to expand their campaign. This adviser, an Urban League official—probably Furman Templeton—would eventually convince the students to picket all the downtown department stores, not just the Hecht Company store and its Rooftop Restaurant at Northwood. By 1963, some steam had gone out of the protest movement around the nation, but Jim Crow remained resilient. Northwood, for example, was situated mere blocks away from a 2,600-student campus, which might have been capable of mounting an overwhelming campaign to open a movie house. With that goal almost embarrassingly within reach, the CIG undertook yet another round of picketing. This time the stars were more closely aligned in their favor.

Beginning in February 1963, fifteen hundred students picketed at Northwood. More than four hundred of them were arrested for violating the state's antitrespass law. Bail was set at $500: a total of $90,200 for the entire group. There was no money, and initial attempts to raise it failed.

Meanwhile, though, students from Johns Hopkins and Goucher College were reinforcing the Morgan group. A few shoppers put down their parcels and joined the marchers. Other Baltimoreans made it clear that their sympathies lay with the students. Political leaders, including Mayor Phillip Goodman, tuned in to what began to look like a groundswell. Goodman was then facing a primary election campaign for mayor. The election was mere days away. He began an effort to find a solution.

Morgan's president, Martin D. Jenkins, meanwhile tried to maneuver between the students and state officials who just happened to be considering Morgan's annual budget request. Jenkins issued orders that might have curtailed the picketing, but he did nothing to enforce them. Later, though, when the heat rose, he suggested that August Meier ought to consider resigning his adviser's post. The students refused to back down, and Meier, too, stood his ground. Jenkins ultimately threw in with the picketers, urging them to cease and desist, and then declaring his support. While all this was evolving, the continued presence of students in the city lockup became an increasingly difficult problem for official Baltimore. The absence of bail forced the city to think of releasing the students, and the students began to see the leverage they held. They began to picket downtown stores as well, further increasing their advantage. Prosecutors wanted to lower the bail; the students demanded no bail at all. And eventually the students' demand was met. Shortly thereafter, owners of the theater announced they were more than happy to join other progressive businesses in dropping their segregation practices. At about this time, Little Willie Adams made one hundred thousand dollars available for bail should it be needed.[24] The students were on a roll.

The incremental success rolled on, emboldening the final assault miles away by the Gwynn Oak army in Baltimore County. The growing involvement of students sparked more adults to enlist. All the resistance, delay, and sham adherence to fairness and the law were pricking the conscience of some Marylanders. Many had lamented the unfairness of their society but had not acted to change it. For many holdouts, the march on an icon of summer, Gwynn Oak Park, made the movement's demands for a universal dismantling of barriers an imperative. Even this symbol of the all-American summer was being forced to change, as if previously it had been or should have been immune. There was a slow-motion domino effect of the movement: from law schools to restaurants, to tennis courts, to amusement parks. It was a headshaker for the most resolute opponents, men and women who continued to deplore the movement's tactics as disruptive and uncivil, as if mere requests would result in doors opened for black kids looking for a candy apple. In jail, Wickwire's crutches were taken from him. Guards taunted Bascom when he asked for a glass of water at lunchtime. "They just poured water in on top of his coffee."[25] The guards were encouraged to be less-than-civil jailers by county executive Spiro T. Agnew, who called the demonstration "hasty and immature," the result of "emotional hypnotism." But hadn't there been efforts over eight long years to bring down the barriers at Gwynn Oak Park? One might ask, of course, what had the county executive done to fend off desperately aggressive efforts? Even the park's resisters had a little more compassion than the county executive, but then, they weren't running for anything.

James Price, one of the park owners, told reporters, "Ordering the arrest of clergymen, whom I sincerely believe were acting on the very highest motivations was the most difficult thing I have ever had to do. But after much soul-searching on the manner in which to protect the equally God-given right of our citizens to their private property, we felt we could not show less courage than the men of the cloth." He predicted "a roller coaster ride down hill for the Negro" as a result of the demonstration. In Price's view, the demonstrators were themselves violating rights, "the God-given right to private property."[26] The inviolability of private property was to be protected by God. This sort of language had worked well enough in the past, but three days later, on July 7, 1963, many members of this contingent were back. The second assault came because strategists wanted to press their advantage. They feared that the remarkable assembly of stars would not be available again to create such excitement and momentum. Better act. The prospect of more massive civil disobedience might miraculously force the gates open.

Peaceful protest had given way to more assertive action. Threats of direct action could be glimpsed on many fronts: in Cambridge, Maryland, for example, where the national guard had been needed as an occupying force. Officials in Washington were weighing in to find accommodations for the protesters. The lesson was finally getting through to the guardians of white privilege. Whites-only golf courses, amusement parks, and burger joints were not going to stand. Thus did Alison Turaj, one of the Gwynn Oak marchers, find herself at the point of more assertive, more direct, more dramatic action at the entrance to Gwynn Oak Park. While the ministers and others waited patiently once again to be arrested and carted off to jail, she recruited several others to make a more probing assault.

Behind the main entrance, across a small stream, was another way into the park. Turaj and others removed their shoes and socks and established a second beachhead. She thought people in the park "could not possibly be as prejudiced as the park's owners thought they were."[27] She ran toward the crowd, joined by George Lottier, whose wife was a great-granddaughter of the *Afro-American*'s founder, John Murphy, the former slave. The web of connection, the historic chain of liberating events and of people, could be traced through generations of men and women who had made their witness as best they could. All this disparate energy and passion and outrage was building to a crescendo.

Lottier had warned Turaj that the presence of white protesters would not be warmly greeted. As she ran forward, a woman in a red dress threw something. Turaj and Lottier fell. He was unhurt. Turaj got to her feet, glasses shattered and blood streaming from two cuts in her forehead. Another of the demonstrators, Arthur Waskow, had predicted such an event, as Wickwire had, followed by escalating anger, the collapse of all civilized restraint, and a murderous passion fueled by mob action. Demonstrators clasped hands while the crowd shouted, "Kill the niggers! Kill the niggers!" It had taken physical courage, a bit of naïveté, and Herculean feats of logistics to mount these actions. It had taken near guerilla warfare over the years to get access to a roller coaster ride for black kids. Barbara Mills, CORE activist and chronicler of these tumultuous days, says, "It was so absurd that we would have to be demonstrating against supposedly educated people to give blacks the right to [visit an amusement park] . . . every now and then [the reality] would just overwhelm you. It's so absurd that we have to do this. There wasn't any answer. It just built up."[28]

No wonder, then, that Alison Turaj and others had waded creeks and braved rock-throwing mobs and scolding county executives. Gitlin later called these days "a weak echo of the bloody movement down South." He wrote that in the South, "an entire social system, fighting for its violent life, went into convulsion. Negroes of the Deep South stepped out of the shadows to shake the pillars, even as they shook with their own fear."[29] Gitlin, who had parachuted in to Baltimore for one demonstration, did not have the benefit of local history to inform his observation. In some sense, the South's revolt was an echo of what had been happening in Maryland since the 1930s. A social system was at stake in Maryland, too, and while the fighting had been less violent, Maryland was no less determined to maintain itself as an inviolable precinct of white privilege. The South and the nation would have the benefit of a nonpareil, incandescent leader, the power of television, and the rising tide of outrage to make it into a national revolution. Maryland had Bill Lee, the CIG, Chester Wickwire, and Alison Turaj—names no one knew outside the Free State.

Two months after the All Nations march, on August 28, the assemblies for justice continued in Washington. Baltimoreans boarded buses for the march in which King delivered his "I Have a Dream" speech. A critical mass had been achieved across the nation, building in Maryland from Pennsylvania Avenue to Northwood, to Gwynn Oak, and now to the March on Washington. Vernon Dobson, pastor of Union Baptist Church, worried that Baltimore might be embarrassed by a low turnout. The sheer backbreaking effort demanded by such actions was hard to appreciate. Walter Carter, the charismatic local CORE leader, had resigned just before the Gwynn Oak march, as he had done earlier in frustration over lack of support.

Hope for masses filling the great national mall between the Lincoln and Washington monuments seemed fanciful. But Dobson, Marion Bascom, and Alison Turaj were not the only Baltimoreans touched by the spirit of freedom and justice. Reverend Dobson remembers the wonder of that moment in August 1963. "All the major churches that went had responsibilities of getting buses together. We stayed up all that night making certain we had people, worried that we had overestimated what we were going to do . . . knowing that if we didn't do a big thing, the whole movement might be in default. So we had to get out. We went to Lafayette Square that morning: buses would pull up and they would fill up. And then another would fill up." The contagion of support that had developed around Northwood continued and built to a crescendo for the march.

"It was just amazing," Dobson said. "It almost made you just teary eyed the whole day, you just couldn't help but thank God . . . They had predicted there were going to be riots, and at times we felt like it. We were all revolutionaries in our souls at that time. We hadn't done enough. And as fast as we loaded a bus up, they'd go. And then when we got on board, the buses were bumper-to-bumper. From Memphis, Tennessee,

Mississippi."[30] Senator Troy Brailey, a sleeping-car porter at the time, says A. Philip Randolph, the union's longtime leader, was ultimately behind the organizational effort across the country.

McKeldin, a black-eyed Susan in his lapel, came to the debarkation point to wish the marchers well. "We cannot hide, even if we wished to do so, the shame we feel before the Almighty and the other nations of the world as a result of the inhumanity which has deprived some of God's children of their rights," thundered McKeldin. "But we can take justifiable pride in the fact that in our land, the right of the citizens to petition their government is sacred, still available, and I would like to predict, still effective."[31] On that same day, as thousands walked onto the mall to hear King, the revolution was having an almost unnoticed moment of triumph on one of the movement's many fields of battle. More unknowns were working things out the way, ultimately, things had to be worked out in society. Charles Langley, a 28-year-old black clerk at the Social Security Administration, put his 11-month-old daughter on the merry-go-round at Gwynn Oak Park. In an era of firsts—first black law student, first black senator, first black mayor, first black congressman—came another: first black merry-go-round rider. Gwynn Oak Park had quietly opened its doors to black families.

Acting as Alison Turaj had assumed white people would act two months earlier, a white woman asked Langley if he would watch her daughter for a moment. And a white boy climbed aboard a painted pony next to Sharon Langley. Vernon Dobson, Chester Wickwire, Alison Turaj, and Todd Gitlin were in Washington that day, listening to Martin Luther King speak about a day when black boys and girls would be judged not by the color of their skin, but by the content of their character. That goal might have seemed to be only a glimmer of hope then, and yet it was reached that very day on a merry-go-round forty miles north in Baltimore County, Maryland. Two kids—one black, one white—doing what kids of all nations love to do.

GLORIA RICHARDSON: FLASH POINT

In the winter of 2004, former Cambridge, Maryland, town councilman Bill Wright once again found himself thinking about the most trying time of his life, a summer forty-two years earlier when the civil rights movement jolted his world. When demonstrators marched and prayed in downtown Cambridge, Wright recalls a local white businessman ran alongside them, shouting epithets.

"He'd come down there and call 'em everything. He'd get right down there. Judge Mason and I would be there near the library, and Judge Mason would say, 'Bill, here he comes.' He'd go along the streets harassing them. It was terrible. It made me feel bad for him. The guy was well educated. He was well positioned. He ran right by Judge Mason and me."[32] Against this standard, many in Cambridge could think of themselves as moderate on race issues, and many did.

At the supermarket a day before a Baltimore writer was coming to talk with him about those tumultuous days, he ran into an old acquaintance. Wright said, "John, don't you remember me?"

"I don't believe I do."

"John, you saw me enough when I was a commissioner."

"Oh yeah, yeah."

It had been forty years since the two had met regularly in Cambridge City Hall or on the demonstration-riven streets of the 1960s. John was a man of some standing in the city, a company executive. "I said, 'John, do you remember when you used to run when they came down High Street?" Wright recounts. The march would end with a prayer meeting in a part of the city known as the valley. Prayer in public became a weapon in those days, a challenge to the conscience and rectitude of the oppressors.

Perhaps it was not surprising that this man did not recognize Bill Wright or said he didn't. Wright had actually been a force for moderation, a man who risked—and quickly lost—his political office by urging Cambridge voters to accept a change in the city charter allowing blacks access to various facilities: restaurants, schools, and movie houses, for example.

The long-running campaign for civil rights in Cambridge, led by the Cambridge Nonviolent Action Committee (CNAC), erupted into near violence even as the Reverend Martin Luther King Jr. led the national nonviolent civil rights movement. The ferocity of protest in Cambridge offered stark counterpoint. Economic conditions and fiercely guarded segregated ways blew to incendiary heights between 1962 and 1964.

At the turbulent center of the Cambridge movement was Gloria Richardson, a tall 41-year-old black woman whose grandfather had been on the Cambridge City Council. She became the embodiment of a small town revolution. People began referring to her simply as Gloria, knowing there was no mistaking which Gloria. Her resolute elegance stood out against the town's implacably defended caste system. She was standing up to the indignities of decades, refusing to let them slide, to accept excuses, to pretend they weren't there.

She was as quietly focused as Lillie May Jackson had been shrill. Both women were unrelenting and fearless. They challenged the historical success of the white opposition's chief tactic, step-by-step accommodation that occasionally appeared to concede the rightness of a challenge without really changing anything. Both women had been drawn into the struggle when their daughters encountered trouble in the school system—were turned away outright, or ran into racially based hazing. Few skirmishes in the national civil rights movement matched the intensity or duration of those in Cambridge.

Crouched along the shores of the broad Choptank River as if to shield itself from the outside world, Cambridge became a flash point in the national drive toward civil rights. It became a testing ground for one of the most famous of Frederick Douglass's maxims: "Power concedes nothing without a demand. It never did and it never will. Find out just what people will submit to and you have found out the exact amount of injustice and wrong which will be imposed upon them and there will continue until they are resisted with either words or blood or with both. The limits of tyrants are prescribed by the endurance of those whom they oppress."[33]

Sharp confrontations in a place like Cambridge were probably inevitable, and they may have represented a crescendo in the outdoor stage of the civil rights movement in Maryland. An outbreak of organized anger by people willing to fight back against those leaders who were willing to flout the law—*Brown v. Board of Education*, for example—seemed overdue. The instinctive shoulder shrugging that met outrages against black citizens was coming to a dramatic end. The Cambridge chemistry was more volatile because, notwithstanding the rabid heckler followed during demonstrations by Councilman Wright and Judge Mason, white residents insisted that race relations were not only good but a model for the rest of the nation. Gloria Richardson contended that life for black residents of Cambridge was good only on paper.

Exhibit One in the city's defense may have been the long-running presence of Richardson's grandfather, Maynadier St. Clair, on the city council, but his position merely created a veneer of tolerance. He had been elected by the virtually all-black Second Ward, making him a misleading symbol of integration and good feeling. Though a deferential manner enabled him to achieve some public works improvements for his community, Councilman St. Clair made few if any inroads in the Jim Crow atmosphere. He was obliged to live with it. When the council met for dinner, he was excluded. A meal was sent around to his house. Just the way it was—and a way he accepted as the price of doing business.

By the 1960s, the validity of Charles Houston's warning against any thought that the battle had been won was demonstrated once again. Six years after *Brown v. Board of Education*'s barrier-toppling ruling, only five of eighteen restaurants in Cambridge would serve blacks. Save for the Phillips Seafood Company, blacks had trouble finding employers willing to hire them. Housing was poor, and black unemployment was twice the national average. There was no school integration, and blacks were not allowed to join the volunteer fire and rescue association, the city's important social, recreational, and civic center.

Thus the Baltimore-based Freedom Riders planned a stop in Cambridge. The white authorities of Cambridge were not anxious for the demonstrators, but they gave no quarter. It was not new behavior. More systematic demands for fairness were coming in Cambridge, and not everyone saw it. Or, if they did, change was beyond them.

After a series of negotiations, Cambridge saw its first sit-ins. On Saturday, January 13, 1962, students from Morgan State College, Swarthmore College, and elsewhere attempted to enter the Choptank Inn. They were met by jeering whites. One of the student group leaders, Bill Hansen, a 22-year-old white student from Xavier University in Cincinnati, tried to enter the inn three times. He was thrown out, kicked, and beaten until a state policeman arrested him for disorderly conduct.

The demonstrations continued, intensified, and in July of the following year, the national guard was called in to keep the angry parties separated. The soldiers remained for more than a year as demonstrators grew more determined. News of the protests brought in reinforcements from universities, civil rights organizations, and citizens seeing an opportunity to become part of the movement.

Months into the tense confrontation, Jim Keat, a reporter for the *Baltimore Sun*, wrote, "In the context of the nationwide Negro rejection of gradualism, time had been running out for Cambridge." A few years earlier, he observed, incremental progress would have been enough to stave off open conflict. Incremental reform and the usual economic threats to those black residents with anything to lose would have been sufficient to preserve the Cambridge way of life. Keat thought outside forces, the Student Nonviolent Coordinating Committee (SNCC), and its firebrand leaders had influenced the Cambridge movement's stoic leader, Gloria Richardson.

But Richardson was a force unto herself, a leader as immovable and resolute on the Eastern Shore of Maryland as King had been throughout the South. If not more so. There was steel in her, the fundamental strength of a woman who, like the sisters Juanita and Virginia Jackson in Baltimore, had returned from college to her hometown with new eyes and new outrage.

Though Cambridge did not achieve the profile of Birmingham or Montgomery or Selma, the movement's most evocative place names, Gloria Richardson and her organization prompted police dogs, baton wielding, and water-cannon action typical of resistance in those southern cities. The Cambridge police chief, Brice McKinnon, was as defiant as the infamous Bull Connor, Birmingham's provocatively named police chief and one of the national movement's most recognizable symbols of white opposition to change.

The police and volunteer fire and rescue departments in Cambridge, civic groups as well as guardians of public safety, mobilized themselves against the black protesters at every turn. Local restaurants and hangouts from the Choptank Inn to an eatery called Dizzyland to the local movie house threw up barriers and manned them against the determination of black citizens to gain admission.

Councilman Bill Wright's moderation put him in the center of all this. He was a target of those who refused to change, and of those who saw that the demonstrations were damaging. Some were ready for someone to act, for some way to ease tensions. Upheaval was not good for commerce. "I had local industry people here, saying you can swing this, get behind it and you can get two more votes. They wanted me to introduce an open accommodations ordinance. They wanted the demonstrations to end. To one of them [the president of Cambridge Wire Cloth], I said, 'Ed, let me ask you something, you're asking me to commit political suicide and you won't even let one black be hired out at Wire Cloth.' And they had six hundred employees out there. It was a big employer. Ted

Phillips of the Phillips Packing Company came up to me later and said, 'Bill, I was proud of you for saying that.' "

But the situation was beyond one man's altering. It was close to being out of hand, not just in Cambridge but elsewhere in Maryland. Only Richardson's trusting relationship with General George W. Gelston, the guard commander, held back open conflict. Box Harris, a black police official from Baltimore, was another important peacekeeper.

The turmoil intensified, though, and the consequences were landing on the desk of J. Millard Tawes, the diminutive Eastern Shoreman who was then governor. When Hotdog Simpkins, one of the governor's aides, arrived for work one day in summer 1963, he got an immediate assignment. "Don't even take your coat off. You're going to Washington."[34] Attorney general Robert F. Kennedy was waiting, he was told. Once again, as it had in the lynching of George Armwood thirty years earlier, Maryland—America in miniature—had gained the attention of Washington.

Simpkins heard this story as he was heading out the door. "This black man stopped at a restaurant on Kent Island," Simpkins recalled. "People said later he was from Chad, but then they said maybe his name was Chad." (A little Eastern Shore humor here.) At any rate, the owner of the restaurant, a popular stopping spot on the way to and from the beach, walked up to him and said, according to Simpkins, "We don't serve -------' " He invited the black man to leave. As it turned out, Simpkins says, a white customer in the restaurant at that moment was protocol chief in the U.S. State Department. A coincidence like that was not unusual in Maryland.

"May I be of any assistance?" the government man asked, recognizing an explosive situation.

"And," said the restaurant man without missing a beat, "we don't serve ------ lovers either." Thus did Maryland provide yet another international incident, one of many that occurred along highways leading from the UN headquarters in New York to Washington. Earlier, in April 1961, black reporters dressed in the regalia of African diplomats were served in restaurants that refused to accommodate blacks. The *Afro* ran their story, making a point that others had made repeatedly over the years: why were people of color from other countries treated with respect while American blacks were barred or required to wait for food they bought to be handed out the back door?

Simpkins met first with the Justice Department's civil rights chief, Burke Marshall, who became a famous name as he tried to negotiate settlements in potentially violent places across the nation. At the end of their talk, Simpkins says, Robert Kennedy came into the room. "Mr. Simpkins," he said, "the United Nations is in this country by virtue, until yesterday, of a twelve-vote margin of the nations voting on where it should be located. After yesterday, we've probably lost Chad. You people in Maryland have got to do something."[35] His brother, President John F. Kennedy, had just made his famous Cold War "I Am a Berliner" speech, standing with Germans walled in by Communist Russia. He was not, on the other hand, willing to offer himself as a resident of Cambridge, Maryland. He had begun to urge a more aggressive national civil rights agenda, but he was critical of the Cambridge protestors, suggesting they had "lost sight" of their goals.[36] Hotdog Simpkins returned to the governor's office that day to report what the attorney general had said.

Gloria Richardson was pleased. "One of the things that we had was that, because we were close to Washington, it should be fairly easy, if we could create enough chaos, to attract their attention and kind of force their hand . . . And we happily succeeded in doing that," she recalled years later.[37] Perpetrators had mocked and defied the law and frustrated authorities. The civil rights movement was, in a real sense, a reaction to the failure of political power centers to intercede—to enforce the law.

Richardson's unsmiling resolve infuriated many in Cambridge, including the police and fire departments, both of which seemed unlikely to protect the marching black residents of the city. Restaurant owners broke eggs over the heads of demonstrators. Mobs administered beatings, and the demonstrators were arrested. Two young men were sent to reform school for participating in sit-in style demonstrations. Gelston and his men prevented real violence between the two sides.

One of the marchers in these days was Marc Steiner, then 16 and already a veteran of civil rights marches and sit-ins in Baltimore. Later a talk show host on WYPR-FM in Baltimore, he was one of many young people who spent weekends carrying the protests into the street. "It was because of my mother, who was an antisegregationist. She could not abide racism. I actually started at about age 13. We were shopping one day at Mondawmin Mall in Baltimore, and there was a picket line in front of a White Coffee Pot." Later he joined the Morgan University–based CIG, sitting in at various places in Annapolis, Cambridge, and along Route 40.

On one occasion, U.S. Navy midshipmen stepped between the marchers and a gang of hecklers, "and they [the hecklers] backed down."

In Cambridge, where he remembers being terrified most of the time, he was arrested during a march outside the local jail. "They wanted me to sign a piece of paper saying I was duped by the Communist Party. I refused, so they said, 'What would you do if your sister married one?' I said I'd buy them a present and go to the wedding."[38] In the night, he says, the CIG and others gathered in a meeting house on Race Street, where shotguns were propped against every window in the three-story house. There was more gunfire in Cambridge that summer than newspapers reported.

The marchers did not turn back, so the Maryland National Guard was called in, and it occupied the city for the better part of two years. If martial law were not the order of the day, something very like it prevailed. Schoolchildren walked to and from class past uniformed men with bayoneted rifles. Night-riding vigilantes tore through the black community with guns blazing. Armed black men crouched in fields, weapons at the ready. That pitched gun battles did not occur was remarkable.

Bill Wright was asked by friends and authorities in Cambridge to defuse the atmosphere. His "moderation" vaulted him into the role of peacemaker. His position put painful distance between him and his neighbors, one of whom promised to help vote him out of office. He and a friend, Tom Spicer, a member of Maryland's House of Delegates, simply did not talk about their differences. They hunted and fished together but didn't talk about Gloria and her demands.

"We were close," Wright says. "But there was one thing we never did jell on."

Delegate Spicer had actually made life miserable for the Shore, without intending to, by voting to exclude Cambridge from Maryland's 1963 open accommodations law. "When they passed the public accommodation law, our representatives exempted Dorchester County and the rest of the Shore. Boy, that pointed the gun right at our heads," Wright said.

When the hostilities grew more prominent in the news—when they seemed to undercut the U.S. demands for democracy elsewhere—Richardson, Wright, and others were summoned to Washington for another conference with Attorney General Kennedy. The meeting occurred a day after the national guard used tear gas to quell a disturbance. A leader of the students, Morgan State's Clarence Logan, had been unable to change clothes and walked into the Justice Department reeking of the acrid fumes.

In his book *Walking with the Wind*, Congressman John Lewis offers the picture of the attorney general, then 45, cajoling the civil rights leader into a more tractable position by getting her to change the expression on her face, as if she would not be able to demand and insist and reject and avoid faithless compromise if only she would smile.

Bill Wright saw the same scene and thought Robert Kennedy had put Gloria Richardson in her place. Hadn't taken anything from her. Hadn't been willing to back down. "Kennedy had us up to his office in Washington. He arranged it to bring us up away from the reporters. He took us up in his private elevator, and the first thing when he got us to the table, he said, "Ms. Richardson, may I call you Gloria?'

She said, 'Yes sir, if you wish.' Then he said, 'Gloria the first thing I want you to do, would you put a smile on that face? If you're up here looking like that, you're not going to get anything.'

"She finally cracked a smile. It was a poor one, but she smiled. And he said 'I want you to keep that smile on your face when you talk to these people at the Cambridge City Council when you call on them.' She never said yes or no to that. But he was very firm. More than I expected."

Here the attorney general of the United States was, trying to exact from Gloria Richardson the smile of acquiescence she had been unwilling to grant the city officials of Cambridge. Kennedy was surely a victim of the paternalistic instinct that afflicted much of black-white relations in those days. A parent talking to a child, in this case, the 45-year-old Kennedy insisting on that sort of relation with the 41-year-old Richardson. She pretended to accede, but even Bill Wright knew she had not abandoned her position.

A real smile might come if victory came, but even then, memory of centuries of injustice might not allow Gloria Richardson ever to smile amid those who had held her people in thrall for so many cruel generations, more than one hundred years since the Civil War and the start of Reconstruction, more than eight years since the U.S. Supreme Court's *Brown v. Board of Education* ruling had been ignored by Dorchester County and Cambridge.

Here were the elected leaders of this community, who had taken oaths to uphold the law, asserting some standards of civil discourse with people whose rights had been granted by the highest courts only to be resisted quietly for years and years. The Court's call for desegregation with "all deliberate speed" would be widely reinterpreted in the United States to mean "go slow, go as slowly as possible," at the speed prescribed to the people who had shown for decades that they would never change, as Douglass said, without demands.

Richardson seems to have been a teacher on this day. Robert Kennedy became something like her ally. "Robert Kennedy initially, I guess, was probably infuriated," she recalled. "Once he saw [the conditions in Cambridge], he realized the abject poverty we had, he almost did an about face, and from that time he was very supportive."[39] John Lewis, an ally of King who later became a congressman from Georgia, stood with Richardson. During a break, Kennedy took Lewis aside and said, "John, the people, the young people of SNCC have educated me. You have changed me. Now I understand."[40] And Kennedy was asking Maryland to understand—understand the stakes of continued resistance, at least.

In Annapolis, Governor Tawes responded as best he could to Washington's pressure. He had passed an open accommodations law in Maryland in 1963, but as Bill Wright saw with apprehension, it excluded the Eastern Shore counties. Maryland had always allowed counties to exempt themselves from state law under certain circumstances. What the counties accomplished, however, was very nearly the opposite of what they intended, as again Bill Wright had anticipated: protestors determined to root out the exemption and bring the Shore into the rest of civilized society. Now they had international help.

After Richardson and Wright's Washington meeting with Kennedy, Governor Tawes sent state police cruisers to Cambridge to bring the council to his office. Bill Wright had to close his business that day. "We went up to Annapolis after we met with Kennedy. The public accommodations law had been passed. We got up there, and we hadn't had anything to eat. We parked in the parking lot and headed up to a restaurant near the State House. We went in. We had a black member, Charles Cornish, a member of our council. We sat there and we sat there. I went up to the waitress and said, 'Are you going to wait on us or not?'

"She said, 'We don't serve blacks here.' I said, 'What are you talking about? You're under the public accommodations law.' She said, 'Our manager still won't serve 'em.' And here we were, on the way to see the governor. She said, 'We'll fix you something to go.' I said, 'No, you won't.' I said, 'This man is a member of the council, and he's been ordered over here by the governor.' But they wouldn't do it. So we left. We weren't going to have something without him, make him go out to the car."

"We went up to the governor's office. The mayor did most of the talking. Then Tawes said, 'What can you do to straighten this out?'

" 'Governor if we can get a pledge from Gloria that she'll stop this parading and going down in the valley and praying and just upsetting the people completely,' we said collectively. They had an ear for her. So the mayor said, 'Governor, if we pass a public accommodation ordinance, it would be effective tonight or tomorrow.'

"He said, 'Will you do that?'

"We all sat there, the five of us. I realized what he was doing. Not a one of us spoke. I wasn't about to. I was going to let one of them speak." No one responded, but Bill Wright thought silence amounted to agreement. "He had committed us to an ordinance, passing it. I said, 'Boys, I guess you realize what you've done.' "

By saying nothing at all, by not saying no, Wright thought, the councilmen had assented to the governor's request. On the way back to Cambridge, the council delegation stopped at the Chesapeake Inn on Kent Island. One of the councilmen was so nervous, he rushed into the bathroom to throw up.

Wright says he didn't say anything during the meeting with Tawes because his colleagues knew he would support the new law. What mattered were the positions taken by his less malleable colleagues, he says. "I wanted to see what they would do. If they thought it was right, I would have supported it."

Instead of an ordinance that would have taken effect immediately, they passed the buck to the voters, Wright says. "We approved a public accommodations charter amendment" outlawing discrimination in public accommodations. But, he said, instead of passing an ordinance suggested to Governor Tawes, the council sent the bill to referendum. "I suggested to the council—Gloria Richardson was at the meeting—I said I think we owe it to the people of Cambridge to get out and support it. It would make me sad not to get out and support it. I was kicked out of office for that." Wright says the council's black member, Charles Cornish, declined to campaign with him for approval.

Then Gloria confounded almost everyone. She decided to oppose black participation. She urged black voters to boycott. Many called her a traitor to the movement. How could she ask black people to oppose a measure that would make legal what the civil rights movement was all about, open accommodations? A more conciliatory accession might have worked better for her politically, but she had a point.

"I thought that since we were born in this country that we shouldn't have to [vote to obtain our rights]," she said. "That was the feeling in the community. People like to say I must be putting these ideas in people's heads, but that really wasn't true. I think it was sort of organic, you know, it was always there. And it came out here. There were Korean and World War II veterans, and they really did not see why they should vote on whether they could go, as they said, into a little greasy restaurant. People really felt that if they were born in this country and they had helped to build the country, they had no business voting on rights that should have been there. It should not have been up for question. The only reason why it was because of this racist thing."[41] The open accommodations measure was defeated 1,994 to 1,720, a margin that might have been erased had black people voted for it. The outcome may have demonstrated the erosion of a more moderate electorate in Cambridge, and it left the community without the law it needed—but not for long.

Some semblance of a truce took over in Cambridge, but it was far from permanent. "There is no real peace in Cambridge, nor can there be real peace in Cambridge until there is justice. This white man's peace is for our people a slave's peace. We have nothing to gain from a peace with a system that makes us less than men," Richardson said.[42]

Bill Wright says he understands what Richardson said. "But you know, there comes a time in everything when you have to compromise a little. You can't just be stubbornly against something. And Gloria was stubbornly against everything that wasn't exactly what she wanted."

If it was ego-driven stubbornness in Gloria Richardson, she did not reserve it for dealing with white people. She turned down a belated offer from King to come and help. In Cambridge, he had no role. The absence of his charisma was, Cambridge leaders concluded later, a blessing. Others thought the episode showed Gloria heading off toward the violent side of the spectrum. She saw it as fortuitous, something that forced the Cambridge organization to handle its own affairs.

"We had gone to a [SNCC] meeting and a decision had been made to invite Martin to come to Cambridge to speak . . . We wrote and he sent back that he was very busy, booked for the next couple of years, and that at that time if we still wanted him we would have to have $3,000." It

might as well have been $1 million. Already diverging at least theoreti-
cally from King's nonviolent approach, Richardson ultimately rejoiced
in his absence. His decision not to come "was really a favor as far as I can
see now because then we had to do it ourselves, without that prophetic,
charismatic leadership. So we did."[43] She was also reflecting some deep
fissures in the national movement, cracks that widened as more players
came onto the civil rights field. In Maryland, the differences would be
most apparent in some muted clashes with Cambridge leaders and the
NAACP.

For an incandescent moment, one person and her small Eastern Shore
army of black resistance fighters, aided by Clarence Logan and his Freedom Riders, refused to take a step they regarded as one more bit of proof
that black Americans were willing to accept second-class status—in the
very way that Douglass had warned would simply prolong ill treatment.
Gloria Richardson did not give in to the pressure. Her refusal marked
one of the most public disagreements between the civil right organizations in Maryland.

Richardson's refusal gave further impetus to an open accommodations
bill for the entire state. Cambridge's vote against the local ordinance represented another point of friction to be worried about in Washington.
Kennedy still needed a bill in Maryland, though his meetings with Gloria
Richardson apparently had begun to reshape his thinking. The embarrassing treatment of UN diplomats had created considerable pressure as
well.

But, as always, more work would have to be done. Governor Tawes
wanted house Speaker Marvin Mandel to assure him the expanded bill
covering every county in the state would pass. Mandel told the governor
he could make no such guarantee unless the governor helped him find
two or three more votes, preferably from the Shore. It was a "hard vote,"
meaning the kind of vote that could get you thrown out of office. Mandel
says he told the governor he had done all the pressuring he could do as
Speaker in the rest of the state.[44]

In a meeting with three of the Shore delegates, including Biggie Long, a
chicken farmer from Somerset County, three delegates agreed that all
three would vote yes, an arrangement designed to provide cover: no single delegate could be blamed for the bill if all of a county's representatives
voted yes. Of course, all three of them could be thrown out. But when the
governor and the Speaker are pushing for something, it's hard to resist.

With the vote pending, Lillie May Jackson appeared in Mandel's office, demanding to see the legislators from Baltimore, most of whom were white in those days, and most of whom had gone for the day, Mandel told her. Get them back here, she said. She wanted assurances they would vote for the bill.

Public accommodations restrictions—keeping blacks out of restaurants and hotels—were hateful every day, and particularly so when a family wanted to travel. It became a part of black life to drive all the way through, knowing you couldn't count on finding places to eat or sleep. Thurgood Marshall remembered Sunday drives to the Shore with his parents. They brought food and drink, not knowing if they'd be able to find a place where they could be served.

In time, Frederick's Bill Lee says, there was a Green Book, a kind of Michelin guide for black travelers in the United States, that pointed to the places where black families could have a meal or stay the night. Before that book was out, black travelers just went up to the first black person they saw to ask about accommodations. Just the way things were in Maryland and in the nation. Mandel gave Jackson assurances, but he was not confident the bill would pass either.

Unable to provide a guarantee, he says, he eventually convinced her he had done all he could do. Like other Jewish legislators—men and women who had lived with the sting of prejudice and discrimination—Mandel had been an ally of Jackson and civil rights causes, so she may have been more willing to accept his assurances. She knew that he had taken care to help the few newly elected black representatives from Baltimore as they tried to survive in a still-segregated Annapolis. At one point, he had integrated the Maryland Inn, a historic hotel on Main Street that had refused to accept reservations from a party that would include the new black legislator, Irma Dixon of Baltimore. Mandel simply walked in with her, sat down, and ordered. Here was power, challenging discriminatory custom, cleansing the channels of everyday life.

When the open accommodation vote was taken, two of the three Eastern Shoremen kept their commitments. But Mandel says one of them, Biggie Long, "took a walk"—didn't vote at all, didn't vote nay, didn't vote aye, didn't vote at all, a tepid last hurrah of resistance for the Shore's ethic of exclusion. The bill passed as, perhaps, Long knew it would. Mandel knew how to count, and how to keep an extra vote just in case.

Hotdog Simpkins says businessmen along Route 50 to Ocean City and other Shore points told him later that nothing bad had happened after the new law was passed. Bill Wright says friends who told him directly they were voting against him came to him later saying they'd made a mistake; they apologized and voted him back into office.

Marylanders would boast that their state had been one of the first states south of the Mason-Dixon Line to pass such a bill. It had done so before the U.S. Congress acted in 1964 on the same issue. But it was hard to argue that the state had forged some progressive path, moving ahead of the nation as it did so.

During that year's Democratic presidential primary in Maryland, George W. Wallace took his segregationist appeal to Cambridge, where thousands crowded into the fire-and-rescue lodge to hear him. Wallace soft-pedaled the racial plank in his platform, invoking instead the specter of federal intervention. It remained a resonant theme in Maryland, where leaders such as Governor Albert R. Ritchie had built long careers on the same arguments. Wallace did well. He had 214,849 votes to 267,106 for Daniel B. Brewster, a civil rights advocate who was Maryland's stand-in for his party's eventual nominee, President Lyndon Baines Johnson. Wallace fared better in Maryland than in either of the other two states outside the South, Indiana and Wisconsin, where he sought to find vulnerable favorite-son opponents.[45]

GOON SQUAD: THE WORD ON THE STREET

When President Lyndon Johnson's antipoverty program began in the 1960s, every major American city had an official community action or antipoverty agency with a well-paid director. The Reverend Vernon Dobson and a group of black Baltimore clergymen had a candidate for this bit of patronage: Clarence Mitchell's brother, Parren. A decade earlier, they would have had no hope of coming away with the job.

But these men were beginning to have a profile. They were known to some as the Goon Squad, an ironic tag evoking the deep respect they enjoyed throughout the community. They led influential churches. They had constituents who could be gotten to the polls. They went to city hall to see Mayor McKeldin.

Only a few short years earlier, during McKeldin's first mayoral term in the 1940s, such a mission might not even have been attempted. But they were there to collect on a promise: they knew black votes had given McKeldin leverage in his runs for mayor and later for governor. And President Johnson's antipoverty program had been designed to give black Americans economic and political opportunity, opportunity not available in the bad old days of Jim Crow.

In Maryland under McKeldin, blacks had won access to government officials, but change still came slowly in every institution: public education, the law, and public accommodations. Even in a program designed to help them overcome years of discrimination, Dobson knew he and his squad had to press their advantage. Even with a man like McKeldin, a man predisposed to meet their demands, demands had to be made. They did not come to the mayor with the ancient power of the political clubhouse, a white-dominated sector of public life, but they had begun to demonstrate their ability to move their community with their own rhetoric. They had allowed their power to be borrowed by men like McKeldin, and now they were using it themselves, claiming the spoils. The church was changing, and the Goon Squad was the change agent.

"Ohhh," McKeldin moaned, according to Dobson, a great mimic, "you put me under great pressure. You know I love you, my brothers. But ohhhh." Dobson and the others nodded. "Yes, yes. We love you, too. You're the only white politician who's been with us."[46] It was part of a dance they did. Many black Baltimoreans realized their mayor was as good as it got with white politicians. Many of them thought he was sincere when, as always, he referred to them as "brothers." And for those who were determined to get something tangible in return for the votes they gave him, McKeldin was manageable. You just had to go through the preliminaries.

The mayor began to moan again about the pressure. The ministers did not relent.

"On this one," said the Reverend Frank Williams, head of the Interdenominational Ministerial Alliance, a powerful group of clergymen, "we can't give up. It has to be Parren Mitchell." Parren it was. Even with a progressive civil rights partisan, an appointment that would have been routine in white political circles still had to be petitioned into place for black Baltimoreans. This was called a piece of the pie, a meaningful portion of the spoils, not the leftovers.

More pressure was exerted on McKeldin when the city council considered, once again, its own version of an open accommodations bill. When the negotiations looked difficult, picketers led by Juanita Jackson Mitchell finally found the end of McKeldin's patience. He invited her to his office and vented. "He was damning and helling all over the place," she said after the session. Didn't the picketers realize, he said, that more pressure would make the negotiations more difficult? It was better for him politically to give in on his own—not to look like he was giving in to black pressure.

But, yes, the prodding was necessary, she told him. "We are used to being told actions are ill-timed. The time for being reasonable about constitutional points is over."[47] In this sentiment, she stood with the implacable Gloria Richardson, though the Mitchells and the NAACP were not always supportive of the Cambridge leader's positions. They were expressing the same attitude from different points of view.

McKeldin did not withhold his own feelings. "I have been battling for civil rights longer than some of the pickets have been alive. God protect me from my friends," he said.[48] When CORE made Baltimore a target city, McKeldin was not happy with the suggestion that Baltimore was resisting civil rights action, but he did his best to keep his anger and frustration out of public view. He met CORE representatives quickly, welcomed them, and made a financial contribution—a key to the city, more or less.

His secretary, Mildred Momberger, gave further testimony on the times and their effect on a man who was sympathetic to the cause and involved in it before many black Baltimoreans were ready to jump in. "He'd stand by the window of the mayor's office and look out, and he'd say, 'There's so many things to be done out there, and yet all I've done all day is spend my time meeting such and such a group and trying to satisfy them. Maybe tomorrow I can get busy on so and so.' The next day it would be another problem. Everything had erupted. Of course, he blamed white people that these problems had not been faced sooner."[49]

The ministers were elated by their victories. Success bred more action. These men of the cloth accelerated their involvement, but their decision to step down from the pulpit was not universally applauded. Quite the contrary.

They were regarded in some quarters as disreputable, ungoverned by the conventions of their calling. What they were doing was unseemly. They had gone into the street to raise hell, hadn't they? A bunch of goons, someone said. Hence their name, Goon Squad. Out of the pulpit and moving to the head of the marching throngs, this Baltimore-based band of ministers and university professors embraced the slur, wore it with pride. It proved to them that anyone who stood up for civil rights would be challenged as somehow disreputable—the better to discredit the mission.

These men were running against an even deeper tide than the one governing clerical decorum. "The prevailing feeling here then among too many," said the Reverend A. J. Payne, pastor of Enon Baptist Church, "was that segregation was segregation, and it was going to be that way till kingdom come. The Negro's place was fixed and few had the nerve to try to change it. Some very fine men in the community were just plain afraid."[50] While he was still working for Lillie May Jackson, Thurgood Marshall had been speaking in the churches, confidently and bravely. Jim Crow or not, he would say, we have rights, but we have to fight for them.

The Goon Squad, its members only slightly younger, had heard his message.

"Some eleven kindred souls dreamed of a more perfect city that could be attained by political empowerment," wrote Homer Favor, a Morgan State University professor and member of the squad.[51] It was not a new vision for them. They were reinvigorated by young black people, but they had also been Martin Luther King's confidantes, and historically, their predecessors had set the example for King and others.

Among the earliest Baltimore leaders was the Reverend Harvey Johnson, pastor of Union Baptist Church on Druid Hill Avenue, a gray stone edifice of quiet majesty. Johnson had been an activist minister in the late 1800s. He pushed formation of something called the Order of Regulators, founded for the purpose of demanding civil rights in Baltimore. Its work—building political strength and the strength of black leaders—helped force at least one immediate breakthrough. In 1885, the same year the Regulators were founded, Everett J. Waring was the first black person admitted to the practice of law in Baltimore. Two years later, Reverend Johnson changed the group's name to the Brotherhood of Liberty.

A new spirit of political independence was detected among nineteenth-century black men, a degree of independence that might have accelerated the move toward disenfranchisement of black voters. In a series of essays published by the *Afro*'s publishing arm, Reverend Johnson began to lay down principles that would be echoed a few years later by W. E. B. Du

Bois in the NAACP's founding principles. Johnson wrote, "There are American citizens of African descent who are denied the privileges guaranteed to every American citizen without regard to race, color or previous condition of servitude upon the pretext that they have no rights which the white man is bound to respect." The echo of *Dred Scott* was too clear to be disputed. "We believe [the black man] to be entitled to all the rights of citizenship, and the man or set of men who deprives men of their constitutional rights are traitors to the cause of good government."[52] As he spoke out despairingly of the compelling need to stop a plague of lynching, he was unsparing of white leaders: "Take the white man in any stage of the world in which he has acted a part, and he will show up as a lawbreaker and disturber of the general peace. He is, as a race, cruel, heartless and bloodthirsty."[53]

Johnson urged black Baptists to separate from their white colleagues unless there was cooperation in the pursuit of civil, religious, and educational rights. He demanded trials for lynch mobs "now going unwhipped of justice in the different parts of the country, especially in the South." He wanted "tavern and innkeepers to admit our ministers and delegates to the same accommodation that is accorded to the white representatives" of their church. He wanted cooperation in pursuit of proper marriage laws that forbade interracial marriage—laws that force black women into "illicit relationships" with white men.[54]

Frederick Douglass, who continued to speak occasionally in Baltimore, offered a rationale for the new black political consciousness: "It was a common thing to hear men of his race say," according to an account of a Douglass speech, "that they were under no obligation to the Republican party." Douglass acknowledged that such a break would be remarkable: "If not under obligation to that organization, then in Heaven's name to whom were they [obligated]? If not to the strong arm which rent their chains and set them at liberty, then to whom?" He had an answer, as paraphrased by the *Morning Herald*: "Speaking to those who advise the colored to set up for themselves, in politics, [Douglass] said he would rather be a small piece of something than a large piece of nothing."[55] The Goon Squad was swept up by Baltimore and Maryland history as well as by King and the spiritual drive of the new movement's objectives.

In October 1964, King had come to Baltimore to confer with Dobson, one of Harvey Johnson's successors at Union Baptist, and others: "We were a little further ahead in the work that we were doing in Baltimore in civil rights than he was. So, much of the work that he was doing was empowered by what we were doing here in Baltimore," Dobson said.[56] And so much of the NAACP itself was traceable to the work Reverend Johnson had done in the late 1800s with his Brotherhood of Liberty. Only the brilliance of W. E. B. Du Bois eclipsed the work done by Johnson, Dobson thought.[57]

What the Goon Squad did, though, was a critical step in the recruitment of black participants in the local movement. "We electrified the city by honing the electoral process to place Judge Joseph C. Howard on the then Supreme Bench of Baltimore," Favor wrote.[58] The Goon Squad came together when Howard, then an assistant state's attorney, declared his candidacy. They knew they could win. The prophet Costonie, Lillie May Jackson, the Young People's Forum, and Harry Cole had shown the potential.

The challenge might have been greater for the Goon Squad because the element of surprise that helped Cole was no longer there. The bosses, Pollack and Kovens, and their ward-level lieutenants knew how to deal with challengers. They had perfected the game over many decades, and they had succeeded for much of that period in keeping black candidates from winning—and black voters from voting. As in the state's schools and universities, the political bosses dealt with the demands of black Maryland by accommodating black demands with no or only minimal loss of control.

The Goon Squad wanted more. Men of God for the most part, they were somewhat embarrassed by their failure to exert a more dynamic presence. But many of their black colleagues continued to embrace the idea that black suffering was divinely ordained, God's way of making them earn a place in heaven. According to this view, their parishioners should make peace with the way it was and do their best to survive in a world designed to frustrate almost everything they did.

But King's national profile—his successes across the country—was pushing the black church into activism regarded by many ministers as radical. The church then tended to believe "that the pain that the black community experienced at the hands of white society was . . . a test of character, a test of will—a test that would ultimately prepare them for ascendance to the Kingdom of God."[59] The Reverend W. J. Winston, pastor of New Metropolitan Baptist Church, put it this way: "Adversity and affliction are God's ministers sent out in search of heroism in men . . . When God would make a people great, He calls for the Angel of suffering . . . Suffering takes his orders from God." Winston advised his congregation to lose neither faith, nor pride in themselves.[60]

Dobson went after this way of thinking after King's death, implying at a meeting of the Interdenominational Ministerial Alliance that it was ministerial apathy not white racism that killed King. "He reminded his fellow ministers of their responsibility to fight a system that allowed racists to ignore the rights of black people and to kill their leaders."[61]

In the following days and months, these ministers became social service entrepreneurs. The Reverend Marion Bascom, pastor of Douglas Memorial Community Church, spent church funds to buy a city block along Madison Street and convert it into low-income housing. Bascom had been a key adviser to Morgan State College students involved in the Freedom Rides in many Maryland communities. He had been part of the adult team that integrated the Northwood Shopping Center and downtown department stores. He was the Goon Squad's intellectual, though all its members were steeped in scripture and the social gospel that inspired the Hopkins chaplain, Chester Wickwire. Bascom made his way through the existential miasma of racism and segregation with a simple belief: when people, black and white, see there is nothing to fear from justice and equality, they will ask why so much marching and hatred and brutality were necessary.

Dobson's Union Baptist Church began to provide literacy classes and child care. The Reverend James L. Moore, pastor of Sharon Baptist Church, started a chapter of Opportunities Industrial Center (OIC), a training program initiated in Philadelphia by the Reverend Leon Sullivan. OIC taught carpentry, auto repair, and secretarial skills. Reverend Dobson was the first OIC director in Baltimore. He and others saw Baltimore's black community as "trapped within an economically oriented power structure." Years later, he founded Baltimoreans United in Leadership Development (BUILD), an organization of activists attempting to show a doubting black community that political involvement could pay off for them. BUILD, under another minister, Bishop Douglas Miles, started a housing development program that built and rehabilitated housing all over the city. They managed to convince political leaders they were a potent force, a perception that earned them millions in state money.

Held together by wit, shared outrage, and success, the Goon Squad came from the black clergy's deep reservoir of accomplished leaders. Bascom was an eloquent, scholarly wise man, a thinker with insight and puckish humor. Dobson was a deep-throated jester, a man whose passionate spirituality flew out of aching, ironic laughter. Dobson's testimony suggests an even deeper motivation for his involvement. He revered his mother's courageous involvement in the movement—before it was a movement—and lamented the Jim Crow system's wounding of the black male psyche. "My father couldn't do it because the history of America is that black men responding to our conflict were in danger of being treated as malcontents [losing their jobs in the post office or in the schools—thus the difficulty of finding complainants for the equal teacher pay suits]. A black woman could be in the movement at a time when a black man dared not. Black men did not join the civil rights movement until it had been set up by black women."[62]

Some of these men had done more than march. They were, after all, natural politicians with built-in constituencies. One of these was the Reverend Wendell Phillips, a motorcycle-riding, bearlike man of God, pastor of Heritage United Church of Christ in northwest Baltimore. He was a man of many callings, a man who moved aggressively into the new mold of black leaders. His deeply rounded speaking voice, used often in opposition to the death penalty, helped him get elected to the House of Delegates, where his wit—and his bike—made him a colorful and cherished member. He led the Interdenominational Ministerial Alliance in combat with Mayor William Donald Schaefer, suing the mayor over a failure to promote black employees. Then he became Schaefer's ally.

The Goon Squad number included Favor, passionate, angry, and intellectual, a force at Morgan State University. Their most famous candidate, Joe Howard, was also a member of the squad. He had stunned the white legal Establishment with a study that showed deep disparities in the sentences of blacks accused of raping white women as compared with the sentences for whites who had committed the same crime against black women. Howard's effort was decried but not refuted. His candidacy for the bench seemed like a further assault on the precincts of the bar. But perhaps no one much feared candidate Howard. Sitting judges were seldom unseated: the bosses took care of them.

Howard was a dream candidate for the movement. He had dared to do the study. He was a man of courage and ability. His 1968 campaign was run, in part, by a young Columbia University law school graduate and civil rights firebrand, Larry Gibson. Gibson and others on the squad knew, as Harry Cole had known, that they had to play the game the way it was played by the bosses. It wasn't going to be enough to decry defeat at the hands of ancient powers.

Dobson says the campaign for all three candidates was financed quietly by Peter Angelos, then a councilman who had offered his own public accommodations bill; James Rouse, the developer and visionary who later built Columbia, Maryland; and Robert Embry. Howard won. Mitchell came close and won, narrowly, two years later.

For election day, following another practiced get-out-the-vote method, Gibson had Howard make a recording to be played over loudspeakers mounted on the tops of cars that patrolled the black neighborhoods. The message echoed a plea made openly during the length of the campaign: "Don't vote for three, just vote for me," Howard said over and over on election day.

The voters were being urged to "single shoot"—a machine-honed tactic employed to increase the power of the vote for a selected candidate, in this case Howard. They could vote for as many as five other candidates, but if large numbers of voters went for Joe Howard alone, they were enhancing his chances and denying support to his opponents. Gibson and Howard knew their opponents would do the same thing, so they didn't hesitate. Howard was elected.

The Howard and Cole victories and others made the black electorate look like the electoral force it had always been, which was the big-picture Goon Squad objective. In the courthouse, Joe Howard befriended the clerks and elevator operators and other anonymous workers and went to bat for them on wages and working conditions. He baked for them, adding a down-home touch to his very dignified mien. He was a tall and burly man, with snow-white hair and a wide fatherly smile, the personification of judicial temperament—just the sort of figure canny civil rights activists were always looking for when a formerly all-white bastion was being penetrated. Image was everything even then.

With Democrat Jimmy Carter in the White House, the responsibility—and political pleasure—of making judicial nominations fell to Maryland's Democratic U.S. senator Paul A. Sarbanes. He chose Howard. Maryland had never had a black federal judge. "The African American community in Maryland wanted it very badly. It's one of the things they pointed to when they talked about how they had been neglected," he said. Because of Howard's sentencing study, "a lot of people had it in for him. They thought he was too radical," Sarbanes said. The Maryland State Bar immediately opposed him. "They've been trying to live that down ever since."[63]

Attorney General Stephen H. Sachs supported Howard, too, writing a letter of recommendation to the bar association as it reviewed Howard's qualifications. Sachs pointed out that the judge had been not only a friend of the worker, but on the side of business as well—not simply a revolutionary, in other words, but someone with a wider perspective, someone willing to listen and weigh the equities.

When Joe Howard died in 2000, Goon Squad members hailed his great bearing and judicial temperament. They called him a leader and man of his people. Dobson made a few jokes. U.S. District Court judge J. Frederick Motz spoke, as did Senator Sarbanes. Wendell Phillips had died by then. Homer Favor was there to urge a renewal of the struggle. Still angry, still militant, he stood on the podium with the ministers and raged against what he feared was the coming, once again, of intolerance. In a review of the Goon Squad's contributions, he pointed out that Maryland had by the 1990s many more black delegates and senators in Annapolis—more than most other states. The squad got people into jobs they couldn't have held in the past. It kept watch over agencies to be certain they hired in accordance with the rules.

By then, they were getting high-level help—self-help, you might say. With their assistance, Clarence Mitchell's brother, Parren, was elected to Congress, with a margin of thirty-seven votes. Democratic leaders, who might have supported a recount in earlier days, accepted the result with some relief. Black progress at the polls was important to the maintenance of domestic tranquility. In the U.S. Congress, Mitchell engineered a black set-aside program in which black contractors were to get certain percentages of government work as recognition of the many years in which black Americans had been barred from progress in practice and by law. "A retrospective look at the Goon Squad era quickens the spirit," Favor wrote. "The fresh new bursts of hope, promise and élan proved enchanting. Reflecting, however, upon the current condition is saddening. Contemplate, momentarily, the consequences of right wing mania now engulfing the nation. It has focused upon the abandonment of affirmative action, a reduction in the level of support for public education and an assault upon equality in the dispensation of justice. This ultra conservative madness results in the widening of the income disparity between the rich and the poor and the plundering of the economic system. The widespread hostility toward intellectualism is part and parcel of this nefarious conduct, thereby facilitating broad based endorsement of mediocrity."[64]

At Howard's funeral, Judge Motz spoke of Howard's "strength of conviction, his compassion and understanding"—a man of pride, he said. U.S. congressman Elijah Cummings said Howard had been one of the men he saw as a model, a man of dignity, a man who did not "laugh when it wasn't funny or scratch when it didn't itch." Vernon Dobson thanked God "for Joseph, a man of many colors . . . for the integrity of his heart. Just over the horizon he leads us to follow." Dobson thanked "Paul Sarbanes for having the courage to see in him the intellectual ferment which colors the 7th District for all time."

Sarbanes, a son of Salisbury, remembered his father in tears, recounting the lynching there. Sarbanes's own experience had included a progressive basketball coach who took his team to Princess Anne and the University of Maryland Eastern Shore (UMES) to scrimmage. The all-black UMES team later came to Cambridge for a game and were kept out of the gym until the coach personally escorted them to seats behind the Salisbury team's bench.

When Sarbanes ran for the Maryland House of Delegates in 1966, he and his wife, Christine, were campaigning door-to-door one day in East Baltimore, and at one of the houses, a young student came to the door. Robert Mack Bell, the young sit-in leader from Dunbar, by then a student at Morgan, met the young candidate. "We got to talking," Bell recalls. "I told him what I was doing. He told me how Boston was the best place to go to school. Based on what he said, I only applied to Harvard, Boston University, and Boston College. He was inspirational. He was out running on his own dime, and he spent an hour with me," said Bell, who chose Harvard.[65] Thirty years later, after practicing in Baltimore and serving on all three levels of the state court system, Robert Mack Bell became chief judge of the Maryland Court of Appeals. Joe Howard had spoken at Bell's investiture at the district court level. Bell was at Howard's funeral, too.

The service drew to a close as Gibson played the old election day car tape, with the voice of Joe Howard exhorting the faithful to vote, not for three, just for me.

Funerals such as this are called celebrations of life, and as the first rank of civil rights pathfinders began to pass from the scene, the celebratory quality rose, transforming solemn moments into reflections on a singular period in U.S. history. In Maryland, the civil rights movement became a principled union that bound men and women—black and white—in harrowing moments of commitment. As the twentieth century ended and a new century began, obituaries in the *Sun* began to commemorate other largely anonymous civil rights partisans: Michael G. Holofcener, for example, not a recognizable name in the civil rights hall of fame but an important person whose position put him in conflict with powerful men. He did not flinch. He was chairman of the Baltimore County Human Relations Commission, openly clashing with County Executive Agnew over Agnew's lack of support for civil rights during the Gwynn Oak Amusement Park crisis. Agnew had demanded his resignation. Holofcener had refused to give it.

The Agnew versus Holofcener confrontation perfectly illustrated the strategy of give and retreat: create a commission but keep your foot on the brake; resist any speed. Allow Donald Murray into the law school, but concede no precedent, observe no established principle, dismantle no other barriers to fairness. Forget the findings of illegality and require a lawsuit before opening each of the state university's professional schools, though they were practicing the same sort of discrimination. Recognize *Brown v. Board of Education,* but interpret "all deliberate speed" to mean no speed at all; pass an open accommodations law, but exempt an entire region of the state (the Shore) or an entire industry (bars and taverns). Resist desegregation up to creation of international incidents caused by refusal to serve African diplomats on Route 40. Recognize the justice of equal pay for teachers, but resist it until caught in the act. Bar black people from Baltimore's Pratt Library School, force a court suit, and when you lose, close the school rather than admit black student librarians.

The Goon Squad—joining, over the course of history, people like Eugene O'Dunne, Michael Holofcener, Theodore McKeldin, and Chester Wickwire—refused to go along.

Obituaries offered opportunities to remember or to introduce people who stood up for decency. Funerals were a moment for contemplating progress and work still to be done and for marveling at how ideas and people could drive action. The Goon Squad planted itself by the water. It had not been moved. It had overcome—not just in some distant day, but in its own day. Its leaders knew the struggle would never end, but they knew also that, during their youth, too little had been accomplished, too little had been tried. But the old willingness to accept the way things were had changed, and they had helped change it. The soothing funeral anthem "It Is Well" filled the sanctuary of Union Baptist like a benediction, not for a single person or politician or for a dozen men with a mockingly proud name, but for a generation or more of Americans who had faith in themselves and in the ideals of their country.

CHAPTER 5

Seats at the Table

O n July 24, 1967, a reckless challenge flew into the still-combustible tinder of Cambridge. The notorious H. Rap Brown headed back from New York to address the subject of black power—to revive the CNAC's resistance there and to counter the appearance of Joe Carroll, a white supremacist who had made inflammatory speeches at Patterson Park in Baltimore and in Cambridge.

Gloria Richardson, after speaking with her daughter Donna, who still lived in Cambridge, asked Brown to make the Cambridge speech but urged him to check in with General Gelston. Richardson and the national guard commander had worked well together during the first Cambridge uprising.

Gelston had won the trust of Richardson, the young black woman who had run out of patience with most white officials. She was a more reasonable leader than her stoic resolve led many to believe. She believes others in Maryland attempted to have Gelston replaced because he was regarded as conciliatory or "soft" on lawbreakers.[1] They were headed off ultimately by recognition that Gelston had backers in Washington. Richardson had moved to New York City by then, but Gelston was still on call for Cambridge, still wary of new outbreaks of violence.

Brown refused to meet with Gelston, as Richardson knew he would. He was not going to speak with any white man, she said.[2] Something like the calamity Richardson and her daughter feared came upon the city almost instantly.

On the evening after he arrived, Brown stood on the hood of a car to make a speech. "If this town don't come around," he famously said, "this town should be burned down. Just don't burn your own stuff." It was, Richardson said later, a standard stump speech for Brown—disregarded by most who heard it. It was rhetoric, not a set of marching orders. But Cambridge was a place, Richardson knew, where whites and blacks had armed themselves.[3] People rode through the black neighborhoods during the worst days of that period, shooting from the windows of their cars and being shot at as they sped away.

This time, Brown got his fire. As usual, despite his throwaway warning about "your own stuff," the damage occurred almost exclusively in the black community along Pine Street. An elementary school was virtually destroyed. A black businessman's club, the Green Savoy, burned without interruption by the fire department, which refused to respond. Lemeul Chester, later a minister in Cambridge, says chief Brice Kinnamon told him: "You goddamn niggers started the fire, now you goddamn niggers watch it burn. I don't give a damn if the entire Second Ward burns." This recollection of Kinnamon's language is consistent with his remarks throughout the years of turmoil.[4]

Two weeks later, Hansel Greene, owner of the burned-out Savoy and several other establishments clustered together on Pine Street, grabbed his shotgun and shot himself fatally in the heart. He didn't understand, his wife said later, why such a tragedy should happen to him. "I tried to be nice to everybody," he told her. Greene was punished for the view that every black citizen should be held accountable for the hateful and outrageous comments of one man.[5] Tennis courts were not the only amenity or public service paid for but withheld from black citizens. Surely, Hansel Greene deserved protection of the fire department.

Rap Brown was indicted on arson charges, and soon after, an explosion damaged the courthouse in Cambridge. The prosecutor there wanted the case moved to Harford County. Cambridge had had all the sensational activity it needed. But Brown's defense lawyer, the famous trial advocate for civil rights and antiwar activists William Kunstler, actually hoped the case could be tried in Cambridge because he and Brown felt their situation would not be improved in virtually all-white Harford County. Cambridge was by then their theater, the backdrop with name recognition that would give them some sympathy in the wider world.

Fears that an explosive event would occur in Bel Air, the Harford county seat, were confirmed for some when a car on its way there exploded, killing two of Brown's SNCC colleagues, Ralph Featherstone and

William "Che" Payne. The case was then transferred to Howard County, west and south of Baltimore, and perhaps, in a racial sense, middle ground. There, state's attorney Richard Kinlein investigated the arson charges and found them baseless. Brown had been hit in the forehead by a shotgun pellet and was in the hospital when the fires started. He could not have set the fires in question. He had uttered inflammatory words, but he had not set the fires. By then Brown had fled, assuming that the case against him would go forward, baseless or not. Kinlein, though, thought of himself as an officer of the court, bound to interpret the law accurately no matter who the defendant might be. Like judge Eugene O'Dunne in the *Murray* law school case, he was determined to do his duty as he saw it.

Kinlein's law license was threatened during this process. He had violated a gag order imposed by judges in the case. His friends were so worried, they began to raise a defense fund for him. Neighbors for whom he had cut the lawn as a boy were among those who sent contributions. Kinlein had risked his career to uphold the law.[6] And he had done it in an atmosphere bristling with danger and fear of what were then referred to ominously as "long hot summers." The nation seemed constantly on the brink of urban warfare. The federal government attempted to tamp down tension by pouring money into various job and training programs, but there was a limit to the control it could assert on rioters or on those who sought to confront demonstrators. And yet, while appeals to racial fear and animosity continued, the underlying movement led by Richardson and Jackson continued, almost literally rising from the ashes in some cases.

On the night of the Cambridge fire, Bill Jews found his way to Race Street to see what was happening. He was a tall black kid with a bright future that might have ended on the night Hansel Greene's life went up in smoke. Jews's parents, like Greene, had done relatively well in Cambridge. They had roots in the community. They owned property. They ran businesses. Their son was a good student, a sought-after basketball player only then becoming fully aware that the world he lived in was changing. He was in more danger than he might have imagined on the night of the fire.

He left his house after Brown had uttered his famous taunt. He watched flames consume the elementary school he'd attended, but a more prosaic image remained in his consciousness: someone carried a soda machine from the front of Hansel Greene's club into the middle of the street. In the background, the heart of black Cambridge was becoming an inferno. At one point, the 15-year-old Jews headed back home through a nearby alley. As he came around the corner, he found a national guardsman with a bayoneted rifle. Jews turned and ran back in the other direction. He wondered about it later: if he'd tried to get home, would he have been shot or run through with the bayonet? The whole city of Cambridge had a near death experience.

Jews, who became head of CareFirst BlueCross/BlueShield thirty-five years later, thinks in retrospect that protest in the street was necessary to make any progress in a resolutely white society, a society that seemed incapable of understanding the grievances that led cities to the brink and beyond. What happened, then, in his life reinforces many of the points argued by Marshall and Mitchell and Jackson thirty-three years earlier with "Shop Where You Can Work," the Donald Gaines Murray law school case, the equal pay suit, and so many other chapters in this saga. "I remember life changing with school desegregation in 1969," Jews says. "I thought that was a huge crossover thing."[7]

He wanted to go to college, and he knew he had catching up to do. "I figured out how to get in study groups. We went to [a new friend's] house in a white community. I remember that." He would not have thought of visiting a white classmate's house before that year. He wouldn't have had a white classmate.

For black Americans, the opportunities suddenly available to Bill Jews and others—more than eating together with whites—was the point. Perhaps a clearer understanding of that black point of view would have been helpful to whites who had a real fear of close contact with blacks, something blacks tended to think was lunacy. But a merely gradual concession of rights was not acceptable any longer in Cambridge. Some of the same old segregationist resistance went on after the fire, but change was inexorable, and with it came opportunity.

"By going to an integrated school in my senior year, I probably got a better perspective on the world. That helped me understand that I needed to accelerate my intellectual competitiveness. There were kids there who I thought were, if not better educated, better exposed to the outside world. Kids were talking about going to Europe, flying on planes, doing lots of things I had never done. And I said, 'There's a whole new world out there.' There was a huge gap between where I was [at the black high school] and what I learned my senior year." Jews absorbed the lessons because he was hungry for them and because they were finally available.

He arrived at his new school with confidence and strength learned from his parents. His father was a barber, a carpenter, and a property owner. His mother managed the properties. As life began to change in Cambridge, Willie Jews, Bill's father, became a member of the local hospital board. At some point, he was given a gavel, which, his son remembers, he proudly displayed on the mantelpiece above the fireplace. "I had the best parents in the world. My mother said, 'You don't have to be subservient or take a back seat as long as you live.' She taught me to be prepared for the opportunity, and she dared me to take the risk and be different."

The move was as emotionally challenging for Jews as it had been fifteen years earlier for black students walking into white schools in Baltimore. He had been an outstanding basketball player at Mace's Lane, the black high school that closed the year Cambridge High fully integrated. He remembered the tension that had surrounded the first game two years earlier, the first one permitted between black and white schools. Jim Crow perched on the hardwood, too, in the stands and on the court. When the schools merged, some lingering loyalty to Mace's Lane, perhaps, robbed the game of its attraction for him. He thought about not playing, but he eventually agreed to join the team. And he was elected class president without opposition. He had white study partners. He had a plan for the rest of his life, and he knew the steps he had to take. He ended up with two boxes full of scholarship offers. Loyola wanted him. So did the U.S. Naval Academy. Lefty Driesell, the University of Maryland coach and legendary recruiter, knocked on his door. And a coach from Bowie State, a black school in Prince George's County, came to his house.

"Where are you going to school?" the coach asked.

"Mr. Jordan, I'm going to Bowie.

"And he said, 'No, you're not. You can do better than that.' He said, why didn't I think about Hopkins. I said, 'That's a hospital, isn't it?'

"He said no, there's a university there. You should think about it. You're smart enough." Actually, Jews had been thinking about medical school. One of his neighbors, James Edward Fassett, the only black physician in Cambridge, urged him toward Hopkins, too. "He was always very supportive." And so, in a sense, was the entire community. Basketball coaches, Jews's mother and father, Fassett, the students who elected him class president. And, of course, Jews's success had required an extraordinary young man who was open to the wisdom of his parents and who was ready to take advantage of the opportunities suddenly at his disposal.

And then another coach came to his house in the spring of 1970: Jim Valvano, the charismatic leader who later took North Carolina State to the NCAA Championship, in 1983. Valvano was the coach at Johns Hopkins then. Jews recalls, "My dad was ill. So [Valvano] talked to my mother about the value of being able to come to Baltimore and see the games, and that they were interested in me. And my first questions were, 'Mr. V, don't you just offer athletic scholarships?' and he said, 'No, we don't have any.' And I said, 'Well, then I'm interested.' " Jews and his mother went for a visit. "I went to the guidance office, and I said I want a scholarship, but you're not offering enough money, and I want that room in the corner. My mother looked at me like I was crazy. Two days later they called and upped the number and gave me the room."

Valvano left that year to coach at Iona College, so Jews never played for him. Actually, he came close to staying away from the game altogether. In another risk-taking moment, he decided not to play in his freshman year. He knew the academic going would be challenging. "I had come out of a decent academic environment, but at Hopkins, there were kids from New York; they had advanced placement. They'd had calculus. It was tough. I decided I was not going to play until I got to a real study discipline." At one point, he almost left school, but his mother appealed to his competitive pride. "My mother manipulated the hell out of me when I was about to leave Hopkins. I called her one night crying because I was not doing well. There were some concepts I couldn't grasp. I don't even remember what they were. I said, 'This school is just too hard. I don't know why you let me come here.' And she said, 'Son, I want you to listen to me. If that school is too hard for you, and those white people up there are too smart and you can't compete, you just come home and work in the factory, and your mother will take care of you.' I looked at that phone and said there's no goddamned way I'm going home. I slammed down the phone. I didn't know what had happened at the time. But what she did was challenge me. She knew what she had put inside of me."

When he thinks about the corrosive ethic of those black kids who reject academic advancement as the province of white people—"acting white"—he says, "I think sometimes what we do is make a determination that, unfortunately, to come up to the standard of acceptable behavior in society [we have] to create a black-white divide, and I don't think that's necessary. I think we need to be able to move through that. It creates a huge problem in our society. We ought to urge people to compete at the highest level possible, to raise their academic standing, and you can do that and still be culturally sensitive to the issues of the black community."

He's not sure what his parents thought about the leadership of Gloria Richardson, ultimately, but he's certain they wouldn't have rejected it out of hand. "I don't think they would have been out front on those issues, but I think the value system they taught me was embracing of what integration should be, that I should not under any circumstances be lesser—lesser prepared, lesser able to assimilate than anybody else. In fact they taught me to take the risk."

He graduated from Hopkins in 1974, which was by then more welcoming to black students, and began a career that saw him become president and CEO of CareFirst BlueCross/BlueShield, one of the leading health insurance companies in the nation. He ended up a poster child for opportunity—and for the kind of nurturing and stable family life that makes it possible to take advantage of opportunity and talent. Without the opportunity, though, without the forceful guidance of law and the eventual easing of antagonisms, talented kids were not going to be in a position to take positive risks, to challenge themselves, to believe they could achieve.

BACKLASH: A MARTYRED KING AND THE MAKING OF A VICE PRESIDENT

On April 4, 1968, Martin Luther King Jr. was assassinated in Memphis, Tennessee. Baltimore leaders—the Goon Squad, Mayor D'Alesandro, and Theodore McKeldin—had to deal with a city on edge and feelings of profound, personal loss.

Baltimoreans had been part of King's extended kitchen cabinet of advisers. They had counseled with him over the years, feeling they were— along with Lillie May Jackson—a little ahead of the national movement.

Only recently, they had traveled with him to Florida for a conference on strategy. Which way should the movement go? There was much dissension in the King ranks and anguish in the leader.

"I saw him naked in pain," said Reverend Dobson. "He was a man who was really not in touch with the next steps. And so his death to me was more than the tragedy of one man dying. It was the tragedy of knowing he died not being fulfilled. He had gotten the Nobel Peace Prize and all these other things, but in his own center he was in conflict."[8] Reverend Bascom knew him well, too, calling him by his nickname, Mike.

Young Tommy D'Alesandro had been the city council president when King had come to Baltimore in 1964 to check on progress toward an open accommodations ordinance. Black Baltimoreans had draped themselves over the back of King's convertible, reaching for his outstretched hand. In a sense, though, it was King who was reaching out to Baltimore, to Bascom and Dobson, hoping they could help him keep the movement going forward. Only two weeks before his October visit, King had been awarded the peace prize. He had the high honor, but he knew the work had hardly begun.

One day when Mayor McKeldin was out of town, D'Alesandro got a call from Box Harris, a black colonel in the police department. "He said, 'Tommy will you do me a favor. Will you give a key to the city to Martin Luther King?' I said, 'I'll be glad to.' Harris said he was over at the Lord Baltimore Hotel. He had a couple rooms on the tenth floor. He took me in there and put his arm around me.

" 'Can I call you Tommy?' he said.

"I said, 'Certainly.' "

At King's request, D'Alesandro explained why he had allowed certain amendments to the city's open accommodations bill, how if he was going to get any bill at all, he needed to make compromises. He explained how each of the amendments would lock up a vote or two.

"He said, 'You do what you have to do.' It was a tough fight. That was the time Cardinal Shehan came and was booed at the War Memorial Auditorium [where a hearing was held on the bill]. They spit on him."[9]

The city bill passed, but it left in place a Jim Crow provision that councilman Henry Parks and others had tried for years to remove. The rule said that any establishment that did more than 50 percent of its business in alcohol need not open its door. The alleged reason: blacks and whites could not drink together without trouble.

The argument drew derision from councilman Solomon Liss, a mirthful man of intellect who went on to be a judge on the Court of Special Appeals. Apparently, there was fear the bill would have Baltimore bars overrun by black drinkers. "I can't conceive that the Negroes of this city are going to run down into East Baltimore and shout 'Give me liquor or give me death.' That argument is a lot of hooey."[10]

The *Baltimore Sun* editorial page gave the bill guarded support. "In choosing to attack simultaneously the disabilities imposed on Negroes in housing, employment, education, public accommodations, health and welfare," they wrote, "McKeldin has charged the council with a necessary though difficult task. There are limits to the ability of legislation to achieve social reform. But it is a powerful weapon which must be available for use."[11]

The agonizing progress toward fairness gained momentum with the urging of King and others, but every step was greeted with a ploy to buy time, to hold off the inevitable. Like opening Ford's Theater, or integrating the law school or the undergraduate college or Gwynn Oak Park. Every battle seemed interminable.

After King's visit and D'Alesandro's maneuvering, Mayor McKeldin's bill passed. City council members could have lunch in a restaurant with their black colleague, Henry Parks, but there was, as always, a limit, a preposterous gimmick. He could not accompany his colleagues into the bar if the restaurant wanted to exclude blacks—which many still did—if the establishment made more than half its income in liquor sales. That was the law. The logic lay only in the power of ten votes on the council—ten of nineteen to make a majority.

Every effort to preserve the exclusions, not just in Baltimore but throughout the state, had been made also in the State Senate. East Baltimore bar owner and state senator Joseph J. Staszak urged his colleagues to allow individual bars to take themselves out of the law if they wished. He was asked after the debate if his amendment did not represent a conflict of interest, since he owned a bar. "No conflict with my interest," he said. The bill passed by a slim majority.

These incremental advances, and the leadership of D'Alesandro, McKeldin, and the ministers, led some to hope Baltimore might escape the unrest that gripped cities all over the country after news of King's death spread. Ralph Moore remembers the mood—the fear—that began to seize the city. Already there had been a controversy over the emergence of Stokely Carmichael and other black power advocates. "I asked one of my teachers at Loyola, 'Mr. Dow, is there really going to be blood in the street?' Dow said, 'Don't worry about it. There's no such thing as black power.' "

But there was blood and fire, looting and many days of unrest.

"When we had martial law here, I can remember looking out the window, seeing tanks and people with bayonets. I would walk past that stuff to get my Number 30 bus and then transfer to the Number 11 to Loyola," Moore said. "There was some tension up there. Somebody decided to have a mass in honor of MLK. That acknowledged at least that he had been killed."[12]

Mayor D'Alesandro's son was one of Moore's classmates. Here was a comforting thought at last. The mayor was one of the white men Moore's father admired. John Lindsay, then the mayor of New York, was another. Lindsay had walked through the riots in Harlem in the 1960s, offering himself as a conciliator. D'Alesandro had done similar things in Baltimore, following the leadership of McKeldin—and D'Alesandro's own conscience. The compassionate images of these and other men eased matters to some extent.

But Republican governor Spiro T. Agnew felt compelled to find culprits, local and national. He blamed "outside agitators." Then he invited black ministers to a meeting that turned out to be a staged tongue lashing. The speech, which he had been working on long before the King assassination and the riots, worried his aides because, they thought, it ignored the anguish of a grieving black community and might have triggered more violence. D'Alesandro heard of Agnew's plan and tried to head him off: he failed.

"He personified the thinking and the values of suburban America vis-à-vis the city. He never got the feel of it. I called him. I tried to dissuade him from making that statement. He said, 'No, it's the way I feel.' " D'Alesandro had observed before that Agnew was new at governing and politics. He was willing to act on personal feelings without weighing the risks that might be involved.[13]

Thus, the angry governor of Maryland, bent on making a point publicly, took the black ministers to the woodshed (a state office building, actually) for a public excoriation: they had fallen, he said, before "a circuit-riding, Hanoi-visiting, caterwauling, riot-inciting, burn-American-down type of leader"—meaning Stokely Carmichael. Agnew accused the ministers of lacking the courage to condemn Carmichael. Many of the ministers got up and left after Agnew's first remarks.

They might have known what to expect. On his way into an earlier meeting, Agnew had stopped Bascom and said, "You repulse me."[14]

The governor was putting the ministers in the same pew as Brown and Carmichael. He indicted his allies. Theirs had been a difficult mission: they did not want to suggest black people were not righteously angry, but they wanted to prevent damage to life and property. For their pains, they were accused to doing nothing, of failing to urge calm, a return to order. The ministers were helping, but he chose to call them irresponsible, captives of the revolutionaries. They were anything but—nor were many of the city's black residents, who looked upon the rioters with the same fear and anger as Agnew.

D'Alesandro and others say the governor of Maryland was personally offended, but he was as removed from the long suffering and humiliation of black people as Robert Kennedy had been before he met Gloria Richardson. Unlike Kennedy, he was willing to risk an even more ferocious period of rioting by scolding the ministers as if they were schoolboys. He was continuing his long record of harsh pronouncements, such as the ones he had made after the Gwynn Oak Park confrontation. One Baltimorean quickly hailed his courage. He had been willing, she said, to denounce "not just the white man's racism but the black man's racism too."[15]

Critics said Agnew was pandering to those who simply hated black people. Some thought his rhetoric marked a change in the national dialogue, a moment when purely racial animosity was replaced—or obscured—by a new set of code words. "Law and order" and "work" became veiled ways of complaining about black people who, regardless of Jim Crow and slavery, were guilty of upsetting the peace of hard-working, law-abiding Americans who felt they had no responsibility for the damage done to their black neighbors over generations.

Baltimoreans, subscribers to the American values of honesty and hard work, felt betrayed and abandoned by "moneyed people," who expiated their guilt by suggesting that others allow their blocks to be integrated, their jobs made available to black people, and their schools opened to black students—all of which could be avoided by the wealthy. This treachery was aided and abetted, it was said, by liberals, university professors, and college students, whose criminal and antisocial behavior was tolerated. The little guy had no equivalent rights except "to pay taxes" that provide "goodies for the loafers and goof-offs who loot and riot, whose only philosophy is to get what you can without working." Agnew, they thought, had said "what had to be said."[16]

Governor Agnew spoke as Baltimoreans contemplated the wreckage of their city. Residents of Bolton Hill looked out over Baltimore from their rooftops to contemplate the haze of still-smoldering fires. A half-dozen people had died. Dozens had been injured, though most of the injuries were slight. Damage ran to $10 million at least. Hundreds of young black people were herded into the Civic Center to be held until their legal status could be sorted out. Black as well as white Baltimoreans looked at the carnage with shock. A black employee of a downtown department store contemplated his burned-out house on Whitelock Street, wondering, as Hansel Greene had in Cambridge, what he had done to deserve such a fate.

Larry Gibson remembers those days with a shiver, as if he had barely escaped catastrophe. The day before the rioting, he was playing softball with a group of lawyers at the Gilman School—until he ran into a soccer goal post, giving himself a prodigious cut that required numerous stitches. The next day, with his head bandaged, he borrowed a small television set so he could watch the news. As he was walking out of the Beethoven Apartments, the borrowed TV in his arms, he suddenly realized how he must look in a city plagued by looting and lawlessness.[17]

Understanding in such a period came with great pain and bewilderment. The grievances of black citizens counted for nothing compared with property destroyed and the good name of Baltimore up in smoke. People with no active role in the great civil rights movement, people who were beginning to look with sympathy on that movement, were shaken.

Baltimore councilwoman Rochelle "Rikki" Spector says Jewish merchants in parts of town where fire and looting struck were terrified. Many were survivors of the Nazi death camps. Were the forces of anti-Semitism rampant in the land once again?[18]

There was a differential awakening of racial awareness, of sensitivity to the trauma of segregation experienced by black Americans. Many white people simply had no knowledge of their black neighbors' lives, no glimmer of the daily difficulties they faced as a result of segregation and racism. If they had begun to emerge from that lack of awareness, they were likely educated by Martin Luther King and Chester Wickwire and so many others who marched to raise consciousness. They were not so far along this path of enlightenment, however, to be sympathetic to burning and rioting. It is clear at almost every step of the way in the long journey toward fairness that black leaders from Douglass to King understood that violence would be self-defeating.

In the succeeding days and years, blacks and whites looked back at these days through different lenses. Gibson sums up the differences: "I remember that Dr. King was killed. White people remember looting."[19] It's a generalization, of course, but it probably has some truth in it.

Murderous violence was not, in those cataclysmic days, limited to black leaders. Robert Kennedy, who had made long strides in his own level of understanding, was shot to death later that summer by Sirhan Sirhan in Los Angeles. The ranks of understanding men, black and white, in high-level leadership positions were falling with alarming frequency.

Juanita Mitchell, who stayed to hear all of Agnew's speech, declared that Baltimore's move toward fairness and justice had made "burners and looters" of black children. Her mother had predicted that result years earlier, urging white authorities to act more quickly on legitimate grievances before the fires of frustration left a generation of disaffected black children. Bob Watts, the NAACP lawyer, said the nation's resistance to *Brown v. Board of Education* left black Americans with a feeling that the law offered no protection for them. If black leaders could be assassinated and if white Americans felt they could ignore a ruling from the U.S. Supreme Court—if men like Bascom and Dobson could be abused by a governor—how could anyone have much faith in the system?

The irony of this episode was rich: Agnew had won his race for governor over a Democrat, George P. Mahoney, who had appeared to seek the governorship on an avowedly antimovement platform. "Your home is your castle. Protect it," declared Mahoney. Agnew looked like the liberal choice. George Russell insists he saw through Agnew from the start. Russell had stood with the supporters of Mahoney, much to the chagrin of other black leaders in the city. "I knew what Agnew was," Russell said.[20]

Later that summer, with the irony deepening, Spiro Agnew's name made it to the short list of potential running mates for Richard M. Nixon. This recognition came on the strength of Agnew's tough talk to the ministers and on his actions on other occasions. In exchange for Strom Thurmond's support in the South, Nixon had given the South Carolina senator a role in the selection of a vice presidential running mate. In what came to be known as Nixon's Southern Strategy, Thurmond had been a major player in the movement of the South from solidly Democratic to Republican, opposing in 1964 the seating of black delegates at the Democratic National Convention in Atlantic City, New Jersey.

Agnew had considered endorsing Nelson Rockefeller for president but changed his mind after conferring with various political figures in Maryland, including Marvin Mandel, then Speaker of the House of Delegates. Mandel was a Democrat, but Agnew sought him out for advice on politics, Mandel's forte. Agnew was, relatively speaking, a babe in the woods. What should he do, he asked Mandel. "Who do you think will win?" Mandel says he asked. "Nixon," said Agnew. "Do you think he'll forget that you supported Rockefeller?" Mandel asked. Agnew said, "No, of course not." "Well then?" said Mandel.[21]

Agnew's name subsequently went into the circle of speculation, pushed there, in part, by Louise Gore, Maryland's GOP committee member and later an unsuccessful GOP candidate for governor. Gore said she and Thurmond had been dating. She was sought out by Nixon emissaries to see if she would try to sell him on the idea of Agnew—as the sort of tough-on-crime candidate Thurmond would approve. Tough on crime, in this case, was almost surely code for tough on blacks and on civil rights. Gore's entreaties, Nixon's favorable impression of him, and Agnew's record no doubt swung the nomination to the man from Maryland. He immediately became "Spiro who?" to the national press. But lightning had struck.

"He was a phenomenon," says D'Alesandro. "In six years, he went from the Loch Raven Improvement Association, to Baltimore county executive, to governor, to vice president of the United States. It was unbelievable." It had a down side, though, says D'Alesandro, who had been weaned on ward-level politics when his father was mayor and he was a precinct captain in Baltimore's Little Italy. "Without a lot of experience, you don't really grasp politics. A lot of people, they're elected and they get awed by a different lifestyle."[22]

Agnew's rise was part luck, part political calculation, and part sincere outrage at the tactics of civil rights leaders. "He was not crudely bigoted like George Wallace. On the contrary, Agnew supported the essential goals of the civil rights movement. [But] he insisted that the American way was the best one in the world and he defended the U.S. government passionately against those who deemed it illegitimate and who considered violence a necessary means toward achieving a more just society . . . he resented those who condemned him as a symbol of white privilege. Raised in a world in which civility mattered a great deal, he was aghast at its rapid decline . . . Agnew enabled the Republican Party to wedge whites, especially working and middle class males, away from the Democratic Party . . . Many saw him as a more legitimate representative of their views than was Wallace." He was, suggests Peter Levy in his book on Cambridge, one of the most important figures in the shift of America to a far more conservative nation.[23]

There was a further irony. Maryland had finally gotten someone on a national presidential ticket. Governor Albert Ritchie had come close in the 1930s. McKeldin had been on the vice presidential short list of Dwight D. Eisenhower in the 1950s, coming in behind Nixon. McKeldin, whose progressive advocacy was driven by a spiritual sense of brotherhood, had no use for either man.[24] Agnew moved ahead on the suddenly buoyant tide of law and order, while McKeldin watched with rising concern for his party.

After the 1954 ruling in *Brown v. Board of Education*, McKeldin was asked how he would proceed. "I represent the law," he had said. McKeldin's declaration came during a campaign swing to the Eastern Shore, where desegregation would be resisted fiercely in the coming years, and was another illustration of his determination to lead in the right direction. When Arkansas governor Orval Faubus opposed integration of his public schools, McKeldin called him "the sputtering sputnik of the Ozarks."

Fifteen years later, testifying before the Kerner Commission on Civil Disorders, a panel appointed to document causes of the summer riots of 1960s, the unique character of McKeldin's leadership came through. Jersey City, New Jersey, mayor Thomas J. Whelan put McKeldin's progressive views in sharp relief. Riots, he said, are the work of "agitators who hate our country" and are best addressed with "a massive show of force" as soon as trouble breaks out. McKeldin by contrast was willing to say then that tough-on-crime was often code for antiblack leadership. "We must not neglect to act positively," McKeldin said, "for fear that we may appear to be rewarding rioters."[25] But the New Jersey mayor's remarks spoke to a prevalent view—one that took Spiro Agnew to the vice president's office.

THE BALLOT: SIT-IN SALADS AND LAWN SIGNS

In the era of civil rights militancy, University of Maryland School of Law professor Larry Gibson looked to some like a bomb thrower. Maybe it was the colorful dashikis purchased in West Africa. Maybe it was his penetrating gaze that made him so fearsome. He was as resolute as Gloria Richardson.

But Gibson challenged stereotypes. He more often dressed in the suits and ties of conservative lawyers. He questioned the existence of a movement that could be defined precisely with a 1950s or 1960s starting point. A movement had been under way for decades, if not a century or more, he thought. If there was such a starting point, it would be marked in Maryland by the admission of black lawyers to the state bar at the turn of the century. They were the modern movement's vanguard. But, like Houston, he knew that the law was only one of the avenues toward equal justice. He saw how housewives and judges and students had changed the country. He was determined to take advantage of the change, the new prospects for success.

Like state senator Harry Cole—like Frederick Douglass—Gibson saw raw, unused power in his people. Gibson thought he could take the potential demonstrated so gloriously in the movement and translate it into political power. That was the prize you got for marching, for enduring the police dogs and the hangman's rope.[26]

He knew the prize was not going to fall into his lap. He would have to earn it. He would be a nuts-and-bolts, old-fashioned organizer who could turn out the black base for black candidates. He was, says his ally and sometime rival Arthur Murphy, a political mechanic. He knew the fundamentals. He was a transitional figure, someone who built on the techniques of the clubhouse bosses and of the earliest black political figures.

Murphy remembered what Harry Cole, the first black Maryland state senator, used to say: "I didn't know enough to know what I didn't know." Black Republicans, before Cole, thought they could win simply by announcing their candidacy. This was the most rudimentary expression of what the political professionals called name recognition. Gibson would take it to the level of art form. "Larry was into showing. He was making sure that the last thing you didn't know was who your candidate was," Murphy said.[27]

Gibson called himself a disciple in the "church of Sign-tology." Every lawn on selected blocks would have a campaign picture of his candidate, creating a kind of visual echo that ran beyond where the eye could see. The sleeping, discouraged, and indifferent black voters—shown over and over that their votes brought little value—began to stir. Gibson was tapping them on the shoulder, helping them to their feet, giving them direction. He used sound as Joe Howard had in his "Don't vote for three, just vote for me" campaign slogan of 1968.

Gibson would not hesitate to use the colors of the African liberation movement to energize his black constituency—even when the tactic made white opponents call him a racist. Records showed repeatedly in Baltimore elections that white voters did not vote for black candidates, even when the black candidate was beyond reproach. So Gibson did the pragmatic targeting every campaign manager demands: appeal to your base, don't waste your resources. Old-time white bosses had done the same things for generations. Kelly green appealed to the Irish, didn't it?

With a succession of good candidates and the support of the Goon Squad, Gibson became a force in the 1960s. He began to get black faces onto the "Vote for so and so" posters and then into the decision-making councils in Maryland. He and other black leaders were pressing their demands, and Gibson was backing them with the ballot, the power Frederick Douglass had yearned to secure.

The political phase of the civil rights movement began for him in the summer of 1964. He was working in Washington as the head of D.C. Students for Civil Rights, an organization deployed on several fronts, including the landmark open accommodations bill then pending in Congress. Southerners were trying to kill the legislation. Students from area universities, including some from the South, were mounting counterfilibusters in support of the bill.

Gibson's teacher turned out to be Clarence Mitchell, the NAACP's chief Washington lobbyist, who was working then to extricate the bill from a filibuster-extended debate in the U.S. Senate designed to kill it. "That was the first time I met Clarence," Gibson said. It was April 1, 1964. "I'll never forget him meeting with my students. He told these black kids from the Deep South to visit their senators." The degree of their disaffection from the democratic process was immediately apparent.

"I'm going to see Eastland?" asked a young man from Mississippi.

"You must," Mitchell said.

"Why?"

"He's your senator."

"Not my senator," the young man said. Mitchell explained that, whatever James Eastland's beliefs, he represented everyone in his state. "Clarence was giving them a lesson in the essence of democracy," Gibson recalls. It was a system from which many black Americans felt profoundly disaffected, not a system many really believed had a place for them. "I don't know how many of those kids did it, but it would never have crossed their minds to approach one of those segregationist senators as a constituent asking for a vote favorable to them."

Gibson, too, made a call on Eastland.

In the summer of 1975, he taught at the University of Mississippi School of Law and later was appointed associate deputy U.S. attorney general. In that post, meeting with Mississippi senator Eastland was a mandatory courtesy. Unlike his young charges, Gibson relished the opportunity to see one of the old Segs up close and personal. Eastland was cordial, though the conversation seemed to carry a veiled message. Gibson might be black, he might have taught at the University of Mississippi, but he ought to realize that some things had not changed.

"We got to talking about agriculture. I observed how soybeans seemed to be replacing cotton. He said, 'Yeah, they make a lot of money off them sy'beans, but I don't care how much money it makes, I got to have some cotton around for sentimental purposes.' " Was cotton inescapably connected to the old segregated ways, the ways of slavery and southern opposition to progress for young men such as Larry Gibson?

All these experiences had shaped Gibson's approach to black progress. He was out of the Jackson-Marshall-Mitchell-Douglass school of equal justice under law, through the courts and the ballot box. The street demonstration had its role, but for the long haul, the permanence of the law seemed to hold the most promise.

Lillie May Jackson, who died in 1976, remained the emotional leader of the movement in Baltimore. Her daughter Juanita had taken her place, becoming the first black woman lawyer to practice in Maryland and a bold practitioner of her mother's insistent importuning. In an editorial written after Jackson died, the *Evening Sun* proclaimed her a heroine of the movement, someone who had sacrificed much for *her* people. Hans Froelicher, a social activist in the city, wrote the editors to say they had missed the point. Jackson had sacrificed not simply for black people, but for the soul of the nation, for whites and for blacks. Froelicher's chastisement went to the heart of the nonviolent campaigns insisted on by Douglass, Jackson, and King. The idea was to lead America toward its unmet goal, to give the argument legitimacy with civil disobedience, prayer, and the shunning of violence—even violent talk.

The approach had considerable success, but it began to lose focus even before King's assassination. The leader was determined to continue his campaign for the poor, but others in his army wanted to pursue different objectives. Again Reverend Dobson says part of the tragedy of King's assassination was that it came during the movement's period of stumbling toward a new identity, an identity that might carry it beyond the street, the mass rallies, and the speeches.

In Baltimore, operating independently of the national leaders as Richardson had done in Cambridge, Larry Gibson charted his own course. He saw opportunity in the Voting Rights Act, in the unrealized power of the black vote. Like Richardson, he was driven by a certain negative nostalgia. His own personal movement would need some hope of success, but it would draw energy from memories of exclusion. He had plenty of those.

"Every day in high school, I got off the Number 8 street car in front of the Boulevard Theater. Then I went and caught the 22 or the 3 over to City College to hear my classmates talk about what was playing at the Boulevard. I could never go to the Boulevard Theater. Most of the movies were totally segregated. Some had balconies where you could sit. The restaurants you simply could not eat in.

"My principal employment in high school was setting duck pins in bowling alleys, and I never set pins in a bowling alley where I could bowl. I didn't like it, but I also found it a good job." Like Thurgood Marshall accepting the twenties on Gibson Island, or Bill Lee in Frederick, taunting the policeman at Baker Park, he sublimated his anger, used it to stay focused.

The 1933 lynching of Armwood was a galvanizing event in Maryland civil rights history, helping Jackson marshal her troops, but passage of the Civil Rights Act of 1964 and *Brown v. Board of Education* were more potent bits of leverage. They might bring black leaders into the courts, the city councils, and the legislatures, where the concerns of the black community would have voices. Over the years, Gibson and the Goon Squad members debated endlessly about what moved people to action. The ministers thought, for the most part, that ill-treatment stirred the soul to resist. Gibson didn't agree.

"It seems there's almost no limit to the degradation people will accept. But when folks say 'Hey, this can change. Let's get on with the business of changing it,' that's when you get the highest militancy." His view was close to the famous Douglass observation about confronting power, drawing lines and pushing back by whatever means seem most likely to be effective. Without that, people try to maintain whatever grip they have on life. To move beyond that understandable concern, people needed support from leaders who won in the public arena—the courts, sports, entertainment, and politics. The national movement led by King proceeded for years on the momentum generated by a bus boycott.

Gibson had helped his father, Benjamin Franklin Gibson, on cleaning jobs. His mother, Daisy, urged him to study, and he excelled at academics—and politics. He became the first black person elected to student office at Baltimore City College. At Howard University, he was student body president, and he did well at Columbia Law School.

When he and the Goon Squad helped Joseph Howard win a circuit court seat, Gibson thought the political phase of civil rights had asserted its importance. He and the preachers had hoped to elect Parren J. Mitchell to Congress along with Joe Howard in 1968—the year of Rap Brown and the assassination of King and Kennedy. Parren Mitchell lost by a handful of votes, but two years later he won. In that same year, 1970, Gibson had a significant role in the successful campaign of Milton Allen for state's attorney.

Gibson came back to Baltimore to live, breaking a promise to himself never to come back to the city that he, like the Jackson sisters before him, regarded as backward and stubbornly resistant to change. He had many opportunities to join important silk-stocking firms suddenly in need of black faces in an era when their absence had become a social and business liability. The finalists for Gibson were Frank Murnaghan's Venable, Baetjer and Howard and the firm headed by George Russell, Robert Watts, former judge Bill Murphy, and Milton Allen.

"I thought, if I go with Venable, who are my clients going to be? The big banks? I joined the black firm and never regretted a day of it. Frank

Murnaghan remained very supportive of me. He was a good man in so many ways."

Murnaghan and his unofficial civil rights partner, Melvin Sykes, another young Baltimore lawyer with a social conscience, had attempted to steer Maryland schools around resistance to the U.S. Supreme Court integration orders under *Brown*. They argued that segregation had occurred not by the accident of where families lived, but as a result of government plan and policy. Schools were segregated by law, in other words, and should be desegregated by affirmative action of government. Had this strategy worked—had there been more federal muscle behind the high court's decision—the deflecting and diluting tactics of diehard *Brown* resisters might not have been so effective. The suit was never filed because neither lawyer had the money needed to proceed, nor did the NAACP.

The injustice of segregation drew both men to the legal barricades. Sykes had the added motivation of a brief personal acquaintance with Charles Hamilton Houston in 1950. Sykes was in law school. Houston was still working Maryland cases in those years. "I was proud to have been a gofer for him," Sykes says.

During their partnership, Sykes and Murnaghan would often walk to work from Bolton Hill, the near-to-downtown neighborhood where Murnaghan lived in those years. He was by then on the U.S. Fourth Circuit Court of Appeals. The court was located in Richmond, Virginia, but he had offices in Baltimore. Sykes says Murnaghan—a big red-haired Irishman with a rollicking wit, a good lacrosse player in his youth—was the court's most distinguished liberal. He wrote many dissenting opinions on a court increasingly noted for its conservativism.

Murnaghan thought of running for governor in 1968, Sykes said, but decided not to because he had four children to raise. "He always blamed himself," Sykes says, "for the election of Spiro Agnew. He thought he might have been able to beat Mahoney and his 'home is your castle' campaign theme, and then Agnew."[28]

Later, Murnaghan filed to run for mayor of Baltimore but saw that Young Tommy D'Alesandro had it pretty much sewed up. After D'Alesandro's election—in which he validated Murnaghan's judgment by winning every precinct in the city—the new mayor made him chairman of the school board. Murnaghan quickly informed the mayor that he wanted the firebrand Gibson on the board. D'Alesandro remembers the shock wave that appointment triggered. "But let me tell you something, I explained it to people who opposed it. It was better to have this discourse inside the framework of government rather than outside. Larry had an opportunity to sit down with peers and explain. That helped. That got it going. It was a reflection of what was on the street, articulately presented by Larry Gibson. He had grown. He always showed me that talent."[29]

Some council approval was needed, and Gibson says he secured important votes when D'Alesandro, bowing to a councilman's desire, allowed a pool hall to stay open later. There was always going to be vote trading. "I ended up contaminating the young people who stayed up to play," Gibson says.

After D'Alesandro left office, Gibson and mayor William Donald Schaefer became antagonists. D'Alesandro had hired Roland Patterson to be the city's school superintendent. Patterson began to order changes that unsettled just about all the power sources in the city. Schaefer wanted to get rid of him and began to restrict his spending ability. "It was really a fight between the school board and Charlie Benton [the city's finance director]. Patterson was doing what the school board wanted, which was to protect the board's independence," Gibson says. "There was a big fight that went on for quite a while." It ended with Patterson's dismissal on Schaefer's orders. "Up until then," Gibson says, "Schaefer and I had a good relationship."

In those days, Gibson's nerve—and successes—made him a kingmaker and a bit of a threat to the city Establishment leaders, some of whom opposed him. Others—like Clinton Bamberger, another passionate radical like Murnaghan and Chester Wickwire—were with him.

Gibson was a threat because he was winning public office for one black candidate after another: Howard to the court in 1968; Allen to state's attorney in 1970; Mitchell to Congress in 1970; and on to the school board, where his implacable expression made him almost as fearsome as the more radical black activists. Gibson was looking like someone who could successfully challenge men like Schaefer. He was also called, over a decade of his most intense political activity, a Rasputin, a puppeteer as well as a skilled practitioner. His ascendancy to the status of real challenger— derogatory descriptions were a kind of respect, after all—seemed uncommonly rapid.

Baltimore had been run by Jack Pollack, the power-mongering northwest Baltimore boss surprised in 1954 by Harry Cole and then by Irv

Kovens, a scowling merchant called the Furniture Man by insiders, who had lined up with Schaefer and Willie Adams to control much of the city. Kovens and Adams were backers of Schaefer, and they were not of a mind to concede much to any challenger, black or white. Schaefer, whose own record of racial tolerance was occasionally questioned, joined those who accused Gibson of playing divisive racial politics, a charge Gibson called offensive and untrue.

In truth, white candidates always ran better in black districts than blacks did in white areas. Schaefer benefited from this pattern, defeating a black candidate one year without the votes of white precincts. But Schaefer was incensed that Gibson had used African liberation flag colors for mayor Kurt L. Schmoke's reelection campaign. From almost anyone else, that raw volley would have been remarkable. Most Marylanders saw it as part of Schaefer's cranky lexicon, which was getting a sharper edge with every passing year. Schaefer always marveled that Clarence Mitchell and his wife, Juanita, had been his supporters. He asked Mitchell why. "Because you voted right," Mitchell said. Schaefer had been moved toward a solid civil rights record by his mates in northwest Baltimore, the largely Jewish, pro–civil rights clubhouse controlled by Kovens.[30]

Gibson had usually ignored Schaefer's taunts without saying anything. This time, he fired back: "I find the governor's remarks offensive. That's 1970s racial rhetoric that Schaefer should be ashamed of. The nation, and certainly the state, is beyond that type of stereotyping. I supported black politicians. I supported white politicians." Ron Shapiro, Gibson's law partner and friend, also responded: "His political opponents are going to call him every name they can because . . . he shakes them up and, in the end, he wins most of the time."[31] Gibson's success included his law partnership with Shapiro and a professorship at the University of Maryland School of Law.

Schaefer had seen his rival's growing organizational strength in the black community. When he ran for mayor in 1983, he wanted Gibson's endorsement. Gibson was looking ahead. All he wanted was the election of a black mayor in Baltimore. He toyed with Schaefer, insisting he would be taking very little if any role in the 1983 election.

All this inside political baseball certified the arrival of black political power in Baltimore. If Gibson had been a nonfactor, William Donald Schaefer would not have bothered to negotiate with him. Gibson was leveraging the successes of Lillie May Jackson, Thurgood Marshall, and Clarence Mitchell. Jackson's contributions are remembered on the façade of a new African American history museum in Baltimore, and there is a Lillie May Carroll Jackson museum on Eutaw Place in Baltimore. Her legacy is an America in which people like Larry Gibson and her most famous protégés, Marshall and Mitchell, could flourish.

An array of local and national luminaries came to the city after Clarence Mitchell died in 1984 to inaugurate the renamed Clarence M. Mitchell Jr. Courthouse. A kind of shrine was constructed in the stately building near the center of the city. Mitchell would have enjoyed the historic symmetry: In this very building, as a young reporter for the *Afro-American,* he had heard Judge Eugene O'Dunne declare an end to the state's aggressively enforced policy of segregation at its school of law, a first-step decision that echoed through segregated America. Mitchell had run all the way to the *Afro-American* newsroom with his story. Many felt the long national road to *Brown v. Board of Education of Topeka* started right there in that Maryland courtroom.

Baltimore's Clarence Mitchell had been there at the creation of the modern-era drive for equality. He had written about the callous revelry of the lynch mob. He been there in the temple of the law, a place where black and white spectators were as separated from each other as blacks were from equal justice, listening with disbelief to the declarations of Judge O'Dunne in favor of Marshall's client. For the rest of his life, he had labored in Washington to end the hateful practices of Jim Crow. A year after the courthouse was renamed for his mentor, Larry Gibson engineered the election of Kurt Schmoke as Baltimore's first elected black mayor.

President Lyndon Johnson famously called Clarence Mitchell the "101st senator." It was no patronizing, throw-away encomium from Johnson, a notorious schmoozer who, said Mitchell, had "forced down my door more than any other person."[32] Over a long career and by virtue of his grace and acumen, Mitchell had become an almost permanent part of the world's greatest deliberative body. He was beyond the political forces that could end any elected official's career.

He knew more about the U.S. Senate than many who served there. Tennessee senator Howard Baker called him a "lion in the lobby." Mitchell had the advantage of time. He had seen the importance of relationships and trust in a collegial body that operated on the basis of custom,

seniority, and idiosyncrasy—nuances that only long study could per-
ceive and use to good effect. Attorney general Ramsey Clark of Texas,
son of the Supreme Court justice Tom Clark, marveled at Mitchell's
standing. "I don't know how many people can get senators to sleep on
cots [while they waited to vote on civil rights bills] for something that's
going to cost them votes," he said.[33] Mitchell knew his business the way
every experienced lobbyist does, but he was black, working in a U.S.
Senate whose members were still in the grip of segregation. He had no
money to buy influence, and he was asking senators to risk deep displeasure among voters back home. Mitchell's passion came to him from the
grotesque aftermath of the Armwood lynching, but he knew when and
how much to show it—and to whom.

After the watershed Voting Rights Act of 1964 passed, Mitchell skipped
a victory party in the office of ally Senator Hubert Humphrey. Instead,
he got on the small subway that runs between the Capitol and the Senate
office buildings. He rode with Richard Russell, one of the most implacable of his foes, but also, Mitchell thought, a man of intelligence and decency, a gentleman. "He was enough of a senator in his mentality to
understand the sort of local pressures a senator was under," said Joseph
R. L. Sterne, who had reported on the U.S. Senate for the *Baltimore Sun*
when Mitchell toiled for the NAACP.[34] With some other white southerners, opposition to civil rights went beyond politics to visceral antiblack
feeling.

If Russell was on the wrong side of the issue, Mitchell thought, he was
there by the force of history—something he would not have said about
some of his other opponents. When one of the southerners, Mississippi's
James Eastland, became chairman of the Judiciary Committee, Mitchell
said, "A mad dog has been loosed in the house of the people."[35] A man of
patience and understanding, Mitchell had his limits.

He wanted Russell to know he was not gloating. He knew the process
at a profoundly deep level, written and unwritten. He knew there would
be other battles. Mitchell's grace and Johnson's crowding insistence produced a wonderful synergy in Washington. Maryland's Mitchell, like
Maryland's Douglass, had influence at the pinnacle of national policy
making.

And yet his work seemed somewhat underheralded in his hometown
and in the rest of the nation. It was 1985, more than thirty years after
Brown, more than twenty years after the voting rights and open accom-

modations bills that Mitchell had shepherded through Congress. Recognition was coming finally, but even then it was difficult for Baltimoreans to believe. "I never expected to see this," said Lawrence W. Hughes, a black sheriff's deputy. "I guess all that suffering, all that humiliation, had to lead to something better."[36]

U.S. Supreme Court justice William Brennan accompanied Marshall to the courthouse inauguration. Asked how he felt on that day by a *New York Times* reporter, Marshall said, "I joined millions of other people who felt they were born in Baltimore, were raised in Baltimore, but were not going to die in Baltimore."[37] He surely included himself in that legion of black men and women who were, directly or indirectly, denied admission to the state's law school. Asked to enlarge on his comment, Marshall declined. The high court justice had not come back to Baltimore, as Mitchell had done almost every day, traveling back and forth from his home on Druid Hill Avenue to Capitol Hill. Mitchell had seen some change in the city of his birth that Marshall may have missed. Mitchell had served on the University of Maryland's board of regents, and he had had a hand in the appointment of a black chancellor at the school in College Park. Marshall's honors had been, for the most part, national—insufficient to ease the enduring pain inflicted by his hometown. Some in Baltimore held these hard feelings against him, as if the city did not deserve some high-level chastisement.

Marshall had always referred to Baltimore as "Up South," a venue for discrimination and segregation as resolutely pursued as in any southern state. In the 1930s, Marshall recalled for an interviewer, the Urban League found segregation was more rigid in Baltimore than in any other city in the country. But one day at Lincoln University, while he was explaining the old South city of Baltimore to a friend, he began to get angry. There were all these things you couldn't do in Baltimore, he said. His friend threw it back at him. "It's terrible, but did you ever try to change it?" Marshall was embarrassed. "Why not do something about it?" he asked himself. "My first idea was to get even with Maryland for not letting me go to law school."[38]

And so he did. He and Charles Hamilton Houston had breached the wall of segregation in 1935, securing the admission of Donald Gaines Murray to the School of Law. The great edifice of American apartheid had begun to shake. With Larry Gibson leading the effort, the University of Maryland School of Law and the state of Maryland attempted to make amends. Its new law library was named in Marshall's honor. He said no thank you. But Clarence Mitchell intervened and the renaming went forward. Marshall did not attend the ceremony. His enduring pique, though formidable, could not erase the pride many Marylanders took in their favorite son's accomplishments.

EXQUISITE BALANCE: TANEY AND MARSHALL IN ANNAPOLIS

A bronze sculpture of Chief Justice Roger Brooke Taney, seated and pensive, commands the small, steep hill on the east side of the historic Maryland State House in Annapolis. His likeness faces the Chesapeake Bay and the Atlantic Ocean, waters that bore black slaves to Maryland shores.

On the other side of the building stands the image of a lean and youthful Thurgood Marshall. The statue, sculpted by Tobias Mendez, presides over Lawyers' Mall, an elegant, tree-lined promenade leading to the State Senate, House of Delegates, and the governor's offices. Just behind the Marshall statue stood the Maryland Court of Appeals building where Marshall's earliest civil rights victory, the 1935 Donald Gaines Murray law school case, was upheld over the State of Maryland's objection.

Adversaries across the decades, Justice Marshall and Chief Justice Taney might have agreed it was fitting for both of them to be honored on hallowed ground where the laws of their state are made, where Marylanders strive to perfect their democracy. There was no more dramatic illustration of the nation's struggle to reconcile democracy with the long prevalence of slavery and discrimination.

The diverse and sometimes troubling directions of American history may never have had such a tidy resolution as they enjoy here—in statuary at least. Taney had declared American citizenship beyond the reach of black men and women, slave or free, drawing that conclusion from drafters of the U.S. Constitution. Marshall objected, laboring for a lifetime to make the law a truer reflection of the founding spirit as he understood it.

Like everything else in the history of civil rights, the achieving of statuary balance called for persistence, wise leadership, and reverence for the process of lawmaking and history. As it turned out, two sons of Maryland—the author of *Dred Scott* and the architect of *Brown v. Board of*

Education—sustained each other. Protectors of Maryland's most famous U.S. Supreme Court justices reached an accommodation that resulted in having both Taney and Marshall statues on the state capitol grounds. The Taney image was undisturbed, and a plan was made to add a Marshall statue.

The story unfolded this way. In the winter of 1994, a member of the House of Delegates from Montgomery County urged a Baltimore colleague, delegate Tony Fulton, to join him in an effort to raze the Taney statue. The Montgomery delegate was finding considerable support for his idea in the beginning. State treasurer Richard Dixon agreed with him, and others might have lined up in support as well. Over time, various Marylanders have suggested some radical end to the Taney statue.

But the state's archivist, Edward C. Papenfuse, called upon often to counsel against erasing reminders of unhappy chapters of our history, took his concerns to Appropriations Committee chairman Howard Peters Rawlings, the most influential black legislator in the history of the General Assembly and one of the best of any color. That ranking is a tribute to his particular acumen as well as an accurate reflection of the black politician's short history of influence in Maryland lawmaking.

Rawlings acted quickly. He was wary of what he saw as a cheap political maneuver—statue bashing in this case. Nor would he allow some lower-ranking member of the assembly, from Baltimore no less, to make him look as if he had failed to act on an insult to black Marylanders.

Any effort to erase history, he observed, would fail by virtue of the volume of work alone. To achieve a balance in statuary, he reckoned, "We'd have to strike down a whole lot of monuments."[39] Baltimore has its own Taney statue, for example, standing in the shadow of the Washington Monument on Mount Vernon Place. And, he thought, there was some educational value in this scattered pantheon. "You want people to be aware of your past and also of your present and your future," Rawlings says. "We needed Taney to stay where he was to show the dichotomy between Taney and Marshall. With Taney gone, you don't have that. So I convinced my members that we had to kill the bill."[40]

And he saw an opportunity. A plan to tear down the Taney image, however unlikely of success, provided leverage for a more positive and constructive idea, an unprecedented project: a statue of Marshall, grandson of a slave and architect of *Brown v. Board of Education*. Marshall had died in 1993. Thus did supporters of these two Maryland figures form a kind of posthumous protection society: saving Taney from the wrecker's ball provided an opening for Marshall.

Rawlings and others decided they would provide funds for the project in the capital budget, the annual spending document that provides for construction projects. Senate president Thomas V. Mike Miller, famous in Annapolis for his attention to history, might go along as a way to protect Taney and history. By then, Maryland had forty-one black legislators with reliably black Democratic voting constituents, none of whom Miller would want to offend. He loved the Marshall-Taney balance.

Rawlings was in a position to authorize the necessary funding in the assembly and to get endorsements from the governor, William Donald Schaefer. Appeals court judge Harry Cole, the former senator who had pushed through political barriers in 1954 to become the state's first black senator, served as chairman of a committee that would plan the statue. Rawlings, though, was the power—the brains, the money, and the will that made it happen.

The Marshall project would showcase the meaning of all the struggles and achievements that gave it momentum, Chairman Rawlings's in particular. A master legislator, Rawlings embodied the objectives of those who knew politics was an avenue—a superhighway—toward equal rights in day-to-day life. He had been a protégé of Lillie May Jackson, calling on her in her Baltimore offices as a young man. She had nurtured many leaders, including the young Pete Rawlings, who was then headed for a career in the classroom. He later broke off study for a PhD in mathematics to become a legislator. He showed dexterity in handling complex policy matters and a talent for interpreting the political significance of these issues to his white legislative colleagues and his black constituents in Baltimore. He knew he had to have power, and he went about accumulating, and using, it. Over the years, people came to understand that Howard Peters Rawlings—known as Petey in his family—was someone to be dealt with. He was a bear of a man, with a deep voice and an ironic sense of the world around him. No one worked harder or demanded more of people—particularly of young black people he saw performing well. He was openly scornful of those new black leaders whose performance fell below his standards, and he did not hesitate to say so publicly.

He seemed to relish risky political activity when he thought he was right. On the night when Rawlings was awarded the President's Medal at the Johns Hopkins University, president William R. Brody recalled their first meeting. "He glowered down at me and said, 'Hopkins is double dealing, promising one level of support and offering a lesser level.' " Rawlings's friends laughed. They had been there. "Pete was holding me accountable. It was tough love." Brody said he'd learned "the ethical framework taught by Pete's parents when they lived in the Edgar Allan Poe public housing project" in Baltimore.[41]

Rawlings thanked Brody and others who had come to the ceremony. "I was an activist some people were not happy with," he said. Again there was laughter. A man of wit and humor, he loved understatement when it involved his power and willingness to use it. He told the story of his work in the South for the NAACP's legal defense fund, the famous Inc Fund. "I couldn't go to them in Maryland for help on my issues if they didn't see me doing things," he said. He was dispatched to a number of southern capitals to assist legislators. One Christmas, he arrived by bus at 2 a.m. in Selma, Alabama. It was an uncomfortable moment for a black man in the Deep South. "I called my contact and said I was there. Then I prayed." He thanked the woman who had inspired him to take the assignment, Jean Fairfax of the NAACP Legal Defense Fund. "A lot of people have had a significant impact on my life, but none of you sent me to Alabama in the middle of the night." He would send others to the equivalent of Alabama: he committed the impolitic act of ordering millions of dollars withheld from his city when he thought the city had failed to meet its obligations. He got frustrated when he thought people were not demanding enough of themselves or others. "To accept less than the best," Rawlings thought, "is demeaning."[42]

Black Americans had been looking for a place at the central policy-making table for all the decades after Abraham Lincoln's death had robbed Frederick Douglass of the role he might have played in national affairs. Whether Douglass would have been able to translate his extraordinary White House access to something tangible cannot be known. His great faith that he might have been adequately compensated was overly optimistic if not naïve given his lack of political experience.[43] What he needed was the kind of experience men like Rawlings developed over a lifetime in politics and government.

Rawlings had moved irrepressibly, even arrogantly, beyond some black legislators who had come rapidly upward without an opportunity to learn how the process worked personally and politically. As gifted a communicator in the political world as black ministers had been from their pulpits, he could synthesize complicated matters in colorful, incisive language, essential to reporters who, without trying, made important figures of people. If you were quoted often, you were somebody—somebody who would be not just worthy, but recognized as worthy, and fully capable of handling the eminence.

He was not even slightly deflected by subtly or not so subtly perceived infirmities of race. He assumed his ability and acumen would be respected by most of his colleagues quickly, and eventually by any who might have thought a black man was not up to the demands. As chairman of the House Appropriations Committee—the budget-making committee that decides which projects will be funded at what level—he became one of the most powerful legislators of the 1990s and would have remained so had cancer not claimed him in fall 2003.

The committee chairs manage all their committee's bills when those bills come to the full house for approval. Rawlings never lost a bill. "He would stand on the floor of the house in the beginning and toy with people for a bit before blowing them away," says his House of Delegates colleague Anne Perkins.[44] He enjoyed those moments but seldom overplayed them, pushed them to the point of humiliating the vanquished. He developed a reputation for arrogance and sometimes peremptory decisions, which made him a player in the political lists no different from the white autocrats who had preceded him. No different except that he had to accommodate himself to the unique challenge of black Americans, to the duality articulated by W. E. B. Du Bois, a way of proceeding that was different for black political figures. Rawlings had no problem with that dilemma. He simply said what he thought, trusting that the truth came without color.

As he moved up in the house leadership, he knew he had two constituencies—his home-base voters in central and northwest Baltimore and his colleagues in Annapolis. Sometimes, to retain the faith of the house, he seemed less responsive to the voters at home, as when he arranged to withhold those millions earmarked for Baltimore because the city had not lived up to commitments it had made to improve the special education system. Had he allowed the money to flow uninterrupted in the face of such failures, he thought, he would have been less able to win approval for outlays in the future. He faced these challenges because he had learned the process over many years, because he was the obvious choice for his chairmanship, and because he had been a remarkably disciplined and energetic student of the process.

One important area of concern to him was higher education and the continuing failure of attention to minority concerns at the University of Maryland. Some important large battles had been won over an agonizingly long period of time. Far more work was needed. "The University of Maryland had always been this kind of entity that black folks would rail against and get mad about, but they never knew how to deal with," he said. Rawlings knew how. "I organized the first meeting between the board of regents of the University of Maryland and leaders of the black community. The regents had never seen any black people. And black people had never seen the University of Maryland's board of regents in operation. It was just unbelievable. Early 1970s. It was an experience to behold. We got on their agenda. By then it was 'Put me on the agenda or I will be there.' They needed those steps that could be taken from the inside by someone who knew the system."[45]

The movement was about getting men and women like Rawlings to "the table." This was the real meaning of affirmative action in policy making. You had to be there, on the various policy-making boards, in the meeting rooms of the conference committees that decided ultimately how much money would be spent on which projects—a statue of Thurgood Marshall, for example. "I don't think my colleagues would ever do anything to hurt me or my city. But if I'm there, I know they won't."[46]

What difference had it made? "It's not an accident that the University of Maryland graduates more black PhDs, more black dentists, more other professionals, some of the highest enrollments in the nation. That is not an accident. It's not because they just decided one day they were going to do it. It was an evolution of a process from those days, and it involved everybody: the Urban League, the NAACP, church leaders, and political leaders. They were stuck. Look at where they were. Look at where they are." Rawlings's success was traceable to his own diligence and determination, but it came as part of the struggle after Donald Gaines Murray was admitted to the law school, after Lillie May Jackson's shrill imprecations to the powerful, after Thurgood Marshall's frightening trips to the South to document poor conditions endured by black students.

Affirmative action must end eventually, Rawlings thought. It had its demeaning aspects. "But you see what you're talking about in the statistics, where large numbers of white folks believe blacks are treated fairly and very low numbers of black folks believe that. I would suspect to a large degree that there's no historical reference in the minds of people when they say these things. When you live an ordinary life, you can be misled by what you see on television . . . People are seeing these realities, commercials, blacks and middle-class settings, so the perception that things are going well is out there. When you have round-table discussions, there are always blacks involved. The perception again. So there's this sense that we're doing better than we really are. In Maryland we're making a lot of progress, but too many black kids are in jail. You start off at a disadvantage because of our history; these groups are in the prison system because historically there were advantages and disadvantages." Too many of those who are not committing crimes, he said, "think they're going to get rich playing basketball."

He found himself in important councils, some of them having to do with sports and the prospects of young black men: the Orioles, for example. "We negotiated certain agreements with Larry Lucchino [then a lawyer for the team owner, Edward Bennett Williams]. When the team was sold, the new principal owner, Peter Angelos, tried to shoot them down. Nobody was going to tell him what to do." Angelos could be as demanding and imperious as Rawlings. "It got pretty intense. We became good friends afterward. He admired someone who was as nasty as he was."[47]

Rawlings was as good an operator in the political traffic as any. His legacy can be found in many things, including a major infusion of money for public secondary education. The so-called Thornton Plan for increasing aid to the poorer school districts ought to be called the Rawlings Plan because he had labored over it and so many other educational spending measures over the years.

But the Marshall statue is perhaps the most visible symbol of the progress Douglass and so many others were after for so many years. As with anything related to black history, though, it did not proceed without its measure of controversy. The bronze image of Marshall, briefcase in hand and striding toward the U.S. Supreme Court, commands a circular memorial with bronze likenesses of children sitting on a brick wall. Governor Parris N. Glendening presided at the unveiling in December

1995. Glendening had been elected governor twice. His narrow first victory had been by fewer than six thousand votes. Politically, he owed his success to the black vote, which went overwhelmingly to him. He'd always had plenty of black support, but he was not taking it for granted. His maneuvering to secure that support was another indication of the degree to which black voting and black representation had evolved.

By the end of his two terms, Glendening was not a beloved figure, but Rawlings was not focused on Glendening's popularity or lack of it. He was the man with the power, and Rawlings needed his approval. "He was much focused on what he wanted his legacy to be," Rawlings said. "He had named an African American chairman of the board of regents of the state's university system. His chief of staff was an African American. And he had appointed many blacks to the district and circuit courts."

At this point in his tenure, Glendening presided over the last ceremonial moment in a rare political opportunity: he could appoint almost simultaneously the chief judge of the vast statewide district court system, with its many employees, and of the prestigious Court of Appeals. It was a unique patronage moment. The two incumbents, Robert Murphy and Robert Sweeney, had to resign by virtue of age. Both were 70. At least one of them tried to have the law changed so he could stay on. Both wanted some role in the appointment of a successor. The governor, who enjoyed pushing past powerful people when he thought he had the better of things, headed that off too.

What he wanted was to put one black judge in the chief's office. For the Court of Appeals, Glendening was urged to appoint Alan Wilner, a respected jurist with administrative as well as legal skills. The governor could then make his black appointment in the district court. But to do that he needed a contorted manipulation of circumstances difficult even for a governor. Years later, Glendening acknowledged his plan: he dispatched an emissary to circuit court judge William Missouri, a black jurist from Prince George's County, with a proposition. If Missouri would resign from the circuit court, Glendening would instantly appoint him to the district court and make him its chief judge.[48] That maneuver was necessary because only district court judges could become chief of that court. Missouri was the last best hope, but he said no.

So Glendening tapped Robert Mack Bell, who had won a measure of civil rights fame almost by accident. The *B* in Bell meant the famous restaurant sit-in case would bear his name: *Bell v. Maryland*. "Several names were suggested to me, but he was the most prominent and most experienced. He'd been a judge at all three levels: district court, circuit court, and Court of Special Appeals. And there was a great sense of pride in the black community. At Morgan State University, there was a feeling of overwhelming pride. A sense that we had reached a level of fairness," Glendening says.[49] In a very political sense this was true as well: black voting power and black power as represented by Pete Rawlings gave Robert Mack Bell the fruits of political patronage—fruits out of black people's reach for most of the nation's and Maryland's history. Perhaps there was a bit of manipulation here, but in years past, blacks would have been manipulated out of the process, not into it.

Bell says Harry Cole had one last moment of glory in the matter. In a sense, it was the former senator, the man who beat the Pollack machines and went on to serve on the Court of Special Appeals, who made Bell's appointment possible. His role developed over the question of mandatory retirement. Murphy and Sweeney wanted to stay to the age of 75, but Cole saw that desire as selfish—and destructive. Blacks and women, worthy candidates for these high court positions, would be denied. He set about opposing the change, and voters ultimately defeated it by a two-to-one margin.

At Cole's funeral, Bell told Glendening: "You appointed the first black chief judge, but this guy made it possible."[50] Glendening might have made such an appointment without the urging of Rawlings, but, as in the matter of affirmative action, Rawlings knew his presence made an enormous difference. A moment of that sort had been years in the making. Frederick Douglass had been certain it would come one hundred years or so sooner, flowing naturally from the ballot. But the black vote had been granted on a limited basis, periodically diluted, withdrawn and distracted from throughout most of the years since Douglass had appealed for it so passionately. Now, all on the same day, a black Marylander became the state's highest-ranking judge and one of Maryland's most famous native sons, and Thurgood Marshall was commemorated on Lawyers' Mall, a few steps from the state house, mere steps away from the old appeals court building, where the march toward *Brown v. Board of Education* had begun.

The two statues make a dramatic statement. There could hardly be a more dramatic clash of ideas than the one created across the span of a century by the two Marylanders honored there. Between their statues stands the old building where George Washington resigned his commission in the Continental Army, the building where every Maryland law passed before and after had been debated, voted on, and signed into law. The Taney statue represents Maryland's past, Marshall's its more enlightened present.

Rawlings found the scene at Marshall's bronze feet exhilarating. "It's on the people side of the building, not the Taney side. It's unprecedented in the country. You can't go anywhere in the country and see such a prominent display of an African American on statehouse grounds. Even in Georgia they just have a bust of Martin Luther King Jr. somewhere in the hall."[51] The grand statues of Marshall and Taney represent the labors of men and women committed to the rule of law. They make a bold promise that the nation's most vexing problems, including the continuing problems of race, can be confronted and solved, however imperfectly, within a democratic system.

Marshall's law school mentor and partner Charles Hamilton Houston's famous declaration—"Mrs. Jackson, we can sue Jim Crow right out of Maryland"—was the ultimate profession of faith in a citizen's ability to make the law serve everyone. What he said turned out to be understatement. Starting in Baltimore with the 1935 law school case of *Murray v. Pearson,* Houston and Marshall began to unmask the false justice of separate but equal. They evicted Jim Crow, not just from Maryland, but from the entire nation. They forced open the doors of a law school and started the nation on its march to *Brown v. Board* in 1954.

Their 1935 victory did not lead to an immediate and comprehensive capitulation by the enablers of Jim Crow. In Maryland, established power held out against equality and justice for decades, stepping back from its opposition only under further pressure, further lawsuits, and persistent demonstrations of resistance. Official power wielded by white elected officials gave ground slowly, only grudgingly, even after the highest court in the land had ordered the officials to do so. Even after *Brown,* they sought ways to delay final concessions. With the local white press virtually silent and with no television, the Maryland movement did not get the early attention it might have. The South, perhaps deservedly, became the eye of the storm.

A more vigorous and feeling press might have seen and reported the extraordinary partnership of Lillie May Jackson and Theodore R. Mc-Keldin, who began to break through the barricades. There may have been no more important white apostle of change in any state than McKeldin. He trumpeted the value of brotherhood and apparently believed it in his heart. In his Republican candidate's mind, to be sure, he saw that the black vote could be his ally in a state that had always been overwhelmingly Democratic.

Maryland and the nation had missed a splendid opportunity to convert the sordid history of slavery into a foundation for men and women emerging from servitude. Eager black voters were not welcomed into the democracy. The potential bonanza of a new constituency of black voters, headed for the party of Lincoln, was sneered at by Democrats as a stain upon the GOP and a threat to the common good. Pushed away from the voting booth and from the holding of public office, black men and women could not participate fully in the American democracy. They were in no position to bargain over statues or anything else. By the year 2000, though, there were enough black votes to achieve progress for black voters in many areas.

Marshall's bronze image on Lawyers' Mall makes the point with sublime eloquence.

DEAN SCHMOKE: RENEWING HOUSTON'S CHALLENGE

In the spring of 2005, the Howard University School of Law in Washington was looking for a new dean, someone to stand in the halls where Charles Hamilton Houston had taught, someone to inspire a new generation of young lawyers. A nationwide search had ended without an acceptable candidate.

The recruitment process continued informally, however, and Baltimore's former mayor, Kurt Schmoke, heard of it. Since the end of his last term as mayor, he had been a lawyer at Wilmer, Cutler and Pickering, one of Washington, D.C.'s pre-eminent firms. He had made more money in three years than in all the previous twelve years as mayor of Baltimore combined. He was, by then, an almost unremarkable symbol of the nation's progress in race relations, a man with a resume that would have been impossible for a black man to compile short decades earlier.

But for him, something was missing, something in which the ideals of Houston and Marshall might be served more directly. He made some inquiries. Would Howard be interested at all in a candidate from a nonacademic, real-world background? The answer: it would. Within weeks the search was over. Howard Law had a new dean.

An engaging, thoughtful man, Schmoke had lived a life Houston might well have anticipated as he went about demolishing the Jim Crow structure. Schmoke had stepped up for the opportunities denied earlier by law and custom. He had taken on the demands of public life theretofore unavailable to black Americans. Schmoke had sometimes seemed ill-suited for the hurly-burly of politics. He was an athlete and the beneficiary of a first-class education: a political candidate of sublime qualification. He was the ideal "first black mayor." So he had run. Like other talented black leaders, he had done what he felt obliged and proud to do. He had served. But now he could be himself. Now he could teach. He could be a mentor. He could nurture young lawyers. He could prepare them for the new frontier of civil rights.

He found himself in awe of his new surroundings and thrilled to be another Maryland link in the chain of connection to the school that had nurtured Houston and Marshall. Schmoke moved into the dean's office in the Houston Building, on the old Dumbarton School campus, at Van Ness Street near Wisconsin Avenue in northwest Washington.

His secretary began to hang some of the former mayor's artwork, paintings done by a one-time *Afro-American* artist. She was about to move portraits of Houston and Marshall when another former dean happened into the room and stopped her. "Deans come and go," the man told Schmoke later, "but those paintings are history. They're permanent."[52]

If Schmoke felt somewhat chastised, it was clear in his telling of this story that he was happier than he had been in years. The job of dean seemed made for him. He and other professors at the school continued to assert Houston's challenging dictum: if you are a black lawyer and you are not involved in the struggle, you are a parasite.

The work of black lawyers in the early part of the twenty-first century would often be markedly different from the work undertaken by Houston and Marshall. But there was plenty of room in cities like Baltimore for work that grew out of the history of race relations and civil rights. In a sense, the job would be more difficult. Many have observed that the discrimination is less visible and therefore more complicated to confront—but no less urgent. Real change can be obscured by the persistence of a lamentable history. The words of Roger Taney, fated to be widely misunderstood and damaging, for example, may never die because they are part of history, available for introduction in current discussions.

For example, you couldn't miss Taney's legacy one night in Baltimore at an NAACP forum in late 2005. A black minister invoked *Dred Scott* (inaccurately, yet again, but powerfully), as if the decision had been rendered yesterday. The meeting was called to discuss a police practice in which many black young people—guilty of no more than rude behavior but suspected of criminal drug activity—were being rounded up in large numbers by police and taken to jail. At least half of them were being released without charge, let alone conviction. They left jail with a potentially crippling arrest record. That record—readily accessible on-line in the computer age—became a dead weight for some when they tried to find work. An arrest record, conviction or not, can block acceptance in public housing as well. And the effort to have such tracings removed from the computer network was Byzantine, Kafkaesque, defeating. In some cases, the person with the debilitating record had to agree not to sue for false arrest if he wanted the record removed immediately. Some were so certain of losing the bureaucratic battle, they didn't even try. Wasn't this another example of the enduring white-over-black conspiracy? Probably not, actually, but therein lay the complexity of race relations in the world a half century after *Brown*.

A well-known Baltimore defense lawyer, Warren Brown, said it was a way for employers to do what they might want to do anyway—discriminate against a black kid. A record was a convenient pretext, a way to hide racial animosity. And when the various authorities asserted they could do nothing about the policy of somewhat indiscriminate arrests without a change in state law, the audience sagged into a posture of muted anger, of discouraged affirmation that for whatever issue they faced, there would be a reason why it could not go away. Just the way it was—and still is.

But as always, there were those who would not accept the way it was. As in the past, the NAACP had allies outside the black community. As in the past, though, these allies were up against a society with no real sensitivity to the issue. These arrests brought "some very serious consequences, because people who lose their liberty for any length of time have suffered real damage," says Doug Colbert, a white professor at the University of Maryland School of Law. "If this were happening to you and me, if this were happening to our children, it would be an outrage. It's only that it's happening in the poor neighborhoods. It's happening to African American people. It's not happening to other people who are guilty of the same crime. The college students who come into town and party and get drunk . . . they're not going to wind up in central booking most of the time."[53]

But where are the voices of the black elected officials? Should they be readily identifiable as advocates for reform of this process? Where were they on the night of NAACP chairman Marvin "Doc" Cheatham's meeting at Union Baptist Church?

Colbert says the Maryland General Assembly's Black Caucus has tried many times to deal with the expunction-of-arrests issue, among others.[54] Assembly leaders—committee chairs and others who often decide whether a bill lives or dies—have not helped. Legislation that would have helped passed both houses but was vetoed by then-governor Robert L. Ehrlich Jr.—Ehrlich, who had chastised Mayor O'Malley for needlessly compromising the lives of young black men by arresting so many of them.

The NAACP meeting was held in what may be thought of as the mother church of the NAACP in Baltimore, Union Baptist on Druid Hill Avenue. This had been the Reverend Harvey Johnson's church in the 1880s, and it was Johnson who had helped shoulder Maryland's first black lawyer into the state bar. On the night of the NAACP forum, there was a conviction palpable in the audience that the fix was in once again. The Reverend Daki Napata, a local activist with roots in the civil rights movement, invoked the words of Taney. There was still no respect, he said. His pleas came cloaked in the grievances of history, knowledge of abusive police practices not unlike those that had helped galvanize Lillie May Jackson's march on Annapolis in the 1930s after a policeman shot a black soldier on Pennsylvania Avenue. There was muted outrage in the church basement meeting room and discouragement, a kind of sad and incredulous statement: Don't you see what's going on here?

But there was a difference. The arrest policy was affirmed in effect—certainly not lamented—by a black city official, police commissioner Leonard Hamm, who said he was retraining his troops in the art of report writing. Many police officers, he said, hadn't learned to prepare reports, offering insufficient probable cause. Over the next few hours, though, an array of witnesses suggested the reports were thin because there *was* no probable cause. The police were using arrests as a crime-suppression tactic, sweeping potential troublemakers off the street, and to hell with the Constitution.

Hamm was accused of being in league with the white mayor who could have—with a single phone call—ordered an end to what everyone (everyone but the commissioner) agreed was a troublesome police practice. Quickly the petitioners were encountering the complexity of their campaign. Many constituencies and interests were in the mix: black, white, and old and young of both colors.

Mayor O'Malley was trying to stop the sort of drug dealing and gang violence that seemed to spring from loitering: loitering was the charge frequently lodged against the arrested young men and then dropped. Surely there was a dilemma here, and it was partly a dilemma for the black community to solve. The police—with urging from other sectors of the black community, sick and tired and frightened of the crime in their midst—were sweeping people off the streets, hoping to reduce violence by reducing the number of players. And, the theory went, if there is a backwash for the young black man, well, we have to deal with the violence, and if they weren't involved in it when they were arrested, they would have been eventually. It was not a sentiment exclusive to white officials. Black inner city residents suffered more than most Baltimoreans by the plague of violent crime, including murder.

This "arrest meeting" was held at time when members of the Maryland judiciary in Baltimore's courts were despairing that anything could be done about the carnage of drug abuse in Baltimore. The courts were almost sinking under the weight of drug arrests. Worse than that by far, wrote circuit court judge Thomas E. Noel, was the damage to the inner city black community. Entire generations of young men were losing their lives to drugs, dying instantly on the streets of the city in drug killings or dying slowly in the grip of the toxic lifestyle.[55]

Blacks and whites were jailed for drug offenses at an increasingly high rate, in pursuit of a policy that had no slowing effect on drug addiction while filling the state prisons—mostly with black offenders. Judge Noel saw history repeating itself. Many of those convicted of drug crimes— often petty drug crimes—lost their voting rights. "The importance of voting rights truly warrants a brief discussion of its history. Disenfranchisement laws in many states in the South were designed to impact primarily upon blacks. Offenses that were thought to be committed by blacks or enforced against blacks were designated as a basis to [deny them] the right to vote. The effect was to disenfranchise ten times as many blacks as whites . . . Often, the offenses that led to losing the right to vote were not serious enough to warrant incarceration." The real objective, the judge wrote, was to remove voting rights. "These obvious discriminatory enactments were not ruled unconstitutional in some cases until as late as 1985."[56]

A similar result was flowing from the drug war, he said, intended or not. It is believed that at least 13 percent of black males in the United States have lost their voting privileges as a result of drug convictions, often minor ones in which an array of experts in the criminal justice system say treatment was the appropriate sanction. A University of Maryland law school professor, Michael Pinard, urged Maryland to join many other states in restoring the franchise to offenders who had paid their debt to society—in jail time served and parole. Only ten other states permanently cancel voting rights for some residents. In many other states, the route back to full voting privileges is almost impossibly complex, as difficult to navigate as the old South's aggressive disenfranchising. Pinard joined Colbert and Schmoke in attacking this barrier to full citizenship. "Dis-enfranchisement often frustrates constructive re-entry from prison to the community," he wrote. Social science research suggests that ex-prisoners who vote are 50 percent less likely to end up back in prison.[57]

The transformation of the city's courts into processors of drug offenders (and into disenfranchisers) had come to present a picture of profound catastrophe in the life of the community. Judge Noel, in one of many reports on the quality of justice in the 1990s, painted this daily courtroom tableau, a window into the world of drug crime and drug punishment. "The [courtroom] usually contains friends and family of those incarcerated. The girlfriends with babies and young children in tow is a constant sight. Many of these children are of school age and one wonders why they are here and not in school, but this is the opportunity for the defendant to see the child and the mothers are encouraged to bring them to court."[58]

What Baltimore clearly did not need was another way for young black men to be ensnared in the criminal justice system. They were doing a good job of that all by themselves. The NAACP's newly elected chairman, Doc Cheatham, said black parents and ministers and other leaders had to step up and own their share of the problem. Like Commissioner Hamm, Cheatham was conflicted. A successful voter-registration campaigner for years in the city, he was trying to resuscitate an NAACP chapter as moribund as the one Lillie May Jackson had rescued in the 1930s. He was leading the effort to have the debilitating charges expunged, but he was asking for help from parents and others in the black leadership of Baltimore.

The meeting place he chose, Union Baptist, resonated with the history of the struggle. He convened his discussion there for a reason. Parishioners of that church had gone to court in 1914 against a local steamship line after they were forced to travel below decks with the cattle. They had won. More important, the women and the minister had organized Baltimore's NAACP chapter, the one that had fallen into disrepair before Jackson revived it. Now, though, almost one hundred years after its founding, the organization might have had more hope of success because it could call on black elected officials in Baltimore to help.

When she was getting in the face of a reluctant, mostly white, official Maryland, Lillie May Jackson occasionally gave a warning: failing to undo grievous wrongs would have enduring consequences for the society. She urged white officials to be pragmatic at least, to see that continued denial of rights would lead to corrosive despair among black Americans and real problems for whites as well. Without justice, she said, the nation would find itself dealing with legions of disaffected citizens who felt alienated from the political system. Her warning may have been too late. One of her lawyers, the affable Bob Watts, for example, thought the nation's grudging acceptance of *Brown v. Board of Education,* along with the assassination of Martin Luther King, led to the riots of 1968. If the U.S. Supreme Court could be ignored and circumvented, and if black leaders could be assassinated, what hope was there? Why not torch everything?

Of course, Jackson was never an advocate of violence or criminal behavior. She had no patience for those in the movement who gave up on the idea of overcoming via prayer and nonviolence—and the effort to help others find their better selves. Her lawyer, Thurgood Marshall, lamented the street demonstrations that came along when the law did not change quickly enough, but he also knew that the nation had sometimes changed the law without finding a way to put the law into everyday practice.

Yet change did come. Attitudes among Americans, particularly white Americans, are altered from the days in which Roger Taney could quote the framers of the Constitution without shame or fear of contradiction, saying that whites owed black people no respect. The vicissitudes of discrimination—in law and custom—helped to produce a continuation of the struggle begun in Maryland by Benjamin Lundy, Harriet Tubman, Frederick Douglass, the Reverend Harvey Johnson, Isaac Meyers, and so many others. Maryland produced Kurt Schmoke, and it had as many black state legislators, women and men, as any other state.

But black elected officials were not rushing in numbers to join the struggle for felony voting rights or the expunction of arrest records, possibly for fear of alienating black voters by seeming to blame the victims. They were also hemmed in by political considerations that obliged them to be careful lest they be marginalized in the legislative process by powerful forces with no real commitment to further evolution of black rights.

Cheatham said he would be urging black leaders and black parents to take some risks, to become part of a new movement that would employ the power of political office with a moral authority akin to the challenges made by Jackson and later by King and Rosa Parks. Cheatham had stepped up to assume his role in the perpetual civil rights cycle, the constant effort to confront issues of race, class, and discrimination. The arrest problem was merely another manifestation of the same problem. Still, some of the crushing dynamic had changed, making the solution more difficult.

He did have allies. State's attorney Patricia C. Jessamy professed deep concern about the problem. "It causes a pain in my heart," she said, "to see black men in shackles and chains lined up each morning" outside Baltimore's Clarence M. Mitchell Jr. Courthouse, named for the civil rights leader.[59] But, as a guardian of the law and of due process—denied black Americans for so many years—she could not go forward with too little evidence to warrant prosecution. A black police commissioner was bringing a multitude of cases to a black prosecutor in a world where black Baltimoreans had often been victimized by officials with no regard for their lives. She knew, as did Commissioner Hamm, that the black community was divided on the proper course. Many black citizens wanted action against drug activity that was ruining the quality of their lives, stealing from them the participation in society they had worked so hard to attain for themselves and their children.

Jessamy and Hamm had adopted at least some of the self-help demands of the comedian Bill Cosby, long before Cosby had offered them so controversially from his unique platform. Here was a challenge for them, for Doc Cheatham, and for the white community as well. Here were issues that could be seen as further steps in the ongoing struggle for civil rights. As Jackson had observed decades earlier, here was a problem that affected the entire society, white and black. White academics and white judges might enlist in the struggle, but the burden would have to be borne by the lawyers and the laboring sons of a new century.

Just the way it is.

Epilogue

The national civil rights movement was part of a historic process, not an event. The struggle for freedom and for civil rights in what became the United States arose surely from the first day of slavery. It trickled to the surface of national life inexorably, like the headwaters of a river, gathering momentum and depth. Gross imperfections were deposited—and mitigated—as the waters passed over the filtering rocks and pebbles of heroic action and patience. Many Americans, white and black, made brave witness for decency. They were all part of the critical, cleansing mass. Each of these lovers of freedom fought on in faith, trusting that victory would be, if never final, as sweet as honey in the rock.

Lillie May Jackson was pre-eminent among those Marylanders who gave the movement momentum and whose leadership sustained others. She was fearless. She hectored black and white, famous and anonymous. She persevered for a lifetime. A large photograph of the national civil rights icon Rosa Parks hangs in the entryway to Jackson's house on Bolton Hill in Baltimore. Ma Jackson is standing next to her in the picture. Rosa Parks's movement was just beginning when Jackson was decades into hers. Parks had come to recognize her leadership.

Jackson and Parks had labored to erase the force of Chief Justice Roger Taney's words in *Dred Scott*. They were almost always outnumbered and confronted with massive institutional opposition, determined to show that Taney's words were an accurate reflection of the state's attitude. After the Civil War, Maryland's political Establishment put up barricades against newly freed black people, denying them the place made at such a high cost for them in the American system. Slavery and Reconstruction were not mere historical earmarks but continuing echoes of disdain and disrespect. Like *Dred Scott,* they had enduring resonance. People who see a surgical end to these periods of national life have not had to find their way in a life shaped by discrimination.

Lillie May Jackson and Theodore R. McKeldin broke through these barricades. There was no more important white apostle of change in Maryland than McKeldin. And yet, real change came slowly. In the meantime, there was the matter of daily coping, of making your way with dignity.

Frederick's Bill Lee enjoys telling the story of the new house he built in the 1970s, not far from Taney's historic manse, with its slave quarters, on Bentz Street. Lee and a friend bought lots there, and while they were lining up a building loan, they periodically cut the grass on their new property. A neighbor lady would come out with lemonade for them. After a few meetings, the woman asked, "Who owns the lots?"[1]

"We do," they said. The lemonade stopped coming, and the woman eventually moved away.

Bill Lee smiles in the telling. If someone wanted to leave such a pretty place to him, fine. He knew the old attitudes were not gone. The bigotry of a neighbor was only the first bit of resistance he encountered. He had a good income, but he was denied a building loan in Frederick. He got one in Baltimore. He didn't make much of it. After he resigned from the school system and left the board of aldermen, he joined the historical society and wrote a book about his life.[2]

While growing up in Frederick, he had learned where he could go, where he couldn't go, and how he would be received. Blacks could not be treated in the nearby whites-only hospital. Black gatherings to celebrate Emancipation Day could be held only if there was white supervision. Public parks, department stores, and restaurants were for whites only. Change came slowly. Personal leadership at every level was critical for epochal change. The people may be chafed raw by a system such as Jim Crow, but the survival instinct makes them properly suspicious of mere gesture. Bravery, insight, passion—and success—are necessary to make the risk worth taking, to show us that we can overcome.

Bill Lee told of daring integrated play periods at one of the local elementary schools. He and a white colleague conspired to let their kids play together on the same playground. No one intervened. In such ways was progress achieved.

In the last years of his life, he helped push the City of Frederick, under mayor Jennifer Dougherty, to identify those black city residents who had been interred—and reinterred by bulldozers—at the old Laboring Sons Cemetery. The movement toward this belated justice came from a white woman, Martha Reynolds, who lived nearby. In a letter to city hall, she wondered why the City had taken down the Laboring Sons sign. That inquiry led to a series of investigations. How many bodies had been buried on the site? How many had been removed? The answers were vague, but there was agreement that a wrong had been committed.

Names of the organization's official founders, at least, had been preserved in the records. Under Chapter 343 of the state laws, the legislature in 1836 had granted incorporation in the names of "Cyrus Brown, president; Perry G. Walker, vice president; Isaac Prout, treasurer; James Weems, chaplain; William Brown Jr., chief manager; James Brown, Reuben Taneyhill, and Thomas Lyles, assistant managers (all colored persons)." Here were proud sons of Frederick undertaking as much of the care and support as they could and doing it within the laws of the state. They were far more meticulous in meeting their obligations as citizens than the state and some of its citizens were willing to acknowledge.

The incorporated group was to be known officially as the Beneficial Society of the Laboring Sons of Frederick City. The incorporation entitled the organization to "have, purchase, possess, enjoy and retain to them and their successors lands, lots and tenements in fee simple, sufficient in their judgment to accommodate the wants of the society." The document gave these sons of Frederick "the power to . . . defend and be defended in all or any Courts of Justice and before all or any judges, officers or persons whatsoever in all and singular actions, matters or demand whatsoever." The society would have, finally, the right to "execute all things touching and concerning the design and intent for the benevolent succor and relief of persons belonging to said society in accordance with their Constitution and by-laws not in violation of the Constitution and laws of this state or of the United States."[3] Such a document was possible—and dutifully obtained—during the tenure of Governor Thomas Swann, who had declared his state to be the preserve of white people.

Fifteen hundred people may have been buried in the block-sized cemetery, but only 161 names were found in city records. Nothing could be learned of others whose final resting place it may have been. The story of the cemetery was deeply unsettling to some in the city.

"It really touched a nerve," said Jackie Berry, who believes her great-great-uncle, Zachariah Daley, is one of the unknowns. She was appalled, she said, to learn that the City had bulldozed the graves and the gravestones. "It brought back old memories of the way it used to be in Frederick in the '50s for African Americans." Berry searched the records to find some trace of her Uncle Zachariah, a blacksmith. His brother, Benjamin, was a carpenter and wheelwright. These were among the trades plied by the Laboring Sons. As she worked on the memorial ground issue, she realized more clearly that "final resting place" was in her hands for many people, not just her uncle. She welcomed the opportunity. "It's as though a whole generation of my ancestors have been lost. I feel they are so close . . . I don't want to forget about them."[4]

She had allies. A reporter, whose name—Patience Wait—was almost too fitting, wrote a number of stories, laying out the offense. Editorial writers had their say. City officials, historians, and others in Frederick brought the Laboring Sons back to the city's collective consciousness and conscience. "It was a mistake to have it as a playground, and we're proud to rededicate it now," said Mayor Dougherty when the memorial grounds were officially unveiled. "It was a promise from the City to the descendants, and to the neighbors, and it is a promise kept."[5]

A plaque dedicates the park to the 161 souls whose names were found in the records and to those others who may have been interred there. It does not mention the how and why it was important to erect such a monument. Jackie Berry thought the omission was a mistake. People should know what happened, she thought. Bill Lee, consistent with his way of seeing such things, said, "We're just glad [the memorial] is being done. We didn't find it necessary to rehash what happened forty-eight, fifty years ago. What's important is what's happening now."[6]

It was happening as part of the continuing evolution of thought and attitude about race in U.S. society—and because Houston and Marshall and others had managed, via *Brown v. Board of Education,* to sue Jim Crow out of Maryland and the nation. Something like the transformation of thinking Charles Houston thought essential was there in the response to the lost Laboring Sons. Just as the *Murray* law school case in Maryland led to *Brown, Brown* led to an array of laws on voting rights, employment, public accommodations, and the like. Said the legal scholar Alan Morrison, "I don't think we would have had the civil rights laws we have without *Brown*. It made people think differently."[7]

Many in the nation endured and even prevailed as change came slowly. One of these was Bill Lee. His grandparents had sheltered him, and like Frederick Douglass, he grew up playing with white kids. He grew up to become, in a new day, one of the city fathers of Frederick. In recognition of his life as a teacher and coach, his stewardship at Asbury United Methodist Church, and his eight years as a Frederick alderman, a public housing project's community center was named in his honor. In Frederick, as in Annapolis, echoes of the past are always within earshot. The center is located in a public housing project named for Roger Brooke Taney.

Acknowledgments

I'm grateful to many people for invaluable help in the preparation of this book. The initial research was supported by a grant from the Meyerhoff Family Fund of Baltimore. My editor at the Johns Hopkins University Press, Robert Brugger, the nonpareil chronicler of Maryland history, was the book's steadfast champion. I am, once again, grateful to Paul McCardell, librarian par excellence at the *Sun* in Baltimore. He upholds the standards of that newspaper's many gracious and generous researchers, men and women who found what was needed with a smile of encouragement. As the final touches were put on the manuscript, I was reminded yet again of how important it is to have a meticulous and well-organized text editor. I have been blessed with the careful, exacting efforts of Melanie Mallon, a masterful accountant of the repetitive phrase or passage. The rigor of her work is here on every page.

I would also like to thank the staff of the Marylandia Collection at the University of Maryland, College Park. I am particularly indebted to Rachel Kassman of the Jewish Museum of Baltimore. Research librarians at the Maryland Historical Society were unfailingly helpful, as were those at the New York Public Library's Schomburg Collection.

My friends Louise White, Tim Phelps, Antero Pietila, Gilbert Sandler, Patricia Cushwa, Fred Rasmussen, Bill Thompson, and David Bogan were kind enough to read various versions of the manuscript. Their perceptive, insightful, and gentle comments were much appreciated. Josh Tong, Bob Brugger's assistant, helped to keep the book's photographs in good order. Thanks also to Marilyn Benaderet, archivist at the AFRO-American Newspapers in Baltimore, and Chris Kintzel, of the Maryland State Archives in Annapolis.

I owe the usual debt of gratitude to those who were willing to answer my questions, but I am particularly grateful to the many nonagenarians in that group. They include Walter Sondheim Jr.; Peggy Waxter, who spoke with clarity and joy at 102, and stood up for human rights long before most Americans did because it was simply right to do so; Richard McKinney, who interviewed W. E. B. Du Bois, later marveled at the very existence of the Reginald F. Lewis Museum of Maryland African American History, and as a member of the museum board was there in the blazing sun on the day the museum opened officially; Lord Nickens, longtime head of the NAACP in Frederick, who maintained his proud demand for respect from the day, at age 6, he was kicked by a railroad station attendant; Sam Hopkins, who has copies of the *Genius of Universal Emancipation,* the abolitionist sheet once edited in Baltimore by William Lloyd Garrison; Sidney Hollander Jr., son of the daring Baltimore civil rights champion and a man possessed with the same passion for peace and brotherhood; and Mildred Momberger, longtime personal secretary to Mayor Theodore R. McKeldin.

I'm also grateful to Bill Thompson and Susanna Craine. For their patience and support, I wish to thank my children, Jennifer, Ali, Jake, Anna, and Emily, and my grandchildren, Hannah, Ryan, Zoe, and Alex. I am blessed to be in the midst of loving young people unencumbered with the myth and misunderstandings that have, in the past, diminished our nation.

Appendix: Author Interviews

Adams, Victorine Quille, September 2005, Baltimore
Adkins III, William L., September 2006, telephone
Angelos, Peter, March 1998, Baltimore
Barrow Jr., Joe Louis, August 2004, telephone
Bascom, Marion C., September 2004, Baltimore
Bates, Milton, December 2003, Baltimore
Bell, Robert Mack, March 2006, Baltimore
Berk, Lane, June 2004, Baltimore
Bogen, David S., December 2005, Baltimore
Cohen, Robert R., March 2004, Baltimore
Colbert, Doug, September 2006, Baltimore
Crenson, Matthew, July 2003, Baltimore
Crockett, James, May 2005, Baltimore
Culotta, Samuel, June 2004, Baltimore
D'Alesandro III, Thomas, December 2004, Baltimore
Dobson, Vernon, May 2006, Baltimore
Doyle, James, January 2004, Annapolis
Gibson, Larry, July 2005, Baltimore
Glendening, Parris N., October 2006, telephone
Glover, Ruby, September 2004, Baltimore
Grubb, Enez, April 2004, Cambridge
Gunther, Nattie, August 2005, Baltimore
Harris, Lucretia, October 2001, Princess Anne
Haysbert, Raymond V., March 2004, Baltimore
Henderson, Sally, May 2005, telephone
Hollander Jr., Sidney, June 2003, Baltimore
Hopkins, Samuel, October 2005, Baltimore

Jews, William L., March 2006, Owings Mills
Jones, Ross, September 2006, Lutherville
Kaufman, A. Robert, November 2004, Baltimore
Kerpelman, Leonard, November 2004, Baltimore
Kinlein, Richard, December 2004, telephone
Lee Jr., William O., September 2001, Frederick
Lewis, David Levering, October 2005, telephone
Logan, Clarence, September 2004, telephone
Mandel, Marvin, August 2001, Annapolis
Marriott, Salima Siler, January 2006, Baltimore
Mathias, Charles McC., August 2001, Chevy Chase
McCready, Esther, March 2004, Baltimore
McKeldin Jr., Theodore R., October 2005, Towson
McKinney, Richard, November 2005, Baltimore
Mills, Barbara, August 2004, Warwick, Rhode Island
Mitchell III, Clarence M., December 2003, Baltimore
Mitchell Sr., Keiffer, July 2007, Baltimore
Mitchell Jr., Keiffer, November 2004, Baltimore
Mitchell, Michael, September 2005, Baltimore
Mitchell, Parren, March 2003, Baltimore
Montague, Ken, June, 2005, Baltimore
Moore, Ralph, June 2005, Baltimore
Morrison, Alan, October 2007, Baltimore
Murphy, Arthur, December 2005, Baltimore
Murphy, Camay, May 2004, Baltimore
Murphy, Frances "Frankie," April 2004, Baltimore
Oliver, Jake, April 2004, Baltimore
Perkins, Anne, November 2003, telephone
Rawlings, Howard P. "Pete," March 2002, Baltimore
Rienhoff, William, May 2005, telephone
Russell, George, February 2005, Baltimore
Sachs, Steve, June 2002, Baltimore
Sarbanes, Paul, December 2006, Baltimore
Schmoke, Kurt L., September 2006, Washington, D.C.
Shifter, Richard, January 2005, Bethesda
Simpkins, Lloyd "Hotdog," July 2001, Princess Anne
Somerville, Frank, September 2003, Baltimore
Sondheim Jr., Walter, March 2004, Baltimore
Spector, Rochelle "Rikki," March 2005, Baltimore
Steiner, Marc, March 2004, Baltimore
Sterne, Joseph R. L., February 2006, Baltimore
Sykes, Melvin, November 2005, Baltimore

Watkins Jr., Levi, November 2005, Baltimore
Waxter, Peggy, March 2006, Baltimore
Wickwire, Chester, August 2004, Cockeysville
Wright, Bill, July 2004, Cambridge

Notes

PREFACE

1. Albert Murray, *South to a Very Old Place* (New York: McGraw-Hill, 1971), 176–78.

PROLOGUE: LABORING SONS

1. Ira Berlin, *Many Thousands Gone: The First Two Centuries of Slavery in North America* (Cambridge, Mass.: Belknap Press of Harvard University Press, 1998), 62.

2. Denton L. Watson, *Lion in the Lobby: Clarence M. Mitchell Jr.'s Struggle for the Passage of Civil Rights Laws* (New York: William Morrow, 1990).

3. *Frederick News-Post,* June 2, 2000.

4. William O. Lee Jr., interview by the author, September 2001, Frederick.

5. Woodward, *The Strange Career of Jim Crow,* 3rd ed. (New York: Oxford University Press, 1974), 7.

6. Ibid., 18.

CHAPTER 1. TANEY AND DOUGLASS

1. *Dred Scott v. Sandford,* 60 U.S. 393 (1856).

2. Lee interview.

3. Typescript lyrics, published by the club, from the collection of Bill Lee.

4. Lee interview.

5. Ibid.

6. Mathias, Charles McC., interview by the author, August 2001, Chevy Chase.

7. Ibid.

8. Ibid.

9. Bernard C. Steiner, *Life of Roger Brooke Taney, LLD, Chief Justice of the Supreme Court of the U.S.* (Baltimore: John Murphy, 1922), 188.

10. Berlin, *Many Thousands Gone,* 38.

11. Ibid.

12. Roger B. Taney, *Memoir of Roger Brooke Taney, LLD, Chief Justice of the Supreme Court of the U.S.* (Baltimore: John Murphy, 1872), 20.

13. Carl Brent Swisher, *Roger B. Taney* (New York: Macmillan, 1935), 4.

14. Taney, *Memoir,* 65.

15. Swisher, *Roger B. Taney,* 13.

16. Ibid., 19.

17. Ibid., 12.

18. Taney, *Memoir,* 87.

19. Swisher, *Roger B. Taney,* 96.

20. Steiner, *Life of Roger Brooke Taney,* 78.

21. Ibid.

22. Ibid., 96.

23. Swisher, *Roger B. Taney,* 97.

24. Ibid., 82.

25. Dickson J. Preston, *Young Frederick Douglass: The Maryland Years* (Baltimore: Johns Hopkins University Press, 1980), 93.

26. Frederick Douglass, *My Bondage and My Freedom* (New York: Dover, 1969; first published New York: Miller, Orton & Mulligan, 1855), 147.

27. Gunnar Myrdal, *An American Dilemma* (New York: Harper, 1944).

28. Preston, *Young Frederick Douglass,* 92.

29. Douglass, *My Bondage and My Freedom,* 35.

30. Berlin, *Many Thousands Gone,* 113.

31. Primo Levi, *Survival in Auschwitz* (New York: Simon and Schuster, 1993; translated from *Se questo è un uomo,* 1958, by Giulio Einaudi), 27.

32. David S. Bogen, "Race and the Law in Maryland," draft manuscript, 37. Lundy was not the only walker for an end to slavery. Bogen cites the case of John Woolman, who traveled the Eastern Shore in 1766, declaring slavery injurious to the Society of Friends and America itself.

33. Henry Mayer, *All on Fire: William Lloyd Garrison and the Abolition of Slavery* (New York: St. Martin's Griffin, 1998), 51.

34. Eric Robert Papenfuse, *The Evils of Necessity: Robert Goodloe Harper and the Moral Dilemma of Slavery* (Philadelphia: American Philosophical Society, 1997), 58.

35. Mayer, *All on Fire,* 75.

36. Douglass, *My Bondage and My Freedom,* 135–36, quoted in Christopher Phillips, *Freedom's Port: The African American Community of Baltimore, 1790–1860* (Urbana: University of Illinois Press, 1997), 57.

37. Mayer, *All on Fire,* 85–86.

38. Ibid., 76.

39. Ibid., 85.

40. Ibid., 92.

41. Ibid., 94.

42. Phillips, *Freedom's Port,* 30.

43. Taney to Secretary of State Edward Livingston, May 28, 1832, quoted in Don E. Fehrenbacher, *The Dred Scott Case: Its Significance in American Law and Politics* (New York: Oxford University Press, 1978), 69.

44. Geoffrey M. Footner, *Tidewater Triumph: The Development and Worldwide Success of the Chesapeake Bay Pilot Schooner* (Mystic Conn.: Mystic Seaport Museum, 1998), 153.

45. A song signaling impending escape, Preston, *Young Frederick Douglass,* 136.

46. Frederick Douglass, *My Life and Times,* quoted in William S. McFeely, *Frederick Douglass* (New York: Norton, 1991), 71.

47. Ibid., 72

48. Ibid. 88–89.

49. McFeely, *Frederick Douglass,* 91.

50. Quoted in *The Frederick Douglass Papers, Series Two: Autobiographical Writings,* vol. 1: narrative, ed. John W. Blassingame, John R. McKivigan, and Peter P. Hinks (New Haven, Conn.: Yale University Press, 1999), xxxix.

51. Ibid., xl.

52. Preston, *Young Frederick Douglass,* 171.

53. "A Simple Tale of American Slavery: An Address Delivered in Sheffield, England, on 11 September 1846," *The Frederick Douglass Papers, Series One: Speeches, Debates, and Interviews,* vol. 1: 1841–46, ed. John W. Blassingame (New Haven: Yale University Press, 1979), 400.

54. Quoted in Eric Foner, *The Story of American Freedom* (New York: W. W. Norton, 1999), 402.

55. *New York Tribune,* March 7, 1857.

56. Swisher, *Roger B. Taney,* 100.

57. McFeely, *Frederick Douglass,* 382.

58. Samuel Tyler, *Memoir of Roger Brooke Taney, LL.D.,* 2nd. ed (Baltimore: J. Murphy, 1876), 60–64.

59. From Taney's decision as quoted in Fehrenbacher, *The Dred Scott Case,* 355.

60. David S. Bogen, "The Maryland Context of Dred Scott," *American Journal of Legal History* (Oct. 1990): 382.

61. Bogen, "Maryland Context," 382.

62. *Dred Scott v. Sandford.*

63. Vincent C. Hopkins, *Dred Scott's Case* (New York: Fordham University Press, 1951), 61.

64. From Taney's decision as quoted in Fehrenbacher, *The Dred Scott Case,* 343.

65. Ibid., 364.

66. Fehrenbacher, *The Dred Scott Case*, 861.

67. Daniel to Van Buren, Nov. 1, 1847, Martin Van Buren Papers, Manuscript Division, Library of Congress, quoted in Fehrenbacher, *The Dred Scott Case*, 561.

68. Fehrenbacher, *The Dred Scott Case*, 560.

69. Hopkins, *Dred Scott's Case*, 61.

70. *New York Tribune*, March 9–12, 1857; *Constitutionalist*, March 15, 1857.

71. Paul Finkelman, *Dred Scott v. Sandford: A Brief History with Documents* (Boston: Bedford Books, 1997), 174. From a speech in New York on the anniversary of the founding of the American Abolition Society, July 1857, and a lengthy reaction to *Dred Scott*, recently decided and announced. *New York Tribune*, March 7, 1857.

72. Blassingame, *Frederick Douglass Papers*, 2:157.

73. George William Brown, *Baltimore and the Nineteenth of April, 1861: A Study of the War* (Baltimore: Johns Hopkins University Press, 2001; first published Baltimore: N. Murray, 1887), 114.

74. Lincoln rebounded dramatically for the 1864 election, defeating George B. McClellan handily, with 40,169 votes—a vast improvement over his earlier showing in Maryland, and a statement of endorsement for his prosecution of the war—despite his incarceration of Mayor Brown and his disagreement with Justice Taney over habeas corpus.

75. Douglass to Theodore Tilton, October 15, 1864, quoted in McFeely, *Frederick Douglass*, 235.

76. Blassingame, *Frederick Douglass Papers*, 3:606–7.

77. Ronald C. White Jr., *Lincoln's Greatest Speech* (New York: Simon and Schuster, 2002), 161.

78. Ibid., 18–19.

79. Douglass, *Life and Times* (New York: Macmillan, 1962), 366, as quoted in White, *Lincoln's Greatest Speech*, 199.

80. Robert J. Brugger, *Maryland: A Middle Temperament, 1634–1980* (Baltimore: Johns Hopkins University Press, 1988), 308.

81. *Baltimore Sun*, May 14, 1866, as quoted in Margaret Law Callcott, *The Negro in Maryland Politics: 1870–1912* (Baltimore: Johns Hopkins Press, 1969), 15.

82. Callcott, *The Negro in Maryland Politics*, 22.

83. McFeely, *Frederick Douglass*, 240.

84. Ibid., 244.

85. Ibid., 243.

86. Charles L. Wagandt, *The Mighty Revolution: Negro Emancipation in Maryland 1862–1864* (Baltimore: Johns Hopkins Press, 1964), 40.

87. Callcott, *The Negro in Maryland Politics*, vii.

88. Ibid., 3. Before 1810, blacks could vote in Maryland under certain circumstances, primarily having to do with ownership of property. In 1810, the state constitution was amended, excluding blacks entirely.

89. *Baltimore Sun,* Aug. 31, 1870.

90. *Chestertown Transcript,* Sept. 2, 1870.

91. Leroy Graham, *Baltimore, the Nineteenth Century Black Capital* (Washington, D.C.: University Press of America, 1982), 40.

92. Ibid., 208.

93. Ibid., 209–10.

94. Ibid., 186.

95. Ibid., 187.

96. Ibid., 138.

97. Ibid., 190.

98. McFeely, *Frederick Douglass,* 243.

99. *Baltimore Sun,* Feb. 9, 1885, quoted in David S. Bogen, "The First Integration of the University of Maryland School of Law," *Maryland Historical Magazine* 84, no. 1 (1989): 39.

100. *Baltimore Sun,* Oct. 22, 1889.

101. McFeely, *Frederick Douglass,* 379.

102. Ibid., 380.

CHAPTER 2. SUING JIM CROW

1. From *Plessy v. Ferguson,* as quoted in Richard Kluger, *Simple Justice: The History of* Brown v. Board of Education *and Black America's Struggle for Equality* (New York: Vintage Books, 1975), 80.

2. Ibid., 81.

3. Walter Carr interview, Baltimore Neighborhood Heritage Project, 1979–1980, Maryland Historical Society, Oral History 8297.

4. John Marshall Harlan quoted in Kluger, *Simple Justice,* 82.

5. Brugger, *Maryland,* 420.

6. Woodward, *Strange Career,* 54.

7. *Baltimore Sun,* Aug. 31, 1938, quoted in Henry Bain, "Five Kinds of Politics: A Historical and Comparative Study of the Making of Legislators in Five Maryland Constituencies" (PhD diss., Harvard University, March 1970), 870.

8. Charles J. Bonaparte to George McAneny, Nov. 23, 1899, quoted in James E. Crooks, *Politics and Progress: The Rise of Urban Progressivism in Baltimore, 1895–1911* (Baton Rouge: Louisiana State University Press, 1968), 57.

9. *Laws of Maryland* 1908, chap. 26, 300–304, quoted in Callcott, *The Negro in Maryland Politics,* 127.

10. Victorine Quille Adams, interview by the author, September 2005, Baltimore.

11. Brugger, *Maryland,* 422.

12. Manuscript, folder 9, box 252, Blair and Lee Family Papers, Firestone Library Special Collections, Princeton University.

13. Ibid., 15.

14. David S. Bogen, interview by the author, December 2005, Baltimore.

15. Woodward, *Strange Career*, 108.

16. Garrett Power, "Apartheid Baltimore Style: The Residential Ordinances of 1910–1913," *Maryland Law Review* 43, no. 2 (1983): 289–328.

17. Memo from city solicitor Edward Allan Poe to mayor J. Barry Mahool, Dec. 17, 1910, quoted in Power, "Apartheid Baltimore Style," 300.

18. Power, "Apartheid Baltimore Style," 302.

19. Ibid., 305.

20. H. L. Mencken, "The Freelance," 137 (1911–1915), unpublished collection, Mencken Room, Enoch Pratt Free Library, Baltimore, quoted in Power, "Apartheid Baltimore Style," 307.

21. Power, "Apartheid Baltimore Style," 314.

22. Garrett Power, "Prelude to *Brown v. Board of Education*," speech given at the College of Southern Maryland, La Plata, October 29, 2004.

23. Ibid.

24. Ibid.

25. Lloyd "Hotdog" Simpkins, interview by the author, July 2001, Princess Anne.

26. *Baltimore Sun*, Oct. 23, 1933.

27. Simpkins interview.

28. *Baltimore Afro-American*, Oct. 21. 1933.

29. *Baltimore Evening Sun*, Dec. 7, 1933.

30. For a detailed account of Ades's encounters with mobs and the sometimes embarrassed bar of Maryland, see *In re Ades*, 6 F. Supp. 467 (D.C.D. Md. 1934), H. no. 978.

31. *Baltimore Sun*, Oct. 21, 1933.

32. Doris Kearns Goodwin, *No Ordinary Time: Franklin and Eleanor Roosevelt: The Home Front in World War II* (New York: Simon and Schuster, 1994), 163.

33. U.S. Senate, *Hearing on Costigan-Wagner Federal Anti-Lynching Bill* (S. 1978), 73rd Cong., 2nd sess., Feb. 20–21, 1934.

34. Ibid.

35. Watson, *Lion in the Lobby*, 46.

36. Senate, *Hearing on Costigan-Wagner*.

37. Lucretia Harris, interview by the author, October 2001, Princess Anne.

38. From a conversation between Adele Holden and Sheri Parks on WTMD-FM in 2005.

39. Camay Murphy, interview by the author, May 2004, Baltimore.

40. David Margolick, *Strange Fruit: The Biography of a Song* (New York: Ecco Press, 2000), 5.

41. *In re Ades.*

42. Watson, *Lion in the Lobby,* 88.

43. Clarence M. Mitchell Jr. interview, July 1976, MHS OH 8154, cassette 1, side 1:6.

44. Ibid.

45. Ibid., cassette 1, side 1:4.

46. Parren Mitchell, March 2003; Keiffer Mitchell Sr., July 2007; and Keiffer Mitchell Jr., November 2004, interviews by the author, Baltimore.

47. *Baltimore Afro-American,* Dec. 16, 1933, box 67, assorted meeting notes, newspaper clippings, letters from civil rights activists, and magazine articles, August Meier Papers, Schomburg Center for Research in Black Culture, New York Public Library.

48. Juanita Jackson Mitchell interview, July 1975, Theodore R. McKeldin–Lillie May Jackson Civil Rights Era Oral History Project, MHS OH 8094, II:22.

49. Ibid., II:24.

50. Ibid.

51. Michael Mitchell, interview by the author, September 2005, Baltimore.

52. Juanita Jackson Mitchell interview, July 1975, MHS OH 8094,

53. Michael Mitchell interview.

54. Phillips, *Freedom's Port,* 171.

55. Juan Williams, *Thurgood Marshall: American Revolutionary* (New York: Times Books, 1998), 73.

56. Ibid., 72.

57. Kweisi Mfume, with Ron Stodghill II, *No Free Ride: From the Mean Streets to the Mainstream* (New York: One World, 1996), 56–57.

58. Kluger, *Simple Justice,* 184.

59. W. M. Hillegeist to Roger Howell, July 13, 1932, printed in the *Baltimore Afro-American,* Nov. 29, 2003.

60. *Baltimore Afro-American,* Nov. 29, 2003.

61. Copies of the covenants are on file with the Gibson Island Historical Society.

62. *Baltimore Sun,* Sunday magazine, March 14, 1971.

63. William Rienhoff, telephone interview by the author, May 2005; Sally Henderson, telephone interview by the author, May 2005.

64. J. Clay Smith Jr., review of *Groundwork: Charles Hamilton Houston and the Struggle for Civil Rights,* by Genna Rae McNeil, *Harvard Law Review* (Dec. 1984): 482.

65. As quoted in ibid., 482.

66. H. L. Mencken quoted in Kluger, *Simple Justice,* 193.

67. From remarks at a retirement testimonial for O'Dunne, June 25, 1945, in Baltimore.

68. Robert Cohen, interview by the author, March 2004, Baltimore.

69. From the program during which Judge O'Dunne's portrait was dedicated, Oct. 6, 1994, at the Clarence M. Mitchell Jr. Courthouse.

70. Cohen interview.

71. Williams, *Thurgood Marshall*, 77.

72. Cohen interview.

73. Larry Gibson, interview by the author, July 2005, Baltimore.

74. *Baltimore Afro-American*, June 22, 1935, as cited in Kluger, *Simple Justice*, 190, 819.

75. Peter Kumpa, "Eugene O'Dunne: The Judge Who Rocked Boats," *Baltimore Evening Sun*, July 8, 1981.

76. Kluger, *Simple Justice*, 190.

77. Ibid., 191.

78. Watson, *Lion in the Lobby*, 89–95.

79. Williams, *Thurgood Marshall*, 78.

80. Ibid.

81. *Baltimore Sun*, Sept. 23, 1935.

82. Watson, *Lion In The Lobby*, 95.

83. *Baltimore Afro-American*, Dec. 5, 2003.

84. Williams, *Thurgood Marshall*, 78.

85. Mencken quoted in Kluger, *Simple Justice*, 193.

86. Michael Mitchell interview.

87. Juanita Jackson Mitchell and Virginia Kiah, interview by Richard Richardson, June 1976, MHS OH 8136 and OH 1079, cassette 1, side 2:16.

88. Kluger, *Simple Justice*, 197.

89. Charles Hamilton Houston, "Don't Shout Too Soon," *Crisis*, March 23, 1936.

90. *Baltimore Daily Record*, Nov. 5, 1945.

91. James Crockett, interview by the author, May 2005, Baltimore.

92. Vernon Dobson, interview by the author, May 2006, Baltimore.

93. Theodore R. McKeldin Jr., interview by the author, October 2005, Towson.

94. *Baltimore News-Post*, Nov. 2, 1958, and March 12, 1956.

95. *Baltimore News-Post*, Jan. 15, 1954.

96. Sam Culotta, interview by the author, June 2004, Baltimore.

97. A. Robert Kaufman, interview by the author, November 2004, Baltimore.

98. *Baltimore Sun*, March 29, 1953.

99. Lane Berk, interview by Ellen Paul, 1976, McKeldin-Jackson Project, MHS OH 8146, cassette 1, side 1:16.

100. Ibid., cassette 2, side 2:21.

101. Ibid., cassette 2, side 1:11.

102. Culotta interview.

103. Ibid.

104. Lane Berk interview, cassette 2, side 2:22.

105. Culotta interview.

106. John R. Hargrove, interview by Michael Louis, June 1976, Jackson-McKeldin Project, MHS OH 8132, cassette 245, side 2:1.

107. Ibid.

108. Crockett interview.

109. Leon Sachs, interview by Richard Richardson, 1976, McKeldin-Jackson Project, MHS OH 8136.

110. Recollection of former Maryland attorney general Stephen H. Sachs, son of Leon Sachs, interview by the author, June 2007, Baltimore.

111. Ibid.

112. Ibid.

113. Raymond V. Haysbert, interview by the author, March 2004, Baltimore.

114. W. E. B. Du Bois, *The Souls of Black Folk* (New York: Library of America, 1968), 364.

115. Berk interview, MHS OH 8146, cassette 1, side 1:10.

116. William L. Adams, interview by Charles Waganett, August 1977, McKeldin-Jackson Project, MHS OH 8210, 1:16.

117. Ibid., side 1:11.

CHAPTER 3. DIFFERENT DRUMMERS

1. Maryland Commission on Interracial Problems and Relations, *An American City in Transition: The Baltimore Community Self-Survey of Inter-Group Relations* (Baltimore: Commission on Human Relations, 1955), 62.

2. Salima Siler Marriott, interview by the author, January 2006, Baltimore.

3. Victorine Adams interview. All Victorine Adams quotations and paraphrases in this section are from this interview.

4. Crockett interview.

5. George Russell, lawyer for numbers man Willie Adams, interview by the author, February 2005, Baltimore.

6. Crockett interview.

7. I grew up in Pinehurst. After many years, the Pinehurst Country Club installed a caddy hall of fame in its clubhouse.

8. Michael Mitchell interview.

9. William L. Adams interview, MHS OH 8210, 1:18.

10. Joe Louis Barrow Jr., telephone interview by the author, August 2004.

11. *Baltimore News-Post,* July 6, 1940.

12. *Baltimore Sun,* Nov. 9, 1948.

13. Marion Bascom, interview by the author, September 2004, Baltimore.

14. Russell interview.

15. Ibid.; Robert Mack Bell, interview by the author, March 2006, Baltimore.

16. Haysbert (one of Henry Parks's partners) interview.

17. Quoted in Vivien Thomas, *Partners of the Heart: Vivien Thomas and his Work with Alfred Blalock: An Autobiography* (Philadelphia: University of Pennsylvania Press, 1985), 92.

18. Ibid., 95.

19. Ibid., 81.

20. William Rienhoff, telephone interview by the author, May 2005.

21. Katie McCabe, "Like Something the Lord Made," *Washingtonian* (August 1989): 80, 97.

22. Levi Watkins Jr., interview by the author. All Watkins quotations and paraphrases in this section are from this interview.

23. Williams, *Thurgood Marshall*; and Williams, interview by WYPR, September 2006. Michael Mitchell, son of Clarence M. Mitchell Jr., the NAACP's Washington lobbyist, insists Marshall did apply, but no record can be found of an application.

24. Esther McCready, interview by the author, March 2004, Baltimore. All McCready quotations and paraphrases are from this interview.

25. Houston, "Don't Shout Too Soon."

26. Quoted in Frederick N. Rasmussen's Back Story column, *Baltimore Evening Sun*, Feb. 11, 2006.

27. Gilbert Sandler, "Baltimore Glimpses," *Baltimore Sun*, Jan. 4, 1994.

28. Du Bois, *The Souls of Black Folk*, 369.

29. Jake Oliver, interview by the author, April 2004, Baltimore.

30. Frances "Frankie" Murphy, interview by the author, April 2004, Baltimore. All F. Murphy quotations and paraphrases in this section are from this interview.

31. David Levering Lewis, telephone interview by the author, October 2005.

32. *Crisis,* April-May 1932.

33. Lewis interview.

34. Richard McKinney, interview by the author, November 2005, Baltimore.

35. Lewis interview.

36. Michael Mitchell interview.

37. Howard Pindell's account, offered to the Frederick Historical Society, courtesy of Mark S. Hudson, executive director.

38. Lee interview.

39. Kluger, *Simple Justice,* 195.

40. Sidney Hollander Jr., interview by the author, June 2003, Baltimore. All Hollander Jr. quotations and paraphrases in this section are from this interview.

41. Arthur Murphy, William H. Murphy Sr.'s son, interview by the author, December 2005, Baltimore.

42. Chester Wickwire, interview by the author, August 2004, Cockeysville. All Wickwire quotations and paraphrases in this section are from this interview.

43. From the report of the Senate Foreign Relations Committee, Subcommittee on the Investigation of Loyalty of State Department Employees, February 1950, quoted in Richard M. Fried, *Nightmare in Red: The McCarthy Era in Perspective* (New York: Oxford University Press, 1990), 124.

44. Ross Jones, interview by the author, September 2006, Lutherville.

45. Dave Brubeck interview on the *Marc Steiner Show*, December 2005.

46. Frank Somerville, a reporter and later an editor at the *Baltimore Sun*, interview by the author, September 2003, Baltimore.

47. Samuel Hopkins, interview by the author, October 2005, Baltimore.

48. Peggy Waxter, interview by the author, March 2006, Baltimore.

49. *Baltimore Sun*, May 22, 1944.

50. Milton Bates, interview by the author, December 2003, Baltimore.

51. Quoted in Barbara Mills, *"Got My Mind Set on Freedom": Maryland's Story of Black and White Activism* (Bowie, Md.: Heritage Books, 2002), 215.

52. From an Enoch Pratt Free Library colloquium on Baltimore's segregated tennis courts, April 26, 2003. All M. Swann remarks and paraphrases are from this colloquium.

53. Frances Murphy interview.

54. Paul A. Kramer, "White Sales," in *Enterprising Emporiums: The Jewish Department Stores of Downtown Baltimore* (Baltimore: The Jewish Museum of Maryland, 2001), 41.

55. Lee interview.

56. Bascom interview.

57. Madeleine Murphy to Hochschild-Kohn, Sept. 12, 1956, Walter Sondheim Jr. Papers, University of Baltimore, quoted in Kramer, "White Sales," 43.

58. Baltimore native who requested anonymity, March 2004, Baltimore.

59. I remember daring to drink from the green (blacks only) water fountains on the golf courses at Pinehurst, North Carolina, where I grew up. It was an adventure across the color line, not the only one and not one I really thought would be fatal or even harmful. That such a trespass would hold such drama seemed to me later a reflection of how powerful ways of thinking, corrosive myth, and prejudice can become, burrowing deeply into consciousness in a way that probably exceeded the results intended by the agents of Jim Crow.

60. *Baltimore Sun*, Nov. 9, 1948.

61. Leon Sachs interview, MHS OH 8136, 1079.

62. Larry Gibson, interview by the author.

63. Peter Angelos, interview by the author, March 1998, Baltimore.

64. Jim Doyle, interview by the author, January 2004, Annapolis.

65. Ibid.

66. Russell interview.

67. Ibid.

68. Jacques Kelly, *Eight Busy Decades: The Life and Times of Clarence W. Miles* (White Banks, Md.: n. p., 1986), 65.

69. Russell interview.

70. James B. Crooks, *Politics and Progress: The Rise of Urban Progressivism in Baltimore, 1895 to 1911* (Baton Rouge: Louisiana State University Press, 1968), 66. It is important to note that "progressivism" in these times meant, in some cases, removing blacks from the democratic process on the theory they were a danger to the system.

71. Russell interview.

72. Ibid.

73. William L. Adams interview, MHS OH 8210, 42.

74. From a series of interviews with William Donald Schaefer between June 1995 and January 1998 for C. Fraser Smith, *William Donald Schaefer: A Political Biography* (Baltimore: Johns Hopkins University Press, 1999).

75. Lee interview.

76. Nattie Gunther, interview by the author, August 2005, Baltimore.

77. McKinney interview.

78. Ibid.

CHAPTER 4. ROADBLOCKS AND RESISTANCE

1. Kluger, *Simple Justice*, 708.

2. Ibid., 705.

3. Lee interview.

4. Alvin Thornton, speaking at a University of Maryland Law School forum celebrating the fiftieth anniversary of *Brown*, March 9, 2004.

5. The following account is offered by Ken Montague, June 2005, and Ralph Moore, June 2005; interviews by the author, Baltimore.

6. Walter Sondheim Jr., interview by the author, March 2004, Baltimore.

7. Thomas D'Alesandro III, interview by the author, December 2004, Baltimore.

8. Sondheim interview.

9. Richard Shifter, interview by the author, January 2005, Bethesda.

10. Kluger, *Simple Justice*, 718.

11. Walter Sondheim Jr., speaking at the fiftieth anniversary of *Brown* forum. Sondheim prefaced his remarks with this observation: "What happens to your memory is that insufficient recollection is replaced by imagination. I know I imagine things that happened and that I hope really did happen."

12. Sondheim interview.

13. Ibid.

14. Sherrilyn Ifill, speaking at the fiftieth anniversary of *Brown* forum.

15. Alfreda Hughes, speaking at the fiftieth anniversary of *Brown* forum.

16. Ibid.

17. Dwight Petit speaking at the fiftieth anniversary of *Brown* forum.

18. Ibid.

19. Shifter interview. All Shifter quotations and paraphrases in this section are from this interview.

20. Gwynn Oak wasn't the only park still closed to blacks. A "white only" sign was posted also at a Braddock Heights amusement park, a few miles from Bill Lee's house in Frederick.

21. From a speech by William Carson Blake, July 4, 1963, quoted in Mills, *"Got My Mind Set on Freedom,"* 170.

22. Todd Gitlin, *The Sixties, Days of Rage* (New York: Bantam Books, 1987), 132.

23. Bell interview.

24. August Meier, *A White Scholar and the Black Community, 1945–1965: Essays and Reflections* (Amherst: University of Massachusetts Press, 1992), 147.

25. Wickwire interview.

26. *Baltimore Sun,* Aug. 23, 1998.

27. *Baltimore Sun,* Aug. 24, 1998.

28. Barbara Mills, interview by the author, August 2004, Warwick, Rhode Island.

29. Gitlin, *The Sixties,* 310.

30. Quoted in Mills, *"Got My Mind Set on Freedom,"* 179–80.

31. *Baltimore Sun,* Feb. 26, 2006.

32. Bill Wright, interview by the author, July 2004, Cambridge. All Wright quotations and paraphrases in this section are from this interview.

33. Frederick Douglass, "West India Emancipation," speech, August 4, 1857, in *The Life and Writings of Frederick Douglass,* vol. 2, ed. Philip S. Foner (New York: International Publishers, 1975), 437.

34. Simpkins interview.

35. Ibid.

36. Quoted in Peter B. Levy, *Civil War on Race Street: The Civil Rights Movement in Cambridge, Maryland* (Gainesville: University Press of Florida, 2003), 2.

37. "Interview with Gloria Richardson," *Maryland Historical Magazine,* special issue (Fall 1994): 346.

38. Marc Steiner, interview by the author, March 2004, Baltimore.

39. "Interview with Gloria Richardson," 351.

40. John Lewis, *Walking with the Wind: A Memoir of the Movement* (San Diego: Harcourt Brace, 1999), 215.

41. "Interview with Gloria Richardson," 354.

42. Quoted in Levy, *Civil War on Race Street*, 381.

43. "Interview with Gloria Richardson," 352.

44. Marvin Mandel, interview by the author, August 2001, Annapolis. All Mandel quotations and paraphrases in this section are from this interview.

45. John T. Willis, *Presidential Elections in Maryland* (Mt. Airy, Md.: Lomond Publications, 1984), 123.

46. Dobson interview.

47. *Baltimore Sun*, October 12, 1963.

48. Ibid.

49. Mildred Momberger, interview by Richard Richardson, August 3, 1976, McKeldin-Jackson Project, MHS OH 8155, cassette 2, side 1:29.

50. Kluger, *Simple Justice*, 184.

51. Favor, "Whither Goes the Black Church: The Black Church and Social Reform: The Goon Squad," a brochure on the history of the Goon Squad, distributed in 2002, during Union Baptist's 150th anniversary celebration.

52. Harvey Johnson, "The White Man's Failure in Government," p. 4, from the *African American Perspective: Pamphlets from the Daniel A.P. Murray Collection*, Library of Congress American Memory Project.

53. Ibid., 3.

54. Ibid.

55. *Morning Herald*, April 17, 1881, 4, quoted in Graham, *Baltimore*, 243–44.

56. Mills, *"Got My Mind Set on Freedom,"* 149.

57. Mills interview.

58. Favor brochure.

59. David Milobsky, "Power from the Pulpit: Baltimore's African-American Clergy, 1950–1970," *Maryland Historical Magazine* 89 (1994): 279.

60. Ibid., 280.

61. Ibid., 282.

62. Mills, *"Got My Mind Set on Freedom,"* 149.

63. Paul A. Sarbanes, interview by the author, December 2006, Baltimore.

64. Favor brochure.

65. Bell interview.

CHAPTER 5. SEATS AT THE TABLE

1. "Interview with Gloria Richardson," 351.

2. Ibid., 358.

3. Gloria Richardson says the movement included people who saw nonviolence as religion, but others armed themselves against the provocations they saw around them. Clarence Mitchell had taken a gun when he went to cover the Armwood lynching aftermath. Carl Murphy kept a pistol by his bed. "Interview with Gloria Richardson."

4. Lemeul Chester, interview on WYPR-FM, May 2004.

5. Levy, *Civil War on Race Street*, 144.

6. Richard Kinlein, telephone interview by the author, December 2004.

7. William L. Jews, interview by the author, March 2006, Owings Mills. All Jews quotations and paraphrases in this section are from this interview.

8. Dobson, interview with Hopkins students, September 1999.

9. D'Alesandro interview.

10. *Baltimore Sun*, June 15, 1964.

11. *Baltimore Sun*, Jan. 21, 1964.

12. Moore interview.

13. D'Alesandro interview.

14. Bascom interview.

15. Kenneth Durr, *Behind the Backlash: White Working Class Politics in Baltimore, 1940–1980* (Chapel Hill: University of North Carolina Press, 2003), 144.

16. Ibid.

17. Gibson interview.

18. Rochelle "Rikki" Spector, interview by the author, March 2005, Baltimore.

19. Gibson interview.

20. Russell interview.

21. Mandel interview.

22. D'Alesandro interview.

23. Levy, *Civil War on Race Street*, 144.

24. McKeldin interview.

25. *Baltimore Sun*, Oct. 5, 1967.

26. Gibson interview. All Gibson quotations and paraphrases in this section are from this interview.

27. Arthur Murphy interview.

28. Melvin Sykes, interview by the author, November 2005, Baltimore.

29. D'Alesandro interview.

30. Schaefer interview series.

31. *Washington Post*, April 27, 1998.

32. Watson, *Lion in the Lobby*, back cover.

33. Ibid., 620.

34. Joseph R. L. Sterne, interview by the author, February 2006, Baltimore.

35. Robert Caro, *The Years of Lyndon Johnson, Master of the Senate* (New York: Vintage Books, 2003), 784.

36. David Margolick, "A Courthouse in Baltimore Named for Black Leader," *New York Times*, March 9, 1985.

37. Ibid.

38. Mark V. Tushnet, ed., *Thurgood Marshall: His Speeches, Writings, Arguments, Opinions and Reminiscences* (Chicago, Ill.: Lawrence Hill Books, 2001), 418.

39. Howard P. Rawlings, interview by the author, March 2002, Baltimore.

40. Ibid.

41. From Brody's remarks at the Hopkins Club, March 2003.

42. Rawlings interview.

43. See McFeely, *Frederick Douglass.* The great black emancipator had thought he would be rewarded by Republican administrations under the usual dictates of the spoils system. But, except for his ambassadorship to Haiti and a few relatively minor appointments in Washington, he was allowed to twist in the wind.

44. Anne Perkins, telephone interview by the author, November 2003, Baltimore.

45. Rawlings interview.

46. Ibid.

47. Ibid.

48. Parris N. Glendening, telephone interview by the author, October 2006.

49. Ibid.

50. Bell interview.

51. Rawlings interview.

52. Kurt L. Schmoke, interview by the author, September 2006, Washington, D.C.

53. Doug Colbert, interview by the author, September 2006, Baltimore.

54. Ibid.

55. Thomas E. Noel, "Baltimore: A City in Crisis," May 2004 unpublished court report.

56. Ibid., 32.

57. Pinard, "Don't Deny Maryland's Ex-Convicts Right to Vote," *Baltimore Sun,* October 17, 2006.

58. Noel, "Baltimore," 32.

59. *Baltimore Sun,* Nov. 26, 2005.

EPILOGUE

1. Lee interview.

2. Ibid.

3. *Laws of Maryland* 1867, chap. 343, passed March 15, 705–6.

4. *Washington Post,* Jan. 12, 2003.

5. Ibid.

6. Lee interview.

7. Alan Morrison, interview by the author, October 2007, Baltimore.

Index